CP Stylebook

A Guide for Writers and Editors

Peter Buckley
Editor

The Canadian Press

36 King Street East, Toronto, Ontario M5C 2L9

Telephone: (416) 364-0321   Fax: (416) 364-0207

First printing 1940
Revised and extended
1947, 1954, 1957, 1966, 1974
Sixth impression of 1974 edition,
with minor changes, 1978
Further revised and extended 1983
Reprinted with minor changes 1984
Reprinted twice 1987
Revised and extended 1989
Extensively revised 1992
Reprinted with minor changes 1993, 1995
Copyright, 1995, by The Canadian Press

ISBN: 0-920009-12-3

Contents

Introduction 1
What is CP? 3
Notes: Why CP style is the way it is 5

CP policies

Principles 13
    Staff responsibility 13
    Ethical behavior 15
    Impartiality 15
Quotations 16
Sensitive subjects 19
    Age 19
    Disabilities 19
    Race 20
    Names of races 21
    Native peoples 21
    Sexism 22
Sources: Unnamed sources, Ethics 25
Taste and tough calls 30
Terrorism, hostage-takings 33

General

Analyses 37
CP Backgrounders 40
Business news 42
Columns 46
Elections 47
Entertainment 51
Flashbacks 55
Foreign news 56
Labor 59
Lifestyles 66
Obituaries 68
Polls 72
Profiles and Newsmakers 75
Sports 80
Statistics 89
Travel 91

Legal

Dos and don'ts 95
Criminal cases (includes Young persons) 96
Civil cases 108
Contempt of court 110
Libel (includes Privilege) 112
Copyright 119
Privacy, wiretaps 121
Press and police 122
Legal vocabulary 124

The working journalist

Writing
    Breaking news 129
    Common faults 135
    Locating the news 146
    Writing 148
Editing 157
Writing for broadcast 162

Some useful tools

Grammar and style
    Abbreviations and acronyms 169
    Capitalization 177
    Compounds 202
    French 204
    Government 210
    Names, nicknames, initials 215
    Numbers 217
    Plurals of nouns 222
    Possessives 226
    Punctuation 228
    Singular or plural 245
    Spelling 248

Some technical guides
    Aircraft, ships, guns 249
    Metric 253
    Military 260
    Native peoples — Indians, Metis, Inuit 267
    People, places 270
    Placelines (Canadian, U.S., Other foreign) 278
    Place names 282
    Technical terms 285
    Time 289
    Titles 292
    Trade names 296
    Weather 299
Access to information 303
Words 306

Illustrating the news

    Pictures (includes Sending photos, Captions) 329
    Graphics 346

The CP news report

Main Desk and bureaus 351
Keeping editors advised 354
    Advisories 354
    Calendar and Look-Ahead 360
    Fronts advisories 361
    News Budgets 363

Packaging the news
    At-a-Glance, Highlights, Quicks 367
    Editorial symposiums 373
    Newspage copy 375
Dealing with members 376

The way we do things
    Advances 378
    Bylines 382
    Completes 387
    Corrections (includes Withholds, Kills, Subs) 389
    Correctives 392
    Slugs and coding 396

Handling vital routine
    Handling business news 408
    Foreign filing 411
    Sports handling (includes Agate) 415
Writing for cable and other services 444

Bibliography 446
Acknowledgments 449
Index 451
Maps 469

Introduction

The *CP Stylebook* began life as a modest little pamphlet more than a half-century ago. It was a sort of operator's manual for staff at The Canadian Press, Canada's national news agency.

It has blossomed since then into a comprehensive reference work used in newsrooms and business offices across Canada.

In 1992, it was redone from intro to index. Every chapter was freshened or revised to reflect the priorities and sensitivities of today's world, in a co-operative effort that enlisted dozens of members of CP staff. Two subsequent editions have ensured the book has remained up-to-date. The emphasis on getting real people and real pocketbook issues into the news, in a readable style, has not changed.

The stylebook is also designed to be friendly to the many outside CP who have come to consider it a standard reference. The language should be understandable to anyone who picks it up.

The stylebook has been organized into these main sections:

Policies: The standards that guide the work of collecting and distributing news. Basic journalism ethics, but also specific help with sensitive areas like racism, sexism, misquotes and anonymous sources.

General: Hard news and soft news, from news analysis to foreign reporting and sports coverage. CP's perspectives on the different types of basic news stories.

Legal: Libel. Copyright. Court coverage. Police searches of the newsroom. Contempt. The rights — and limitations — that govern the everyday work of reporters and editors.

The working journalist: Communicating clearly. Down-to-earth advice on writing and editing, with common pitfalls identified and lots of examples to illustrate each point.

Some useful tools: The nitty-gritty. In one subsection, punctuation, capitalization and other grammatical elements. In another, information on aircraft names, military ranks, weather and other technical matters. Also, a how-to guide for access-to-information laws and 20 pages of tricky words.

Illustrating the news: Pictures on the page. Practical information about getting photos and graphics into print.

The CP news report: Primarily for CP staff. Sets out procedures for advisories, packaging the news, coding and slugging of copy, the handling of corrections and other important elements of the agency's news report.

At the back of the book, the index is expanded to help find specific advice and style rulings faster. Some basic maps have been added.

For those who judge a book by its cover, there's a fresh look and a tougher, more resilient binding. White space is provided throughout for notes and observations — particularly helpful at newspapers that modify or expand on CP style.

CP's basic style changes cautiously: evolution, not revolution. Thus, while this edition contains many changes of emphasis and detail, there are few departures from long-standing fundamentals. CP continually assesses its style to keep it up to date and sensible. Suggestions for improvement are always welcome.

What is CP?

The folklore of The Canadian Press tells of a publisher in Atlantic Canada who, frustrated by some fault with the service his newspaper was receiving, was heard to exclaim: "The trouble with CP is that it has no soul to curse, nor ass to kick."

There is probably no other organization that has made such an ongoing contribution to Canadian life and yet has had so little public profile. Since its founding in 1917, CP has directly played a crucial role in the growth of the Canadian newspaper industry. It has helped shape the way Canadians see themselves and the world. Yet CP remains largely mysterious to most of the people it serves.

The Canadian Press was created by newspaper publishers to provide a flow of news across the sparsely populated regions of the country. Before 1917, newspapers exchanged news within regional associations and received international news from The Associated Press on north-south telegraph circuits. But they had no ready means of sending news east and west across Canada.

Part of CP's early financing was a $50,000 federal grant to pay for telegraph circuits linking the Maritimes to Quebec and Ontario, Central Canada to the Prairies and the Prairies to British Columbia. The government offered to help because of CP's potential to serve the cause of national unity during the First World War.

The funding ended in 1924 by mutual agreement and CP's founding publishers voted never again to risk the appearance of compromise by accepting government money for any news purpose.

The logo (**CP**) appears on hundreds of newspaper pages every day. If despite that, the organization is not generally known or understood by the millions who read its work, the country's news-makers are well aware of CP's reach, whether a prime minister on tour or a Mountie on northern patrol.

What is CP? Its definition is a mouthful: **the national news-gathering not-for-profit co-operative owned by the daily newspaper industry.** The newspapers are not shareholders, but rather are *members* of the co-operative. Each member pays a fee based on circulation to meet CP's costs, and contributes news of its area to the common pool.

Since its early days this exchange of news via CP has been at the heart of the co-operative: Le Soleil in Quebec providing coverage of a big downtown fire and in return getting a story about a waterfront strike from the Vancouver Province.

However, from the beginning CP has assigned its own reporting and photo staff in major Canadian cities and they produce about 50 per cent of the agency's domestic-news content.

CP also provides full coverage of world news. The bulk of the international file originates with The Associated Press and Reuters. This material is edited by a foreign desk at Toronto and supplemented by CP reporters working out of Washington and London, plus correspondents in major world capitals.

An important milestone occurred in 1951 when CP's French service was established. Although some of the French report is translated from English, the co-operative's policy ensures that important stories anywhere in Canada of direct interest to Quebec are covered by French-language reporters. And La Presse Canadienne compiles a world-news report from its own correspondents and from French-language services of AP and Reuters.

Since the early days of public and private radio in the 1930s, CP has served the broadcasting industry. An early task was preparing scripts for Lorne Greene and other well-known voices who read the latest dispatches from Second World War battlefronts over the fledgling Canadian Broadcasting Corp.

Currently, service to private broadcasters is provided by Broadcast News Ltd., a wholly owned subsidiary of CP. BN microphone flashes are a common sight at news conferences and major events as material is collected for the hourly newscasts and other information programming of BN Audio, the largest radio network in the country.

On the technical side, in 1973 CP became the first news organization in Canada to make extensive use of word processors to write and edit stories. In the mid-1980s, CP and BN switched from land circuits to satellite for delivery of stories, photos and audio reports to about 450 satellite dishes.

Past generations of CP journalists who practised their craft to the click of Morse code and the beat of teletype machines would disagree with the publisher who searched for CP's soul. They built a service organization driven by a quest for good journalism and the needs of its newspaper members. That tradition is carried on by CP's modern reporters with their silent laptops.

Keith Kincaid
President

Notes

Why CP style is the way it is

The SWAT team moved in, frisking the rappers for crack.

Several words in that sentence would not have made sense to an average reader a generation ago. Most of today's readers would find the phrasing normal in a news report.

That's one of the reasons why stylebooks are needed. If a SWAT team turns up in a front-page story about a local hostage-taking, and again on the entertainment page in a movie review, the capitalization should be the same in both cases. (And in both cases, **SWAT** needs to be explained as meaning **s**pecial **w**eapons **a**nd **t**actics.)

English is a fluid language, but it's bound by complicated rules of grammar. Working reporters and editors don't have time to research decisions on vocabulary and capitalization and grammar every time a problem arises. A stylebook presents such decisions in logical, handy form.

Whimsy is found in every stylebook. But style decisions overall are based on sound reasons. Most are basic grammar and common sense, with the stylebook simply a reminder. Other decisions involve choosing from among a range of valid alternatives, and at that point a number of factors come into play.

Among the ones that have influenced CP style over the decades:

Preferences of Canadian newspapers

The newspapers own The Canadian Press and most of them follow CP style in their handling of local news. It's only common sense to accept their preferences in terms of story presentation and typography. And if there's an important style change being considered, the papers are consulted. The majority preference becomes CP style.

An example:

CP became the first western news agency to drop the courtesy titles **Mr.**, **Mrs.**, **Miss** and **Ms.** from all copy. Over the years, the use of such titles had become erratic. For men, the **Mr.** was omitted in stories from outside Canada as well as from sports and crime news. For women, the title tended to be dropped from sports and crime copy and in referring to some widely known celebrities, but it was retained in all other stories from Canada and abroad. The result was news columns with a **Mr.** here and not there, **Mrs.** and **Ms.** in stories where the **Mr.** was dropped and so on. Finally, most papers agreed the rules needed change, and the soundest course was to drop all such titles. Some papers continue to use them, either throughout the paper or in particular sections.

Consistency

A style that is full of exceptions is difficult to use. If Canadians write **theatre** and **centre**, in the name of consistency it's not a great leap to write about the **Lincoln Centre** in New York, even though the sign outside says **Lincoln Center**.

Maintaining consistency can be troublesome. In general, if there's an option, CP prefers lowercase initial letters to capitals. That meant CP did not capitalize federal and provincial government departments until fairly recently. However, with the naming of such departments as Environment Canada, and the proliferation of Crown agencies like the Canadian Wheat Board which demanded capitalization, it seemed inconsistent to keep using lowercase. Up they went.

Popular usage

News reporting is meant to inform the public, not to score points with language experts. Outdated expressions can get in the way of that goal. Many of the changes in the meaning of words are not for the better, but if most readers are led to believe that **presently** means **right now**, rather than **soon**, there's no point in using the word in a news story and risking misunderstanding.

CP won't be the first to accept the misuse of a word, and occasionally we're a bit stubborn about changes that seem to debase the language. But eventually a misused form can take on a life of its own and CP bows to the inevitable. We have reluctantly accepted the word **gender** in such phrases as **gender politics** or **gender equality** although **sexual equality** makes more basic sense. (**Gender** is primarily the word used by grammarians to distinguish masculine, feminine and neuter words; **sex** is what distinguishes males from females. But **gender** has gradually accumulated a variety of nuances in popular usage that go beyond the strictly grammatical.)

Sensitivity

Today's perfectly normal word can be tomorrow's flagrant example of sexism, racism or other abuse. In particular, people who feel put upon by society are likely to reject labels that seem to limit their potential or lock them into hurtful self-images.

People who are identified by certain words (**cripple, housewife, colored**) can easily believe that the language is insensitive and prefer another description (**disabled person, home-maker, black**). In time, those labels may also fall out of favor.

CP believes that people's preferences should be respected when new forms are adopted by a significant number of those concerned and become familiar to the general public. But we don't want to be faddish, accepting words for routine use that are so *sensitive* that they have little clear meaning left — expressions like **developmentally challenged**. Nor will we go along casually with new labels that are politically controversial among the people most concerned.

Words like **spokesman** and **chairman** cause resentment when applied to women, but the search for alternatives has led to forms that CP and the public have not warmed to. We use **spokeswoman** and **chairwoman** and other **-woman** forms where appropriate, but consider words like **alderperson** and **chair** (as an all-purpose description for the person presiding at a meeting) to be clumsy or artificial. We won't adopt them unless they gain wider acceptance.

Because we think we're right

Almost all Canadian newspapers use the *-or* ending in such words as **favor, honor, labor** and **vapor**, following a long-standing CP style. Many Canadian schools and government departments prefer *-our* endings: **favour, honour, labour** and **vapour**. The reason most often given is that the *-our* ending is Canadian (or British) and the *-or* ending is American. To give up *-our* endings, it's often said, would be another blow to Canada's heritage.

CP believes it's far from being that clear-cut.

For centuries, the tendency in written English, in Britain and elsewhere, had been toward *-or* endings. Otherwise, we might be writing **errour** and **terrour, governour** and **oratour**. The Shorter Oxford Dictionary of 1933 notes, for example, that **color** has been used at times instead of **colour** in England from the 15th century.

*Sir John A. Macdonald had strong views on many topics, including spelling. In 1890 he decreed that Canadian government documents should use **-our** spellings of **honour** and the like.*

(Canapress)

But the trend was derailed when Americans began using *-or* endings almost exclusively in the last century, and it became almost a matter of honor to retain the examples of *-our* that remained. Sir John A. Macdonald wrestled with the issue and in 1890 decreed *-our* endings for Canadian government documents in line with the practice in Mother England, so that **"the same system should obtain in all portions of the British Empire."**

The Queen's Printer of the day in Ottawa, Brown Chamberlin, responded spiritedly with a raft of citations and arguments against the -*our* endings. But the federal government has generally continued Macdonald's preference. Newspapers, on the other hand, increasingly used -*or*.

There are now about 40 words for which British spelling decrees an -*our* ending. (A complication for users of -*our* is the fact that English spelling drops the *u* in variations for about half of those 40 words. It's **honour**, but **honorary**; **colour**, but **coloration**; **humour**, but **humorist**; **labour**, but **laborious**; **glamour**, but **glamorous**.)

Anyone who has Henry Fowler on side in a debate about language has a respected ally. Fowler's Modern English Usage has been a great, droll authority on the language for generations.

Of the -*or/-our* question, Fowler writes:

Those who are willing to put national prejudice aside and examine the facts soon realize, first, that the British -our words are much fewer in proportion to the -or words than they suppose, and, secondly, that there seems to be no discoverable line between the two sets so based on principle as to serve any useful purpose. By the side of favour there is horror, beside ardour pallor, beside odour tremor, and so forth.

Having decided basically that -*or* will be preferred, should CP make exceptions? This is a treacherous area, one where decisions on style can seem most arbitrary.

Except for geographical names (e.g., *Harbour Grace, Nfld.*), CP has decided that we will use -*or* spellings come what may. We call it the **Labor** party in Britain, we write that the word on the Victoria Cross is **valor** and that members of the Privy Council are entitled to be styled **Right Honorable**. We do it in the name of consistency.

If it seems arbitrary, consider some of the alternatives. Imagine that we decided to prefer -*or* spellings, but would make an exception for normal preferences. In that case, how do we report on an international seminar on political ethics in Britain? We should logically follow the printed text of the **Labour** leader's speech and report his remarks about **honour** and **fervour**. Then, the guest speaker from the American Federation of **Labor** might improvise some remarks about (as we would have to spell it) **humor** and **candor**. Then which form do we use when reporting translated remarks by the traditionalist French delegate or the technocratic Swede?

Similarly, for a convention of Canadian grammarians, do we switch from -*or* to -*our* according to each speaker's preference? One organization of English teachers in Canada had a **programme** of events one year, and a **program** the next — deliberate choices of different presidents in each case.

If CP's policy on this can seem insensitive at times, the alternatives don't seem much better.

Names

Another troublesome area concerns capitalized or lowercased letters in proper names. These can be exploited for promotional purposes – an all-caps product name tends to jump out at the reader.

CP aims to spell names correctly, but for purposes of readibility, we do not go along with either all-capitals or all-lowercase names of corporations, products and cultural output. So it's Scrabble (not SCRABBLE); Velcro (not VELCRO); 5th Estate (not 5th estate), Via (not VIA) Rail.

One exception is the names of people and performing groups, where CP generally follows their preference, as long as it is consistent. So it is k.d. lang (not K.D. Lang) and bp Nichol (not B.P. Nichol).

➤ See **Capitalization**, page 189.

We don't expect everyone to agree with all of the style decisions we have made. They have been carefully thought out, but we welcome discussion of our style from the news industry and the public.

CP policies

Principles
    Staff responsibility
    Ethical behavior
    Impartiality
Quotations
Sensitive subjects
    Age
    Disabilities
    Race
    Names of races
    Native peoples
    Sexism
Sources
    Unnamed sources
    Ethics and sources
    Involving Head Office
    Describing unnamed sources
    Women as sources
Taste and tough calls
Terrorism, hostage-takings

Principles

The Canadian Press exists for one purpose: To serve in English and French the newspapers that own it, and through them, the Canadian public.

We serve by offering minute-to-minute news, information and illustrations crafted to help Canadians know and understand each other, and the world beyond their borders.

What we present daily is like a giant's photo album. There are snapshots of the cities, the regions, the provinces, the country, plus images of the world. We focus on real people — not just institutions — to show in human terms how events affect our individual and collective lives.

But these are snapshots, not portraits, because no news agency can hope to present a complete picture of the country, let alone the world, on any given day. We can and we do link the snapshots and compare them, pulling together for readers some trends that they can contemplate and perhaps use.

Straight news-of-record reporting certainly, but enhanced by innovative packages of modern living news, views and commentary, columns, graphics and special reports, all made possible through CP's unique strength — the right mix of strong member-exchange and CP staff work.

Although our role continues to evolve, the principles that guide our work are unchanged. Everything that we do must be honest, unbiased and unflinchingly fair. We deal with facts that are demonstrable, supported by sources that are reliable and responsible. We pursue with equal vigor all sides of a story.

Accuracy is fundamental. Discovery of a mistake calls for immediate correction. Corrections to stories already published or broadcast must not be grudging or stingy. They must be written in a spirit of genuinely wanting to right a wrong in the fairest and fullest manner.

Our work is urgent. Speed must be a primary objective of a news service committed to the deadlines of newspapers and broadcasters in six time zones. But being reliable is always more important than being fast.

Good taste is a constant consideration. Some essential news is essentially repellant. Its handling need not be.

Staff responsibility

Responsibility for upholding CP standards developed over 75 years rests with our reporters, editors and supervisors. So much individuality is involved in reporting, writing and editing news that it is impossible to have precise rules covering every eventuality. Being guided by proven practices is the surest way of meeting the standards that Canadians have come to expect from CP.

Among the most important of these practices:

1. Investigate fully before transmitting any story or identifying any individual in a story where there is the slightest reason for doubt. When in doubt cut it out. But never make this an excuse for ditching an angle without thorough checking. The doubt must be an honest doubt, arrived at after examination of all the facts.

2. Cite competent authorities and sources as the origin of any information open to question. Have proof available for publication in the event of a denial.

Reporters, photographers and TV crews encircle a soldier and Mohawk Warrior in September 1990 during the standoff at Oka. Journalists will have opinions and a point of view, but these must not get in the way of balanced reporting.

(CP—Frank Gunn)

3. Be impartial when handling any news affecting parties or matters in controversy. Give fair representation to all sides at issue.

4. Stick to the facts without editorial opinion or comment. Reporters' opinions are not wanted in CP copy. Their observations are. So are accurate backgrounding and authoritative interpretation essential to reader understanding of complicated issues.

5. Admit errors promptly, frankly. Public distrust of the media is profound and troubling. The distrust is fed by inaccuracy, carelessness, indifference to public sentiment, automatic cynicism to those in public life, perceived bias or unfairness and other sins suggesting arrogance.

6. CP can help overcome such public attitudes through scrupulous care for facts and unwavering dedication to fairness. We must not be quick to dismiss criticism and complaints, a trait journalists refuse to accept in others.

7. The power of news stories to injure can reach both the ordinary citizen and the corporate giant. CP's integrity and sensitivity demands that supervisors and staff respond sympathetically and quickly when an error has been made. It doesn't matter whether the complaint comes from a timid citizen acting alone or from a powerful figure's battery of lawyers.

8.   Every story shown to be erroneous and involving a corrective must be drawn to the attention of supervisory staff. Each bureau is responsible for the copy it files whether it is written by its staff or by travelling staffers assigned to special events.

Ethical behavior

Part of our responsibility as journalists is to ensure we don't do anything that demeans the craft or weakens our credibility. Because we deliver the bad news about politicians who turn dirty, care-givers who abuse their trust and business people who discard ethics for gain, we must observe stringent ethical practices, and be seen to be doing so.

It is impossible to raise all potential ethical challenges in this book. But the following guiding principles are offered in the spirit of wanting to advance, not restrain, our work.

1.   Pride in yourself and in the practice of journalism nourishes ethical behavior.

2.   CP policy is to pay its way. Staff should not accept anything that might compromise our integrity or credibility.

Impartiality

Impartiality is somewhat like exercise. You have to work out regularly to build tone and strength.

The best exercise for impartiality is to stop regularly and ask yourself: "Am I being as impartial, honest and fair as I can be?"

Some other guides to impartiality:

Parties in controversy, whether in politics or law or otherwise, receive fair consideration. Statements issued by conflicting interests merit equal prominence, whether combined in a single story or used at separate times.

But always try to get opposing sides for simultaneous publication.

If an attack by one group or person on another has been covered, any authoritative answer is also carried. If a proper source cannot be reached, say so, and keep trying.

When a comparative unknown expresses controversial views, question his or her expertise on the subject. If there is no expertise, or the individual does not have an official position that puts weight behind the views, consider carefully whether the report should be carried.

Quotations

Quotes are the lifeblood of any story. They put rosiness into the cheeks of the palest stories. They add credibility, immediacy and punch.

They can also bring grief to writers and editors who play loose with them. Some news organizations permit liberties with quotes. CP takes a somewhat stern approach to any tampering with just what was said.

In general, we quote people verbatim and in standard English. We correct slips of grammar that are obvious slips and that would be needlessly embarrassing. We remove verbal mannerisms such as *ah's*, routine vulgarities and meaningless repetitions. Otherwise we do not revise quotations.

While we don't routinely use abnormal spellings and grammar to indicate dialects or mispronunciations, they can have a place in helping to convey atmosphere.

Cleaning up this quote from a concerned unionized fisherman would have taken some of the heart out of the story:

"We don't want our money took to Toronto and not spent on behalf of our members," said Eric Miller. "The few dollars that I makes, I want it spent on behalf of my family, my friends and my brothers and sisters in Newfoundland."

And obviously Jimmy Durante's *Dese are de conditions dat prevail* would be worse for a quick tidy-up.

Quotes containing bafflegab are routinely paraphrased in plain English, no matter how eminent the speaker.

Other points to remember about handling quotes:

1.   Getting exact quotes without shorthand or tape is not easy. When there is risk that a quote is not exact, for whatever reason, a paraphrase is safest.

2.   When exactness is essential — if it's one person's word against another's — quote verbatim.

3.   When a speaker uses what is obviously a wrong word, check back when possible. When a quote does not make sense, check back with the speaker or ditch it.

4.   Misquotes result not only from tampering or carelessness. Failure to place a quote in context can have the same eroding effect on credibility. For instance: **"If our tax revenues allow it, I'll repave all secondary highways"** should not be parlayed into the bare reported statement that the speaker promised to repave all secondary highways.

Similarly, failure to indicate tone can skew a quote. A speaker's jocular comment may need to be reported with an explanatory **she said with a smile** or some such. There are other occasions when the bare words benefit from addition of a brief description: **"I'm not guilty," he said, glowering at the jury.**

5.   When clear and concise, a full quote is preferred to a partial quote. But a partial quote can be useful for spicing a lead, setting off a controversial statement or giving the flavor of a speaker.

6.   Make only cosmetic changes to quotations from a text: changing spelling and capitalization to CP style, for example.

7.   If words are left out of a text or middle of a quotation, show the omission with an ellipsis.

8.   Long bracketed explanations and paraphrases should not be inserted at the beginning or end of a quote.

Not: "(The new program) is imaginative, realistic and worth the time and money invested," Scott said.

But: The new program "is imaginative, realistic and worth the time and money invested," Scott said.

9.   Guard against attributing one person's quote to several speakers.

Not: Most retailers surveyed condemned the new tax, saying that "it will mean working half a day a week for the government."

10. Do not include in a quote words that the speaker could not have spoken.

Not: Davis said he "was delighted that the prize is going to the American."

But: Davis said he was "delighted that the prize is going to the American."

Davis's words were "I'm (not was) delighted."

11. Provided the meaning is clear, use slang or other substandard language when it suits the context. Set it off with quotation marks only if it is to be explained. **He said he held up the bakery for "bread" —** **meaning money.**

Language

A reminder to be careful with translations. We should not imply that someone is speaking English when he is not.

In interviews and speeches, make clear what language is being used unless it is obvious. At a news conference where both French and English are used, specify when French was the original language. When reporting the shouts of a crowd or the wording of protest signs that are in other languages, specify that a translation is involved.

Readers are entitled to know when a direct or indirect quote is based on translation rather than the exact words used.

Obscenity

Casual obscenity, blasphemy and vulgarity are not wanted in the news report. Four-letter words shouted from a crowd or muttered by an angry demonstrator add nothing useful to a story.

There are few exceptions. A prominent figure who uses obscene language in a public situation is one. An interview subject may use obscenities in such a way that leaving them out would paint a false picture. Or a quote that includes a vulgarity might be the most effective way to connote certain emotions. But these are the exceptions, not the rule. Always consider other ways of getting across this element of the story before resorting to the use of obscenities.

Obscenities or vulgar language should always be flagged with the following slug:

EDS: Note language in para 3.

If the language or topic is exceptionally offensive, a **Borderline** slug is required:

BORDERLINE
Eds: Note language in para 3.

When an obscenity or vulgarity must be reported, do not use the prissy device of replacing some letters of the offensive words with hyphens. Put the questionable language in a separate paragraph that can be readily deleted by editors who do not want to use it.

Sensitive subjects

Potential to offend lurks in every news story. Age, race, sex, disabilities, religion are often pertinent to the news but must be handled thoughtfully.

Use fairness, sensitivity and good taste when identifying age, color, creed, nationality, personal appearance, religion, sex and any other heading under which a person or group may feel slighted.

Age

Often age is relevant as part of a personal description or for identification. Ages also help readers to relate to people in news stories.

In general, give a person's age rather than imprecise and possibly derogatory terms such as **senior citizen, retiree, oldster, elderly, middle-aged, teenager, youngster**.

Put the age in the lead only when it is significant, such as in obituaries or when an 80-year-old is cycling across the country, or when a three-year-old child is missing. Guard against the formula lead — **a 30-year-old dentist; a 52-year-old fisherman; a 23-year-old convict** . . .

Writing **Mario Lalonde, 30**, is usually preferable to the more cumbersome **30-year-old Mario Lalonde**.

If age is missing for an obituary, give an indication of it from the person's activities, such as year of graduation or year of retirement.

Males up to 16 are called **boys** and females to that age are **girls**. Use a phrase like **young people** for those of both sexes who are somewhat older.

First names may be used in subsequent references for children under 18, except in sports stories.

Youth in general includes both sexes: **the youth of Canada**; applied to individuals, it means males: **Four youths gave the officer a hand**.

Disabilities

Be accurate, clear and sensitive when describing a person with a disability, handicap, illness or disease. They are people first; their disability is only one part of their humanity.

Mention a disability if it is pertinent. Never dismiss someone with an unqualified **disabled, crippled** or the like. Write **Romanov, whose hands are twisted with arthritis,** . . . And perhaps indicate to what extent a person has overcome a disability or how she copes with it: **Girushi uses a wheelchair once she leaves her studio**.

Be specific. **Afflicted with** suggests pain and suffering. It doesn't always apply. Nor does **suffering**. People who use wheelchairs are not necessarily **confined** to them. **Crippling** can be a temporary or permanent condition. People may be **deaf, slightly deaf** or **hard of hearing; blind** or have **poor eyesight**. A **patient** is someone under a doctor's care or in hospital.

Victim connotes helplessness. A child who is **mentally retarded** (slow) is not necessarily **mentally disturbed** (ill). Epileptics have **seizures**, not **fits**.

Avoid defining people by their disorders: **the disabled, the blind, the retarded**. Writing **people with disabilities** emphasizes the human beings and not the disabilities.

Describe disabilities in detail, when appropriate. For instance, it is often relevant to mention whether an amputation is above or below a knee or elbow.

Race

CP news reports should reflect the racial diversity of Canada in a natural way, free of explicit or unconscious racism.

Identify a person by race, color or national origin only when it is truly pertinent. It is appropriate to report that a woman facing deportation is Polish. Similarly, the victim of hate mail may be referred to as a Jew. A full description, including color, may be used if the person is at large.

The appearance of racial minorities in news reports should not be confined to accounts of cultural events, racial tension or crime. A Korean shopkeeper's reaction to a sales tax is just as valid as a Scottish stockbroker's. Include comments from various races in matters of public interest such as federal taxes or national surveys on general topics.

Remember that what is obvious to a university-educated Christian of British stock might need explanation for persons from a variety of other backgrounds. And, it should not be taken for granted that a Muslim ceremony needs explanation while the Roman Catholic mass does not.

Race is pertinent when it motivates an incident or when it helps explain the emotions of those in confrontation. Thus references to race are relevant in reports of racial controversy, immigration difficulties, language discussions and so on.

Race is not included when the context makes it obvious. Readers are safe to assume that people rioting in a predominantly black country are black.

When an incident cuts across racial lines, say so, as when a sizable number of whites join Pakistanis demonstrating against immigration procedures.

That a man found guilty of shoplifting is, say, an Indian is usually irrelevant and he should not be identified as such. However, revealing his race may be unavoidable, through giving a reserve as his address or identifying him as the son of a chief.

It is not objectionable to report that Sons of Freedom have been found guilty of burning a house to protest compulsory education.

Race is pertinent in reporting an accomplishment unusual in a particular race: for example, if a Canadian of Chinese origin is named to the Canadian Football Hall of Fame.

Beware of playing up inflammatory statements at the expense of the main story. Be certain that a spokesman indeed speaks for a community or organization, and give a brief description of that organization, its aims and number of members.

Don't always turn to the same minority spokesmen and organizations for reaction. This can give unwarranted standing to groups that don't necessarily reflect the full range of views of their communities.

Let people speak for themselves. In particular, avoid stories about aboriginal people in which all or most of the talk is provided by white bureaucrats.

Arguing that humor was intended is no defence for a racial slur. Threadbare attempts at humor to be avoided include expressions such as **ah so, ugh** and **firewater**.

Use racially derogatory terms like **honky** and **nigger** only when part of a direct quotation and when essential to the story. Flag such a story:

BORDERLINE
EDS: Note racial slur in para 15.

Names of races

1.   Capitalize the proper names of nationalities, peoples, races and tribes.

Aboriginal Peoples, Arab, Caucasian, French-Canadian, Inuit, Jew, Latin, Negro, Asian, Cree

2.   Note that **black, mulatto, red, yellow** and **white** do not name races and are lowercase.

3.   The term **black** is acceptable in all references in Canada and the United States. In the United States **African-American** is increasingly in use. In Bermuda, **colored** is correct usage for both black and mulatto. In South Africa, the **Cape Colored** are regarded as an ethnic group of mixed blood, and the term is capitalized. In the United States there is a National Association for the Advancement of Colored People, usually identified as the NAACP.

4.   There is usually no need to use hyphenated descriptions such as **Polish-Canadian** or **Jamaican-Canadian**.

Native peoples

In Canada, there are status (or reserve) Indians, non-status Indians (living outside reserves), Metis (people of mixed white and native origin) and Inuit. Collectively, they are known variously as Aboriginal Peoples, original peoples, aboriginals, indigenous peoples, the First Nations and other variations.

Some points concerning Aboriginal Peoples:

1. CP uses uppercase for **Aboriginal Peoples**, which includes all Indian, Métis and Inuit people in Canada. **First Nations** is also uppercase. Other variations – **indigenous people**, **aboriginals** (except for Aboriginals of Australia), **native peoples** – are lowercase.

2. In all references, be guided by the preference of those concerned.

3. Use **Indian** with discretion. Some people object to it because it originated with the European explorers' misconception that they had landed in India. Others, especially status Indians, prefer it to be used.

4. Use **native** advisedly. **Aboriginal** is more specific and is preferred by many in the community.

5. Where reasonable, prefer the actual name of the community – Cree, Mohawk, Blackfoot, Ojibwa – to a generality. For band names, use the spelling the band prefers, which is also the spelling used by the federal government.

6. The word tribe in its original sense was reserved for primitive peoples. Some natives use it casually and it need not be entirely avoided. But community, people, nation, band, language group are alternatives.

➤ See **Native peoples**, page 267.

Sexism

Treat the sexes equally and without stereotyping. A woman's marital or family status — single, married, divorced, grandmother — is pertinent only to explain a personal reference or to round out a profile. The test always is: Would this information be used if the subject were a man?

Referring to a woman gratuitously as **attractive, leggy** or **bosomy** is as inappropriate as describing a man as **a hunk, hairy-chested** or **having great buns**. But there are stories beyond the routine in which such adjectives might be appropriate.

Readers are interested in what people wear. For example, a change of hairstyle or new fashion for Diana, the Princess of Wales, always attracts people's interest. Always apply the test: Would the information be used if the subject were a man?

Never suggest surprise that a woman has talent. Not: **You would never guess from Adriana Hosek's appearance but she is a highly regarded brain surgeon.** Similarly, a woman who has achieved success in public life should not usually be referred to on first reference as **a housewife**.

Do not assume a woman uses her husband's last name. Check.

Use parallel references to the sexes. Not **the men and the ladies** but **the men and the women** or **the women and the men**. Prefer **husband and wife** to **man and wife**. Do not treat **lady** as a synonym for **woman**, or **gentleman** for **man**.

Avoid stereotyping jobs and careers.

Shoppers (not **housewives**) are paying more. If statisticians speak of **a family of four**, don't translate it into **a worker with wife and two children**, unless that's exactly what is meant. More commonly, given the uncertainty about a family's source of income, it should be **husband and wife with two children**.

Only write **female doctor, female lawyer, male nurse, male secretary** and the like when it is essential for clarity.

When writing in general terms prefer **reporter** to **newsman, police officer** or **constable** to **policeman, firefighter** to **fireman, mail carrier** to **mailman, flight attendant** to **air hostess** or **stewardess**.

But if sex is pertinent, masculine and feminine forms are proper: **postman, newswoman, policewoman, air steward**.

Use only established feminine variants ending in **-woman**.

Write **businesswoman, Frenchwoman, newspaperwoman, spokeswoman** but not **journeywoman, linewoman, second basewoman**.

Avoid other feminine variants unless they are so well established that a substitute rings false.

Thus it is proper to describe a woman as an **actress, hostess, masseuse, princess, seamstress** or as an **author, comedian, Jew, murderer, poet, sculptor**.

Do not use cumbersome coinages like **alderperson, chairperson, salesperson** and **spokesperson**.

Often a plural construction solves the sex problem: **Retired officers are not usually referred to by their former rank**. Avoid: **A retired officer is not usually referred to by his or her former rank**.

It is proper English to let **he (him, his)** stand as a word of common or indeterminate gender.

Write **Each student must bring his lunch**. Write **his or her** and the like only if there is a danger that women may seem excluded: **Whoever is promoted will have $50 added to his or her pay**.

The generic **man** is regarded by some as excluding women. Instead of **man** or **mankind**, you can write **people, human beings, humanity, human race**. Alternatives to **manmade** include **artificial, constructed, manufactured, synthetic**. But don't get carried away. To write **human energy** or **human resources** to avoid **manpower**, or **person-eating tiger** to avoid **man-eating tiger** is being hypersensitive.

Gay may be used as an alternative for **homosexual: two gay men**. Some lesbians prefer the term **gay women** or **homosexual women**; follow an individual's preference when it is known. Prefer **sexual orientation** to **sexual preference**; gay people do not view their sexuality as an option. Don't refer to a gay **lifestyle** or suggest that the majority of homosexuals routinely live unorthodox lives; most don't. Consider using **same-sex** as an alternative to **homosexual** or **gay**.

Beware of leaving the impression that homosexuals alone, and not heterosexuals, are at risk to AIDS. Simply say that the disease is caused by a virus that attacks the body's immune system. It is spread most often through sexual contact, needles or syringes shared by drug abusers, infected blood or blood products and from pregnant women to their offspring.

When writing about abortion, the terms **pro-life** and **pro-choice** can be used if they are preferred by the person or organization involved. When writing about a movement in general, it is better to use a neutral phrase, such as **abortion-rights advocates** or **opponents of abortion**.

Sources

Cultivating knowledgeable sources who can provide the background and insight necessary for delivering a complete story is the trademark of the excellent reporter.

Without good sources — be they the town clerk in the small northern mining town, or the fast-moving executive assistant to a cabinet minister — CP cannot hope to craft a comprehensive daily picture of life in Canada and the world.

Getting and keeping good sources is hard work. It involves patient telephone work plus breaking free from our desks to get out and meet people.

CP reporters, editors and supervisors are encouraged to pull back from the front lines occasionally to spend time with people who know what's happening in the world beyond our own limited horizons. Special efforts should be made to develop contacts in non-urban areas, ethnic communities and other places beyond the bright spotlight of big-city journalism.

It is the job of journalists to meet a variety of people. We should all take a special interest in people and listen to what they have to say. Developing good sources is a way of living to the committed journalist.

When dealing with sources, remember that many people are not used to dealing with the media. Ensure they understand they are being quoted, and their words or picture may appear in many newspapers.

And, a cardinal rule with sources is to avoid close personal involvement. There is nothing wrong with social contact with sources, but close personal relationships can lead to conflicts of interest.

Unnamed sources

Democracy works best when someone with facts or opinions to make public is identified by the press by name and qualifications. Readers need to see named sources to help them decide on the credibility and importance of the information.

Regular use of unnamed sources weakens our news reports. CP should be firm in discouraging the quoting of sources who want to hide their identities. Leaks, especially in government and business, are sometimes designed to undermine new policies or to damage rivals.

There are of course many situations when persons with information important to the public insist on concealing their identity for understandable reasons. CP would be foolish, and in some cases irresponsible, never to grant anonymity in news copy, but it can show leadership in working to stop misuse of unnamed sources.

Some guidelines:

1. Push sources hard to understand that putting their names to what they say is important to freedom of information. This is especially important in dealings with public servants who demand anonymity in routine circumstances.

2. Beat reporters should regularly test the willingness of their sources to be named.

3. Information from unnamed sources should be confirmed whenever possible by one or two other sources (always respecting the original source's anonymity, of course). Try to get supporting documentation. One-source stories are rarely acceptable these days.

4. Reporters writing stories containing unnamed sources must be able to demonstrate: (a) The information is of genuine public interest; (b) The information can be verified by at least one other source, even if unnamed; (c) The source is known to them; (d) There is no real possibility that the source is using CP for selfish purposes; (e) Normal standards of fairness and balance are followed.

5. Bureau supervisors must be consulted before a story with unnamed sources is released. Names of sources will be given to Head Office when requested.

6. Direct quotes should be avoided unless the actual words have unusual significance. This is especially important when opinion is being expressed and the sources might be tempted to use bolder language than if they were being named.

7. If the source is presenting one side of a controversy, the opposing side's views must be sought and presented fairly in the original story.

We don't have to tie every bit of information to a named source. Naming the airline employee who hands out a list of dead and injured in a plane crash adds nothing to the story. The government official who provides routine background or uncontestable fact need not always be named.

But always note names, just in case. And a reminder that prudent reporters always store their notes and tapes in safekeeping for one year at least. In extremely important matters, tapes and notes should be kept indefinitely.

Government officials often insist on anonymity at information briefings, such as in the locked room where reporters write federal or provincial budget stories in advance of delivery. CP abides by such restrictions if necessary, but will not go along with deliberate misrepresentation, such as when a cabinet minister wishes to pass as a civil servant.

Statements from such briefings should not be passed off as general knowledge or undisputed fact. The reader should be told as much as possible about the source and the circumstances should be described.

It is not unheard of for a source to give information confidentially, then deny it by name. If CP feels obliged to carry such a denial, it will identify the original source as the person denying it, provided we are confident the original story accurately reflected the source's information. Consult Head Office before proceeding.

Ethics and sources

When we do promise anonymity we must scrupulously respect that pledge. But it cannot be absolute and it is only fair to tell potential sources so. The courts may require reporters to disclose sources.

Verbal contracts with sources are enforceable in court. Make sure both you and your source understand precisely what that agreement is before you get the information. Do not make promises you cannot keep.

For instance, you can promise not to identify the source in your story and to not willingly make the identity known beyond your employer. You cannot promise to protect the source from any damages that result if the name does become known, through accident or through court order.

CP will not require or advise an employee to balk at the court's direction. It will provide counsel who can advise the employee and who will seek to persuade the court that the public interest does not require disclosure, or who will plead for a closed hearing.

Sources also should know that reporters must identify their sources to their supervisors. This could include anyone from a bureau News Editor to the President. This does not mean that everyone in the chain of command must know. A staffer in a delicate circumstance may go directly to the Vice-President, Editorial or the President.

In extreme circumstances the President might have to inform the Chairman of the Board of a CP source because the member newspapers are legally responsible with CP for the CP news they publish.

If a source must be disclosed beyond the level of the President, senior management will make a concerted effort to advise the originating staffer in advance.

There may be cases where 100 per cent confidentiality is essential on an extremely sensitive news tip and CP is unable to confirm the information with other sources. In such a case senior management will consult the originating staffer. If the problem is insurmountable, CP will not carry the material.

Good reporting dictates that readers be given as much information as possible about the unnamed source's background. This helps readers judge why the story is worth their attention. Qualifications ascribed to the unnamed source must never be misleading. A bit of thought should produce a description helpful to the reader yet protective of the source.

It may be necessary to consult the source about the wording of such a description so the story can inform the reader without revealing the identity.

Other details should be clarified with sources. May all material be used, or must some be treated as only for the reporter's information and guidance (called *background* or *deep background* in the jargon of officialdom)? Are direct quotes permissible or only paraphrases?

Some phrases like **off the record** can have different meanings to different people. Be sure everyone is operating under the same meanings. Consult Head Office when someone proposes unusual restraints.

Some informants may provide information that may be attributed by name, then insist on anonymity for additional information. Attributing this confidential information is tricky: it would be misleading to specify that it came from someone else (**another Finance Department official, who asked for anonymity, said**). Usually it is preferable to rely on phrasing such as **It was also learned.**

Other guides to dealing with unnamed sources:

1.   Don't use others' unnamed sources as if they were CP's. Unnamed sources in stories picked up from newspapers or broadcast should be specifically tied to the paper or broadcaster: **The News quoted an unidentified official in the Energy Department as saying** . . .

2.   Stories should specify that the source requested anonymity and explain why.

3.   Spokesmen and officials should not be confused. A spokesman puts forward the position of others; an official actually helps formulate that position.

4.   Where a fictitious name is being used — for instance, in the case of a juvenile in trouble or a family on welfare — or where a composite person is created to represent a variety of similar individuals, the artifice must be explained promptly. It is a device that cannot be used often without losing impact.

Involving Head Office

Stories from unnamed sources pack much potential for harm against an individual or an institution. Thoughtless journalism damages careers, personal lives, companies and public faith in the media. It also can hurt CP's reputation and its legal position in any suits that might arise.

Safeguards have been designed to help ensure that major stories with potential for harm get plenty of thoughtful evaluation before being rushed into print.

Bureaus with major news breaks involving unnamed sources and with legal and ethical implications must follow these steps:

1.   Have counsel review the story.

2.   After legal checks, the bureau supervisor must set up a telephone conference with the Vice-President, Editorial, the General News Editor and a Main Desk editor.

3.   The conference will answer questions such as:

(a) Who are the sources? How credible are they? What motives exist for a leak of information? Can further verification be obtained?

(b) What public good will the story serve? What are the legal risks? What ethical considerations are involved?

4. Every opportunity to respond must be given to the person or institution involved. Where conscientious effort does not produce a response, the story must detail the attempts made and the reasons why no response was provided.

A final caution: The source who does not want to be named in copy will rarely be available for CP's defence in the event of court action. This could leave us with no defence and lacking any ability to prove what we distributed for public consumption.

Describing unnamed sources

News sources given anonymity should be identified as specifically as possible.

Sources said is bare bones and lacks credibility. Also don't use the hackneyed or meaningless phrases **political observers** and **senior officials** and adjectives like **key, informed, veteran**.

Use specifics that give readers reason to read and believe the story: **An industry source who has been involved in the negotiations, a west European diplomat familiar with the case, a Finance Department official who worked on the draft.**

Computer sources

Online services and the Internet allow an array of information to be gathered quickly in the form of raw data, official records and electronic mail.

In all such cases, the material must be verified before it is used. Human error is a major problem in computerized records. It is also necessary to check the identity of an electronic-mail sender, just as it would be essential to check the identity of a phone caller.

Women as sources

A balanced news report will provide a full range of voices and perspectives, including those of women. Reporters should make a conscious effort to broaden their usual lists of sources to include the women experts in every field. That means not just for topics like child care, equal pay and family violence but also the economy, sports, commodity trading, science, the law and all other news areas.

A well-equipped news desk should include the *Media Directory of Women* and other compilations of contact numbers for women in a variety of spheres.

Taste and tough calls

Today's public demands that the media do their work with more compassion, exhibit more good taste and intrude less on individual privacy. On the other hand, some segments of the public dote on gore and salacious detail.

How far to go in informing the public is a dilemma faced every day.

Do we publish the photo of the University of Montreal student slumped dead in her seat while a plainclothes police officer pulls down holiday decorations in the background?

Strong opinions arose about the publication of this photo. It shows a man removing holiday decorations as the body of a woman lies slumped in a chair— one of 14 women shot in December 1989 at the University of Montreal.

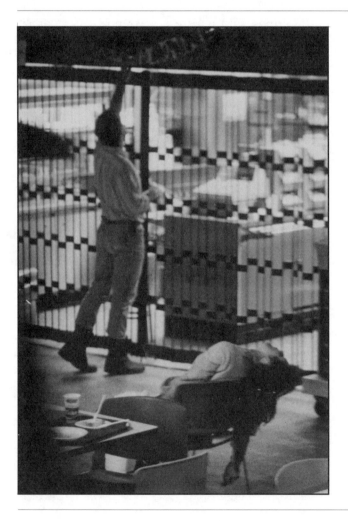

(Montreal Gazette—
Allen McInnis)

Some newspapers did, arguing that the dramatic illustration made readers stop and think about the enormity of the Montreal massacre. Other editors said the photo intruded without sufficient cause on the privacy of the young woman's family and friends.

Were the bounds of decency overstepped by publishing the photos of Rajiv Gandhi's shattered corpse after the former Indian prime minister was assassinated with a bomb?

When a Pennsylvania civil servant, distressed by his own wrongdoing, puts a revolver in his mouth at a news conference and pulls the trigger, what restraints should we use in publishing the photos and in describing the scene?

What about the photo of the nude Vietnamese girl fleeing a napalm attack? Or the shocking photo of a South Vietnamese police chief executing a Viet Cong prisoner by shooting him in the head with a handgun?

These are tough calls, with strongly felt opinions on each side.

At CP we approach each tough call thoughtfully, relying on our experience, good taste and news judgment to help us make the right decision. We weigh carefully what the public needs to know and wants to know against what some might consider repugnant.

CP does enjoy some protection in that it does not transmit directly to the public except in its cable television and radio news operations. We expect that our member newspapers edit our stories and review our photos before deciding whether to publish them.

We must not act as their censors, rejecting material based on standards that are much higher than they, or their reading public, are willing to accept.

That said, our members pay us to select and edit and we must not abandon journalistic standards and principles on the premise that the final gatekeepers are the newspaper editors.

Some guidelines:

1.   An individual's grief is personal and private. CP respects privacy and does not exploit grief to enhance the news.

2.   That applies to funerals. Before covering any funeral, we must ask ourselves: What possible important information will we gain for the public by intruding on this intensely private event?

➤ See **Obituaries**, page 68.

3.   Flag questionable stories and photos with an editor's note to alert newspapers that the material might offend some readers.

4.   When dealing with grieving sources, be respectful and understanding. Don't push your way in. Most people are willing to share their thoughts in situations involving grief, provided there is legitimate public interest. Don't ask people how they feel about a loss.

5.   Public interest must also be carefully weighed when deciding whether to publish the identity of a victim. Details of some crimes are so graphic that naming the victim can only cause more anguish to the innocent party. This can be especially harmful when publishing the victim's name serves no public purpose and adds nothing to the story.

Terrorism, hostage-takings

No news story is worth someone's life. Going for the scoop at any cost when lives are at stake belongs to a time long past.

Ottawa police grab a suspect outside the Turkish Embassy at the end of a hostage-taking incident in March 1985. CP has a clear policy on handling breaking news of terrorist activities.

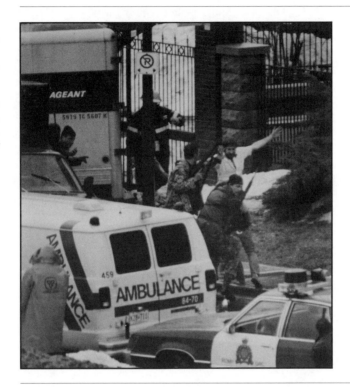

(CP—Fred Chartrand)

That's why we treat terrorist incidents and hostage-takings with extreme caution: They are life-and-death situations.

We have a responsibility to report the news but we have an even greater responsibility to ensure that our actions in news-gathering and reporting do not endanger human lives.

We do not want to become an open publicity line for terrorists, give unwitting support to terrorist causes or impede anti-terrorist efforts.

Some specific guides for dealing with terrorist incidents and hostage-takings:

1. Notify police immediately when you receive a phone call, fax or note about an unpublicized hostage-taking or other terrorist act. Make all information available to police.

2. Do not move a story before checking a senior editorial supervisor at Head Office.

3.   If the story is approved, write that the information was given to **a news organization** without naming CP. Naming CP would risk having it become an outlet for terrorist publicity.

4.   Never telephone the terrorists or their hostages without the approval of a senior editorial supervisor at Head Office. If approval is received, consult the same supervisor again before moving a story.

5.   Do not detail police or security countermeasures or any other information that might aid the terrorists.

6.   We will not tailor or distribute terrorist demands or platforms without Head Office approval. Head Office will not give approval without consulting police or government, or both.

7.   Translate the language of terrorists and police for readers: use plain English such as **note** and **kill** for **communique** and **execute**.

8.   Also consult a supervisor on how to handle terrorism stories received from foreign agencies such as AP and Reuters. What's acceptable to other agencies might not fit CP standards and ethics.

9.   Keep our newspapers informed by advisories when policy restraints affect coverage.

For additional details consult the July 9, 1987, written policy on Reporting on Terrorism and Hostage-takings.

General

Analyses
CP Backgrounders
Business news
  Business reporting
  Business terms
  Company meetings and reports
Columns
Elections
Entertainment
  News
  Awards
  Features
  Reviews
Flashbacks
Foreign news
  Principles
  Chasing news
Labor
  The new workforce
  The new workplace
  Conditions of work
  Labor organizations and affiliations
  Union membership
  Laws and courts
  Conciliation
  Strikes and lockouts
  Vocabulary
Lifestyles
Obituaries
  Cause of death
  Language
  Prepared obits
  Funerals
Polls
Profiles and Newsmakers
Sports
  Points to watch
  More than a game
  Women in sports
  Thinking visuals
  Sponsorship in sport
  Metric, measurement and numbers
  Records
  Spellings to watch
Statistics
Travel

Analyses

The CP News Analysis tests the best qualities that reporters and editors can bring to the news report.

The writer must know the subject intimately to give the reader an informed, intelligent and reasoned assessment of the issues involved. Newspapers look to the CP News Analysis to give their readers a clear and unbiased understanding of what has happened or may happen — and why.

An analysis cannot be done on the run. It demands careful thought and unhurried discussion with a number of outside experts.

Most important: an analysis is not a soapbox. It can focus on a single perspective or point of view, but that perspective must be dispassionate and logical. Opposing views must not be neglected.

Some guidelines:

1. The CP News Analysis is usually built around a single thesis: The new tax will have little effect on consumer spending; the Opposition leader's staff are hurting her image. The thesis is supported by material marshalled in logical order. Objections can be noted, experts cited and secondary angles explored a bit. But the analysis should never lose sight of the main theme by jumbling it with distractions.

2. The analysis should open the reader's eyes, not belabor the obvious. Worthwhile analyses can be built on an unconventional viewpoint, a perspective that hasn't been explored much in the past, a prediction that seems calm when others are confused or even hysterical.

3. The analysis should strike the right balance and tone in the first paragraph. It should not be cute or hyper. Get right to the point:

CP News Analysis
By Kirk LaPointe

OTTAWA (CP) — In the couple of kilometres circling Parliament Hill — bureaucracy's distinct society known as Official Ottawa — there is a deep-running shudder and shake about the Mohamed Al-Mashat case.

Beyond the bruised egos, there is a betrayed trust and brittle suspicion that has paralysed parts of the public service and poisoned aspects of its relationship with its political masters.

---

4. The CP News Analysis is not a substitute for the CP Backgrounder. The analysis focuses more on perspective than on factual background while the backgrounder leans more toward straight-ahead treatment of the major issues in a complex news story.

5.   Analyses do not float a writer's pet theory. They do not pass judgment. They do not offer the writer's solutions. These are **CP** News Analyses and writers should consider every line of them from that perspective. Some newspapers, in fact, remove individual bylines and attribute analyses to CP, period. CP must be able to stand behind every word of every analysis. That means editorializing — or anything that can be construed as editorializing — is out.

Unacceptable: Wilson, publicly crippled by his inability to get fellow Conservatives on side, now must start a new round of negotiations with special-interest groups.

Acceptable: Wilson must now resume negotiations with special-interest groups in the knowledge that his previous efforts failed to draw support from fellow Conservatives on this specific aspect of his tax-reform package.

Never try to build a case with adjectival powder when mortar in the form of facts and thoughtful opinion is lacking. Keep digging or abandon the story as a lost cause.

6.   Keep loaded phrases and words out of analyses. They can turn a sound argument into instant rhetoric — and send a reader away.

Unacceptable: The decision to impose the GST during a recession was based strictly on political considerations, but it will haunt government candidates in the next election. (Two errors: CP is speculating on motivation and CP is making a hard prediction.)

Acceptable: Opposition MPs see pure political strategy behind the decision to impose the GST two years before an election even if it worsens the recession. Among government MPs, there is fear that even two years won't be long enough to soften voters' anger about the new tax. (The information is the same, but the sources for it are people in a position to say.)

7.   Many analyses lend themselves to human touches. In a piece dealing with a major corporate shakeup, for example, a reader might wonder what elements in a new chief executive officer's background particularly qualify her for the top job. Who are the political winners and losers in a federal throne speech? What is the likely impact of a cabinet shuffle on the new or shifted ministers' prospects in the next election?

8.   The one-voice *analysis* has no place in the CP news report. Instead, analyses should attempt to synthesize opinion and be as well sourced as news stories. They should give the reader a sense of the sources who have been consulted, even if they must be unnamed. In an analysis on native issues, for example, it makes a big difference whether the issues are looked at through the eyes of academics or natives themselves.

9.   Avoid over-attribution — a constant **he said, she said**. Often a general line early in an analysis can help.

> . . . **interviews with several senior Liberal party members.**

This gives the reader a sense that the writer has done his homework.

10. The CP writer's own observations and conclusions can be helpful in shaping some analyses. For example, a reporter who has covered a major environmental story from its beginnings to a key development months later should have the background and understanding to assess the situation fairly and from all perspectives. More often, however, the analysis flows from exhaustive research, an uncluttered understanding of the issues involved and solid contact with sources on all sides of those issues.

11. Analyses should be written as close as possible to the news event to heighten their impact. Many papers use CP News Analyses on their front pages, sometimes as the main story.

12. A writer assigned to an analysis on a fixed time event, such as an election night, should not be assigned other duties. He or she will require an uncluttered mind (and desk) to concentrate on the event and its meaning for readers.

In these cases, it should usually be possible to rough out a couple of potential analyses based on different outcomes. If, for example, it appeared possible that the NDP could be elected for the first time in a province, some obvious questions could be explored in advance. What will an NDP government mean in everyday terms for everyday people in that province? Are the New Democrats likely to make major changes? Will people lose their jobs? Will the new government have difficulties dealing with the old-line parties in Ottawa? What has been the experience of other provinces with NDP governments?

13. No analysis should be distributed without being seen by a senior supervisor such as a News Editor or Bureau Chief.

14. Copy should be slugged **CP News Analysis**. There should always be a double keyword slug — one word indicating the subject, the other identifying the piece as an analysis. The label CP News Analysis is intended to be publishable. It goes directly above the writer's byline separated by a space from photo and other service slugs.

BC-Filmon-Analysis, Bgt
Budget
See CP Photo WPG7

> **CP News Analysis**
> **By Scott Edmonds**

WINNIPEG (CP) — . . .

CP Backgrounders

When it's time to pull a maze of news threads together or to stand back from a particularly confusing story, the CP Backgrounder is the vehicle of choice — and a welcome friend to the reader.

Above all, the CP Backgrounder gives the reader the answers to basic questions: What's really going on here? What does it mean to me and my families and my neighbors?

CP Backgrounders, formerly known in-house as *situationals*, differ from CP News Analyses. Essentially, the analysis builds a structure of interpretation upon a foundation of factual material. The backgrounder focuses on the foundation stones through an orderly assembly of factual detail and perspective.

The backgrounder provides historical context, sets out the whys and wherefores of a complicated issue in the news, explores legal questions or lists the pocketbook impact of the development under review.

Where appropriate, the backgrounder will also quote knowledgeable authorities — or everyday people with first-hand experience in similar circumstances — about future implications for the lives of readers.

A strong sense of a key player's human side is usually needed to give the reader an understanding of the personalities involved.

There is no practical limit to the kinds of situations that can be served by a well-thought-out backgrounder:

• The history of Dr. Henry Morgentaler's battles with the legal system, as a scene-setter for his latest court test.

• How Prairie farmers are coping with a string of bad luck: drought, debt, coyotes and grasshoppers.

• How the premier has pulled her party together at the last minute to head into an election, with the story focusing on her persuasive personality and political savvy.

• Why some major corporations are lopping off subsidiaries after years of bigger-is-better thinking.

• What's behind a new NHL rule on facemasks, reviewing a rash of facial injuries from a doctor's perspective.

Effective backgrounders can often be worked up on matters that might otherwise receive only passing attention in the spot news report.

An example:

Business interests, local residents and nature lovers are locked in a battle over a proposed tourism development in the North. What is at stake? Why are the various sides in conflict? How have the battle lines been drawn?

The story could include interesting sketches of people on each side of the dispute, description and history of the area being fought over and some sense of the values being promoted — a rare breeding ground for song birds versus jobs in a high unemployment area, for example.

The writing approach to such stories is as wide open as the imagination of the writer. It often helps to focus on a specific element in a many-sided situation or on a single human being directly involved.

Be wary of the grab-bag lead that tries to gather in a large number of major components. It is an approach that rarely works.

Point form can be especially effective in setting out key issues or background to give the reader some fast and tidy context.

A backgrounder on the Atlantic provinces, for instance, could hit points like this high up in the story:

• The four provinces have 194 legislature members and 34,000 civil servants for a population of 2.2 million. Alberta, with a population of 2.4 million, has 83 legislature members and 12,000 civil servants.

• Newfoundland gets 47 cents of every government dollar from the federal treasury; P.E.I. 46 cents; New Brunswick and Nova Scotia 39 cents each.

• The cap on federal transfer payments has already cut $400 million from the amount the region had been counting on, and more cuts seem certain.

Style

The label CP Backgrounder is intended to be publishable. It goes directly above the writer's byline, separated by a space from photo and other service slugs.

AM-ENVIR-Tourism-Bkgrndr, Bgt
Budget
See CP Photo CPT17; CP Graphic CPT3

CP Backgrounder
By Ian Bailey
SIOUX LOOKOUT, Ont. (CP) — . . .

Business news

Business news is about companies, industry, trade, commerce, finance and the economy. But ultimately it concerns people — their jobs, mortgages, bank accounts, investments and long-term prosperity.

Changes in economic conditions affect people. And people's behavior can influence the economy.

• The merger of two companies, for example, may combine their strengths and improve production efficiency. But it may also mean lost jobs.

• Consumers continuing to spend despite signs of an impending recession may temporarily delay the start of the downturn.

• Higher interest rates could mean a higher Canadian dollar, which benefits someone travelling abroad but hurts exporters. Closer to home, higher interest rates may mean a bigger monthly mortgage payment, but savings in the bank may earn a bit more interest.

Business news deals with fluctuations in financial markets. As much as possible, business stories should explain what the price movements indicate. To what extent do they reflect investors' perception of economic conditions or a company's prospects? How much of the change is affected by political events? By sheer speculation? Is there a herd mentality at work? How about the interplay of greed and fear?

Like other news, business news occurs within the context of society. Bottom lines can be affected by developments in areas not traditionally associated with business. Environmental concerns, new standards of ethics and morality, the spread of AIDS, an aging population — these are some of the factors that can affect a company's prospects.

Similarly, business news in Canada is affected by what goes on elsewhere. A war in the Middle East could improve the economic outlook of oil-producing western provinces. The discovery of a cheaper and better substitute overseas may hurt the prospects of Canadian producers of, say, lumber or steel. Eventually, people who work in these industries feel the effect.

Business reporting

Business news is judged like other news, on reader interest.

Discard the assumption that business writing has to be staid, uninteresting and faceless. The best business stories are often dynamic and colorful, and focused on people and companies making their way through a constantly changing economic landscape.

The business writer should keep in mind two levels of understanding:

• General readers who want to keep up with what is happening in the business world.

• Business readers who want information on the economy and developments in fields related to their own.

Always try to write the story in an easy-to-read way. Even highly specialized readers appreciate a clear and accurate story.

The basic requirements of business reporting are similar to those for other news — accuracy, clarity, speed, balance, relevance to readers and freedom from jargon. Accuracy and clarity are especially important in business news, which deals frequently with figures, names and complex concepts.

Common pitfalls:

1.   Check all figures. One extra digit can throw a number off completely. A single letter turns million into billion.

2.   Watch accounting terms. **Net operating income** and **net income**, for example, can be quite different things.

3.   Verify corporate identities. Some companies have similar names but are not directly related, or one may be a subsidiary of another. **Camco Inc.** and **Cameco Corp.** are in quite different lines of business; **Montreal Trust Co.** is a subsidiary of **Montreal Trustco Inc.**

4.   Companies change hands, product names are bought and sold. Check with the company concerned if at all possible.

For example, a fictitious company called **Really Clean Products International** changes its name to **RCP International** after selling its soap-making division along with the brand name, **Really Clean**. The buyer, wanting to capitalize on the well-established name, sets up a company called **Really Clean Inc.** Despite the similarity in names, there is no corporate link between the two companies.

5.   Watch percentages. A statement that a company's profit is **up 50 per cent** isn't helpful: $150 is 50 per cent more than $100, and $1.5 million is 50 per cent more than $1 million. Include actual figures.

Some suggestions:

1.   Keep human faces high in the story whenever possible. It's a way of saying a corporate development affects people in real life. For example, if Really Clean Inc. announced a layoff of 150 employees, an effective approach to the story might be:

James Lee walked home from work to save bus fare. He and 149 of his co-workers at Really Clean received layoff notices Friday.

2.   Always ask how any development is likely to affect the reader. Some events, like GATT negotiations, may have no immediate impact on readers but their long-term impact can be significant. Explain why: protectionist walls may go up around countries that buy Canadian products, and jobs in the export sector may be jeopardized.

3.   Keep long corporate names or unfamiliar acronyms out of the first paragraph. Instead, use a short name that may be readily recognized, or a quick explanation of the type of business. The full name can be included a bit later in the story.

4.   It sometimes helps to mention a company's best-known products. For example: **Scott Paper, the company that makes White Swan tissue** . . .

5.   Complex corporate relationships or long lists of names and numbers might best be laid out in a sidebar, a chart or a QuickFacts box. This allows the story to deal with the impact of a development.

6.   Translate business jargon into plain English. If a technical term must be included, explain what it means.

Business terms

Bonds, debentures
The buyer of **bonds** or **debentures** is a creditor who lends money to the company for a fixed term at an agreed interest rate.

Debentures are unsecured promises to repay the loan. Corporate **bonds** are ordinarily secured by fixed assets. Although government securities are often called bonds, they are actually debentures — guaranteed by the government but without assets being pledged. If a company goes out of business, secured creditors' claims on its assets have priority over claims of other creditors and preferred shareholders, who in turn are ahead of common shareholders.

Cash flow
Refers to a company's cash resources. **Cash flow** is different from **net earnings** because accounting items like depreciation are deducted from earnings but do not result in actual paying out of cash. Cash flow can be calculated by adding non-cash expenses — usually depreciation and deferred taxes — to net income. It gives an indication of a company's ability to earn money and meet its obligations.

Consolidated statement
A financial statement that includes the results of subsidiary companies. This is usually done when the parent company owns 50 per cent or more of the subsidiary.

Extraordinary items
Year-over-year comparisons of net profit can be distorted in a year when, for example, plants and equipment are sold. These one-time events are called **extraordinary items**. For a meaningful comparison from year to year, it is usually necessary to look as well at net profit before extraordinary items. Wherever possible, try for longer-term comparisons such as a five-year range or average. Figures should be given for comparable previous periods.

Financing

Equity financing means raising money through the sale of common shares. The buyer becomes a part-owner of the company.

Debt financing means raising money through bonds and debentures. The buyer lends money to the company, which promises to repay the amount in the future with interest.

Net profit, net income, net earnings

The three terms mean the same thing — a company's profit (or loss) after all expenses and taxes have been paid. It is out of net profit that dividends are paid — first to preferred shareholders, then to common shareholders.

Net operating profit

Money earned from a company's operations — the sale of its products or services. It should not be confused with **net profit**, which includes both income from operations and non-operating sources like rents, interest and investments.

Net earnings per share

Obtained by deducting from net profit any amount paid to preferred shareholders, and dividing the resulting amount by the number of common shares outstanding.

Share, stock

A part-ownership of a company obtained by providing capital to the business. **Common shareholders** have the right to vote in the company. If the company performs well, shareholders benefit from the rise in the value of the shares. The term **a share** refers to a common share unless otherwise stated.

Preferred shares entitle the holder to a fixed dividend from net profit before common shareholders are paid. Preferred shares generally carry no voting privileges as long as promised dividends are paid.

Company meetings and reports

Some Canadian companies date to the early days of Canada and have played important roles in the country's economic development. Other firms have been the economic bedrock of their community, providing both employment and tax dollars. Some occupy pivotal positions in their sector of the economy. Their financial health and future plans are often news of wide interest.

Company meetings and reports can provide information on how these companies are doing and where they are going financially.

Stories based on company reports need not be dry recitals of statistics. Many companies explain in their reports why profits are small or sales have increased. This kind of information, along with background on the company and its products, can brighten the story and give it depth.

➤ See also **Handling business news**, page 408.

Columns

Unlike a standard feature, a column permits the writer to express opinion. The level of personal opinion or analysis depends on the expertise of the author. A regular columnist is assumed to have greater expertise than a guest columnist, and therefore would have a freer rein to offer personal views.

Whether writing about food, fitness or finances, basic rules of journalism apply: watch for the hard-news angle; balance the piece with both sides of a controversial story; seek out multiple sources; inject healthy doses of color and personality.

Favor active adjectives and description. Don't say the blues singer has a low voice when you can say he **croaks in a deep-fried rumble**.

Avoid alienating the reader with inappropriate use of the first person or an elitist tone.

When possible, use specific, everyday situations or terms that will help the reader relate to the topic.

So you stayed up till midnight and finally finished that income tax return.

Reporter-columnists who are actively involved in gathering news in the field, not just sitting back passing editorial judgment, should always try to see and present all sides of the story. Expressing opinions can be an important part of a column — crucial to a review — but the columnist must be seen to be fair.

Elections

Public-opinion polls and clever election strategists have dramatically changed the election process in Canada. So have skeptical and savvy voters.

Fund-raising has become an art, candidates' personalities are carefully polished, campaigns are stage-managed for maximum television exposure, news is manipulated. And yet the voters grow ever more wary of elections and intolerant of manipulative politics.

News coverage must adapt to the changes, looking for more effective ways of describing the process and involving the voters. Television has become a more influential factor in campaigns, but print reporting still has an important role.

Some of CP's criteria for an effective news report on an election:

1. **Let the voters, not the politicians, decide what the issues are.**

Campaign coverage that is focused heavily on candidates' travels and statements may be irrelevant to readers. For example, if all the major parties are concentrating on constitutional issues, where does that leave voters worried about their jobs or the air they breathe or the fact that their kids have trouble reading?

Political reporters need to recognize that getting the *tough* one-liner snapped off by a cabinet minister with an eye on the 6 o'clock TV news is often less important than spending 20 minutes talking to voters in the minister's riding.

If reporters listen to what's on the voters' minds, and put those concerns to the candidates, readers may decide the press is worth paying attention to.

The alternative is to allow politicians to decide what's news.

A sound election file can be built by focusing on the party leaders and the apparent issues in the first week or two of the campaign. From then until the final days, the focus should shift to pinpointing what's bothering the voters, explaining the background to the big issues and clarifying the parties' stands on voter concerns.

2. **Be prepared.**

Surprise elections are rare. Supervisors and political reporters aware of an impending election will (a) set up a clear organization for covering the campaign; (b) establish their news priorities; (c) put profiles of the party leaders and other basic backgrounders *in the bank* for use when the election is called.

As the campaign unfolds, measure out special takeouts on the issues dear to the voters' hearts. Some regional issues become important enough to swing whole areas, so they need sensitive explanation. Some unlikely candidates will come on strong and need profiling. Issues like party funding, television ads, all-candidates debates, minor parties and historical trends are often worth looking at.

Election campaigns are also a test of CP's relationship with newspapers and broadcasters. Getting their news supervisors on side ahead of time can mean timely reports on major developments and a consistent supply of spot and feature material from all over a bureau's region.

Being prepared also means recognizing that the general public has lots of other interests besides politics. Campaign coverage shouldn't deprive readers of other news that's important to them.

3. **Don't forget the libel laws.**

Statements are sometimes made in the heat of an election campaign that in other circumstances would be pretty good grounds for a libel suit.

Some basic legal ground rules:

a) A fair and accurate report of public statements made at a meeting that's open to the general public isn't usually risky. But that may not apply if only some members of the public (say, one party's members) are allowed into the meeting. And if a person attacked at the meeting wants to respond, the response must be reported.

b) Potentially libellous statements made in other circumstances — even a radio broadcast — are not safe to publish. Get legal advice.

c) Federal law bars publishing or broadcasting poll results in the last three days of a campaign. That includes mentioning or analysing earlier polls. Some provincial and federal laws limit certain forms of campaigning and advertising just before voting day. Check election laws for pitfalls.

4. **Provide context, color, detail.**

Reporting on campaign activities means making sense of the political statements. It also means bringing the campaign to life.

Context: What would the promise of a new housing policy mean for house prices? Construction jobs? Increased government debt and taxes? How does the new policy compare with past promises, the other parties' positions? What do outside experts think of it? Not all such questions will be worth answering, but few political statements of any importance should be left to stand alone.

Color: Most politicians are scarcely known to the public. They often need to be described in action, gesturing and raising their voices to emphasize a point or laughing at the hecklers or making small talk on the street. The towns and crossroads where they campaign should be sketched. The campaign audiences should be shown responding or watching skeptically.

In both context and color, be specific.

Not: The premier promised to cut government spending.

Instead: For the farm crowd in Ruralia, the premier promised to cut loan guarantees for big business. At the Middleton Rotary Club, she said there would be fewer tax concessions for shopping malls. Back in the capital, she worried about the cost of irrigation projects and secondary roads.

5. **For election night, again be prepared.**

Smooth, comprehensive coverage of election results depends on thorough advance work. It's too late to look for background information when the voting results are flooding in.

Prepare: profile material on the leaders and any candidates important to the overall coverage; background on the major issues and how the parties stood on them; the range of public-opinion poll results; the best of the campaign anecdotes to lighten up the stories.

Also: statistical histories of which parties have formed the government and when; figures on the size of majorities for past governments; information on minority governments, the defeat of governments and their leaders, the national situation for each major party.

CP gets continuous reports from returning offices to prepare progressive tabular results on election night.

```
{u

{↑AM-TAB-ELXN-Standings↓
¶  CP Standings--National
{  at 01:45 am EDT
{    Elected Leading Total
{PC   130       36      166
{Lib   59       28       87
{NDP   30       12       42
{Ind    0        0        0
¶  Totals: 295 in 1988
{after redistribution;
{282 in 1980 and 1984.
¶
```

(Most newspapers and broadcasters depend on CP for detailed results, gathered progressively at a single election centre. The results are delivered in ready-to-use formats from a computer programmed to make instantaneous adjustments in vote totals, winners and losers, party votes and other categories. The material is invaluable for those writing lead stories and separates at CP and other media.)

6. **Down with hype.**

The frenzy of election night can be the enemy of clear thinking.

It's common in Canadian elections for one party to win a substantial majority of seats with barely 40 per cent of the votes. That doesn't constitute a **landslide** of popular support. Stories about the result need precise wording.

And sweeping statements about the voters' feelings or intentions are risky. Each voter in a federal or provincial election makes a choice among local candidates, period. Each constituency result is probably influenced by broader issues and the popularity of the party leaders, but they aren't on the ballot.

It's stretching things to write baldly that voters **rejected a spending freeze** or **punished the government for failing to cut unemployment.** The effect of all those individual votes will be a government with some stated commitments. That's the surest way to describe the election result. Informed political observers can help keep the influence of national or provincial factors in perspective.

7. **The cleanup.**

Election campaigns don't end on election night. The days immediately following an election bring some of the most significant stories.

Supervisors need to ensure that fresh staff is available for two or three days after an election to complete reporting on how the results will affect voters.

Working from notes left over by election-night supervisors, the next-day staff should clean up loose ends — late polls, possible recounts, missing ballot boxes.

They can also concentrate on reaching the experts who will help make better sense of the results. They can examine the detailed results more closely for victories and defeats that were overlooked. And CP staff can exploit newspaper material that was neglected in the rush of election night.

8. **Plan for the next one.**

The start of good coverage of the next election begins with a thoughtful file on this one. Before the ink is dry on coverage of any election, a file should be opened that includes:

•   Careful notes from supervisors on everything that went well and everything that went wrong — and why.

•   Notes from reporters and deskers on how to improve election coverage. Everyone who took part should have something to contribute.

•   Examples of the best and the worst stories from the campaign, your own or others'.

•   Copies of all the memos, circulars, letters and other paperwork that will be needed as reminders the next time.

Entertainment

Entertainment is a catch-all title covering a broad range of activities and interests. For so-called popular tastes, there are television and radio, pop music and movies, circuses and standup comedy. For the highbrows, there are books and plays, operas and concerts, museums and balls.

Each of these categories can produce a hard-news story on any given day — everything from a fund-raising crisis at the art gallery to the arrest of a prominent actress. On other days, they'll merit a profile or feature.

Or they may be dealt with in a review or column.

News

It's often regarded as soft news, but basic principles of journalism apply to entertainment coverage.

1. **Look for hard news:** Ask the TV actor if and when he plans to move on from his current sitcom. When the tour of a controversial rap group is announced, ask police whether they'll have extra patrols when the musicians hit town. Ask the author of the new best-seller her opinion of sales taxes on books.

2. **Strive for balanced coverage:** If a songwriter complains that music royalties in Canada are tiny, check copyright laws and how royalties compare with those in other countries. When an author trashes a celebrity in a book, get comment from the star or his representatives. In articles about the state of a particular art form in Canada, include representatives from across the country.

3. **Avoid single-source stories:** When the artistic director of a theatre announces a new stage season, some insightful comments may be provided by actors, directors or even academics and drama critics about the choices. In a profile of a sexually provocative singer, talk to others — his parents, perhaps? — about his image.

4. **Inject color and personality:** Don't say Madonna wore a bathing suit and shoes when she entered the press room. Say The former Material Girl wore very little of it, except for the teeny weeny polka-dot bikini, black spike heels and a gleaming white smile. In reviews of new works, describe the atmosphere in the hall and the reaction of the opening night audience. If a usually suave young actor trips and falls at your feet when you come to interview him, don't brush it off — include it in your article.

Think pictures and graphics. Nothing sells a story like a good illustration.

Keep section deadlines in mind. Deliver a time-sensitive story well in advance of deadline to help editors making up pages. Keep editors advised of late-breaking or short-notice material they can expect soon.

Awards

Industry awards are among the highest profile entertainment events. There are so many of them, the challenge is to determine how much and what type of coverage to give each awards event and how to develop lively, interesting copy from it.

Singer Celine Dion hoists two Juno Awards at the Canadian music industry ceremonies in March 1991. Entertainment awards are often big news to readers.

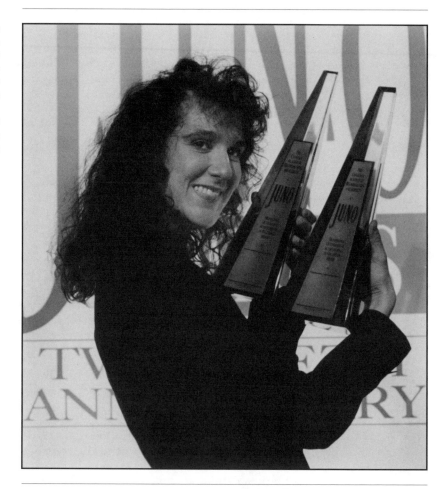

(CP—Tim Pelling)

Entertainment awards tend to be self-serving. Major events such as the Emmys, Grammys, Oscars, Junos, Geminis and Genies are of interest to the average reader and merit extensive coverage. Lesser-known events may warrant little or no coverage.

A little homework in advance can be valuable. For example, research may turn up that the director of a film on long-distance running suffered polio as a child.

Complete lists of winners are an important companion to stories on the event. The list should give the category first, preferably in boldface. Then on a separate line, indented, the name of the winner.

Top Female — Country
     Anne Murray

Some category titles may have to be shortened to fit a single column. **Outstanding Performance by a Lead Actor in a Drama Series** might be changed to **Best Actor — Drama**.

Features

Entertainment feature-writing generally allows more freedom to inject color, personality and imaginative writing.

Colorful metaphors or similes can sometimes paint a vivid mental image. **Rock music on television is a lion in a cage. The BMW on Rodeo Drive glistened like a well-buffed Gucci loafer.**

Summing up a well-known person in a choice phrase can do two things: distil the subject's personality for the reader, plus set a tone for the article. **The artistic film director is a 32-year-old bundle of neuroses.**

While actors may make for identifiable hooks for a story, producers and directors are often more articulate about a project and can provide fresh insight. A good entertainment story often mixes the creative insights with the star quality of a Hollywood figure.

Reviews

In a world teeming with entertainment choices, the thoughtful review is especially important to help readers decide how to spend their leisure time.

Basically, a review gives the reader a synopsis of the work with some commentary on its artistic merit or entertainment value.

Full-time reviewers have more credibility and leeway than part-timers — who would do well to approach the assignment as a news event, describing it and getting audience comment or quoting newspaper reviewers.

➤ See **Columns**, page 46.

Reviewers should avoid cheap shots or gush. While someone like George Bernard Shaw could get away with a demolishing review, readers can be turned off by harshness or apparent unfairness.

Commentary needs to be grounded in specific detail. Saying a rock band's show was atrocious means nothing. Rather: **The lead singer was off-key on three numbers, the lighting failed during another and people at the rear of the hall complained they couldn't hear the lyrics.**

Give readers a signpost: **The band conjures up the driving rhythm of the early Rolling Stones.**

When reviewing drama or books, reveal only as much of the plot as necessary to set the scene for the review. Readers will be annoyed to have the ending revealed by a thoughtless reviewer.

Resist adopting the vocabulary of the industry. Terms such as **genre** and **film noir** smack of trendiness and they're not used by the average reader.

Flashbacks

The key to Flashbacks is to make clear why the events were important when they happened and why they deserve to be remembered now.

Newspapers always seem to have space for a nicely written historical piece on anything from Louis Riel to the October Crisis, especially one sprinkled with human touches and appealing anecdotes.

1. Flashbacks tied to anniversaries should note that connection somewhere in the first two or three paragraphs: **It was 60 years ago this week that . . .**

2. The successful Flashback starts with a strong idea, usually in one of these two categories:

a) Recognizable historical events like Prohibition and the conscription crisis, tied to a specific anniversary, or an event like the Korean War that is tied to a veterans reunion.

b) All-but-forgotten happenings that can be successfully revived for today's reader — events like the Frank landslide of 1903 that killed at least 70 people in the territory that in 1905 became Alberta.

3. Flashbacks on historical figures should usually be tied to a specific anniversary as well (birth, death, special honor, etc.) — the anniversary of Sir John A. Macdonald's first election, for example.

Lesser-known individuals can serve as the focus point for Flashbacks on major events — the coal miner who survived the 1958 Springhill disaster, the diary of a policeman who battled rioters during the 1919 general strike in Winnipeg.

4. Look for topics with some direct effect on people — then or now.

5. Try to find someone who was around at the time. That will be impossible in some cases, of course, so it will mean a trip to an archives or a library — public, university or newspaper — to search for contemporary accounts or comments on the incident being recalled.

6. Opportunities for color are rife in such stories. Sometimes personal scrapbooks or letters can be helpful. Quoting the flowery language of the day can bring a dusty piece of history to life.

7. If the subject is controversial, check at least three different sources to ensure you're not quoting someone with an axe to grind.

The label **CP Flashback** is intended to be publishable. It goes directly above the writer's byline, separated by a space from photo and other service slugs. See page 41 for a comparable example.

Foreign news

Gunfire in Jerusalem . . . A Canadian gold medal for swimming in Nairobi . . . A riot at a rock concert outside Buenos Aires . . . An international arms conference at Geneva.

Whatever the event, Canadians will know about it within hours.

Few countries are better served on world news than Canada, with its instant access via satellite to countless reliable sources of information. And CP contributes in a major way to that flow of news and photos.

CP has its own network of staff and freelance correspondents abroad, sending stories to central desks in Toronto for English-language services and in Montreal for La Presse Canadienne, CP's French-language sister service. Staff from CP's bureaus in Canada travel abroad regularly on assignment.

In addition, both world news desks have instant access to reports from two of the most important news agencies in the world, The Associated Press and Reuters. Their news is delivered directly to CP's computers, to be co-ordinated and edited by people experienced in making sense of complicated foreign developments.

And the world report is supplemented with news gathered through phone calls from Toronto and other Canadian bureaus to trouble spots abroad, adding a Canadian dimension to reports of storms, coups, shipwrecks and other urgent developments.

That Canadian dimension justifies CP's special efforts in shaping the world news report. Canada's interests don't exactly coincide with any other country's: we have a different history, different perspective on the world, different trade and cultural traditions, different political system, different internal tensions and problems.

News written for readers in other countries cannot entirely satisfy a Canadian readership. Canadian reporters abroad are more likely to notice parallels of interest to Canadian readers. They'll pay more attention to Canadian activities on the international stage. And they can make foreign developments understandable in Canadian terms.

The international agency copy received in Canada is reported and edited by a cosmopolitan mix of nationalities — including many Canadian expatriates — and the agencies' credibility depends on copy that is free of bias.

However, the copy is largely written for an American audience, and its political and cultural context is tuned to American interests. CP's editors must be alert for bias in any copy from abroad. And they should balance the American influence with background and explanation designed for Canadian readers.

Guiding principles

A few basic principles should guide those putting together a foreign news report:

1. Canadians are entitled to be well informed on events abroad that affect their own lives or that can influence the course of world history.

2. International news is not only the doings of political leaders — *President X* said this, *Foreign Minister Y* arrived there — along with some riots and civil wars, hurricanes and earthquakes. It is also ordinary people doing extraordinary things anywhere in the world. It is the small triumphs and defeats of the human spirit. It is social and cultural trends that can reach across borders and continents to interest readers elsewhere.

3. Canada is a player on the world stage, and its efforts abroad deserve coverage. Its influence and activities need to be kept in perspective, however. For example, at a conference of the Group of Seven, the Canadian delegation's views are worth reporting in detail by Canadian correspondents. But a balanced report will also focus on the most important overall developments and the most thoughtful or provocative positions of other countries.

4. A complete news report will include a look at how other countries try to solve issues that Canadians also face. The common problems found in health care, pollution, tax levels and other areas can be tackled in a variety of ways. A report on how other countries are coping with such problems can provide Canadians with fresh alternatives to consider.

5. The role of Canadian correspondents or travelling reporters abroad is not to take Canada's side in international disputes — how, for example, other countries may be using unfair agricultural subsidies that hurt Canadian farmers. A more important function is to explain to Canadians why others see and do things differently — the importance of farm communities to another country's social texture. The Canadian viewpoint is usually well presented by officials in Canada.

6. In the same way that Canada isn't just Mounties and snow, other countries are more than their folklore and eccentricities. Emphasizing the cliched elements in another country — the stiff upper lip in London, the volubility of Parisians, carved temples in India, carnivals in Rio — can distract readers from the fascinating complexity of other societies.

7. Effective coverage of the Third World involves more than buses falling into ravines, coups and rebellions, soccer riots, chronic misery and government corruption, with a bit of witchcraft thrown in. A balanced foreign report will also look at ordinary peoples' concerns, new agricultural practices, self-help programs, the leading pop singer or poet, traditional religious influences, unusual pastimes and other aspects of daily life in the Third World. The international agencies' files should be watched closely for such copy. And travelling CP staff can be used to fill the gaps, where possible.

Chasing news

The CP World Desk uses the phones to provide a steady source of news on Canadians abroad. Its efforts can be duplicated by reporters anywhere with some resourcefulness and patience. Whenever Canadians are at the centre of developing stories overseas — earthquakes, fires, revolutions, plane crashes or whatever — they can be a vivid part of the story for Canadian readers.

Some useful basic resources:

1. A telephone with automatic redial capability. When calling an overseas number with 14 digits and a half-dozen intermediate points that could give a busy signal, it saves time to let a machine do the dialling.

2. A Foreign Affairs Department booklet of Canadian ambassadors and other representatives abroad. It includes business phone, fax and Telex numbers as well as some home phones.

3. A travel agency book with hotel numbers from around the world.

4. A Telex machine, with directories. Telexes are widespread in other countries, easy to use and effective for prompting others to reply. It's often possible to make Telex contact with a distant country when telephone lines aren't working. Newspapers, radio stations, hotels, private companies and government ministries usually have Telex connections. Telex also has a directory-assistance service to provide additional help.

5. A good filing system of names and numbers overseas, listed by country, with brief notes about previous contacts. The hotel clerk who was so helpful with the earthquake two years ago may again be invaluable tracking down Canadians missing during a military coup.

Remember when calling abroad that almost anyone you reach is likely to know more about the country and its information sources than you do. Many strangers will try to be helpful to someone calling from overseas with a legitimate need for information.

Even try asking a private company whom they would call if they were trying to get the information you need. If they don't know, they may be able to suggest someone who can help.

Which leads to a key bit of advice: Always ask the person you've managed to contact for the names and numbers of anyone else who might also be able to help. Some terrific contacts have been made by the CP World Desk that way.

Labor

General

Most people spend more of their waking hours at work than at anything else, including time for friends, family or leisure. They can have strong opinions about work.

That's one of the factors that makes reporting on work and the workplace so demanding. There are many other complications that increase the need for accuracy and fairness.

For instance, relations between employee and employer, between labor and management, tend to be complex and sensitive.

And despite its reputation, work isn't always something people perform numbingly. For many, work is how they define themselves. For others, it's something they regularly discuss with friends and family and continually contemplate.

Workers go through periods of great ambition and satisfaction and swings of unproductiveness and discontent. They are often part of a business or profession that can boom one year and go bust the next.

And they are an increasingly transient and adapting force. Where a generation ago someone had a lifelong career, this generation of workers can expect to have two or more different careers.

That means workers, and people seeking work, must be thoughtfully portrayed. Stories about work need to reflect that work is a focal point for many and a diversion for others. Stories need to vividly represent work's role in society and examine the many aspects of the work environment.

The new workforce

1. Although contract disputes provide the most drama, coverage of work needs to go far beyond the union-shop floor. The rapid growth of service industries, small businesses and self-employed enterprises has fuelled job creation in the last decade. Most of these workers do not have a contract and are not part of a union. Indeed, roughly 60 per cent of the workforce is not unionized.

2. Two-income families are the norm, not the exception, and the two-worker phenomenon has as much to do with economic necessity as it does with career aspirations. Having a job doesn't mean having economic security — a significant number of people using food banks in cities are the working poor.

3. An increasing number of skilled workers and skill-seeking businesses are looking for ways to alter the employee-employer relationship. With initiatives like *flex time*, more people would work from home, more would have flexible or reduced work hours, more would share jobs, more would take leaves of absence for retraining and professional development. Workplaces increasingly offer such benefits as on-site child care or fitness centres.

4. At either the urging of employees or the concession of employers, a number of highly prized workers are engaging in the process called *downshifting*, named after the tactic a Formula One driver uses to go around a hairpin curve. By reducing hours of work or taking less demanding jobs, they are trying to get out of the rat race.

5. There has been steady growth in the number of term contract employees — people hired for a specific function for a specific time. They are often paid a lump sum in lieu of benefits or pensions.

The new workplace

1. If the nature of labor is changing, so is the nature of management. Experts say more duties are being delegated, more decisions are being made by workers and more ideas are working their way up to the boardroom from the office or factory floor.

2. Consultation between workers and managers is becoming more common. The *us-against-them* approach is slowly breaking down, and partnerships among business, labor and governments in industrial and professional risk-taking have begun to appear.

3. These changes in turn produce other changes in traditional practice. Workers make concessions on salaries in exchange for bonuses tied to performance. Managers make concessions on professional leaves even if that creates short-term expertise problems.

Coverage of news about work and the workplace has to reflect such changes.

But even when covering more traditional union-management situations, the goal should be perspectives that are tied to human beings: how someone is making ends meet during a strike; how a local merchant is coping with a lockout; what prompted someone to become active in the labor movement.

Conditions of work

The basic document governing conditions for employees and workers in unionized plants and offices is the contract. Non-unionized workers generally live under more casual arrangements. Complicated economic times bring complex work arrangements that require careful, clear explanations.

Some general guides:

1. **Wages:** In contracts, always compare the previous basic or average wage with the new rate, using a recognizable job (a bricklayer in the construction industry, a production line employee in an auto plant, a senior reporter at a newspaper). When wage changes vary according to the job category, the range should be specified.

When using percentage changes in wage stories, always use actual examples of change. And compare like elements: report a $50 weekly increase in a $500 weekly salary, not a 50-cent hourly increase in a $500 weekly salary. Beware of baldly totalling percentage increases. An increase of 10 per cent now and 10 per cent next year is not a 20 per cent increase; compounded, it is 21 per cent. Don't make readers do math.

2. **Dates:** In contract stories, spell out the starting date to indicate how much retroactivity is involved in a contract settlement. Spell out the dates of further changes in the contract during its identified full term. Don't say a new contract gives workers $4 an hour more, when in fact it gives $2 now and $2 in two years' time.

3. **Inflation protection:** Mention when wage arrangements provide for additional increases if inflation is a specified rate, commonly called **indexation** or a **cola (cost-of-living-allowance) clause**, terms to be avoided except in quotes and to be explained no matter what.

4. **Job protection:** Summarize measures that shield workers from unemployment, including advance notice of layoffs or plant closings, guaranteed payments for those laid off, retraining programs, pension protection, offers of corporate transfers to other communities.

5. **Worker concessions:** In contract stories, summarize changes that might limit strikes or other activities to protest work conditions, or agreements to limit salary increases in order to protect jobs or increase the workforce.

6. **Pay equity:** Roughly defined as **equal pay for work of equal value**, pay equity is part of some provinces' legislation. It compels employers to pay women the same as men for similar work. Many contracts now feature a catch-up clause for women in specific jobs; any breakthroughs in this area should be mentioned.

7. **Non-statutory holidays:** Mention should be made of companies that provide workers with a fixed number of days off to be taken in observance of their religious or ceremonial holidays.

8. **Non-monetary issues:** Some contracts are now fought over conditions of work, including the flexibility of work hours, the ability of workers to curtail their work hours or to share jobs, the amount of continual worker training a company will provide, or health and safety issues.

These should be highlighted as interesting elements for readers with similar or contracted jobs. When estimates of the value of these benefits are carried, the source of the estimate must be given: **The company says the new child-care provisions are worth $50 a week per employee.**

When neither workers nor companies mention these aspects of a contract, try to get the information independently.

Labor organizations and affiliations

Federations

Unions are grouped in national and regional groups but have a large measure of autonomy within them. The main federations are:

Canadian Labor Congress, with 2.5 million members, formed out of the 1956 merger of the Trades and Labor Congress of Canada and the Canadian Congress of Labor. The CLC counts among its affiliates more than 50 international organizations, 20 national, three provincial and 80 directly chartered local unions. Affiliated secondary bodies include 12 provincial federations, 120 local labor councils and one labor committee. CLC headquarters is in Ottawa.

People are members of the CLC only through their affiliated unions. In larger provinces, such unions are grouped in provincial federations — the Saskatchewan Federation of Labor, for example. CLC unions also maintain local labor councils in most urban areas.

It is correct to describe the CLC as the **Canadian counterpart** of the American Federation of Labor-Congress of Industrial Organizations, but the CLC is autonomous and doesn't regard itself as affiliated with the AFL-CIO.

Canadian Federation of Labor, formed in 1982 by U.S.-based construction unions that left the CLC. It consists of 10 affiliated unions with a total membership of 200,000 and has headquarters in Ottawa.

Confederation of National Trade Unions — in French, **Conseil des syndicats nationaux** — formerly the Canadian Catholic Confederation of Labor. The CNTU developed in Quebec from a Roman Catholic labor movement into a broad-based organization with 259,000 members. It has member unions in Newfoundland, New Brunswick and Ontario as well as Quebec, and headquarters in Montreal.

Centrale de l'enseignement du Quebec is a federation representing teachers and others in French-language Roman Catholic schools and junior colleges in Quebec. It represents 107,000 members in more than 130 affiliated units and has headquarters in Quebec City.

Centrale des syndicats democratiques, an independent federation formed in 1972 by unions that broke away from the CNTU. It represents 59,000 members in 490 unions and is based in Quebec City.

Confederation of Canadian Unions, a federation that often clashes with CLC affiliates that are U.S.-based. It consists of about 20 member unions with 21,000 members, mostly in British Columbia, and has headquarters in Toronto.

Unions

Large unions in Canada, especially those spread over a wide area, are usually broken down into locals. For example:

Canadian Union of Public Employees — 406,000 members in 1,700 locals, with headquarters in Ottawa.

National Union of Public and General Employees — 307,000 members in 860 locals, with headquarters in Ottawa.

United Food and Commercial Workers — 180,000 members in 150 locals, with headquarters in Toronto.

Public Service Alliance of Canada — 165,000 members in 1,400 locals, with headquarters in Ottawa.

United Steelworkers of America — 160,000 members in 975 locals, with headquarters in Toronto.

Canadian Auto Workers — 153,000 members in 120 locals, with headquarters in Toronto.

Independents

Independent unions are occasionally regular labor organizations, but many are company sponsored and were organized to keep out regular trade unions.

Note: When writing about a union that has a French name only — **Syndicat des fonctionnnaires provinciaux du Quebec**, for example — avoid using the French name unless the story requires it. Paraphrase the nature of the membership — **Quebec civil servants union** — rather than invent a capitalized English name.

Union membership

Specific terms describe the various forms of union membership.

Closed shop: an employer may only hire people who are members of the union.

Union shop: an employer may select employees but all are obliged to join the union within a specified time.

Maintenance of membership: employees must retain membership for the duration of the contract.

Open shop: employees are free to join or not join a union. Workers who don't join are commonly called **free riders**, a term to avoid.

Rand formula: named after Justice Ivan Rand, who arbitrated a 1945 Ford strike. It requires all members of a bargaining unit to pay union dues but makes membership in the unit voluntary.

Checkoff: The employer acts as a collecting agent for a union by deducting dues from the employee's pay.

Laws and courts

Labor relations in Canada are divided into federal and provincial jurisdictions, each governed by a labor code.

The Canada Labor Code covers employees of federally chartered companies like banks, Crown corporations and those in such regulated businesses as transportation and communications that have interprovincial dealings. Provincial codes cover all others.

The federal code is enforced by the Canada Labor Relations Board, a quasi-judicial body that investigates and rules on union accreditations and violations of the code, such as illegal strikes and lockouts, unfair labor practices and inter-union membership raids.

Similar bodies exist in the provinces. Such functions in Quebec are filled by a labor court.

Federal civil servants are governed by the Public Service Staff Relations Board and disputes are regulated by a special act.

Conciliation

When the federal government intervenes in a dispute, there are several stages:

Stage 1: A **conciliator** is appointed who tries to get the sides talking.

Stage 2: A **conciliation commission**, often the original conciliator, is next appointed. The commission studies the issues and, unless it is felt the sides are too far apart for agreement, writes suggestions for a settlement.

Stage 3: A **mediator** goes back and forth to the parties and tries to craft a report for a vote by management and union membership.

Stage 4: An **arbitrator** can be brought in to devise a binding settlement. Arbitrators are also used in grievance procedures and, on occasion, for contract negotiations.

Provincial governments intervene in different ways, and a reporter covering a dispute under provincial jurisdiction should be aware of specific procedures that apply.

Strikes and lockouts

Strikes are the cessation of work to press the workers' position. **Lockouts** are the closure of all or part of an establishment to counter a work slowdown, to gain concessions from workers or to resist their position. Always distinguish between the two.

The reasons for a dispute must always be at the top of a story. Every story should say how long the strike or lockout has been in effect and the number of employees involved. Specify the average or base wage before the dispute — preferably the average.

As with any labor story, reporters should seek out the human elements when strikes or lockouts occur. There are economic consequences from a prolonged dispute for both the workers and their industry, and occasionally there are moments of violence and high drama. Less well explored are the psychological impacts for healthy workers to be away from their jobs and for managers to be in open conflict with employees.

Vocabulary

Labor-management reporting is loaded with pejoratives, so tread warily.

1. People are not **terminated** and workforces are not **downsized** or **consolidated**. People are **laid off** or **fired** and workforces are **cut**. (Avoid the term **cutbacks**. It's simply **cuts**.) Always say whether layoffs are temporary or permanent.

2. Employees are not **engaged in study sessions** or **job actions**. They have **stopped work** or **slowed work**.

3. **Scab**, a term used since 1777 for a worker who refuses to join a strike or who takes over the work of strikers, is permissible only in direct quotes; even so, use with discretion. **Strikebreaker** is a vague, rarely accurate term — a strike is seldom broken by the hiring of people to replace striking workers. A more accurate term — even though it doesn't reflect the hostility of strikers that can accompany such hiring — is **replacement worker**. In Quebec, companies are forbidden to hire outside workers to do the jobs of strikers.

4. Avoid **company offer** and **union demand**. **Proposal** and **counter-proposal** are neutral terms.

5. A **picket**, borrowed from the military term for a small body of soldiers on guard duty, is a force of workers stationed outside an establishment to dissuade customers or workers from going in. A **sympathy picket** involves people outside the bargaining unit joining in. A **demonstration picket** is a temporary form of protest by workers about employment conditions or bargaining talks. An **electronic picket** involves a striking union tying up all incoming lines to an establishment relying on telephones for business.

Avoid the term **honor a picket line**. It implies some legal obligation which may not exist. Report that someone or some group **refused** or **declined to cross a picket line**. Similarly, do not write that pickets **barred access** to a struck establishment unless someone was actually prevented from entering.

6. Avoid the term **union bosses**. Union leaders in some cases may not legally order members to walk off the job. Strike decisions and executive appointments in unions depend by law on a majority vote of union members or of members present and voting at a union meeting.

7. A **wildcat strike** is a strike for which union leaders disclaim responsibility.

8. A number of specialist terms deal with workforce reduction. **Attrition** involves reduction through normal retirement, leaves of absence and resignation. A **buyout** involves a company offer to pay special compensation — improved pension, generous severance or the like — to employees who will retire early or quit. In some cases, if attrition or a buyout doesn't achieve the desired workforce reduction, **layoffs** would be the next step. But a buyout is not a layoff.

Lifestyles

Lifestyles coverage should be a mirror on how our society is changing — how we take care of ourselves, how we relate to each other, what we eat, wear, do for fun.

It is a broad field that includes health, fitness, medicine, food, fashion, leisure, human interest, gardening, homes, psychology, social affairs and science.

Lifestyles stories are not fluff. They are often tied to the day's news and can hit page 1.

A graphic like this puts information in a convenient and useful form. Many of the best graphics on Lifestyles pages are clipped by readers and posted on refrigerator (or boathouse) doors.

Water SAFETY

• Wear your life jacket.
• If you drink around water, be responsible.
• Supervise your children when near water. Don't leave young children unattended near water, even for an instant.
• Learn to swim.
• Cold water kills. Know the facts to avoid hypothermia.
• Don't dive — go in feet first, the first time.
• Know your craft. Keep low to avoid capsizing or falling overboard.
• Play and swim in supervised areas.
• Have a water-smart "buddy" near the water — don't go alone.
• Be your own lifeguard by learning water rescue skills and being responsible for others.

RESCUE BREATHING *six basic steps*

1. **Shake gently and shout.** Shake to see if person is conscious. Ask, "Are you OK ?". **If there is no response:**

2. **Call** for help and tilt the head back gently, lift the chin to open the airway.

3. **Look, listen and feel.** Look at the chest to see if it is rising and falling. Listen for the sound of breathing. Feel for air escaping the mouth with your hand or cheek. If you cannot see, hear or feel breathing:

4. **Pinch the nose** and make a seal with your mouth on the victim's mouth and **give two full breaths.**

5. Turn your head and look, listen and feel.

6. Give a breath every five seconds. Continue until someone takes over from you.

(CP—Andrée Lachapelle)

Source: The Royal Life Saving Society Canada (CP)

An inquest into the death of someone following liposuction, for example, calls out for an article outlining the procedure. The closing of a department store chain's fur salons could be accompanied by a story examining trappers who relied on the stores for their livelihoods. A piece on gardening trends could focus on concerns about pesticides.

In short, basic rules of journalism apply in lifestyles coverage: Watch for the hard-news angle; keep copy tight; strive for balance; avoid single-source stories.

Aim for QuickQuotes, QuickFacts and graphics that can help an editor lay out a page attractively.

On an ongoing topic, always seek a new angle or twist. A look at the dangers of suntanning may turn up an angle that some sunscreens do little to decrease the dangers of skin cancer.

Remember to include cross-sections of society — both sexes, various age and racial groups, geographical regions and income levels.

Avoid stereotypes. Not all grandmothers are silver-haired matrons in aprons.

Write in simple language. When technical terms must be used, explain them in plain English. Don't talk about **in vitro** fertilization if most people are more likely to understand **test-tube babies**.

Lifestyles basically breaks down into two types of stories: the exotic and the everyday.

Trends

While readers want to keep abreast of the latest trends, guard against inventing trends by exaggerating their scope. Two or three men seen wearing eye makeup doesn't mark a trend toward men wearing women's cosmetics.

On the other hand, keep an eye out for larger changes in society that narrowly focused writing may overlook. Changes in the family unit, living arrangements, family size and division of work are constant. These changes are worth writing about and should also influence writing on society as a whole.

Use personal observation as a tipoff, then seek out research material and Statistics Canada data to gauge how widespread a trend may be.

Promotion

Guard against promotion. Manufacturers and retailers have an outlet for promoting new goods and services — it's called advertising.

Be wary of the public relations practitioner's sales pitch. Some new products or services are newsworthy. Others are not. Be wary of claims for health treatments, parapsychology, the latest How-To books and so on. The litmus test is: Who will benefit from the story — the source or the reader? Always aim to include comments from outside sources.

Obituaries

Survey after survey has shown strong reader interest in obituaries.

Readers are attracted to obits for many reasons, some of the main ones being simple curiosity; wanting to learn the secret of the person's success, happiness or failures; or wanting to know what kind of person society has lost.

Obituaries are stories about life — about recognizing a life for what it was and what it meant.

They should be portraits, with brush strokes provided by friends, family, colleagues or acquaintances who can provide insights into the person's personality and life. Sharp quotes add color and depth.

But the portraits should be exact, with no attempt to brush out wrinkles and warts. Resist the tendency to canonize the departed; very few are true saints.

Some general guidelines:

1. Report deaths of newsworthy people. Don't limit obits to lawyers, politicians and other automatically prominent members of society. Be on the lookout for the deaths of average folk: the waitress who worked 30 years at the town's most popular diner to put seven foster children through university; the amateur philosopher who operated a downtown newsstand for many decades.

2. Often an obituary item of 50 to 100 words will suffice, but it should include a significant fact or two about the person and his or her life.

3. Unsavory details may be pertinent as part of a life story but should be kept in perspective.

4. The spot story opens with the simple facts — the name, other identification, notable achievements, cause of death and particularly age — the first questions that a reader wants answered.

Glenn Gould, the world-famous Canadian concert pianist, died early today in hospital, a week after a stroke from which he did not regain consciousness. He was 50.

5. After the lead paragraphs, details of the subject's life are given in inverted-pyramid style rather than chronologically. The early years and schooling are rarely as interesting as later accomplishments.

6. For a next-cycle story, a featurish top may be the best approach in the absence of worthwhile developments.

Glenn Gould was remembered Monday as a child prodigy who could read music at age three, as a 21-year-old pianist who recorded Bach "the way the old master himself must have played," and as an eccentric who wore gloves the year round.

7.   The length of an obituary depends on the person's newsworthiness. In addition to the lead information, longer obituaries should include biographical facts, the names of survivors and funeral arrangements.

8.   For unusually prominent public figures, as well as for people in the news business, include precise details of funeral arrangements.

9.   At some point — but preferably not in the lead where it might confuse readers — include the full name of the subject: **Alexander Young Jackson** for the painter usually known as **A.Y. Jackson**.

10. The identifying feature in the first paragraph should be the one that best highlights the subject's life and career. Often it is something that happened years ago.

A.Y. Jackson, a father of modern Canadian painting and last survivor of the original Group of Seven artists, died today in a nursing home at age 91.

11. In reckoning age, take into account the birth month and day. A person born Dec. 27, 1927, who died Oct. 1, 1987, was 59, not 60. To say **She was in her 60th year** is correct but confusing.

12. When the precise age is not available, give some indication of it from the person's activities, such as the year of graduation or the setting up of practice in law or at the newsstand.

Cause of death

1.   The cause of death should be given, except when the story makes plain that death resulted from the complications of old age. When the cause is not available, say so, and why.

2.   Never speculate about the cause. If information doesn't come from someone clearly in a position to know, it is irresponsible to speculate.

3.   When the cause is suspected to be a disease like AIDS, which carries certain connotations, respecting the wishes of the family can normally be justified. However, in the case of someone clearly in public life, the right to privacy in such matters can be outweighed by the public's right to know. If in doubt, consult Head Office.

4.   In listing the cause of death, prefer a plain term to medical jargon: **heart attack** and **heart disease** rather than **coronary thrombosis** or **coronary occlusion**.

5.   Explain unfamiliar scientific terms: **Hodgkin's disease — an uncommon disorder of the lymph nodes and spleen**.

6.   Taste and redundancy often rule out detail when death resulted from violence.

7.   When suicide is suspected but not officially confirmed, it may be possible to report that a note or a gun or an empty barbiturate bottle was found near the body.

Language

1. Write **die, bury, coffin** and **undertaker** or **funeral director** rather than **pass away, inter, casket** and **mortician**. Do not use **resting** for the dead, or other euphemisms.

2. Write **die of**, not **from**, an illness.

3. Use **widow** and **widower**, but **wife** and **husband** until after the funeral. Guard against the redundant **widow of the late**. Write **wife of the late** or **widow of**.

4. Do not describe people as **late** when referring to something they did while alive. Not: **The late doctor fought the epidemic alone.**

5. In general, use **the late** only of a person who died recently. It is not needed, for instance, in **the late John Lennon**.

6. Beware of such common non sequiturs as **Born in Calgary, she was an ardent skier.** The two ideas are not linked by meaning and do not belong in the same sentence. Better: **She was born in Calgary. Six years later, the family moved to Collingwood, Ont., where she soon developed a taste for skiing.**

Prepared obits

1. When an obit shows up in a newspaper's electronic return news, always check with the paper by telephone. The story may be one prepared in advance.

2. Each bureau prepares biographical sketches of its most prominent citizens. The Main Desk in Toronto keeps copies on disk.

3. As with spot obituaries, prepared obits are made interesting by quotations and anecdotes bringing out the character of the subject.

4. To make an obit stand up for use at any time, avoid past tenses except when tied to a specific date or time. Include religious affiliations or activities if newsworthy.

Funerals

1. On those rare occasions when CP does staff funerals, do not sentimentalize the dearly departed. Plain language is best, avoiding any attempt at tear-jerking.

2. Do not suggest that the remains are in any way the person.

3. There is generally little need to staff show funerals, such as the funeral of a police officer killed on duty, except through photographs.

Polls

Public-opinion polls are like snapshots: it's not always obvious what they're showing. Is that woman on the right smiling or grimacing? Is she the mother of the young girl in the centre with the same blond hair? Some mysteries there, and opportunities for misinterpreting the scene — particularly if you try to speculate that the snapshot is typical.

There's another similarity between polls and snapshots: there are too many of them, but no one wants to be the first to give them up. CP reports on reputable polls dealing with topical issues, leaving it to individual newspapers to decide when they've had enough.

By canvassing the opinions of a relatively small group of people, pollsters are able to calculate how a larger population feels about a topic. But reputable pollsters would never state that the smaller group's views exactly mirror the larger one's, nor that there isn't a possibility of being wildly wrong once in a while.

1.   Stories about polls should use verbs like **indicate** and **suggest**, rather than **show** or **report**.

TORONTO (CP) — Liberal support appeared to be holding stable across Canada in March as measured by the Angus Reid polling organization.

Reid's poll, published Tuesday in the Toronto Star, suggested little change from February for any of the major national parties among voters with an opinion: Liberals 38 per cent support versus 39 the previous month, Conservatives 32 (35), NDP 28 (26).

---

2.   An essential qualification is called the *margin of error*. It needs to be spelled out in stories on polls and its significance explained. Where changes in comparative figures are smaller than the margin of error, public opinion cannot be said with any certainty to have moved up or down.

Angus Reid said the poll was reliable within 2.5 percentage points 19 times out of 20. That means, when applied to the population at large, Liberal support in March could have been as high as 40.5 per cent or as low as 35.5 while Tory strength could range between 29.5 and 34.5 per cent. In one case in 20, the figures could be substantially different.

Changes from February figures that are smaller than the margin of error have no polling significance. The apparent drop in Liberal support, for instance, is meaningless.

---

3. A national census is the ultimate poll. An election is a close second: it registers the opinion of all who vote. Comparing a poll on party popularity with the most recent election result is sound practice. When comparing one poll with earlier polls on the same topic, however, don't assume that similar results make the polls more accurate. They don't.

4. Polls, like snapshots, show a moment in time. By the day after the questions were asked, people have already begun to change their minds. So it's wrong to suggest that a poll result can predict how people will behave — for example, a June political poll that's used to forecast an October election result. And it's wrong to take polling figures from the past and write about them in the present tense as if they are still just as valid.

5. National poll figures will usually be out by no more than two to four percentage points. But when the national figures are broken down into regions, the risk of error is much greater. The difference needs to be explained.

By regions, the poll indicated NDP support was at a peak of 38 per cent in Ontario and a low of 12 per cent in Prince Edward Island. However, since the poll's accuracy depends on the number of people surveyed, the Ontario figure might range anywhere from 32 to 44 per cent while the P.E.I. sample was too small to be considered reliable.

---

6. There's a big difference between **per cent** and **percentage points**. The poll is accurate within 2.5 percentage points, not per cent. A political party whose support has apparently gone from a level of 16 per cent to 24 per cent has registered an increase of eight percentage points but its support has increased 50 per cent.

7. Statistical studies produced by Statistics Canada and other reputable organizations are routinely based on a sampling of the general population. They are polls. That means they may not accurately reflect what's happening in the population as a whole; the margin of error needs to be specified and explained, just as in a political poll. And suggest, not show, is still the verb of choice.

➤ See **Statistics,** page 89.

8. Some published polls cover a wide range of issues. In reporting on them, it's better to sacrifice polling results on secondary questions than to skip over essential information about the basic poll and its accuracy. Take a narrower focus and do it right. Consider using a Quick-style box to summarize some of the secondary results.

Some other pitfalls

Public-opinion researchers recognize a number of other elements in polling that can affect the accuracy of a poll's results.

1.   The sponsor of a poll may influence the questions asked and other aspects. The story should say if the poll was paid for by a political party, a lobby group or someone else with a vested interest in the outcome. And results from two different polling organizations can't be compared unless they were asking the same questions: for example, about the popularity of **the Conservatives** rather than **Brian Mulroney's Conservatives**.

2.   The dates a poll was taken can affect the outcome. If there was a significant event before or after the poll that could have colored the result, say so.

3.   A poll that requires members of the public to make a specific effort is likely to attract those who feel strongly about an issue. Specify whether the poll was conducted by personal interview, by phone or by mail. Phone-in or mail-in polls are of dubious value.

4.   If the people polled aren't a random selection — that is, with every person having an equal chance of being picked to respond — the results may be skewed. If there were a disproportionate number of middle-class people sampled on the question of income tax rates, the poll might not give a true picture of society's attitudes as a whole.

5.   The question asked can influence the result. Polls suggest most Canadians don't support abortion on demand, but a majority believe a woman whose health is at risk should be able to get an abortion. Depending on the question, poll results can claim to support almost any position in the abortion debate.

6.   If 40 per cent of a random selection of people can't be contacted, or refuse to answer a particular question, or don't know the answer, the significance of the remaining responses is reduced. They may not represent society at large. This aspect needs increasingly careful attention since polling organizations report that the growth in answering machines and people's irritation with phone canvassing are leading to more difficulty getting accurate samples.

Profiles and Newsmakers

Profiles and Newsmakers tell people about people. They put human beings into news pages.

Profiles usually deal with people who may not be in the public eye but whose lives, jobs, hobbies or thoughts are interesting and appealing. Newsmakers focus on people in the day's news — the new leader of a national native organization, the provincial cabinet minister whose public statements have caused a furore, the unlikely hero of a Stanley Cup championship game.

Except for the time element — or *peg*— Profiles and Newsmakers have much in common. At their best, they leave the reader with a sense of knowing the subjects as individuals — the next best thing to meeting them in person.

Like all CP stories, the Profile and Newsmaker must be fair and in good taste. They should never be a vehicle for cheap shots, sexist comments, irrelevant detail or clumsy description that can be embarrassing to CP and its newspapers as well as the subject.

These stories should skilfully blend background, color, personality touches and newsy tidbits about the subject. They should avoid logjams of detail and gratuitous information. Good quotes which convey the mood or personality of the subject are particularly helpful.

Stories such as Profiles and Newsmakers offer a great opportunity to take the reader where the TV camera can rarely go. They also go beyond the canned biography of *Who's Who*.

Look for telling actions that would probably not take place before the cameras: a federal cabinet minister gets upset when he can't get into his hotel room because he's misplaced his key; a notoriously tough football coach spends his days off as a volunteer art instructor for inner city youngsters.

The keen-eyed reporter can also sketch things a TV viewer might miss: the politician's aide always wears red neckties and combs his hair exactly like his mentor; the baseball player warming up for the all-star game keeps a jealous eye on the television camera.

Profiles and Newsmakers should be tight and bright. They should tell readers something about who the subjects are, how they got where they are, a little about what makes them tick. Friends and colleagues can be helpful in providing perceptive insights and anecdotes. So can enemies, but only if they're named.

Did the subject grow up on a farm and save egg money to buy books? Did she run three newspaper routes at the same time to buy a bicycle? Does she read books for blind people at a seniors home?

Let the reader in on your subject's home surroundings, revealing his likes, dislikes and interests.

The late New Brunswick premier, Richard Hatfield, with some of his collection of dolls. Often people can reveal interesting hobbies and interests which lend color to a Profile or Newsmaker.

(CP—Jann Van Horne)

Stephen Lewis, when he was Ontario NDP leader, had office shelves filled with children's picture books, an interesting touch. Richard Hatfield, when he was New Brunswick premier, kept all his mementoes at home — every picture the Rotary Club ever gave him, campaign posters, a model of the infamous Bricklin sports car. And a doll collection.

Interesting mannerisms, speech patterns and habits can speak volumes about a subject. Singer Rita MacNeil performs in front of thousands but is painfully shy and reluctant to talk about herself offstage. Joe Clark frequently punctuates what he is saying with air-chopping hand motions. Even before he became Nova Scotia premier, Don Cameron always referred to himself in the third person, saying things like "Don Cameron is not going to waste the taxpayers' money."

Color and description

1. Description should be fresh, imaginative and relevant. It should help the reader get a sense of the subject's appearance and personality or to feel what it was like to be at the news scene.

2. A string of generalized adjectives is usually less effective than active and specific words.

Not: He laughed heartily as he watched the Three Stooges on TV in his wood-panelled library.

But: His laughter rumbled so forcefully as he watched the Three Stooges on TV that a photograph of his yacht wobbled on the wall of his wood-panelled library.

3. A basic description of physique or character should be provided when it is pertinent to the news event. The lined faces and baggy eyes of the first ministers were worth noting during the endless Meech Lake talks in 1990. But readers do not need to be told that Brian Mulroney has a prominent chin or that Robert Bourassa wears glasses.

4.   Description should always serve a purpose. Saying that a businessman wore a pinstripe suit will seem unimaginative unless there is a specific reason — for instance, a former athlete's deliberate attempt to create a new image.

5.   Watch for chances to use a description that will work better than a bald statement:

Not: The prime minister was angry.

But: The prime minister's face tightened with anger as he spun on his heel and strode quickly off the platform.

6.   It sometimes helps to encourage subjects to talk about themselves. Ask lots of questions about childhood, hobbies, former jobs, dreams and hopes. Many people will be refreshingly open when given the chance.

Sometimes even the well-known public figure will reward the reader with something new and different. For instance, Jerzy Urban, the official spokesman for the former hardline Communist government in Poland, was asked in an interview what the worst day of his life was. He replied it was when his sombre weekly news conferences were cancelled and he ceased being "a TV star."

7.   Subjects who are naturally reserved and taciturn are particularly challenging. So is the individual who dislikes media attention. Look for body-language from such people. Some of them convey a wealth of information even though their actual answers may be sparse or even gruff.

A media-hating tycoon whose speech is closely clipped can still leave a trail of visual images.

He's big and rough-looking, a yep-and-nope type who seems to shun even those monosyllables if a shrug or nod will do for an answer. She shifted impatiently and constantly during the brief interview, drawing squiggles on a yellow pad on her desk.

8.   Comparisons can be helpful in giving the reader a mental image. *Lincolnesque*, for instance, implies tall and craggy.

Or compare a person's appearance or character with natural objects: granite-jawed; reed-like; limbs like oak; built along the lines of a water buffalo.

9.   Technical references can even be helpful: nimble as a Porsche; he was well put together, like a neatly constructed Lego man; Tammy Faye Bakker's industrial-strength eye makeup.

10. When it comes to effective use of color and description, one trick is working it in without making it look forced. A paragraph devoted entirely to color to the exclusion of news, quotes or anything else to inform the reader will seem distracting. Laborious descriptive clauses are also discouraging.

11. Color should be woven into a story in a natural way:

The defendant, lean and erect throughout the trial, watched without apparent emotion as the jury announced its guilty verdict. Hands clasped behind him, he glared at the judge as she imposed a life sentence without possibility of parole for 15 years.

His wife and two children wept quietly as he was handcuffed and led past them on the way out of the courtroom.

12. But don't fall into the trap of tediously substituting bits of background for the person's identity:

Para 1:   John Simpson said Tuesday . . .

Para 2:   . . . the former Vancouver engineer added.

Para 3:   The lanky, grey-haired bureaucrat insisted . . .

Instead, consider giving readers an early mental image that can stay with them as they read on:

Simpson, lanky and grey-haired, is a former Vancouver engineer who in 1986 joined the federal Transport Department and rose quickly to the No. 2 spot. In that job he is now insisting that the harbor project be shelved.

Slugs

Profile:

BC-CPE-Alomar-Profile
SEE CP Photo CPT27

By Steve McAllister
    TORONTO (CP) — The first time Roberto Alomar remembers dreaming about being in the big leagues . . .

Newsmaker:

PM-Chretien-Newsmaker, Bgt
Budget
SEE CP Photo OTT11

Newsmaker: Jean Chretien
By Gerry Arnold
    OTTAWA (CP) — Jean Chretien never said it would be easy. He . . .

A graphic can put the bare facts from a Profile or Newsmaker into an attractive package.

Jean Chrétien

Facts and figures on Liberal prime minister

BORN:
Jan. 11, 1934, at Shawinigan, Que.

EDUCATION:
St. Joseph's Seminary in Trois-Rivières, Que.; studied law at Laval University in Quebec City.

WORK HISTORY:
Practised law in Shawinigan after being called to Quebec bar in 1958.

POLITICAL CAREER:
After winning election to Commons in 1963 for Quebec riding of St-Maurice he was re-elected in seven straight elections. Served as parliamentary secretary to Prime Minister Lester Pearson 1965-66, entered cabinet in 1967. Held variety of posts over the next 19 years in Trudeau governments, including revenue, Indian affairs, Treasury Board, industry, finance, justice, energy, external affairs and deputy prime minister. Ran unsuccessfully for party leadership in 1984, losing to John Turner; resigned from Commons in 1986. Won leadership June 23, 1990, and was re-elected to Commons for New Brunswick riding of Beauséjour six months later. Led his party to a massive defeat of Conservative government in October 1993.

FAMILY:
Married Aline Chaine in 1957 and has three children — France, Hubert and Michel.

HOBBIES:
Reading, classical music.

(CP—Tonia Cowan)

– CP

Sports

General

1.   The standards of good general-news writing apply with equal force to the coverage of sports. People are the focus of reader interest. Bare results are the preserve of the agate page.

2.   The sensitive sports writer should know when a cliche has become threadbare. While athletes still profess to be *taking it one game at a time* and *giving it 110 per cent*, the days of reporting such mundane quotes are over.

3.   When writing game copy, be concise. There's no need to describe every scoring play. Focus on the key play or performer and build the story around it. Pull together the remaining scoring plays into a paragraph or two. Sometimes, one sentence listing the remaining goal-scorers for each team in a hockey game, for example, will suffice. The reader who wants more can find it on the agate page.

Limit game-over stories to 400 words; papers seldom have space for more. If developments warrant, do an add or spin it off into a sidebar. All vital elements of the game must be contained in that initial 400-word story.

4.   Make sure the blinkers are off. Sports is more than what unfolds on the playing field. Capture the mood and size of the crowd and its impact on the game. Were the fans raucous, or sedate? Did they display banners or signs vilifying the visitors?

Watch for the interaction at the bench between players and coach, as well as between teammates. If the coach berates the star defenceman for giving the puck away on the decisive goal, let the reader in on it.

➤ See **More than a game**, page 82.

5.   Be mindful of the competition for sports-page space and write accordingly. Tight writing is particularly needed on weekends when there is a glut of copy for Monday editions. Overwriting hurts a story's chances for publication.

6.   Finally, don't forget something so simple it's often neglected in stories: Was it a good game? Was it well-played? Was it entertaining?

Points to watch

1.   The sport involved must be identified early in every story.

2.   City names used as team names take singular verbs; team titles usually require plural verbs: **Vancouver is last** . . . but **The Canucks are last**. Watch for singular team names like the Toronto Blizzard. Write **The Toronto Blizzard won its third game**.

3.   Avoid unnecessary possessives. Write **The Canadiens centre stole the puck** not **The Canadiens' centre** . . . However, the possessive is required in the following: **The Canadiens' three straight losses are a season record.** When you are unsure whether the possessive is necessary, mentally substitute the city for the team nickname. By substituting **Montreal** in the examples given, it's quickly apparent which requires the possessive.

A reminder that singular nouns ending in *s* generally take an apostrophe and *s*, as in **Jimmy Connors's victory**.

➤   See **Possessives**, page 226, for exceptions.

Plural possessives take only an apostrophe.

4.   Avoid nicknames unless they are long-standing. If a person is known to readers by a given name and nickname, put the nickname in parentheses on first reference: **boxer Thomas (Hit Man) Hearns**. Usually, however, when a person is commonly known by a nickname, it is unnecessary to provide the given name as well: **baseball outfielder Chili Davis** and **tennis player Gigi Fernandez**, not **Charles (Chili) Davis** and **Beatrice (Gigi) Fernandez.**

5.   Long-established and well-known leagues such as the National Hockey League, the Canadian Football League, the National Football League and the National Basketball Association may be referred to in first reference as **the NHL, the CFL, the NFL** and **the NBA.**

Initials are permissible on second reference for well-known minor leagues such as the American Hockey League **(AHL)**, the International Hockey League **(IHL)** and Canada's three major junior hockey leagues. Otherwise, avoid initials even on second reference.

All leagues named in newspagers and other stories that might end up on non-sports pages should be spelled out in full.

6.   Capitalize major events and trophies such as **the Olympic Games, the Olympics, the Pan-Am Games, the Commonwealth Games, the Canada Games, the World Series, the Canadian Open, the Grey Cup, the Super Bowl, the Queen's Plate** and **the Vezina Trophy.** On second reference, refer to them simply as **the Games, the Open**, etc.

National and world championships are not capitalized. Write **the Canadian wrestling championships** and **the world hockey championship.**

7.   Multiple-word names of municipalities in Quebec, France and other French-speaking areas are spelled with a hyphen. Examples: **Lac-Beauport, Ste-Agathe, Val-d'Isere.** Note there is no period after the abbreviation for saint. However, in English-speaking countries and predominantly English-speaking provinces in Canada, a period rather than a hyphen is used. Write **Sault Ste. Marie, Ont.**

➤   See **French**, page 207.

8.   Use the plural of proper nouns advisedly. Write **Boston is a five-time winner of the Stanley Cup** not **Boston has won five Stanley Cups.** Similarly, if referring to baseball's two major leagues, write **The presidents of the American and National leagues** (lowercase *l*) . . .

9.   The word *final*, meaning the last round of a competition, is singular. Write **Pittsburgh reached the Stanley Cup final** not **finals**. An exception: **Five swimming finals were scheduled Tuesday.**

10. Don't expect the reader to have a medical dictionary next to the newspaper. What's an *anterior cruciate ligament* and why is it preventing Wayne Gretzky from playing hockey? Make sure any medical jargon is explained and the extent of the disability is clear.

Sports . . . More than a game

1.   A sports writer who reports only what happens on the field or rink and ignores what takes place off it is being negligent.

2.   On many sports pages today, the daily game is often summarized in a few paragraphs or worked into a roundup. Line stories tend to be analyses, backgrounders and profiles, or else they focus on trades, drafts, salaries, racism, substance abuse and legal problems.

3.   Certain stories invite a blind eye: substance abuse, racial tension, disciplinary problems. These are not merely personal questions for publicly acclaimed athletes. Writing about these issues may require legal advice, but it should be part of the sports beat.

Eric Lindros and lawyer Gord Kirke were never far apart during the NHL draft proceedings in June 1991. Sports is big business and reporters need to keep an eye on the whole story for readers.

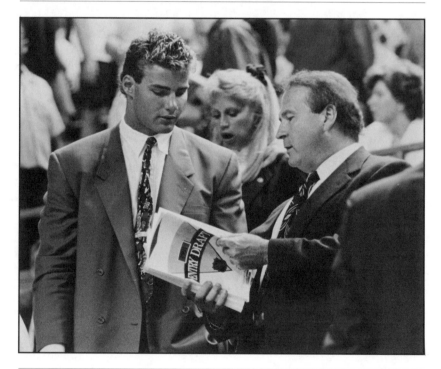

(CP—Hans Deryk)

4.   Sports pages must reflect the evolution of the multibillion-dollar sports entertainment industry. Every sports writer takes time to interview a team's general manager about a new prospect or a hot trade rumor. But a good sports writer will also get to know a team's business manager to write about attendance, television revenue and taxes.

5.   Don't leave the business end of sports out of so-called amateur events. Members of Canada's national teams are no longer amateurs. Appearance money is now the main criterion for most track meets, so don't ignore it in the story.

6.   As well, Canada's amateur sports federations are part of a substantial bureaucracy and should come under the same journalistic scrutiny as any government department.

When 40,000 cyclists roll through Montreal in the annual Tour de l'ile, it's news. Though most of these participants are recreational athletes, alert sports journalists are keeping readers informed of amateur trends.

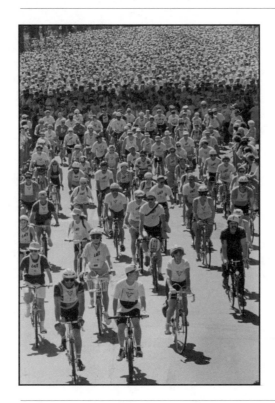

(CP—Tom Hanson)

7.   The only true amateurs left in sports are people like weekend softball players and neighborhood joggers. While recreational athletes aren't usually newsworthy, the sports they play are. Keep a close eye on trends in recreational sports. Why are people willing to spend hundreds of dollars on running shoes? How many weekend warriors are seriously injuring themselves on the softball diamond?

Women in sports

1.   Sports pages tend to be filled with stories about male athletes. Despite that, a survey by the National Hockey League found more than 40 per cent of its fans are women. The crowd at any major sports event can show a similar ratio.

2.   Sexist language, stereotypes and references have no more place in sports pages than in any other part of the newspaper.

3.   A few anachronisms survive in sports: **the Ladies Professional Golf Association**. But generally, female athletes are no more *ladies* than males are *gentlemen*.

4.   There are sports where women excel — tennis, cycling, athletics, golf, to name a few. The complete sports report includes full, well-written stories about such events.

5.   There's no justification for always leading with the men's competition in events, such as marathons, where both sexes compete. If separate stories aren't warranted, the most competitive, exciting race deserves the lead — and that's not always the men's event.

6.   Be on the lookout for sexism in sports. Female athletes, particularly in golf and tennis, get a disproportionately smaller share of prize money compared with men. If an amateur program seems to be devoting more resources to male athletes, find out why.

7.   Physical descriptions of athletes — male and female — are sometimes appropriate, and their personalities and gestures will enliven quotes. But avoid gratuitous descriptions that have sexist undertones. The simple test: Would this type of thing be written about a male athlete?

8.   Finally, any male sports writer who refers to a female gymnast as a **pixie** or a basketball player as an **amazon** is not relying on a cliche, but is being sexist. Don't patronize. Be thoughtful and tasteful in your use of language.

➤   See **Sexism**, page 22.

Thinking visuals

1. When developing a story, think immediately about illustrations. Discuss the story with a staff photographer or photo editor. Rely on their talents to make your story more complete.

Getting statistics out of the story and into a graphic treatment improves readability and contributes to eye-catching pages.

Canada Cup

Here are the results of the last four Canada Cup hockey series:

1987			1984		
Final (best of three)			**Final (best of three)**		
Soviet Union 6	Canada	5 (OT)	Canada 5	Sweden 2	
Canada 6	Soviet Union 5	(OT)	Canada 6	Sweden 2	
Canada 6	Soviet Union 5				
1981			**1976**		
Final (sudden death)			**Final (best of three)**		
Soviet Union 8 Canada 1			Canada 6 Czechoslovakia 0		
			Canada 5 Czechoslovakia 4 (OT)		

(CP—Tonia Cowan)

(CP)

2. The same holds for graphics. Many sporting events leave writers with more statistics than should be used in a story. The unused stats can make a timely graphic. Sports lends itself to graphics and a good one can sell a story to editors and readers.

3. As well, QuickSketches, QuickFacts and QuickQuotes are welcome complements to sports stories. They can spell out essential background material, leaving more room for color and personality in the story.

Sponsorship in sport

1.   Long-standing events and trophies known generally by the name of a commercial sponsor or one of its products are identified as such in first reference: **the Players' International men's tennis tournament, the Sun Life Nationals tennis tournament** and **the duMaurier Classic LPGA tournament.**

2.   National and world championships are usually identified as such in first reference, with the sponsor's name given later. However, the **Labatt Brier** probably carries more reader recognition than the **Canadian men's curling championship.**

3.   Sports are inevitably an advertising vehicle, but references to sponsorship in sports stories should have legitimate news value and not be unduly emphasized. Resist lobbying by sponsors to have their company or product name integrated into the title of the event. Only in cases where the sponsor's name has become synonymous with the event as the result of long-term affiliation should such integration take place.

Metric, measurement and numbers

1.   CP generally uses metric to measure distances and calculate speeds. However, some sports — football, horse racing and certain classes of auto racing, for example — are reported in imperial. (For departures from the metric rule, see sections dealing with individual sports.)

Today's youth have been brought up on metric and to persist needlessly in imperial measures is to risk turning away potential readers. Unless precise imperial field demarcations are involved, as in football, or race distances, such as the Indianapolis 500, use metric wherever it's a sensible option.

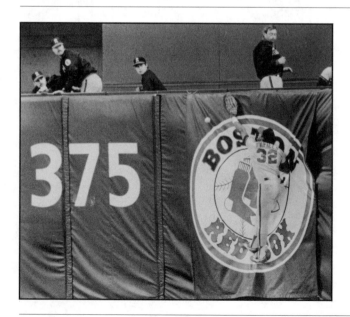

Dave Winfield hits the fence trying for a catch at the 375-foot (112-metre) outfield sign. CP has moved to increase use of metric in sports reporting.

(CP—Scott Macdonald)

Although fence signs in most baseball parks still list the distance from home plate in feet, there is no logical reason why the distance a batted ball carries can't be given in metres. Write **Wilson's drive barely cleared the fence in left-centre field, about 110 metres away.** Should the actual distance sign be pertinent to the story, put the metric equivalent in parentheses: **Wilson doubled off the 360-foot sign (about 110 metres) in left-centre field.**

Similarly in hockey, there's no need to write about a **30-foot slapshot** when **a slapshot from the top of the faceoff circle** or a **10-metre slapshot** is just as descriptive.

Note: Many figures, imperial or metric, are rough estimates. When translating imperial to metric, don't use exact conversions unless precision is essential, such as in field events at an athletics meet. Round figures off.

2.   Personal measurements continue to be imperial. When referring to heights, write **The centre stood six foot three**; as an adjective, it's **the six-foot-three centre**. If it's clear from the context, it's permissible to say **Jones, 6-3, 220 pounds, came to the Blue Bombers . . .**

Don't mix imperial and metric in one sentence: **The six-foot-three forward shot from 10 metres out.** Rephrase it or use separate sentences.

3.   When measurements consist of two or more elements, do not use commas. Write **She stood five foot three** and **She was timed in two hours 15 minutes 35 seconds.**

4.   In times, a colon is used between hours, minutes and seconds; a period before decimal fractions of a second. Write **0:27** (27 seconds), **0:27.7** (27.7 seconds), **2:00.1** (two minutes one-tenth of a second), **3:47:39.67** (three hours 47 minutes 39.67 seconds). Note that times involving only seconds include a zero before the colon.

5.   When not expressing fractions in decimal terms, write **8-100ths of a second** and **3½ minutes**, but **two-thirds of an inning**.

6.   Odds are listed as **20-1**, not **20 to 1** or **20-to-1**.

➤   See **Numbers**, page 217.

Records

When records are established, put them into perspective:

•   Compare a national standard with the world mark.

•   Try to explain why the previous record had been one of long standing or why it has been broken three times in the last year.

Spellings to watch

Allan Cup (Canadian senior hockey championship)
America's Cup (yachting)
analyse (v.), analysis (n.)
Cup-Winners' Cup (European soccer tournament)
defence (n.), defensive(ly) (adj., adv.)
Hamilton Tiger-Cats (Ticats acceptable on second reference)
Hec Crighton Trophy (Canadian university football award)
Oakland Athletics, Oakland A's
offence (n.), offensive(ly) (adj., adv.)
Ottawa 67s, Philadelphia 76ers, San Francisco 49ers, Vancouver
    86ers (no apostrophe)
Pan-American Games, Pan-Am Games
practice (n., adj.), practise (v.)
resign (to quit), re-sign (to sign again)
tiebreaker

➤ For detail on preparing and editing Sports agate, see **Sports handling**, page 415.

➤ See also *(CP) Caps and Spelling* under **Baseball**, **Basketball**, **Football**, **Golf**, **Hockey** and **Horse Racing**.

Statistics

Statistics can be pillars of the day's news. They are also the devil's playground, luring reporters into errors of interpretation, assumption and fact.

Some of the problems with statistics would diminish if the news media would regularly treat them with the care — and the skepticism — they need. The quote credited to Benjamin Disraeli is deservedly famous: **"There are . . . lies, damned lies and statistics."**

The value of statistics, intelligently used, can hardly be overstated. They help to give substance to stories on hundreds of topics. But there are pitfalls:

1.   Some statistical reports rely on actual counts: the number of new cars sold in Vancouver in March, based on sales reports from all dealerships. Some are estimates: the number of unemployed in Canada in August, based on extensive samplings of households. These poll-based statistics are subject to error and reporting on them needs some of the same care applied to writing about public-opinion polls.

➤   See **Polls**, page 72.

2.   Some statistical reports are issued on a preliminary basis, subject to adjustments later. The federal government's figures on international trade are one example. Some of the later adjustments can be substantial. That means the figures must always be described as preliminary, and early in the story the importance of the adjustment process needs to be spelled out each time. When the final figures are available, they should be reported and comparisons made with the preliminary figures. Since the preliminary figures are tentative, it doesn't make sense to attribute great significance to the precise numbers. If that makes a story less interesting and less authoritative, so be it.

3.   Statistics are usually relevant only for the time period concerned. There can be substantial changes from one year to the next in all sorts of statistics. An obvious example: a poll on the number of homes with compact disc players in 1988 says very little about how many families had rushed to buy CDs by 1991.

4.   Comparisons of statistical studies on the same topic can be useful in detecting trends, such as employment in the manufacturing sector over a few months or even years. However, comparisons between one time period and an earlier one should take account of how the population and other crucial factors have changed in the interim. A 25 per cent increase in auto thefts from 1975 to 1985 might actually represent a decline in the **rate** of thefts, if population and car ownership figures are taken into account. (Rates are more telling when they're available: the number of murders per 100,000 population.) Similarly, comparisons of value over time must take into account the decline in purchasing power of the dollar.

5.   The bases of comparison shouldn't be decided routinely. Comparing January retail sales figures with December's can be meaningless because of the Christmas rush; comparing them with the previous January's is usually best. But when the economy is reaching a peak or a trough, a year-over-year comparison may not be as revealing as month-over-month or some other comparison thoughtfully chosen.

6.   The significance of statistics can't be safely stretched. If Canada's overall cost-of-living index goes up mainly because of higher taxes in Ontario, many Canadians wouldn't be affected and a story should make that clear from the start. If a provincial study reports that the number of homeless people in the province has declined eight per cent from a year earlier, that alone can't be taken to suggest declines in other provinces.

7.   Similarly, it's risky to assume that American statistical studies are equally valid in Canada. Some academics find it hard to resist using the floods of American studies to buttress arguments about conditions in Canada, adding casually that "there's no reason to believe the same figures don't apply in this country." Don't believe it. Check some authorities; there are numerous differences between the two societies.

8.   Phrases like **seasonally adjusted, gross domestic product** and the like may be understood by specialists, but the ordinary reader can use help. The methods of calculating changes in such basic measurements as the consumer price index or the unemployment index should also be explained from time to time. When available, sample size — 700 of the 2,000 sporting goods stores, for example — should be mentioned. People want to know how reliable these indicators are.

Travel

Travel stories share many of the requirements of other features: effective use of quotes and people, a lively writing style, a good lead that grabs the reader's interest.

But more than most other features, travel stories must usually convey a sense of place. The writer draws a picture for the reader by selecting vivid detail and using description effectively.

1. Travel writers need to make their stories interesting — a mere listing of information from travel brochures and government tourist boards won't do.

The airily upbeat style more common in promotional travel literature doesn't work either.

2. The proper approach is somewhat sharper and reflects the writer's personal observation.

What is it about a particular place that is distinctive, that catches the writer's senses?

What do the city streets look like? What do the people wear? What is striking about the markets, the countryside?

The writer should try to get one or two real people into the story — a street vendor, a passerby, a museum guide. Anyone but the overused taxi driver or hotel desk clerk.

3. The best travel stories will capture the genuinely interesting aspects of a destination without glossing over harsh reality: poverty, inefficient transportation, anti-tourist sentiment. Experienced travellers expect some discomfort but they also want practical information on what to be prepared for.

At times, the need for plain-speaking will be paramount. When travel is likely to be affected by political developments, earthquakes or floods, terrorist threats or other newspage developments, a travel-page report can hardly ignore it.

4. Good travel topics include an offbeat site, a new attraction, any interesting destination.

Trends that affect tourists are also worth considering: the modernization of British pubs, the renovation of cathedrals in France.

A narrow focus often provides the best opportunity for colorful writing — for example, a market street in Lima, a festival in Barcelona, a museum on cats in Malaysia. But a large-topic story — travel in Eastern Europe, London in summertime, cruising the Caribbean — is also worth while.

If the reporter can add some perspective — a sense of familiarity with the country and the people — all the better.

5.   Business people make up a large part of the travelling public. They want information that can help them travel more efficiently — tips on getting through airports, facts on practical matters like packing, food, ground transportation, foreign customs.

6.   Unlike some magazine material, travel stories for newspapers must be punchy and concise. Interesting historical background can be woven in judiciously.

Facts on accommodation, food, prices and other similar information may be appropriate, especially when organized into an **If you go** Quick.

7.   The use of the first person is occasionally acceptable when giving a personal account of an unusual adventure, but it should not be overdone.

This shot of the Fasal Mosque in Pakistan is an example of a good travel photo. Include people or animals to give a sense of scale. The main subject is off-centre, and foreground detail is included to help composition and provide a sense of depth. Generally, keep the sun behind you and take lots of pictures.

(CP—Chuck Stoody)

8.   The most useful length for travel stories is usually 500-600 words. Photos are essential, and a map may be handy to locate offbeat sites.

9.   Travel stories do not need exotic placelines. Many people want ideas on cheaper or shorter holidays within Canada.

Legal

Dos and don'ts
Criminal cases
  Before charges are laid
  Inquests
  Pré-enquête
  Arraignment and bail hearing
  Change of venue
  Preliminary inquiry
  Trial
  Appeals
  Retrials
  Young persons
  Sensitive cases
Civil cases
  Claims
  Other civil cases
  Appeals
  Examination for discovery
  Damage suits
Contempt of court
Libel
  Privilege
  What's protected
  Provincial statutes
  Special concerns
  Good faith
  Fair comment
Copyright
Privacy, wiretaps
Press and police
  Public notices
  Co-operation with police
  Newsroom searches
Legal vocabulary

Legal

Engraved in the memory of every reporter and editor should be:

1.   Carelessness and bad judgment on legal questions can ruin people's lives. Every journalist must weigh this responsibility when working.

2.   It is dangerous to publish statements that damage a person's reputation or livelihood unless the statements are provably true or unless the law clearly provides a special exemption.

3.   It is particularly dangerous to suggest criminal conduct unless it has been proved in the courts.

4.   Every person charged and before the courts is entitled to be presumed innocent and to receive a fair trial. It is forbidden to publish anything that passes judgment on an accused or that could hinder a fair trial unless it has been admitted in court as evidence. (Of course, the court's judgment is publishable.)

5.   Juveniles involved with the law — accused, witnesses or victims — must not be identified, even indirectly, without legal advice.

Follow these rules:

1.   Check legal authority before writing anything legally doubtful. This stylebook may provide some of the answers, but if there's any doubt check counsel.

2.   Cut out anything that looks legally questionable until it can be cleared for use.

3.   If legal doubts arise after a story has been distributed, order the story killed or withheld immediately until the doubts can be resolved.

Crime

Reporting on crime

No area of reporting requires greater care than crime.

People's reputations and livelihoods are at stake. Concepts of fairness that are at the core of Canadian democracy come regularly into play.

On the other hand, a justice system that deals effectively with criminals is a legitimate goal of every democracy. And one of the bases of an effective justice system is public scrutiny: the public must see justice being done, if not in person then through the press.

Courtrooms are natural theatres of human drama and good court reporting takes the reader to the heart of the drama. But always with fairness and objectivity in the recording of testimony and the description of witnesses.

Reporters and editors should make themselves familiar with the entire legal section of the CP Stylebook in a general fashion. The subsections are set out in such a way that those working on a specific step in the legal process can refer to the portion dealing with that step. The worst pitfalls are highlighted at the start of each subsection.

However, the law is complex. A stylebook is no substitute for legal counsel on doubtful issues.

Criminal cases

Some general rules:

1. Court reporting must be fair and accurate to be legally protected. Otherwise, the protection is lost. That means straightforward coverage of testimony, even-handed descriptions of accused or witnesses, balance between Crown and defence cases, no plain or implied taking of sides.

2. Coverage must also be contemporaneous. It is risky to report well after the fact on a criminal proceeding, particularly if the accused was acquitted. It can seem like an attempt to blacken the accused's name needlessly. Consult counsel before reporting on an old proceeding.

3. Give the exact charge in a criminal case, not a generality. If the charge is sexual assault, don't write **attack**.

4. Don't refer casually to a defendant's religion, race, political party, profession or other qualification unless it's directly relevant. Beware of categorizing an accused in a way that could reflect on an entire group of people.

5. Identifying alleged victims or other witnesses in sexual assault cases and some other sensitive areas may be banned by the court. Even if not banned, such details should be published only after carefully weighing the possible hurt to those who have already been victimized.

6. In important cases, provide the possible penalty, but also mention that the maximum penalty is rarely imposed and prison terms are rarely served in full.

7. When substantial prison terms have been imposed, specify promptly how much time must be served before parole can be considered.

8. Don't total concurrent sentences (**sentenced to a total of 120 years**). Report the individual sentences on various charges and the actual maximum prison term.

9. Don't attempt to pull together two or more court cases into one story unless they were linked in court. Such natural linkages are rare anyway, but on days when a number of parallel cases are going on in different courts — say, concerted disturbances by activists — publishing a roundup can risk influencing a sitting jury or potential jurors.

Some general background:

1. Criminal offences are generally of two types, **summary conviction** (less serious) and **indictable** (more serious). Some offences such as theft under $1,000 may be prosecuted either summarily or by indictment, at the discretion of the Crown.

2. Summary conviction offences are dealt with in a streamlined procedure under which the accused goes directly to trial without a preliminary hearing. Examples include causing a disturbance, indecent exhibition in a public place or being found in what are called **common gaming-houses** or **bawdy-houses**.

3. Summary conviction offences are tried by a justice of the peace or by the lowest of a province's courts. There are no jury trials at this level.

4. Indictable offences generally involve a choice of courts, at the discretion of the Crown, and sometimes a choice of trial with or without jury, at the discretion of the accused.

5. For many indictable offences — including armed robbery, breaking and entering, forgery and arson — the options are:

a) Trial by provincially appointed judge (lower courts) without jury and without first undergoing a preliminary inquiry.

b) Trial by federally appointed judge in a provincial superior court without jury but with a preliminary inquiry.

c) Trial by a federally appointed judge with jury in a provincial superior court. Such courts have a variety of names in different provinces: Court of Queen's Bench, Supreme Court, Superior Court, Court of Quebec, general division of Ontario Court.

6. For the most serious indictable offences, such as murder or treason, there is no option. They must be tried in a superior court. And they must be heard by a jury unless the accused and the provincial attorney general both agree otherwise.

7. Appeals of convictions for indictable offences are heard by provincial courts of appeal. Appeals for summary conviction offences are heard by a variety of courts depending on the province.

8.   The Supreme Court of Canada hears criminal appeals only if a point of law is involved and if leave to appeal is granted by a panel of three justices or by a provincial appeal court. Leave to appeal is not necessary if a provincial appeal court has reversed an acquittal won in the trial court; if at least one justice has dissented in the appeal court's decision; or if a co-accused, having been tried jointly, has had an acquittal sustained on appeal.

Before charges are laid

Dangers:

1.   Naming a person before court appearance.

2.   Providing past criminal record.

3.   Linking a suspect to a crime.

Police take an interest in many people. Often nothing comes of it. But to write that someone **is under investigation** for a criminal offence can cast a cloud over the person's life. The courts consider a false allegation of criminal conduct among the worst forms of libel.

Therefore, special care must be taken with any story identifying a person being investigated but who has not been charged or has not appeared in court to answer a charge.

CP does not normally name individuals until they appear in court to face formal charges. There may be exceptions depending on particular legal circumstances and news value, but the exceptions are rare.

Always check supervisors or seek legal advice before using doubtful information. With that caution, following are some general comments and examples:

1.   Contempt of court — appearing to influence a criminal proceeding — usually becomes a risk only when the case is actually about to proceed in court (**sub judice**).

2.   Even if not contemptuous, a report that police are **investigating** a specific person, or **considering charges** against a specific person, can be libellous in some cases.

3.   Depending on the circumstances, it may be permissible to report that **an investigation is under way** or **searches have been carried out**.

4.   It is proper to publish the fact that a warrant has been issued for the arrest of a named person, or that he or she has in fact been arrested, or has received a summons to appear in court, or has signed a promise to appear.

5.   The exact nature of the charge can be stated if the person has appeared before a judge, or if the charge is outlined in a warrant, summons or other document. It is probably dangerous to go into further detail without documentary evidence or testimony in open court.

6. Occasionally, the criminal record or other background of the accused is virtually inseparable from the description of the crime. A breakout or a riot at a prison or detention centre, for example, is committed by people who either have a criminal record or are held without bail for trial.

7. Trickier is the case of a murder committed by someone on parole. If the suspect's previous conviction was also for murder, a strong editorial case could be made for reporting that fact on grounds of public interest, although legally the information would be totally prejudicial. If the previous crime was petty theft, the record is irrelevant. Consult a supervisor or counsel before including detail of the previous conviction.

8. In cases where the criminal record of the person concerned is essential to understanding the story, after consultation with counsel it is usually permissible to refer concisely and fairly to such background at the time the story breaks. During later court proceedings, there should be no casual references to background that could prejudice the case or be ruled inadmissible at trial. Special care must be taken in the month or so before a trial, so prospective jurors aren't prejudiced.

9. Even when it's permissible to mention the background, a story must never imply that the suspect's record means he or she is guilty of the new offence.

10. Occasionally, a criminal comes before the courts who's so notorious that virtually anything may safely be written about the person's past and character until trial is imminent. Resist the temptation to abuse this liberty. If the criminal is truly notorious, the public doesn't need constant reminders of the reasons. And such stories can send the wrong signal about the press's concern for fair play.

11. On rare occasions — a hostage-taker who surrenders, a bank robber wounded in the act — the suspect's identity may be obvious even before being charged. In such cases, write only that a named person has been arrested or is in custody, without going into detail.

12. A suspect must be kept separate from the crime. For example, it may be all right to say: **A robbery was committed. John Doe is being held.** It is never all right to say: **John Doe committed a robbery.** Similarly, it is not acceptable to write: **A drug ring was broken today with the announcement of charges against three people.**

13. Witnesses can be interviewed when a crime is committed, but their statements should not be used to link a specific suspect to actions that could be disputed later in court. Witnesses must not be interviewed once a suspect has come before the courts.

14. Reporting police statements carries no immunity from the risk of libel or contempt. Such statements have to be weighed as carefully as any other information and checked for accuracy when possible. Whether a particular police force can be depended upon for fairness and accuracy is a matter of past experience. It is no defence against a libel or contempt charge to say the police were thought to be trustworthy.

Inquests

Dangers:
1. Publication bans.
2. Later use of incriminating evidence.

1. Coroner's inquests — or as they are increasingly known, **fatality inquiries** — are held to investigate the cause of a violent death and make recommendations designed to avoid future deaths. They are presided over by a judge or coroner, depending on provincial law.

2. Inquests are usually open to press and public. The general rule holds that public hearings may be reported fairly and accurately.

3. However, the person presiding may order the inquiry closed, temporarily or permanently, because of possible prejudice to a potential accused, national security, public safety or intimate testimony, depending on provincial law. In such cases, whether evidence from the inquiry becomes public later is a matter for the presiding officer and/or provincial law.

4. An inquest may hear evidence that would be inadmissible at a later court proceeding, such as a confession. It may be reported at the time, unless the presiding officer directs otherwise, but it should not be repeated without legal advice once the case is before the courts.

5. Inquest juries are usually forbidden to make any finding of civil or legal responsibility. However, their investigations can sometimes lead to questions of who might have committed a crime, in a way not normally open to the courts, and that could lead to criminal charges. It's unwise to speculate about such possibilities without legal advice, however.

6. Inquest juries, like those at criminal trials, are forbidden by law from disclosing any information about their deliberations.

7. In Quebec, among things the law forbids:

a) Publishing a photograph of the dead body without consent.

b) Publishing any identifying information about a witness under 18 years of age implicated in the events.

c) Publishing autopsy reports.

Pré-enquête

Danger:
1.   Reporting testimony.

1.   A pré-enquête is a rare form of private inquiry by a judge to determine whether a charge should be laid. It is sometimes used when a public figure is implicated, to limit potential damage should the evidence not support a charge. The judge may hear witnesses in private before deciding whether to proceed to a preliminary inquiry or another step in the judicial process.

2.   Procedure can be one-sided (**ex parte**), without cross-examination under oath and other legal safeguards. Thus, testimony may not be reported if it somehow becomes available. It is permissible to report that the hearing is being held, to name the persons against whom charges are being considered, and to report the decision on whether to proceed with charges.

3.   The pré-enquête should not be confused with a preliminary hearing, a later step used in many criminal cases at which the judge decides whether a person already charged should be sent to trial.

Arraignment and bail hearing

Dangers:
1.   Violating publication ban.
2.   Reporting confession or criminal record.

1.   Arraignment is normally the first step in a criminal court proceeding. It usually involves just an appearance by the accused before a judge, reading of the charge, making a plea and selecting a trial option. It's not essential that the accused enter a plea; the court may record a plea of **not guilty** if no plea is entered.

2.   The court may hear evidence from a psychiatrist or other qualified person and order a psychiatric examination to test the accused's fitness to stand trial. The judge usually orders a ban on publication of such evidence; if not, it may be reported. There are normally no other restrictions on reporting arraignments.

3.   A decision on bail may be made at arraignment, or at a separate bail (or **interim release**) hearing. If the accused requests a ban on publicity, the judge must grant it. It is then forbidden to publish testimony or the judge's reasons for granting or denying bail. The fact of whether bail was granted, and any conditions for release, may be reported.

4.   Even without a publication ban, no confession offered in evidence by police or other witnesses may be reported at this stage without legal advice. There should be no mention of a criminal record without approval from a supervisor or counsel.

Change of venue

Danger:

1.   Reporting court decision.

1.   When a criminal case becomes so notorious in a community that it would be almost impossible to find jury members who could be impartial, a change of location (**venue**) can be ordered by the court to ensure a fair jury trial for the defendant. The change is usually to a community well removed from the scene of the crime.

2.   Since the point of changing location is to find untainted jury members, the court may order severe limitations on what can be published about the case.

3.   On occasion, the court may ban publication of anything about the change of location — including the fact that a change of venue has been requested or granted.

4.   When the trial begins in the new location, the court can order a ban on reporting that a change of venue has taken place. The ban remains in effect until a verdict has been handed down or the trial otherwise ends.

Preliminary inquiry

Dangers:

1.   Violating a publication ban.
2.   Reporting a confession.

1.   A preliminary inquiry is held to determine if there's enough evidence to warrant a trial. The accused usually asks for a ban on publicity. The judge is required to grant it on request, and no evidence may then be reported.

2.   What may be reported:

a)   Whether the accused is sent to trial.

b)   The exact charge on which the accused was brought to preliminary hearing and, if appropriate, on which he or she was sent to trial.

c) The number of witnesses heard.

d) Any comment by the lawyers, or the accused, or any part of the judge's decision not referring to the evidence heard.

3.   Even without a publication ban, the Criminal Code prohibits reporting any confession — by the accused at the hearing (rare) or mentioned in evidence by police or other third parties at this stage — at risk of a fine of up to $2,000 or up to six months in jail, or both.

4.   A confession in this context can mean a literal admission of guilt or any statement or action implying guilt. For example, if police testify that the accused led them to the body in a murder case, it should be avoided as an implied admission of guilt.

5.   Any publication ban remains in effect until the conclusion of any subsequent trial, defined as the point at which a verdict is reached, regardless of intention to appeal. At that point, testimony at the preliminary hearing becomes publishable.

6.   If the accused is discharged at the end of a preliminary hearing for lack of sufficient evidence, the banned testimony becomes publishable. An exception is a confession offered as evidence by police but not admitted by the judge; in such cases, consult a supervisor or counsel.

Trial

Dangers:

1. Reporting what the jury hasn't heard.

2. Evidence of criminal record.

1.   The general rule is that any evidence admitted by the judge at a public trial can be reported. This includes confessions and other evidence that may have been excluded at previous stages, if the evidence is presented again in open court.

2.   It is dangerous to resurrect any other previous submissions made at a preliminary inquiry until the trial ends.

3.   Evidence or arguments presented with the jury absent should not be reported, except in the rare cases where the jury has been sequestered. For example, no reference should be made to evidence at a hearing (**voir dire**) held to determine whether certain evidence, such as confessions or wiretaps, may be legally presented to the jury.

4.   If such evidence is admitted by the judge, it can be reported when presented to the jury. If not admitted, it may not be reported until after the trial, and then only with consent of supervisors or counsel.

5.   Statements ordered struck from the record by the judge may still be reported. The judge's ruling has the effect of erasing the statements only from the trial record.

6. Any reporter who starts to cover a trial part way through must confirm that there is no voir dire or other restriction on what may be reported.

7. Evidence of previous convictions is usually not admitted at trial. If an accused presents evidence intended to show good character, he or she may then be asked about any prior criminal record.

8. On rare occasions, the public is excluded from all or part of a trial:

a) Trials of young people under the Young Offenders Act.

b) Trials in which there is risk of disclosing information affecting national security or defence, international relations or the public interest.

c) Cases where the judge orders a trial closed in the interests of maintaining order or the proper administration of justice. No testimony may then be reported, but the verdict can be.

9. If the public is excluded to maintain order but the media are allowed to remain, the proceedings may be reported unless the judge directs otherwise.

10. Immediately after a verdict in a criminal trial has been rendered — and even if one of the parties plans to appeal — it is permissible to report fair and accurate comments by editorial writers, columnists and legal experts on the facts of the case, the parties, their lawyers, the judge's conduct and the administration of justice.

11. There is increasing leeway now to criticize the administration of justice, including the conduct of judges and the validity of their judgments. But to suggest unworthy motives by a judge is courting a contempt citation.

Appeals

Danger:
1. Suggesting bias.

1. Normally, anything and everything said at an open appeal court hearing can be reported.

2. Appeal court judges are generally considered to be above being prejudiced by the publication of comment or opinion about a case being heard on appeal.

3. Nonetheless, to suggest bias or prejudgment on the part of a judge — appeal court or otherwise — is tempting fate.

4. And of course the normal rules of court reporting — fair and balanced coverage — apply to appeal court hearings.

Retrials

Dangers:

1. Recalling previous verdict.

2. Recalling previous evidence.

1.   When a trial ends in a hung jury, or when a conviction or acquittal has been overturned on appeal, a new trial may be ordered. That means that for the accused, the slate has in effect been wiped clean. It is as if the first trial did not take place.

2.   The appeal court's decision may be reported at the time with full background. But well before a new trial begins there must be the same restraint in reporting on evidence or testimony as would have applied before the first trial, especially if a jury trial is possible.

3.   Unless specifically banned, it is permissible to report at any time that a previous trial ended in a hung jury, or that the verdict of the previous trial was overturned on appeal. When retrial is imminent, it is not normally permitted to report what the previous verdict was, since that could influence the new jury.

Young persons

Dangers:

1. Naming young suspects, witnesses, victims.

2. Providing identifying characteristics.

3. Quoting witnesses about juvenile crime.

4. Naming in adult-court transfers.

5. 48-hour deadline on "wanted" notices.

1.   The Young Offenders Act covers people from their 12th to their 18th birthdays, male or female.

2.   The act prohibits publication of the names or other identifying characteristics of young people who appear or are to appear at a hearing, adjudication or appeal under the Young Offenders Act. The prohibition applies to accused, witness or victim, unless a victim is dead.

3.   Among the characteristics that could serve to identify a young person under the act — and are therefore forbidden to be published — would be names of family members, a home location, a sports team, or the name of a school attended or of the institution in which a young person has been detained.

4.   The publication ban applies also to adults who were under 18 at the time of an offence and who are not being tried in adult court.

5.   The ban also applies to a young person who is said by witnesses or police to have committed an offence. It is risky, for example, to quote a witness as saying a named young person was speeding when an accident occurred.

6.   When a young person is suspected in a crime involving members of his or her own family, no story may include *both* the victims' names *and* their relationship with the suspect. That would amount to identifying the suspect. When the first news of such a crime becomes available:

a) Do not either name the victims or describe their relationship with the suspect until it is clear from accumulating details where the chief news interest will lie: in the relationship or in the stature of the family.

b) Try to develop a consensus with other media on what to publicize — the names or the relationship.

c) Once a decision is made on which element to publicize, do not switch tracks without consulting counsel. Anyone putting together the names from one story and the relationship from the other can identify the suspect.

7.   The court can order all or part of a youth court hearing closed to press and public at any time to protect those involved, in the interest of public morals or maintenance of order.

8.   When an application is made to transfer a young person to adult court for trial, the court may order a ban on publication of any information from the transfer hearing until:

a) the last appeal of the order has been exhausted, or

b) until the trial in adult court is ended.

9.   In cases where a possible transfer to adult court is at stake, it is therefore dangerous to identify a young suspect before all appeals are exhausted.

10. Occasionally, police are given permission by a judge to issue a public appeal for a wanted young person, by name, where there is thought to be danger to others. Such court orders are valid *only for 48 hours*. Before publishing anything based on such an order, it's essential to verify that publication won't occur after permission has lapsed. CP news stories must include an editor's note at the top, giving the deadline.

11. Don't be led by the name of the act to refer to accused people as **young offenders**. That phrasing automatically convicts the defendants.

12. The entire issue of young persons and the law is particularly treacherous because of the sweep of the current law and uncertainties about its application. Whenever there is doubt about a particular case, consult a supervisor or legal counsel.

Sensitive cases

Dangers:
1. Identifying victims, witnesses.
2. Suggesting fault in divorce.
3. Naming those with AIDS, STDs.
4. Naming minor offenders.
5. Gruesome or indecent detail.

1. In cases involving sexual offences, extortion or usury, a judge must ban publication of the identity of victims or a juvenile witness if asked to do so by either the victim, the witness or the Crown.

2. In such cases, it is forbidden not only to name the victim or witness but also to provide any information that could disclose their identity.

3. Among information that could reveal their identity would be a family relationship, address, place of employment or other characteristic that could allow some members of the community to make an identification.

4. Even where no ban is in effect, it is usually wrong to identify alleged victims of sexual assault without their active consent. CP does not name minors, even with the consent of their parents.

5. In rare cases, a victim's name somehow becomes widely known in the community and publication of the name is not banned. Nevertheless, editors should still weigh whether using the name will send a signal to readers that the press is indifferent to the problems of sexual assault victims in general.

6. Reporting on divorce and annulment proceedings is subject by law to restraints. Generally, only a bare identification of those involved, the main issues and the judgment can safely be reported.

7. When referring to divorced people, avoid wording that might suggest fault unless the facts are verified. A phrase like **was divorced** might imply adultery, cruelty or some other fault by the person named. Prefer **whose marriage ended in divorce** or similarly neutral wording.

8. Generally, provincial legislation that requires the reporting of communicable diseases also provides for strict confidentiality. It is therefore risky to breach the anonymity of those with a sexually transmitted disease, AIDS or other reportable infection without their consent.

9. Certain offences are regarded by the law as relatively minor, subject to small fines at most. But publicly naming those accused of communicating with a prostitute, indecent exposure or similar offences can have ruinous consequences. It should be done rarely.

10. The law, not just ethics, can determine what gruesome or indecent details to publish in court cases. The law forbids reporting on indecent matters or indecent medical details that could injure public morals — phrases that are vague enough to require legal advice when in doubt.

Civil cases

While criminal cases involve society's attempt to control wrongdoing or protect the public good, civil cases involve disputes between private individuals or corporations. Society provides the court structure and a set of laws designed to make the settlement of grievances an orderly process.

Civil cases require the same care and dispassion of reporters as criminal cases do.

Vocabulary:

1.   In civil cases, there is no **prosecutor**. Nobody is said to be **charged**. At the end of a court hearing, no one is **convicted** or **acquitted**, nor found **guilty** or **not guilty**.

2.   The person initiating a civil case is the **plaintiff** or **petitioner**. The process involves **bringing suit** or **taking action** or **seeking damages**. The other party is the **defendant** or **respondent**.

Claims

1.   Small claims are heard in a variety of lower courts depending on the province. The upper limit for the amount claimed in such cases also varies with the province.

2.   Small claims are usually heard directly by a judge, without lawyers acting for the contesting parties.

3.   Intermediate claims are heard at lower or intermediate court levels, with lawyers representing the parties. Jury trials are rare.

4.   The largest civil claims are heard in provincial superior courts, by judge alone or with jury.

5.   Jury trials are no longer provided for in Quebec for civil suits.

Other civil cases

1.   Surrogate or probate courts exist in some provinces to deal with wills and estates. In other provinces, such cases are heard by the courts that handle other civil actions.

2.   The Federal Court of Canada has jurisdiction over citizenship, taxation, immigration, copyright, trademark and patent cases, judicial review of federal administrative tribunals, and claims brought against the government of Canada.

Appeals

1.   Appeals in civil cases are heard by the appeal division of a provincial superior court or court of appeal. Leave to appeal must almost always be sought from the higher court.

2. The appeal division of Federal Court hears appeals from decisions of that court.

3. The Supreme Court of Canada hears appeals on civil cases if there is a matter of public importance or an important point of law at issue.

Examination for discovery

Danger:
1. Testimony is not safely publishable.

1. Before trial of a civil suit, a process called examination for discovery is normally held. It allows the parties to examine each other's case and to clarify the issues to be resolved at trial.

2. Although the testimony is recorded and those testifying are under oath, the evidence at examination for discovery is not subject to all the normal safeguards of a courtroom.

3. Such examinations are not considered public hearings and cannot be covered by reporters. The transcripts are not public documents and are not normally accessible to the press. Publication of such evidence should not be considered without legal advice.

Damage suits

Dangers:
1. Quoting from one-sided documents.
2. Referring to amount claimed.

1. When one party files suit for damages against another, a **writ** or **statement of claim** is issued and this fact may be reported. But the writ may contain allegations that are one-sided, defamatory and not subject to rebuttal. Statements from writs should not be reported without advice from legal counsel.

2. When a jury is hearing a civil suit for damages, it is not supposed to be informed about the amount of damages sought, for fear it will be misled. There is no real limit to the damages a person can claim and the amount may in reality be ridiculous.

3. As a working (but not infallible) rule, don't report the amount of damages sought during a jury trial or for a month before such a trial. Once a case has been decided, there is no such restriction.

4. The restriction does not apply to cases heard by a judge alone, nor to civil cases in Quebec where there are no longer jury trials in civil suits.

Contempt of court

Every journalist must be on guard against contempt of court in reporting on crimes, investigations and court cases.

Contempt of court doesn't mean despising a judge or the justice system. It's an old usage of the word **contempt**, meaning to **interfere** with the administration of justice or **disobey** the courts.

Controlling contempt is intended to protect a person's right to a fair trial, a cornerstone of democracy.

General guidelines

Dangers:
1. Defendant's confession.
2. Previous convictions.
3. Speculation.
4. Ignoring publication bans.

1. When a story is known to be in contempt, kill it at once. If contempt is suspected, withhold the story from publication, check it with counsel and keep editors advised.

➤ See **Libel**, page 112.

2. It is a basic rule that nothing must be published that interferes with the proper course of justice. That particularly includes anything that impairs an accused person's right to a fair trial.

3. Even if a statement is true and not libellous, it may be in contempt of court if it hurts a person's right to a fair trial.

4. There is a particular risk of prejudice in reporting on a defendant's confession unless it has been accepted as evidence in open court.

5. Check counsel before referring to previous convictions unless they are mentioned in open court. Such information is not necessarily admissible at trial.

6. The publication or repetition of a statement in contempt of court is itself contempt. The source of the statement or its accuracy doesn't matter.

7. Guilt or innocence should not be imputed to any party in a court case. It is also dangerous to speculate on possible motive for a crime, the credibility of witnesses or the likely outcome in a jury trial.

8. Do not report testimony or other material from previous stages of a criminal proceeding — preliminary hearing, death inquiry or the like — unless it is introduced again in open court.

9. At a jury trial, it is a crime to report evidence heard by a judge at a *voir dire,* a hearing held to determine whether certain evidence will be presented to the jury. Such hearings are always held with the jury excluded. However, publication of voir dire evidence may be allowed when it involves a case being tried by judge alone or in those rare cases where a jury is being sequestered. If in doubt, check counsel.

10. Any restriction imposed by a court on publication remains in effect until the court sets it aside.

11. It is a crime in Canada for jurors to disclose any information on their deliberations. While there's no law forbidding reporters to interview jurors, the reporter could be charged with inducing a juror to break the law by encouraging the juror to reveal protected information.

12. Once a case has ended, it is usually permissible to report criticism of the administration of justice or the conduct of a judge. It is risky to suggest the judge had improper motives. In some provinces, a statement may also be in contempt if it villifies a court or judge. Check counsel when in doubt.

Foreign cases

1. Exercise care on any story from abroad that includes out-of-court statements by police or others about Canadian individuals or businesses if a subsequent trial is likely to take place in Canada.

2. In particular, beware of assuming that U.S. laws and legal procedures apply in this country. Statements about an accused person from police and other authorities of a kind that are routine in the United States can be considered contempt in Canada.

Libel

Remember:

1. Statements damaging to reputation must never be published unless there is a clear legal basis for doing so.

2. Anyone who repeats a libel is fully responsible for the libel, no matter what its source.

3. A libel can cause great damage to a person's life.

4. Individual reporters and editors can be sued along with their employers for libels they permit to be published.

Libel is the publication of a false and damaging statement. It is part of the broader legal category known as **defamation**, covering **slander** (ordinary conversation) and **libel** (published or broadcast).

Defamation is a statement that tends to lower a person in the opinion of others, or exposes the person to hatred, contempt or ridicule. Defamation is also a statement that injures another's reputation in a way that affects that person's livelihood — work, trade or profession — or financial credit.

When a story is known to be libellous, **kill** it at once.

> **BULLETIN**
>   EDITORS: Kill Moncton PM-Accusation. No charge laid yet. Story is possibly dangerous. Will be no sub.
>   **CP Halifax**

When even a slight doubt exists, **withhold** the story from publication immediately while a check is made.

> **URGENT**
>   EDITORS: Withhold Brandon AM-Wheat from publication. Contains possibly dangerous quotes. CP is checking with counsel.
>   **CP Winnipeg**

Then either kill it or release it promptly. If a kill is needed, advise whether a sub will be sent. If the story is approved as sent, release it urgently in an advisory.

Note: Don't blame libel or libellous material for a kill or withhold. It might weaken CP's defence against a subsequent suit.

General information

Key Points:

1. Truth difficult to prove.

2. Public interest must be weighed.

1.   Libel has serious potential to harm not only CP and its employees, but any newspaper or broadcaster using the material. A plaintiff can sue everyone, or pick and choose arbitrarily — even to the point of aiming at the weakest links, those with the smallest resources who are most likely to pay to settle a libel suit without contest.

2.   Libel involves an untrue report. Truth is a **complete defence** against a libel suit. A true statement of fact is not vulnerable even if it is damaging. But the one who publishes a damaging statement is responsible for proving the truth of the statement, and that is often extremely difficult. In some cases it may be impossible. It's not up to the plaintiff to prove the statement is false.

3.   In Quebec, in addition to truth, the Civil Code requires that publication be in the **public interest** and **without malice**.

4.   **Public interest** and **lack of malice** are not specified by law elsewhere in Canada. However, professional ethics dictate that before publishing a truthful but damaging statement, the press will weigh carefully whether the public interest is served by publication. And absence of malice must be a foregone conclusion in the publication of any news report.

5.   The Canadian Press and other media whose reports reach an audience within Quebec must take into account Quebec's legal requirements when considering publication of potentially libellous material from elsewhere in Canada, particularly if the report concerns a Quebec resident.

6.   Consent can be used as a defence in a libel suit, but it requires proof that:

a) the person defamed has been informed defamatory information will be published, and

b) the person knows what he or she is consenting to, and

c) the person consents to publication. The proof of consent must be in the form of documents, tapes or a witness.

7.   Except in Quebec, it is virtually impossible to libel the dead. And a libel suit launched by someone who subsequently dies is normally dropped. However, it could be dangerous to defame a dead person in a way that affects the living: for example, suggesting a woman had illegitimate children before she died.

Privilege

Key Points:

1. Fair, accurate, no malice.
2. Right to rebuttal.

1. Privilege means **protection from legal action**, even when defamatory material has been published. Privilege is based on two traditional assumptions:

a) It would be in the public interest for every citizen to attend certain events or read certain reports. Failing that, all citizens should have access to fair and accurate reports of such events.

b) In some cases, the public good is better served through unrestrained debate and the free communication of information than it is through a normal concern about accuracy or defamation.

2. Privilege is never absolute. At its most fundamental, it still requires that any report be **fair, accurate** and **without malice**:

a) **Fairness** means lack of bias, not taking statements out of context.

b) **Accuracy** means reporting the facts correctly. A report need not be textual or complete; it can be a fair synopsis.

c) **Lack of malice** means there is no dishonest or hidden motive nor reckless disregard for the truth.

3. The protection of privilege is also lost as a defence in a libel action if there has been a refusal to publish a reasonable statement of explanation or contradiction despite a request from the person defamed to do so.

What's protected

Key Points:

1. Legislative bodies, courts.
2. Quasi-judicial bodies.
3. Meetings, reports.
4. Public proceedings.
5. Notices to the public.

1. The common law — that is, traditional rights recognized by the courts — and the Civil Code in Quebec provide general principles for the protection known as privilege.

2. In addition, all provinces have specific statutes dealing with libel and privilege. The statutes vary; in tricky cases, get legal advice. However, the following may be considered privileged:

a) Debates and committee meetings of the House of Commons, the Senate and provincial legislatures, as well as public reports and documents issued by these bodies.

   Note: The privilege doesn't extend to statements made outside of a chamber or committee hearing, such as in a scrum.

b) Proceedings heard in public before any court exercising judicial authority, and reports issued by courts. The privilege doesn't extend to hearings from which public and press are excluded, nor to any matter on which the court has banned publication. If a report is not contemporaneous, consult counsel.

c) Death inquiries or coroner's inquests, royal commissions and other commissions of inquiry are not strictly courts but their proceedings and reports or documents are generally privileged.

d) Hearings of federal and provincial regulatory agencies and administrative tribunals, such as labor relations boards, and their reports or documents.

e) Meetings and reports of local government bodies and their agencies, such as municipal councils, municipal planning boards, school boards, boards of health.

f) Public meetings. This broad category can be tricky. It is usually defined as a meeting open to the general public, lawfully convened, to discuss a matter of public interest. It probably doesn't cover a news conference, nor a political meeting to which only supporters of one party have been invited. When in doubt, check counsel.

g) Any bulletin, report, notice or other document issued for the information of the public from any government office or department, medical officer of health or local board of health. This would include, for example, a warning that a particular product is dangerous to health.

h) Any notice or report issued by any government or municipal official, commissioner of police or chief constable for the information of the public, and published at that person's request. The most common example is a police appeal for public help in locating a fugitive or missing person.

Provincial statutes

Key Points:

1. Professional, business, sports bodies.

2. Right of rebuttal.

3. Retraction, apology.

1. Each province in Canada has some form of libel legislation, dealing with issues of defamation and protection from legal action under certain conditions.

2. In addition to the categories of privilege listed previously, most provincial laws extend privilege to the findings and proceedings of professional, business and sports organizations that are formed in Canada. Included would be the disciplinary proceedings of law societies, medical associations, trade and business associations and sports leagues.

3. However, provincial law states that refusal to carry a reasonable statement of explanation or contradiction from the complainant, if asked to do so, will wipe out the privilege.

4. The law also specifies that a full and fair retraction for a defamatory story, if published with equal prominence to the orginal story and within *three days* of receiving legal notice, will reduce damages. The provision doesn't apply to a story that suggests a criminal offence was committed.

5. Damages may also be reduced if a full apology is published either before legal action was started or promptly afterwards.

6. The Quebec Press Act, in addition to most of the above, also extends privilege to the reports of the provincial ombudsman when tabled in the legislature, and to reports by the government or an authorized person about the financial solvency of companies or the value of certain stock and bond issues.

7. The Quebec law provides for reduced damages by apology, but that doesn't apply when a criminal offence is suggested. Nor does it apply when the defamation involves a candidate for Parliament, the national assembly or municipal office and when it is published in the period extending from three days before nomination day until election day.

Special concerns

1. People in certain areas of society make outrageous statements as a matter of course. Politics and sports are prime examples.

2. Public statements from people in these fields are routinely harsh, overstated and malicious. If such statements were made by others under different circumstances, the courts would be much busier.

3.   The fact that political or sports comments rarely result in libel claims does not mean there is no need for caution in reporting them. Libel is libel. Check counsel before taking chances.

4.   A separate concern involves non-Canadians who have business or other interests in Canada. Such people can sue for libel in this country if news from abroad is published in Canada which affects their reputation or livelihood in Canada. Thus, for example, a report from somewhere in the United States that alleges drug-taking by a football player now in the Canadian Football League — or even with CFL prospects — would be dangerous. So would a report from abroad that damages the reputation of a Hong Kong businessman with Canadian business interests.

Good faith

1.   If a statement is false, it is no defence to claim that it was thought to be true at time of publication.

2.   However, the damages awarded in a libel suit may be reduced because of absence of malice and evidence of good faith:

a)   if there were reasonable grounds for believing the defamatory statement was true, and

b)   if an apology was published when the statement was discovered to be false.

Fair comment

Key Points:
1.   Honest opinion.
2.   Based on provable fact.
3.   Public interest.

1.   Commentary involves questions of opinion and interpretation. A different test is applied to commentary than to factual reporting. Comment or opinion (**the government's program is ruining the economy**) need not be proved true in the sense that an objective fact (**the government has increased the sales tax**) is true.

2.   The defence of fair comment has often been applied to editorials and to artistic criticism such as book, film or theatre reviews. But it isn't limited to such material. It can be used to defend any story that mixes factual material with interpretation and analysis.

3. To be defensible, comment must meet these criteria:

a) It must express an opinion honestly held. It can't be presented maliciously or out of a hidden motive.

b) Most important, it must be based on facts *presented in the story* that can be proved to be true. An honest opinion based on false information cannot be defended.

c) It must relate to a matter of public interest, not a purely private matter.

4. Public interest is roughly parallel to news value. But publication in one province on the grounds of public interest could be libellous in another province.

5. The basic rule holds: When in doubt, get legal advice.

Copyright

Dangers:

1. Substantial quotes without OK.
2. Permission not in writing.

1. Copyright is what gives the creator of an original work the exclusive right to benefit from it.

2. Copyright covers such creations as books, films, songs, articles and essays, letters, diaries, pictures or anything else that's original and in some permanent form. It can even extend to distinctive titles.

3. The copyright owner controls the right to reproduce the work, in whole or in substantial part.

4. For the press, this means there can be no substantial quotations from copyrighted material without written permission of the copyright owner. Giving a mere credit to the copyright owner isn't sufficient.

5. *Substantial* has different meanings for different works. A complete stanza from a short pop song could be substantial. Generally, copying the heart of a work would be against copyright law. Check counsel when in doubt.

6. An exception is made for quotations used in a review or critique, but it must be a bona fide review and the quotes should be no more than needed to make a critical point.

7. Generally, government documents, speeches and most other material used in daily journalism are not copyright.

8. Over time, copyright protection is lost and the work falls into the public domain. In Canada, literary and artistic copyright expires 50 years after the author's death. Copyright on photographs expires 50 years after the negative has been processed.

9. Information cannot be copyrighted, only the form in which it is presented. Although newspapers frequently identify a story as being copyright, the actual news in the story cannot be protected. Someone else using an original method of expression may reproduce the information. Making a few changes in expression is not sufficient; the presentation must be substantially original.

10. The Canadian Press has first right to use staff-written local news from newspapers that are part of the co-operative news agency, whether or not the newspaper declares it to be copyright.

11. However, worked-up exclusives or news from beyond the newspaper's normal coverage area cannot legally be distributed in their original form by CP without permission from the managing editor or other senior officer at the paper. Giving credit to the paper is not a substitute for getting permission if there are to be substantial quotes or reproductions from the original.

12. Like anyone else, in the absence of permission, CP may distribute a report based on the information in the copyright story. It must use substantially different words and it should be brief — no longer than needed to report the substance of the story. Direct quotes of more than a sentence or two are not allowed.

13. CP may also not normally use a published feature created by a freelance, even if it involves local news. Freelance work is usually identified by a different credit line (e.g., **Special to the Mirror**) than staff work. Ignoring the copyright owned by a freelance can be costly.

14. The copyright in a Letter to the Editor is held by the letter writer, who automatically gives a right of publication to the newspaper that receives the letter. To reproduce all or part of the letter elsewhere would require written permission from the copyright holder, in strict legal terms. But in practical terms, verbal permission from the newspaper will do. (Few letter writers are likely to sue because their views have been given a wider audience, and if they won a suit the damages would likely be minimal.)

15. Freelance photographers hired by CP negotiate in advance the ownership and resale rights for their film. The work of newspapers' regular freelance photographers is available to CP. In most instances of spontaneous photography — the bystander's shots of a hot news event — the freelance is told by the paper to negotiate directly with CP.

➤ See **Pictures**, page 342.

Privacy, wiretaps

Dangers:

1. Disclosing others' communications.
2. Broadcasting private conversations.

1.   Anyone may record their own conversations, without the permission of the other party, whether in person or on the telephone or other circumstance.

2.   However, it's illegal to intercept or record conversations or private communications of other people without the consent of one of the other parties.

3.   It's also illegal to broadcast on radio (but, oddly, not on TV) any part of one's own conversation with someone else without the consent of the other person. An exception is when the other person has phoned in to participate in the broadcast.

4.   And it's illegal to use or disclose anything about others' private communications without the consent of one of the parties.

Press and police

Police in Canada have shown a disturbing tendency to turn to the print and broadcast media for information and evidence in recent years. They have demanded the use of photographs and film to document charges against possible rioters and others involved in public disturbances, and have made other demands on news people to support police work.

The media have generally resisted. If people come to view the media as an arm of the justice system, they will lose confidence in the media as an intermediary between ordinary citizens and authorities.

Following are normal guidelines for dealings with police:

Public notices

1. The press normally co-operates when police ask for publicity about the hunt for suspects or lost persons. Accuracy in identification is essential. Racial description and other characteristics — not usually part of a news report — are a normal part of such published identification material.

2. Do not casually refer to a person as dangerous. The description would be prejudicial if referring to someone whose jury trial is imminent. It should be based on a *written* release from police intended for the public.

Co-operation with police

1. There is normally no objection to providing police with copies of stories or photographs that have already been published, or other routine material of a non-confidential nature, as a matter of courtesy.

2. However, reporters' notes, unpublished film, background files and other material dealing with ongoing stories or anything of a private or confidential nature should not be provided to police unless they produce a search warrant.

3. Material gathered by reporters and other employees in the course of their work is the property of the employer. No employee has the right to turn over such material to police without permission from a senior supervisor.

Newsroom searches

1. Police will sometimes provide advance notice that they intend to present a search warrant. In any case, police arriving in a newsroom with a search warrant — with or without notice — must not be delayed, obstructed or resisted. They are not obliged to wait until legal counsel is on the scene.

2. However, police should be referred immediately to a senior supervisor, and legal counsel should be informed immediately by phone.

3.   The warrant should be inspected closely to ensure that

a)   all factual references (address, name of company or person, date) are accurate;

b)   a suspected offence is specified;

c)   it is properly signed by a justice of the peace.

4.   If there are errors, the police should be asked to leave. If there aren't, the supervisor can watch any search being conducted. Others on staff can observe and, if necessary later, serve as witnesses about the way the search was conducted, but only the supervisor should talk to police.

5.   While not obliged to assist searchers, the supervisor may decide it is best to direct them to a specific desk or area and otherwise help them if the option is a wide sweep that could uncover unrelated confidential material elsewhere in the newsroom.

6.   The supervisor should ask permission to photocopy any material that is to be seized. If the request is refused, legal counsel should be consulted immediately.

7.   If the searchers intend to take confidential material relating to sources, or unpublished material, the supervisor should insist that it be placed in a sealed envelope until the question of privilege can be decided in court.

8.   Legal counsel should be consulted promptly about any question that arises as a result of being served with a search warrant.

Legal vocabulary

The language of courts and lawyers is extremely precise, but it can be distant from plain speech. Latin terms and jargon abound. Legal language may find its way into a story legitimately for effect or precision, but in most cases a plain substitute or clear explanation is best.

Some standard legal terms:

affidavit: sworn written statement to be used as evidence.

arraign: charge before the courts.

bawdy-house: archaic term still used in Criminal Code for brothel.

common law: unwritten law based on ancient custom and judicial precedent.

> **common-law marriage**: relationship based on living together without legal recognition. (Use phrase with caution.)

concurrent: at the same time; of a number of jail sentences, to be served simultaneously (as opposed to consecutively).

contempt (of court): not disdain for the judge, but interference with justice or disobedience of court order.

copyright: protection of exclusive use of original work.

ex parte (Latin for *from one party*): one-sided; submission by one party in legal dispute without contest from other side.

habeas corpus (Latin for *You have the body*): writ requiring person be brought before court, usually to test whether person's detention is legal.

in camera (Latin for *in a room*): private(ly); hearing with public excluded.

indeterminate sentence: of no fixed term, dependent on prisoner's conduct.

indict, indictment: formally accuse of crime; formal accusation or charge.

> **indictable offence**: more serious level of criminal charge (less serious is called summary offence).

interim release: term increasingly used instead of **release on bail**.

leave: permission, as in **leave to appeal**.

open custody: assignment of offender to group home or other lightly supervised environment, usually for juveniles.

plaintiff: person who brings complaint to court in civil case.

pré-enquête (*pre-inquiry*): rare form of private hearing by judge or justice of peace to decide whether charge should be laid.

privilege: immunity granted under certain conditions to speak without fear, or to report such speech.

sub judice (Latin for *under a judge*): before the courts; for the court alone to decide.

subpoena (Latin for *under penalty*): Writ commanding presence in court.

venue (change of): location; move trial to another community to avoid prejudice against accused.

voir dire (Old French for *say the truth*): hearing within a trial, with jury excluded, to test admissibility of confession or other evidence.

writ: court order requiring specified act or giving authority to someone to have act done.

> **writ of certiorari** (from Latin for *inform*): demand from higher court for records from lower court.

> **writ of mandamus** (Latin for *We command*): command to inferior court, or to person to perform legal duty.

young person: in law, male or female between 12th and 18th birthdays. Covered by Young Offenders Act.

> **child**: person under 12.

The working journalist

Breaking news
   Getting organized
   First steps
   Organizing chaos
   Equipment
Common faults
   Unanswered questions
   Dig for treasure
   Sentences and paragraphs
   Active vs. passive
   More than words
   Trippers
   Front-end loading
   Overloads
   The formula lead
   Jargon
   Everyday words
   Lazy words
   Say and variants
   Attribution
   Arithmetic
   Headline language
   Verbs ending in *-ize*
   Time element
   That
   That-which
   Who and whom
   Cliches
   Word order
   Mind-reading
   Splits and prepositions
Locating the news
Writing
   Be human
   Be specific
   Be clear
   Be direct
   Be concise
   Next-trick stories
   A writing checklist
Editing
   Principles
   How to do it
   Tighten the story
   Brighten the story
   Check accuracy
   Check style
   Make it clear
   Make it fair
   Handle with care
Writing for broadcast

Breaking news

Battle Stations!

The call to action in a CP newsroom when a major story breaks is like a ringing command across the deck of a warship steaming into action.

The fast-breaking story goes to CP's very heart. The Canadian news industry — print, radio and TV — fixes its eyes on the CP computer queue when major news erupts.

CP faces a potential deadline every minute. It must deliver at breakneck speed.

But absolute accuracy and precise attribution rank ahead of speed in handling breaking news.

Slow down, step back, check and recheck if there is any risk of inaccuracy.

Getting organized

There is no textbook on handling the spot news break. Circumstances in any two breaks are never the same.

There may be official sources such as the police to help. But there may not be — at least in the early stages.

Improvisation and resourcefulness are the standards. So are clear-cut organization, precise individual roles, steady direction and cool heads.

Confusion at the scene of events like a plane crash, prison riot or tornado is the norm. Expect it but don't get caught up in it. Officialdom may be in a dither. The *official* version of what has happened may change in minutes. And then change again. Damage estimates and death tolls can swing wildly.

But disorder has no place in a newsroom when a big story is breaking.

Some basic guidelines:

1.   Respond immediately to a tip of a major break. Assign someone to concentrate on getting it confirmed or denied. Notify a bureau supervisor so planning can begin immediately on staff assignments: on-site staff, main lead writer, other writers, chasers, editors; and on logistics like rental cars and chartered aircraft (see *Equipment* below). Tip Main Desk, CP Pictures and Graphics. If a report cannot be confirmed immediately, send an advisory to say CP is checking an unconfirmed (*repeat, unconfirmed*) report or angle, and include the gist of what is involved. If the report is confirmed, send a NewsAlert, Bulletin or Urgent immediately and work on the advisory next.

Note: Don't dredge up the relic *copy will be expedited*. That goes without saying. Do say as precisely as possible when copy is expected. Then deliver it on time. Or, in rare cases, send another note saying why it has been delayed. Never leave editors hanging.

➤ See **Advisories**, page 354.

2. Never move a story on a major break that isn't nailed directly to an identified source. That can be anyone from the prime minister announcing a declaration of war to a tow-truck driver at the scene of a multi-vehicle pileup. Move a Bulletin or Urgent as soon as the report is confirmed. Get the attribution in the first paragraph. Every detail must be secure. Hold back if there is even the slightest doubt about a new development. But don't sit on a hot angle or wait for official sources to return calls. Move immediately to get it confirmed or denied. Nail down all sources. Ask them to spell their names — twice if there is any possibility of error. Ask for precise ranks or titles. This takes only seconds. Corrections take minutes and disfigure the report. Hold on to tapes or original notes of who said what and when.

A typical opening story:

PM-Crash
Code:1
BULLETIN
   REGINA (CP) — An unidentified airliner plunged into a farmer's grain field and exploded in a huge fireball today near the community of Gravelbourg in rural south-central Saskatchewan, the farm's owner told radio station CXYZ.
MORE

Note: The **MORE** slug promises further information in the form of a 1st add (see page 406) within 10 minutes.

3. Move a coverage advisory as soon as plans are firm:

PM-Crash-Advisory
Code:1
   Eds: CP reporter Chris Wattie has left Regina for Gravelbourg, Sask., where an eyewitness has told a radio station that an unidentified airliner has crashed and exploded. Wattie should reach the area at about 11:30 a.m. CST. A further advisory on other coverage plans, including photos, will move within 20 minutes.
   CP EDMONTON

4. Quickly pin down the location, including the nearest town if the site is remote. Tip Graphics so a newsmap can get rolling. Keep the location high in all subsequent leads.

5. Don't wait for local authorities to get back from the scene. Chasers should not stop pressing while waiting for a promised call-back from an official source.

Each bureau should have current telephone books for every community in its region. Scour listings for likely unofficial sources — the local service station or general store. Or if there is nothing obvious, take a stab at random numbers in the book. Chances are most people in the area will know something. Or know someone who does.

Note: Long before authorities were saying anything for the record, an eyewitness to the 1989 University of Montreal massacre told a CP reporter that a man carrying a gun had burst into a classroom.

"Someone asked him if it was a joke and the guy started firing,"
the eyewitness said.
Another said: "It was a human hunt and we were the quarry."

Caution: Don't say witnesses or sources when only one person is being quoted.

6.   Move adds in short takes of a paragraph or two. Aim for a 1st Lead within 20 minutes of moving an Urgent such as the reported plane crash above. Official confirmation or direct word from a reliable witness may rate a Bulletin:

AM-CRASH, 1st Ld
Code:1
1st Lead 601 (police confirm airliner has crashed)
BULLETIN
   REGINA (CP) — An unidentified airliner described by a farmer as "silver with a green tail" crashed in a fireball today in a grain field near Gravelbourg in south-central Saskatchewan, police said. An officer at the scene said there were no signs of survivors.

---

7. Don't bury the news when new — but less important — information becomes available. Survivors found staggering from the scene or casualties on the ground belong at the top. But don't leapfrog the real news with secondary information such as an RCMP announcement of a news conference on the plane crash. That sort of information is vital for the media — but not the reader.

8. Try for fresh information for the top of 1st Leads and all subsequent leads, but it must be pertinent to the main news. If necessary, stay with the original lead and keep later secondary information lower.

Here is an example of a lead that keeps the essentials at the top:

**By Penny MacRae
and
Peter Lowrey**

MONTREAL (CP) — A gunman who yelled "you're all a bunch of feminists" went on a deadly rampage Wednesday at the University of Montreal, shooting 14 female students before committing suicide with his own weapon.

The gunman, who was in his early 20s and wore hunting garb, also inflicted bullet wounds on 13 others — nine women and four men — in the bloodiest mass shooting in Canadian history.

"I saw death close up and I shook," said Vanthona Day, 22, one of scores of horrified students who streamed out of the building after the carnage.

Not all breaking news comes as a surprise and a writer can benefit from advance preparation:

By Chisholm MacDonald

ST. CATHARINES, Ont. (CP) — Helmuth Buxbaum, millionaire businessman, womanizer and patron of dubious drug-pushers, has moved to an even darker level of life — a prison cell for at least 25 years.

Convicted Thursday of first-degree murder in the contract slaying of his wife Hanna, his partner in nursing-home enterprises and marriage for 23 years, Buxbaum insisted to the end that he had nothing to do with her death.

But a jury of 10 men and two women decided it was he — not his drug supplier — who masterminded the murder plot in which the 48-year-old mother of six children was pulled from the Buxbaums' car on a roadside and ruthlessly shot in the head.

9.   Give a wide berth to generalized and vaguely attributed statements, especially related to death tolls and damage estimates:

Not: Witnesses at the scene estimated about 20 people were killed and 40 or more injured.

But: "I counted 20 or 21 bodies and there must have been twice that many people who were showing some sign of life," said Jackie Lo, one of the first to reach the scene.

If the figures prove badly out of line, it was Lo who was wrong — not those reporting her words:

The official toll — 11 dead and 46 injured — was provided by RMCP Sgt. Laura Bridges and coroner Luis Alvarez. Earlier, one of the first volunteer rescuers to reach the area said she had counted 20 or 21 bodies.

Guard against slipping into the present tense on breaking stories, especially when picking up material from radio or TV. Writing in the past tense has two advantages: the story can be quickly led without having to change the tensing of the original; and the story stands up even if the situation changes after a paper has gone to press.

First steps

Major news breaks at any hour of the day. A solo CP staffer who gets word on such a break should:

1.   Move an Urgent.

2.   Alert local supervisors who can call in reinforcements and start making plans for getting staff to the scene.

3.   Brief Main Desk.

4.   Send an advisory on coverage plans, even if it has to be tentative.

Organizing chaos

As noted, no two big news breaks are alike. But there are some tried and proven procedures to follow:

1.   Get a strong lead writer in place immediately and let that person stick with the job. The writer knows what information has been placed where in the story, where figures are first reported and where sources are first named, where new information can be smoothly blended in and where pickups should naturally occur.

2.   The lead writer should be assigned an editor who can work directly with the writer, checking content, smoothing the flow, setting up slugging, coding and headers, ensuring pickups are in the right place and moving Completes. The writer and editor keep the copy moving. A last-minute detail or appealing touch of color can go in the next lead. The editor ensures the writer knows about any major changes being made in the story. Trying to keep the news in proper order and pickups in the right place is hard enough without having the story rearranged without notice.

3.   The writer and editor should **not** be involved in any other news while handling the big break. Their undivided attention is needed.

4.   A bureau supervisor decides how much other copy is to be handled. Depending on available staff, or if the story is big enough, everything else may have to be put on hold. Often, though, the best course is to free one reporter-editor to handle all unrelated copy, likely in bare-bones form.

5.   A supervisor, consulting with the writer and editor, decides what angles need chasing, who should go where and what information is needed for the next main lead or sidebars. If others are providing quotes or other details for the main story, remember this from the Old Lead Writer's Creed: *Don't tell me — write it.*

6.   One supervisor or senior staff member should be the bureau funnel, dealing with Main Desk, the Picture Service, BN supervisors at Head Office and other media to ensure the bureau is getting everything it can from newspapers and radio stations in the area. The lead writer and editor should not be answering phones and worrying about logistics and other details.

7.   An editorial assistant should be freed from routine tasks and made responsible for tearing copy from printers and delivering messages to the editor. The editor should not have to go searching for a hard copy of the last lead or a piece of information messaged from Head Office or another bureau. The editorial assistant may be able to help the lead writer by chasing down a piece of background, checking a map for spelling or digging into Newstex or the morgue files. This staffer may also help Pictures and Graphics if a file photo needs to be transmitted or information is needed for a locator map.

Equipment

Proper equipment and fast action on logistics like transportation are critical when big stories break. Editorial and Communications supervisors should ensure:

1.   That cellular telephones, tape recorders and portable computers are in top shape, fully charged and ready for action at all times. Company credit cards should be available for staff on short notice. There also should be some system in place for supplying cash in off hours.

2.   That each bureau has at hand the after-hours phone numbers for at least two charter plane companies in the bureau's area. Phone immediately and get a quick estimate of cost and availability. Competition for charter aircraft can become intense when a big story breaks. It is often wise to make a tentative booking. Check other local media quickly about possible cost-sharing.

3.   That reporters and photographers have current passports. Even entry to the United States has become stickier. St-Pierre-Miquelon lie just off Newfoundland but belong to France.

Common faults

The most common faults in news writing are lack of imagination, muted curiosity, and a deaf ear and closed eye for the reader's interests.

These faults lead straight to news stories that are predictable, unfocused and boring.

By turn or together, they may confuse readers with conflicting information, leave them gasping for missing facts or infuriated at what they know is misinformation.

Such stories can puzzle readers with fog and bafflegab, and have them wondering what the news means to them and their everyday lives.

Bluntly put, they turn readers off.

Unanswered questions

Never leave basic questions unanswered.

Not: The price of two litres of milk is going up five cents in New Brunswick today.

But: The price of two litres of milk in New Brunswick is going up today by five cents to $3.10 a carton or two-bag plastic pack. It is the second five-cent increase in just over seven months.

Not: She was sentenced to life in prison.

But: She was sentenced to life in prison with no chance of parole for 17 years.

Not: A police officer was shot Friday as two men sped away from the scene of a bank holdup in downtown Brandon.

But: A police officer was shot in the chest and seriously wounded as two men sped away ...

Not: Canadian shoe manufacturers say a federal government plan to lift import quotas on leather footwear will deliver a severe blow to the industry.

But: Canadian shoe manufacturers say a federal government plan to lift import quotas on leather footwear will ultimately lead to higher shoe prices for Canadians, especially women. It will also mean hundreds of Canadians will lose their jobs in shoe factories, they said.

Dig for treasure

Search a story through for hidden angles that would snatch a reader's attention if even a hint of the buried treasure were woven into the lead.

Not: A local man faces three counts of attempted murder and four counts of assault with a weapon causing bodily harm after a hotel brawl at a wedding reception sent seven men to hospital, six with knife wounds, early Saturday morning.

But: A brawl at a wedding reception between friends of the bride and friends of the groom left seven men hurt and a country lodge with a heap of shattered furniture, antiques and chandeliers early Saturday.

Sentences and paragraphs

Readability has never been more important. People are busier and have less time than ever to read newspapers. They will quickly bail out from a story that is heavy and dull.

One key factor in readability is sentence length.

A sentence is more likely to be clear if it is short and conveys one idea:

People with near-death experiences agree about details to a remarkable extent.

A longer sentence which closely connects several ideas also works:

Many of them say they float out of their bodies, encounter God or a spirit figure, meet deceased relatives, review their past lives, feel great peacefulness and finally return to their bodies.

That sentence runs to 32 words, but its meaning never falters because everything relates to the same subject and the language is simple.

Try to begin sentences with words that have punch and power. Avoid starting with phrases, longer clauses or attribution.

Keep paragraphs short and active. Paragraphs of two or three tight sentences are inviting. Long, grey blobs of print are not.

Active vs. passive

Think of active verbs as power words — words that drive your sentences, keep the reader's attention and move her briskly along.

Not: The economy experienced a quick revival.

But: The economy revived quickly.

Not: At first light there was no sign of the ship.

But: The ship vanished in the night.

Use the passive when a switch in emphasis is helpful, for instance, to put the news ahead of the source:

Not: A grievance board has ordered the reinstatement of a counsellor fired for kicking a patient.

But: A counsellor fired for kicking a patient has been ordered reinstated by a grievance board.

And the passive may lighten a sentence by removing secondary information that can wait: **A banker wanted for questioning in the disappearance of $1 million is believed to have flown to Mexico, police said today.** (But be sure a later paragraph gives reasons for the belief.)

More than words

Tell the reader what has happened, certainly. But also help the reader understand why and how it has happened in terms that strike home:

Not: The hurricane caused widespread damage to buildings, farm equipment, trees and hydro lines.

But: The hurricane's winds lifted roofs off houses and barns and flipped over cars, tractors and even lumbering dump trucks used to carry grain. Almost every fruit and shade tree in the region was knocked over, and linemen said about 3,000 hydro poles had been snapped off.

Trippers

Be alert for words, phrasing and sentences that will cause a reader to stumble:

Not: Manness said he met with trucking industry officials earlier this year who said they were concerned about taxes.

But: Manness said he met earlier this year with trucking industry officials who said they were concerned about taxes.

Not: After dining on hundreds of pet cats and dogs, the provincial Environment Ministry has decided to round up coyotes and ship them to remote parts of the province.

But: Coyotes have killed dozens of pet cats and dogs, so the provincial Environment Ministry has decided to round up the predators and ship them to remote parts of the province.

Not: The bears were destroyed when they would not leave a tree in which they were munching leaves.

But: The bears were shot when they could not be coaxed out of a playground tree where they were munching leaves.

Front-end loading

Avoid it like the plague.

Not: United States envoy Herman Cohen said in London after meeting government and rebel representatives at peace talks that the two sides had agreed to a ceasefire.

But: The two sides have agreed to a ceasefire, United States envoy Herman Cohen said after ...

Not: In a telegram to Prime Minister Brian Mulroney urging that the offices Canada Post plans to eliminate be retained, the union said it was appalled by the proposed measures.

But: The union said it was "appalled" by Canada Post's plans to close the offices. It urged in a telegram to Prime Minister Brian Mulroney that all the post offices be retained.

Not: An official of the Nova Scotia Environment Department, who was at the scene on the Annapolis River near the small community of Paradise about 170 kilometres west of Halifax, said both tractor-trailer units were spilling chemicals into the river.

But: Both tractor-trailer units were spilling chemicals into the Annapolis River near the small community of Paradise, a Nova Scotia Environment Department official said from the scene, about 170 kilometres west of Halifax.

Not: British Columbia and Yukon Birders Association executive director Anne-Marie Sheehey will be the featured speaker.

But: Executive director Anne-Marie Sheehey of the British Columbia and Yukon Birders Association will be the featured speaker.

Overloads

The overloaded lead is sure to turn the reader off:

Not: The family and friends of William John Fortune have raised enough money to rescue the stranded Canadian tourist and, with the help of volunteers from the Barbados police department, will send an airplane on Tuesday to lift him and his two daughters, Louise and Samantha, from a tiny sandspit north of the Caribbean island, longtime friend Lorne Pulsifer said today.

But: An airplane will head for a tiny Caribbean sandspit north of Barbados on Tuesday to rescue a stranded Canadian tourist and his two daughters, a family friend said today.

The overblown statement is another turnoff:

Not: Once the wind was at his back, the home-town quarterback wreaked as much havoc on the defence as Hurricane Hugo did in the Caribbean.

But: The home-town quarterback, with the wind now at his back, threw touchdown passes on three consecutive drives.

Overwriting weakens stories and repels readers:

Not: The legislation was greeted with howls of protest.

But: One opposition member after another criticized the legislation, calling it ill-conceived and dangerous.

The facts are best presented in plain conversational style with deft phrasing, touches of human interest, significant details and strong quotes.

Avoid overcharged words: **blast, charged, chastise, flail, flay, lambaste, enraged, lash** and **slam.**

Simply report in an even tone what was said:

Not: Labor leader Bob White launched a bitter attack on the company offer.

But: "It is the most preposterous company offer I've seen in the last 15 years," said labor leader Bob White.

The formula lead

It needs no introduction.

Not: BARRIE, Ont. (CP) — Three men suffered minor injuries when their light plane crashed into a field after striking hydro lines Friday.

But: BARRIE, Ont. (CP) — A light plane hit power lines while taking off in a rainstorm Friday, flipped and crashed upside down in a farmer's potato field. The three men aboard escaped with minor injuries.

Jargon

Bureaucratese and other forms of bafflegab have become an epidemic. Some experts and academics seem bent on smothering readers in phrases like **problemize binary opposition, conceptual signage** and **rethink categoricalism** which frustrate translation.

As if this weren't stifling enough, newspaper people have their own self-inflicted verbiage in the form of *journalese:* MPs **blast** each other; inquiries **probe;** rescuers are **grim-faced.**

Inside language of a profession or any other specialist group should be translated into understandable English. But the translation needs care.

Not: "The bullet lodged in the cerebrum," the doctor said.

But: The bullet lodged in the upper front part of the brain, the doctor indicated.

Not: There was "a severe loss of separation" between the two aircraft, the air traffic controller said.

But: The two planes nearly collided, the air traffic controller suggested, explaining that is what he meant when he used the term "a severe loss of separation" in his report.

Not: Police withheld his identity pending notification of next-of-kin.

But: Police withheld his name.

Abstract nouns, especially ones ending in *-ion* and strung together with prepositions, often signal foggy writing. Passive verbs can be culprits as well.

Short words tend to be concrete, standing for people, places, objects and acts.

Not: Medically speaking, the inhalation of the toxic substance is considered capable of the creation of psychological compulsions resulting in his criminal behavior.

But: Doctors said breathing the poison may have affected his mind and driven him to kill.

Everyday words

Treat the reader to words and phrases that are short and familiar.

About, not **approximately**

Met, not **held a meeting**

Instructor or **teacher**, not **resource person**

Improve, never **ameliorate**

Plan or **program**, not **initiative** or **strategy**

Lazy words

Cast an inquisitive eye on words like **colorful**, **controversial** and **zany**. An editor who asks why Mayor Horsefall is **colorful** may learn Horsefall once ate his hat on the town hall steps when he lost a hockey bet with the mayor of a rival town. Tell the reader.

Say and variants

Early CP stylebooks described **say** and **said** as honest and inconspicuous. They are also not to be toyed with.

Say and **said** should be attached to words and ideas that exactly mirror the speaker's, not an interpretation or extension. Words like **indicate** or **suggest** may be appropriate where **said** is not and are mandatory in stories on opinion polls.

Not: The poll shows fewer than 10 per cent of Canadians believe . . .

But: The poll suggests fewer than 10 per cent . . .

Many substitutes for **say** and **said** are risky or, at best, vague:

Admit implies confession, **affirm** states a fact, **assert** declares strongly, **claim** and **maintain** hint of doubt, **confide** implies a confidence, **declare** states explicitly, **disclose** and **reveal** presume earlier concealment.

Be especially wary of **explain, point out, claim** and **note**. They all imply that what is being said is fact. **According to** and **said she believes** may question the speaker's credibility.

Words like **recalled** and **predicted** can be tricky. Make sure they fit the circumstances.

Attribution

Claude Ryan moves through journalists as he leaves the Quebec Liberal party convention in March 1991. Writers can avoid the hackneyed **told reporters** *and try* **said** *instead.*

(CP—Jacques Boissinot)

Avoid the hackneyed **told reporters**. That the speaker said something after her speech, or after her statement in the Commons, or after a news release was issued is always sufficient.

Told The Canadian Press or **The Canadian Press has learned** should be used sparingly, such as when:

• The same person has said different things to different media and it seems appropriate to spell out the differing versions.

• CP has an exclusive interview with the prime minister or some other high official.

• An interview is obtained from an unusually distant or hard-to-reach point such as a submerged submarine or the tip of Mount Everest.

• Exclusive material has been gained through the Access to Information Act or similar legislation.

Arithmetic

Writers should mind their math when dealing with statistical percentages and other figures. Never make the reader do the arithmetic.

Reporting that the number of flagpole-sitters in Canada has increased 100 per cent in the last year is meaningless without the base figure. An increase from five flagpole-sitters to 10 is 100 per cent but the percentage figure alone suggests a population explosion.

Take care as well in phrasing changes in percentage statistics. A poll that suggests a drop in government support to 25 from 50 per cent does not mean a 25 per cent drop. It's a change of 25 percentage points.

Headline language

Keep headline language out of news copy.

Not: Bell inked a six-year contract.

But: Bell signed a six-year contract.

Not: The commission will launch a three-pronged probe into the fire.

But: The commission will investigate the fire in three ways.

Short general-purpose words may fit in a headline, but not in a story.

Avoid words like:

Ban, beef up, bid, boost, cop, ink, ire, laud, lash, pact, probe, quiz, rap, shun, vow

The headline-writer's practice of dropping **a, the, of** and the like to save space leads to lumpy sentences in the body of a story.

Not: He was intrigued by Canadian Imperial Bank of Commerce chairman Russell Harrison's defence of Dome Petroleum's rescue.

But: He was intrigued by the defence of Dome Petroleum's rescue offered by Russell Harrison, chairman of the Canadian Imperial Bank of Commerce.

Verbs ending in -ize

Trendy verbs ending in *-ize* strike many readers as ungainly.

Accessorize, capsulize, decimalize, definitize, finalize, prioritize, therapize

Accept them cautiously or only when there is no satisfactory alternative.

Time element

Put the time element where it falls naturally in speech, usually right after the verb or at the end of the sentence.

Not: Transport Minister Doug Young Thursday said the new policy . . .

But: Transport Minister Doug Young said Thursday the new policy . . .

Try to put the time element at the end if putting it directly between the verb and its object is awkward:

Not: Finance Minister Paul Martin announced Wednesday a $2-billion job program.

But: Finance Minister Paul Martin announced a $2-billion job program Wednesday.

There are situations where the time element is at home either in the middle or at the end.

Dawn Coe came out of the pack Saturday to score a five-shot victory in the Canadian women's golf championship (Saturday).

That

Dropping **that** often makes for smoother reading, especially in shorter sentences.

She said (that) she wanted to be alone.

But retain it to avoid misleading the reader even momentarily.

Carr said that on May 1 he was in Halifax; Justice Minister Allan Rock warned that the government would step in.

That should also be retained and repeated with two or more clauses.

He promised that the singer would appear and that the evening would be a success.

That-which

When it comes to introducing a clause in the middle of a sentence, there's sometimes confusion about whether **that** or **which** is correct. **Which** sounds grammatical somehow, so it ends up being used too often.

That is generally used when the clause is essential to the noun it defines or narrows the topic: **The movie** that **opened at the Roxy last week.** (It's not just any movie, it's the one that opened last week at a specific theatre.)

Which clauses give a reason or add a new element: **The movie,** which **cost $4 million to make, has done landslide business.** (The assumption here is that the reader already knows which movie is being discussed, and its cost is an added bit of information.)

A helpful distinction: **which** clauses generally need commas, **that** clauses don't. Read the clause over in your mind. If it makes sense using **that** instead of **which**, chances are **that** is the right word to use.

Who and whom

Correct usage of these two eluders can be determined by dividing a sentence in two. Use **who** when it stands for **he, she** or **they.** Use **whom** when it stands for **him, her** or **them.**

The police issued a public alert for a man who they said was armed and dangerous. (They said **he** was armed and dangerous so **who** is correct.)

She took refuge with her next-door neighbor whom she had trusted in the past. (She trusted **her** so **whom** is correct.)

Cliches

Tired expressions are indeed tiresome. No one needs to read about a **hurler** who **toed the slab** or the **red-faced** MP who got a **tongue-lashing** from the opposition.

But use a cliche if it expresses your meaning exactly and if it will spare the reader some cumbersome second choice. It would be hard to improve on such gems as **sour grapes, cry wolf** or **tip of the iceberg** which sum up complex ideas in a few words.

Avoid the automatic or lazy cliche:

Grind to a halt, unveil, in the wake of, launch, seriously consider

And the fad term:

Ambience, greening, infrastructure, peer group, quantify, underachievers

And the fossil that no longer raises the faintest image:

Moot point, short shrift, at loggerheads, by the same token

Word order

Words out of order can create chaos.

Not: Having been born in France 24 years ago, Montreal baseball fans wasted little time picking up on Charlie Lea's French connection.

But: Charlie Lea was born in France 24 years ago and Montreal fans wasted little time picking up on his French connection.

Not: She has a six-figure income as a model, a horse and a Jaguar.

But: Modelling has given her a six-figure income, a horse and a Jaguar.

Mind-reading

Reporters and editors should not consider themselves mind-readers who can somehow measure others' true feelings.

Not: Genereux believes the government is corrupt.

But: Genereux said he believes the government is corrupt.

Not: Iroshima is furious about the layoffs.

But: "We're not taking this lying down," Iroshima said, shaking with anger and smashing his clenched fist into the factory fence

Splits and prepositions

The normal position for an adverb that modifies a compound verb (**is missing, was reached**) is between the parts of the verb: **The plane is still missing. Agreement was soon reached.**

Split an infinitive (**to satisfy, to keep**) rather than create a confusing or unnatural sentence: **The discovery is expected to more than satisfy investors. Godfrey told him to kindly keep his opinion to himself.** But don't split infinitives unnecessarily: **The parents asked the babysitter to quietly leave by the back door.**

If a preposition falls naturally at the end of the sentence, leave it there: **Reuben wants to know which team he'll be on.**

Locating the news

1.   Today's reader is more interested than ever in knowing exactly where the news is happening, both in Canada and abroad. Few Canadians live their full lives in the area in which they were born and brought up. Career moves take them from one part of the country to another and sometimes to still another. And, of course, thousands of Canadians have come here from other parts of the world.

2.   Name well-known streets or areas in stories about major fires and the like. In Halifax it might be: **a block from Barrington Street in the restored Historic Properties district of the waterfront beneath Citadel Hill.** In Hong Kong: **in the heart of the Central District within sight of the Bank of China Tower and just three blocks from the Star Ferry Pier.**

3.   Readers interested in entertainment and celebrities want to know where events are held. In a review of a show or coverage of an event involving a big-name star, try to set the scene for the reader: **the cast met for an after-show dinner at the Bayshore Inn, on Burrard Inlet facing the mountains of West Vancouver.**

4.   But keep in mind as well those readers who are unfamiliar with even the biggest cities. Pause early in the story to set the scene: **highrises on the Toronto harborfront with a view over boat-dotted Lake Ontario and out to the greenery of the Toronto Islands; the shooting at the University of Montreal, whose Art Deco administration tower atop Mount Royal can be seen from all over the city.**

5.   Don't assume readers know precisely where familiar mid-size cities are. Give places like Moncton, Kitchener, Prince Albert and Kelowna a physical presence and geographical location when that would help readers picture an event.

6.   Pinpoint the location of news in remote areas, as well: **The two tankers collided at the tiny community of Purple Springs on Alberta Highway 3 just east of Taber and about a 40-minute drive from Lethbridge; The power station is near Gillam in a rugged area of northeastern Manitoba inland from Hudson Bay and about 14 hours by road from Winnipeg.**

7.   Sometimes referring back to the story's placeline helps: (Glenwood, Nfld.) — **this central Newfoundland logging town about 300 kilometres west of St. John's;** (Mahim, India) — **this seaside town just outside Bombay.**

Nuclear power in Canada

Nuclear power reactors and waste management sites across Canada:

Power reactors	Waste management sites
1 Ontario Hydro *Pickering, Ontario*	**1 Ontario Hydro** *Tiverton, Ontario*
2 Ontario Hydro *Tiverton, Ontario*	**2 Ontario Hydro** *Tiverton, Ontario*
3 Ontario Hydro *Pickering, Ontario*	**3 Atomic Energy of Canada Ltd.** *Douglas Point, Ontario*
4 Hydro-Quebec *Gentilly, Quebec*	**4 Hydro-Quebec** *Gentilly, Quebec*
5 New Brunswick Electric Power Commission *Point Lepreau, N.B.*	**5 Atomic Energy of Canada Ltd.** *Gentilly, Quebec*
6 Ontario Hydro *Tiverton, Ontario*	**6 New Brunswick Electric Power Commission** *Point Lepreau, N.B.*
7 Ontario Hydro *Bowmanville, Ontario*	**7 University of Alberta** *Edmonton, Alberta*

(CP—Andrée Lachapelle)

(CP)

8. Don't assume the placeline is going to give the reader a clear geographic sense of where the news has happened. For example, a story from Edmonton that says a force of specially trained police officers has been set up to give immediate emotional support to battered women must make clear where the force will function. In Edmonton alone? In all major Alberta centres? Or throughout Alberta? Watch phrases like *city police* and *the provincial department* which may be adequate for local newspapers but rarely for CP. Usually it is better to name the city and province in first references.

Writing

The first page of one of the early CP stylebooks had this to say about writing news:

"Every story worth printing can be written for The Canadian Press."

That remains the case, although much about writing news has changed.

No longer is the role of the news writer merely to inform. Readers (call them news consumers, if you will) are bombarded with information.

But what many modern-day messengers fail to provide are context, background, balance and the sights, smells and sounds of the news.

Things that tell readers why this is important and what it means, in terms that strike home.

Newspapers are fighting to attract new readers and hold the ones they have. Some of the forecasts are chilling and the fight seems far from over. To help, reporters and editors must present news stories that are uniformly appealing.

Readability has always been an issue in the newspaper business, but never more than in today's reality: Fewer people are reading newspapers. Those who are reading papers spend less time at it.

Readability is often tied to sentence length. Sure signs of trouble: too many ideas, too many subordinate clauses.

It's possible to write brightly and clearly in sentences that run to 30 words and more. Possible — but not probable.

Be human

Stories must be human, specific, clear, concise, imaginative and factual.

1. Write about people. Personal words like **father, pilot, nurse, welder** put life into news stories:

> An ice fisherman trudging along the edge of an isolated lake found the wreckage.

> A power failure crippled most of Quebec's electricity network Tuesday afternoon. It left about six million people without heat and light in freezing temperatures.

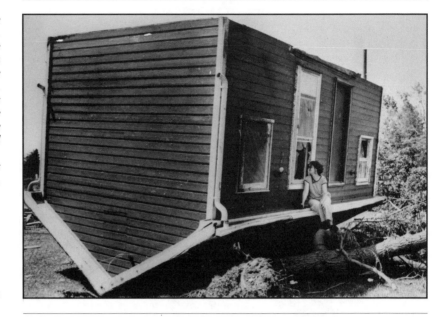

Look for the human angle in every story: the sheet-metal worker replaced by a robot, the single parent whose rent has doubled, the teller robbed by a gunman with a shaking hand. A roundup on unemployment could open this way:

> Like anyone buying insurance, Donald Good hoped he wouldn't need it. He insured himself last March against being laid off. As it turned out, he did need it.

Put things in real-people terms:

Not: An Alberta provincial court judge has thrown out charges against two men, ruling that the six days they spent in a Camrose jail constituted cruel and unusual punishment.

But: Two young Alberta farmhands were freed from jail after telling a judge their cell had a broken window and was so cold the water pipes to the sink and toilet froze for days on end.

2.   Relate the news to the reader's life whenever possible, which is often:

> Air-fare negotiations between Canada and the United States broke down Wednesday, dashing the hopes of thousands of travellers for bargain flights over the Labor Day weekend.

> Scientists believe they have detected the deadly chemical dioxin in the lake, but they say the levels appear too low to harm cottagers who drink its water or swim in it.

> The ruling means the plant workers will be eligible to apply for unemployment benefits within a week.

3.   Enliven the story with quotes that set the scene, capture the flavor of the news or provide insight:

> "He burst through the swinging door and ran straight to the checkout counter," she said. "He waved this baseball bat he was carrying over his head and kept saying: 'Give me the money — all the money.'"

> Asked why he had gone on the radio show after refusing to speak with other reporters, Carter said the open-line show is "unedited and not open to the selective editing that occasionally takes place in other aspects of the media."

4.   Perk up stories that are devoid of anything human, except perhaps some unnamed *spokesman* or *official.* Season them with examples that bear directly on readers' lives:

> Just when you thought you had finally caught up with the Joneses, along came Statistics Canada on Tuesday announcing that 367,000 families have backyard swimming pools.

Be specific

1.   Give the reader specific details. Ask yourself: How does this look? sound? feel?

> But her long slender fingers with dark burgundy nail polish do not tremble as she picks up her glass.

> A Waylon Jennings song is playing loudly on a dusty radio in the corner, a 24-pack case of Club beer sitting beside it. "Beer is my friend in these troubled times," says Martin, an unemployed trucker who lost his $38,000-a-year job five months ago.

2.   Get interesting human nuggets into the lead:

> A prison guard killed in the Archambault Penitentiary last July "was looking at pictures of his family and crying like a baby" when convicts burst in on him, a murder trial was told Tuesday.

> In the land they poignantly call Next Year Country, Prime Minister Brian Mulroney promised drought relief for farmers and a rosy, free-trade future for agriculture.

> Simon Reisman paced the halls like an expectant father on Saturday night. And when the news of the delivery came through, he acted like one pleased pop.

> Quebec's language law, better known as Bill 101, led Eaton's and The Bay to rename themselves Eaton and La Baie. On many menus, hamburgers became hambourgeois and hot dogs became chiens chauds.

3.   Paint word pictures:

Not: The accused were overjoyed.

But: The accused kissed and hugged each other.

Not: The northern cod is found in huge numbers off Newfoundland.

But: The northern cod, a grey-green fish with a barb under its chin, is found in teeming abundance in the chilly waters around Newfoundland.

Not: The MPs showed disgust at a rape scene in one of the Playboy films.

But: The MPs winced as the Confederate soldiers grabbed and raped a black slave in one of the Playboy films.

Be clear

1.   Always organize the story in your mind before you start writing.

Decide what the news is and put that in your lead. Stories with leads like these stand a good chance of flowing smoothly:

> A convicted 50-year-old rapist whose record for violent crimes stretches back to 1963 was sent to jail for at least 35 years Monday. The judge said he was so "sickened" by the case that he would ignore sentencing guidelines.

> American daredevil Maxie Anderson has decided to give up trying
> to fly around the world in a balloon after his third attempt came to an
> abrupt end Monday in the trees of a southern Ontario peach grove.

2.   But there are other ways to a reader's heart as well:

> The old Tory tune played in Alberta again on Thursday, but a lot
> fewer people got up to dance.

> Liberal party policy seems a lot like Scottish weather. If you don't
> like it, wait a few minutes — it's bound to change.

> Lotteries. Those spine-tingling, dream-inducing, pot-of-gold-at-the-
> end-of-the-rainbow lotteries are everywhere.

3.   Use plain words, but always the right words. Make it **wicked**, not
nefarious; **remaining**, not **residual**; **tone down**, not **modulate**.

4.   Use specific words when details are useful. Write **hamburger and
french fries**, not **food**; **shouting and laughing**, not **making a noise**;
a man of 87, not **an elderly man**.

Be direct

1.   Don't write **a number of cars** if you can say **five cars**; **a six-figure
income** if you can say **an income of $115,000**; **a long dry spell** if you
can say **37 days without rain**.

2.   Don't use lazy terms for unknown quantities: **fairly, really, pretty,
few, quite, very**.

3.   Translate pompous phrases.

Not: A poor public response.

But: Only a quarter of the tickets were sold.

Not: There is a doctor availability problem in the health delivery
system.

But: There are not enough doctors in hospitals and private
practice.

4. Avoid putting more than one thought in a sentence. In general, the contents and structure rather than length itself make sentences hard to understand.

Not: Union leader John Dickerson declared, "I have no regrets and would do the same again" as he entered prison today to begin serving a three-month sentence imposed last week for defying the legislature and refusing to call off a strike of civil servants angered by wage rollbacks.

But: Union leader John Dickerson said he had "no regrets and would do the same again" as he entered prison today to begin serving a three-month term.

Dickerson was sentenced last week for defying the legislature and refusing to call off a strike of civil servants angered by wage rollbacks.

5. Beware of too many dependent clauses, especially in mid-sentence where they break the flow. Each clause adds more ideas to the sentence, making it harder and harder to grasp.

Not: The U.S. vice-president flew into Berlin from Bonn, along with the German chancellor, with whom he held talks Monday on disarmament strategy on the first stop of a seven-country tour.

But: The U.S. vice-president flew into Berlin from Bonn on the second stop during his seven-country tour. With him was the German chancellor, with whom he held talks Monday on disarmament.

6. Keep introductory phrases and clauses short and simple.

Not: Noting spirited and repeated suggestions from the floor that the group should press Ottawa for a higher salmon quota for British Columbia fishermen who have complained bitterly about competition from foreign fishing fleets, especially the Japanese and American, but to some extent the Russians, association vice-president Hedley Evansson said ...

But: As for higher salmon quotas, Evansson said ...

7. Sentence length can grow comfortably when the sentence is simply a list of closely linked ideas referring to the same subject:

The Blue Jays pulled off the first triple play of the major league season when shortstop Manuel Lee stabbed what looked like a sure hit to left field by Oakland's Mark McGwire, stepped quickly on second base to double off Harold Baines and then drilled the ball to third baseman Kelly Gruber, catching Dave Henderson as he tried to get back to the bag.

Be concise

Keep your story tight in content as well as phrasing. Stick with the truly significant angles. A *full* report can often mean a dull report.

Be aware that a 1,000-word story in standard newspaper print would cover the back of a corn flakes box. Ask if the story would really hold a reader through an entire bowl of cereal.

If a story threatens to run long, consider whether some of the material could be broken out as highlights, a chronology or a point summary.

Clutter chokes meaning. Simplify:

1.   Ditch the long word that says no more than the short: **attempt** (try), **approximately** (about), **preponderance** (most), **consequently** (so), **substantiate** (prove), **initiative** (plan).

2.   Ditch the laborious phrase: **despite the fact that** (although), **at this point in time** (now), **in the event that** (if), **ahead of schedule** (early), **in the majority of cases** (usually).

3.   Ditch ponderous euphemisms and gobbledegook: **correctional facility** (prison), **job action** (strike, slowdown), **depressed socio-economic area** (slum), **in a classroom setting** (in a classroom), **resource centre** (library or lab), **lower rates of infant mortality** (fewer baby deaths).

4.   Ditch words that aren't doing any work: **He said** (that) **the cut**(back)**s in** (the) **health care** (field) **have put hospitals in a crisis** (situation).

5.   Consider whether the fad word works before using it: **parameter, overview, trendy, viable, motivation, inoperative, strategy, interface, prioritize, supportive.**

Next-trick stories

AMs newspapers are increasingly turning to more analytical approaches on stories, especially staged news events, as a way to attract readers who are likely to have already heard the facts from last night's TV newscast, a 24-hour news channel or a brief radio report. This puts next-day afternoon editions in a tight spot as they seek even fresher angles. Copy for these papers must keep alive a story that may have already been reported for more than 24 hours. Try to avoid past-tense wording as much as possible: **Canada can no longer export goods to Spain**, rather than, **The government imposed export restrictions Tuesday**.

Don't place undue emphasis on minor developments to freshen a story. But do look for a different perspective. For example, on a provincial budget: Were human-interest angles neglected? How will the budget influence the next election? On a disaster, was there an eyewitness who can provide a lively account of what it is like to be caught in such a situation? Could it have been prevented? What are the implications?

The essential details of the news must be covered so it is understandable to readers who may be hearing about it for the first time. If these details are lengthy or complex, they can sometimes be handled in a Quick so they don't burden down a lead that is taking a new approach.

A writing checklist

1.   Is the lead right? Does it capture only the most significant angles? Is there secondary information getting in the way of the main points? Is there an appealing human touch or quotation deep in the story that would fit in the first paragraph? Is the time element placed where it falls naturally in speech?

2.   Does the writing appeal to a reader's senses? Are there gobs of *officialese*, jargon or abstractions? If so, can they be translated into direct language? The language people use when they're discussing events of the day over dinner?

3.   Would a point summary help the reader? With the main news angle covered in the lead, should readers be given a capsule taste of other interesting angles awaiting them lower in the story?

4.   Does the story give the reader any sense of where the news happened and how it happened, how people in the immediate area reacted? Did some of the audience start to leave before the speech was over? Did the speaker seem to notice?

5.   Is there another side to the story? Is one side buried, throwing the story off balance? If someone whose viewpoint is obviously part of the story was unavailable, does the story say so? When pertinent, does it spell out what efforts were made to reach the unavailable source?

6.   Have legally questionable elements in the story been cleared by a lawyer?

7.   Is there overattribution? Are all those *he said*s necessary? Does every direct quote need attribution tacked on?

8.   How about sentences? Is each sentence limited to one thought or a closely connected range of thoughts? Can a subordinate clause be changed into a sentence to give the reader a clearer path? Are the sentences active? Are inactive verbs adding fat to sentences? Is there an idea that needs explaining? If so, find a way to explain it better. Or could the problem sentence be cut without loss?

9.   How about quotes? Could the story be brightened with stronger human voices? In cutting quotes, have the strongest been saved and the weaker sacrificed? Can some quotes be cut because they aren't controversial and don't give any character to the speaker? Is the story sprinkled with fragmented quotes? Is it necessary to say, **He said he was "out of touch"**?

10. Have words been wasted? Can single words replace phrases: **placed under arrest** (arrested), **in the vicinity of** (near), **charged in connection with** (charged), **in the shooting incident** (shooting)?

11. Can shorter or more familiar words be used: **They attempted** (tried) **to expedite** (speed up) **what they perceived** (saw) **as a viable** (workable) **plan**?

12. Has bafflegab been translated? Have **accommodation units** been turned into **houses and apartments**; methods of intercity transportation into **planes, trains, buses and cars**; disadvantaged into **poor**; upwardly mobile into **ambitious**?

13. Does the writing read like normal English? Is any of it unlike anything you would ever say: **the six-foot-eight 290-pound University of Manitoba product**; **Paramount vice-president of corporate communications Deborah Rosen**?

14. Are there stale expressions? Is the story dulled by cliches: **court was told; 14-hour marathon session; grim-faced delegates**?

15. Do the transitions lead the reader smoothly from one idea to the next? Could a bump between two sentences be removed with an **and, but, meanwhile** or some other transition? Would it help to repeat a key word or phrase from the preceding sentence or paragraph? **This new strategy . . . ?**

16. Is the tone right? Is the writing too formal, slangy or trendy? Has sexist, racist or other tasteless language slipped in?

Editing

Few people grow up longing to edit someone else's writing. It's not glamorous work; it is invisible at best and resented at worst.

But some people who love the written language develop a passion for perfecting its use on the page. The best publications rely on such editors for success. The best editors strive for excellence in every story they handle.

Pride comes from turning around a mediocre or erroneous story. The trick is to do more than just catch mistakes but less than rewrite.

As the last ones to touch copy before it gets into the reader's hands, editors have a vital role. They are the watchdogs over clarity, good taste, balance and accuracy.

Editors should be the reader's best friend. They add background and perspective. They make a story relevant and fun. They don't challenge readers to get through a story — they dare them not to.

Principles

1. When time allows, read a story three times: once for content, once to edit and once to clean up.

2. If you don't understand the story, the reader certainly won't. When something is unclear, either get it explained or chop it.

3. Generalities blur the picture; demand specifics for your readers. Make sure the story is animated by human beings.

4. Suggest improvements to the writer: revealing quotes, touches of color, specific details, an example or anecdote.

5. Watch for holes and fill them. Ask the writer. Check reference works. Consult a supervisor.

6. Shorten the story — but not at the expense of human interest, significant detail, daubs of color or meaty quotations.

7. Avoid overediting, which can reduce good writing to mediocrity or headline language.

8. Change copy if you have a good, explainable reason — not just because it's not the way you would have written it yourself. Leave extensive rewriting to the writer whenever possible.

How to do it

Look at the lead. The first sentence is supposed to lead the reader into the story. If it isn't interesting, why would the reader go any further? If readers aren't enticed by the first sentence or two, they're not going to stick around to be informed or educated or provoked.

1. Replace vague or complicated words with simple, specific ones.

2.   Brighten the lead with descriptive verbs and the active voice.

Not: Two men are dead following an avalanche Tuesday on a popular ski slope in the Rocky Mountains.

Better: An avalanche thundered down Mount Norquay on Tuesday, crushing two men who had been learning to ski at the Rocky Mountain resort.

3.   Take a scalpel to long leads. Aim for fewer than 30 words. Cut unwieldy phrases. Remove secondary information or unnecessary attribution from the lead and place it lower.

Not: International Development Minister Monique Landry announced Monday that after six months of study, the Canadian International Development Agency has approved an operating plan, including a $3-million bailout, to ensure the future of the World University Service of Canada.

Better: It took six months of study and a $3-million government bailout, but World University Service of Canada will soon be back at work helping people in poor countries.

The federal government agency that co-ordinates Canadian aid abroad has approved a plan to ensure the future of the service, International Development Minister Monique Landry announced Monday.

4.   Never assume the reader knows the subject as intimately as the writer does.

Not: Joy Medinski was found Thursday in Bienfait, apparently unharmed.

Better: A five-year-old girl who vanished from a family campsite in southeastern Saskatchewan last week was found two kilometres away on Monday, apparently unharmed.

5.   Beware of the double-barrelled lead.

Not: Thousands of seniors angry over federal pension changes marched on Parliament Hill on Monday while their national spokesman condemned Prime Minister Brian Mulroney as the worst threat to seniors in Canadian history.

Pick the most interesting or important element, the seniors or the spokesman, and make that the lead. Put the other one in the second paragraph.

Tighten the story

1.   Keep paragraphs short, usually no more than two or three sentences for newspaper copy. Don't assault the reader's eyes with massive blocks of grey.

2.   Tighten sentences to clarify, inject life and save space. Be ruthless in cutting wordiness and secondary detail.

3.   Replace cumbersome words with short, everyday words that convey the same meaning.

Not: The correctional facility workers voted in favor of a prolonged work stoppage.

But: The jail guards voted to strike.

4.   Cut vague modifiers and qualifiers: **fairly, really, pretty, quite, very**.

5.   Cut overattribution. Are all those *he said*s necessary?

Brighten the story

1.   Prefer one or two interesting angles fully developed to a dull, bare-bones account that touches all bases regardless of merit.

2.   Change passive voice to active where appropriate. **Police took no action** is better than **No action was taken by police**.

3.   Change boring expressions to lively ones. Watch for participles ending in *-ing* or nouns ending in *-ion* — they may signal that a sentence can be punched up. Watch for the weak verb *to be*. Can it be replaced by an active verb?

Not: The government is planning to implement a program aiming for a reduction in the number of alcohol-related deaths this year.

Better: The government aims to cut alcohol-related deaths this year through a new program.

Best: Police will be able to seize the cars of drinking drivers on the spot under a government plan to cut alcohol-related deaths this year.

4.   Translate or cut journalistic hype and jargon, the kind of language you would never use in ordinary speech. Prefer the specific to the general.

Not: Residents of this farming community were reeling in shock Thursday in the wake of the slaying of two respected schoolteachers.

Better: Flags flew at half-mast outside the Shoal Lake elementary school Thursday in tribute to two teachers killed in an apparently unprovoked attack.

Not: A twofold habitat mitigation program is in full swing at the Oldman River dam site.

Better: The provincial government is spending $2 million to preserve the environment for wildlife around the Oldman River dam and create new protected areas to replace those destroyed by the dam.

Best: Ducks will swim in new ponds and deer will munch on their favorite grasses under a $2-million program to preserve wildlife around the Oldman dam.

Check accuracy

1. Check proper names and unusual spellings. Make sure unusual surnames are spelled the same way throughout. Never guess at capitalization. Think of your reader again — few things are as annoying as misspelled names.

2. Check math. Make sure percentages are right. If portions of a total number are used, make sure they add up.

3. Check days and dates for obvious errors.

4. Watch closely for mistakes in the use of *not* in court cases and important judgments: *not guilty, not responsible.*

Check style

1. Strive to retain the writer's tone and choice of phrasing.

2. Fix errors in grammar, style and structure. Watch for mistakes in word order that mislead the reader.

Not: A Winnipeg police officer who shot a man with a toy gun has been cleared of any wrongdoing.

Better: A Winnipeg police officer who shot a man pointing a toy gun has been cleared of any wrongdoing.

3. Check that plural subjects are followed by plural verbs and pronouns, singular by singular. **The government announced its** (not **their**) **long-awaited social reform package Tuesday.**

4. Does punctuation mislead the reader? Fix it.

Not: She said the company is run by men, who have no ethics.

But: She said the company is run by men who have no ethics.

Make it clear

1. Lighten overloaded sentences by putting some of the facts into another sentence.

Not: The Nova Scotia government made controversial deals involving the purchase of toilet-seat-cover dispensers and marketing dogfish in the Caribbean with two companies connected to Halifax businessman Robert Cranston, the province's New Democratic Party says.

Better: Nova Scotia's New Democrats want to know why the province lent money to a man who sold it high-tech toilet seats that have never been used.

NDP Leader Alexa McDonough called Wednesday for the release of all details of a $40,000 loan to Halifax businessman Robert Cranston. The Department of Small Business made the loan to help Cranston's company market dogfish in the Caribbean.

2.   Answer all pertinent questions. Make sure all unusual and technical terms are explained.

Wealthy Britons often buy private health insurance, just as they send their children to "public" schools, which in Britain means fee-paying, private and elite.

3.   Move sentences or paragraphs to improve flow or strengthen emphasis.

Make it fair

1.   Put both sides of a controversial issue high in the story.

2.   Tone down or play up material wrongly treated by the writer. Guard against partial quotes that may create the wrong impression.

The woman was hired for her "talent," the premier said.

3.   Watch for unintentional editorializing.

Not: **The Opposition blamed the government for ruining the economy.**

Better: **The Opposition accused the government of ruining the economy.**

4.   Remove material that is potentially libellous or in bad taste.

Handle with care

1.   When source material is sensitive or confidential, lock it safely away while the reporter works from a copy.

2.   Make sure a supervisor is fully aware of the source material's contents and the source's reliability.

3.   Before an investigative report is published, make every effort to give everyone who may be criticized an opportunity to reply.

4.   Counsel must approve the final wording of any possibly dangerous material.

➤   See **Principles**, page 25.

Writing for broadcast

It's radio — it's the way we speak.

Writing for radio is writing that's meant to be spoken and heard. It requires special style and form.

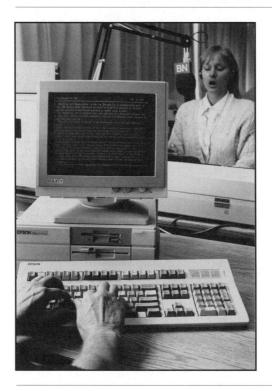

(CP—John Felstead)

1. Write tight opening sentences that grab the listener's attention.

The first sentence should make listeners want to hear more but not confuse them with too many details.

In other words, it serves as a headline.

Never write lead lines on broadcast copy that are over 15 words long. A long lead line can throw an announcer's breathing off for the entire newscast.

2. Write in the present tense or active voice.

It's the way people speak.

Avoid the passive voice: verb forms like **was hit**, **have grabbed**, etc.

Broadcast copy, written in the active voice, should place the verb as close to the subject as possible.

Not: A Hamilton man has been arrested by police.

But: Police arrested a Hamilton man.

3.   Limit sentences to a single idea or closely connected range of thoughts.

Not: Alex Hickman, chief justice of the trial division of the Supreme Court of Newfoundland, has been cleared of any wrongdoing by the Canadian Judicial Council after a review of his financial dealings.

But: The chief justice of the Newfoundland Supreme Court has been cleared of any financial wrongdoing. The Canadian Judicial Council cleared Alex Hickman after a review of the judge's financial dealings.

4.   Simplify complex and wordy sentences.

Not: The minister of employment, Jasper Brown, has established a study group within his department to conduct a review of the principles and objectives of the unemployment insurance program. He told the Commons today he expects to table the findings this fall for further discussion.

But: Employment Minister Jasper Brown has ordered a review of the unemployment insurance program. Brown told the Commons he expects to table the findings in the fall.

5.   Use the subject-verb-object approach to tell the story in as straight a line as possible.

Not: The gunman was shot by the police.

But: Police shot the gunman.

6.   Place the time element, if needed, after the verb.

Don't use **yesterday, last night**, etc. in a lead sentence.

Don't use **continues** in a lead sentence.

Don't start a broadcast story with **as expected**.

7.   For ease of understanding, put a person's identification ahead of the name.

Former dentist Barney Clark has become the first person to live with an artificial heart implant.

Twenty-five-year-old Beverly Amies of Toronto was killed.

8.   Prefer plain words to fancy ones.

Prefer **end** to **terminate, build** to **construct, confuse** to **obfuscate, poor** to **disadvantaged, shops** to **retail outlets**.

9.   Use specific words, not general ones.

Write **rain, snow, fog**, not **bad weather**. Write **one million dollars**, not **financial aid**. Write **She smiled**, not **She looked pleased**.

10. Keep sentences lean. Excess words clutter the facts.

Write **failed**, not **was unsuccessful**. Write **won**, not **chalked up a victory**. Write **lives at**, not **makes her home at**. Write **burned**, not **was devoured by flames**. Write **presided**, not **acted as chairman**.

Eliminate unnecessary and long titles. Would **a union spokesman** serve just as well as **Jean Talon, secretary-treasurer of Local 136?**

11. Write incomplete sentences occasionally. Like this. To make an idea easier to absorb. For a change of pace.

12. Put the source at the beginning of the sentence rather than at the end.

Not: A new wave of violence is showing up, the movie critic added.

But: The movie critic says a new wave of violence is showing up.

13. Use contractions occasionally, as the ear dictates.

I don't know whether he'll come has the sound of everyday English. The formal **I do not know whether he will come** would be starchy in shirtsleeve contexts.

Use **she won't, it couldn't** and other common contractions. Avoid forced contractions like **would've, it'd.**

14. To reflect spoken usage, hyphenate abbreviations that the news reader should pronounce letter by letter.

Write **C-B-C, M-P, N-D-P, R-C-M-P, U-N, U-S** but **NATO, MiG, Sidbec, Stelco.**

Note: BN practice is to hyphenate network abbreviations, **C-B-S, C-T-V,** but to write station call letters solid, **CKLM Laval, CHMM-FM Winnipeg, CJON-TV St. John's.**

15. Guard against a string of *s*'s and other repeated letters.

Sources at city hall say might cause the news reader to stumble or slow down.

16. Round off large numbers to make them digestible and spell out the dollar sign.

The robber got away with more than 13 hundred dollars is easier on the listener — and the news reader — than **$1,335.** For ease of reading, spell out and hyphenate dollars and cents: **The increase will add one-dollar-and-25-cents to the average monthly electricity bill.**

17. For economy and directness, prefer paraphrased speech to direct quotation. But use a quotation if it is unusually forceful.

The judge explained why he had ruled in favor of the 20-year-old cerebral palsy victim. He said: "We have recognized a gentle, trusting, believing spirit who has a part to play in our compassionate, independent society."

18. Repeat key points in major news breaks.

In an airliner crash, for example, give the location a second time for listeners who missed it. Don't hesitate to add a throw-away sentence at the end summarizing the story.

To recap: An airliner has crashed at the Edmonton airport and at least a dozen people are dead.

For a full treatment of writing for broadcasting, see the *BN Style Guide*, also available from The Canadian Press.

Some useful tools (Part I)

Grammar and style

Abbreviations and acronyms
  Style for abbreviations
  Style for acronyms
  Dates and times
  Measurements
  Organizations
  Places
  Titles
  Miscellaneous usages
Capitalization
  Alliances
  Animals and birds
  Awards
  Buildings
  Compositions
  Courts
  CP, PC, AP, AFP, Reuters
  Derivatives
  Food and drink
  Foreign personal names
  Geography
  Government departments
  Historical terms
  Holidays
  Laws and documents
  Legislative bodies
  Military
  Music
  Names
  Nationalities and race
  Newspapers and magazines
  Nicknames
  Numbers
  Organizations
  Plants
  Political divisions
  Politics
  Quotations
  Religion
  Schools
  Slogans and headlines
  Space
  Sports
  The
  Times and seasons
  Titles
  Trade names

Compounds
French
  Names of organizations
  Books, movies, etc.
  Capitalization
  Hyphens in place names
  Saint
  Translation
Government
  National and provincial
    legislatures
  Political affiliations and
    designations
  First minister
  Monarchy
  Succession
  Ceremonies
  First lady
  Nationhood
  Canada
  Government jargon
Names, nicknames, initials
Numbers
  When to use figures
  When to spell out
  Roman numerals
  Large numbers
Plurals of nouns
  Nouns ending in *f, fe* and *ff*
  Nouns ending in *o*
  Nouns ending in *y*
  Nouns ending in *ics*
  Proper nouns
  Compound words
  Foreign nouns
  Nouns with the same singular
    and plural
  Nouns plural in form, singular
    in meaning
  Dos and don'ts
Possessives
Punctuation (alphabetical by
    name of punctuation mark)
Singular or plural
Spelling

continued over

Some useful tools (Part II)

Some technical guides

Aircraft, ships, guns
Metric
  When metric?
  Let logic be your guide
  Sports
  Odds and ends
  Metric conversion tables
  Common metric units
  Different strokes
  Converting
  Recipes
Military
  Bases
  Units
  Ranks
  Titles
  Retired officers
  Courts martial
  Ceremonies
  Miscellaneous
Native peoples
  Indians, Metis, Inuit
  Indian languages
  Writing about Indians, Metis,
    Inuit
People, Places
  Alphabetical list of countries,
    capitals etc.
Placelines
  Canadian placelines
  U.S. placelines
  Other foreign placelines
Place names
  Exceptions
  Regions
  People and places
  Place names to watch

Technical terms
  Scientific names
  Drugs
  Medical
  Condition
  Burns
  AIDS
  Richter scale
Time
  What day is it?
  What time is it?
  What zone is it?
Titles
  Courtesy titles
  Professional titles
  Religious titles
  Honorable, Lady, Lord
Trade names
Weather
  Weather in metric
  Terminology

Access to information
  What you can get
  Tips
  When you feel cheated

Words
  Alphabetical listing of tricky
    words

Abbreviations and acronyms

General

1. Use only abbreviations and acronyms (abbreviations pronounced as words) that are familiar to ordinary readers.

CN, CTV, MP; Stelco, NATO, radar

2. An abbreviation is sometimes acceptable to avoid an unwieldy lead: a PLO rocket attack. But in general, provide the full name later: Palestine Liberation Organization.

3. Abbreviations that have become household terms are acceptable in all references. That is, they need not be spelled out, though the full word or phrase may make for more graceful reading.

CBC, MP, NATO, NDP, PoW, RCMP

Note: As to familiarity, it is impossible to set lasting rules. The once-familiar **RAF** (Royal Air Force), for instance, no longer commands widespread recognition, whereas **BBC** does. When in doubt, spell out.

4. In general, do not put a bracketed abbreviation after the name of an organization: Transportation Safety Board (**TSB**), Liberation Tigers of Tamil Eelam (**LTTE**).

Abbreviations that need this device to be clear should rarely be used.

5. For ease of reading or variety, a general term is often preferable to an abbreviation.

the labor relations board, the arms talks, the union, the autoworkers, the company, the association instead of CLRB, SALT, CAW and the like.

6. Do not spell out common abbreviations if the full term is not in general use or is hard to pronounce: TNT (for trinitrotoluene), KGB (for Komitet Gosudarstvennoi Bezopasnosti).

Where necessary, include a brief description to help the reader: KGB, the Russian secret police and intelligence agency.

7. Abbreviations suitable in one context may be unsuitable in another. MLA, for instance, might puzzle readers in Newfoundland, Quebec and Ontario, and should be spelled out for general service: member of the legislative assembly, or member of the legislature.

Similarly: MHA — member of the (Newfoundland) house of assembly; MNA — member of the (Quebec) national assembly; MPP — member of the (Ontario) provincial parliament.

8.   Non-English abbreviations that may be unfamiliar to English-speaking readers should be explained at some point.

the terrorist group ETA, the acronym for the Basque name meaning Basque Land and Liberty; the French union federation CGT, short for Confédération générale du travail; the Quebec steel company Sidbec; Soquip, which stands for a French name meaning Quebec Petroleum Development Corp.

9.   Text studded with abbreviations is hard to read and unsightly.

Style for abbreviations

1.   Omit periods in all-capital abbreviations unless the abbreviation is geographical or refers to a person.

AD, CST, PLC, UBC, UFO, VIP; B.C., P.E.I., N.W.T., U.S., U.S.S.R.; J. R. Ewing, J.R., E.T., good ol' J.B.

Note 1: Some public figures become known by initials without periods.

FDR (Franklin Delano Roosevelt), JFK (John Fitzgerald Kennedy), PET (Pierre Elliott Trudeau), GBS (George Bernard Shaw)

Note 2: Put a *thin space* between a person's initials, G. K. Chesterton, except where they stand alone, G.K.

Note 3: Compound abbreviations are written without space.

B.Comm., P.Eng.

Note 4: Omit periods from currency abbreviations.

$500 US, $800 Cdn

2.   Most lowercase and mixed abbreviations take periods.

f.o.b., Jr., lb., Mrs., No., m.p.h., B.Comm.

Note: Metric symbols are not abbreviations and take periods only at the end of a sentence.

m, L, km-h

3.   Mixed abbreviations that begin and end with a capital letter do not take periods.

PhD, PoW, MiG, U of T

4.   Single-letter abbreviations are followed by a period.

36 King St. E. (for East)

But brand X, the letter E

Style for acronyms

1. Acronyms formed from only the first letter of each word are all capitals.

NATO (North Atlantic Treaty Organization), **a CAT** (computerized axial tomography) **scan**

2. Acronyms formed from initial and other letters are in caps and lowercase.

Dofasco (Dominion Foundries and Steel Corp.), **Nabisco** (National Biscuit Company)

3. Acronyms that have become common words are not capitalized.

radar (radio detection and ranging), **scuba** (self-contained underwater breathing apparatus), **snafu** (situation normal, all fouled up), **laser** (light amplification by stimulated emission of radiation)

Dates and times

1. For months used with a specific date, abbreviate only **Jan.**, **Feb.**, **Aug.**, **Sept.**, **Oct.**, **Nov.** and **Dec.** Spell out standing alone or with a year alone.

Oct. 1, 1982, was a Friday. January 1981 was wet.

Note: Do not abbreviate a month spelled out in the name of an organization: **the November 17 terrorist group**.

2. In tabular matter, use these forms without periods:

Jan, Feb, Mar, Apr, May, Jun, Jul, Aug, Sep, Oct, Nov, Dec

3. Days of the week are abbreviated only in tabular matter and without periods.

Sun, Mon, Tue, Wed, Thu, Fri, Sat

4. **AD** is acceptable in all references for **anno Domini** (Latin for *in the year of the Lord*) and **BC** for **before Christ**. AD precedes the year; BC follows it.

AD 410, 55 BC

But write **12th century AD.**

5. Write **10 a.m., 3:30 p.m., EDT, AST**

➤ See **Time**, page 289.

Measurements

1.   In general, spell out such terms as **foot, hundredweight, kilogram, metre** and **minute.**

A five-kilogram packet costs $2.

2.   A few common terms — **km-h, mm, m.p.h., c.c.** — are acceptable on second reference when used with figures.

70 km-h, 105-mm cannon, the old 30-m.p.h. limit, 2,000-c.c. engine

3.   Terms may be abbreviated in tabular matter.

kg, L, cwt., min.

4.   Use this style for imperial abbreviations, both singular and plural, in tabulations:

in., ft., yd., mi.; oz., lb., cwt.; sq. ft.

Similarly: sec., min., hr.

5.   Use this style for metric symbols, both singular and plural, in tabulations:

mm, cm, m, km, kg, g, t, mL, L, ha, kPa

➤   See **Metric**, page 253; **Numbers**, page 217.

Organizations

1.   Use **Bros., Co., Corp., Inc.** and **Ltd.** with corporate names and without commas.

General Motors Acceptance Corp., Canadian Pacific Ltd., Texaco Inc.

Note: Spell out **company**, etc., in the names of entertainment groups unless the group name includes an abbreviation.

Canadian Opera Company, Smothers Brothers

2.   Do not abbreviate other terms — **association, department, division, organization** and so on — in corporate and government names.

Reader's Digest Association, Justice Department

3.   Spell out **United Nations** as a noun, but the abbreviation **UN** may be used as an adjective with well-known organizations.

The United Nations will meet. The UN Security Council voted no.

Places

1. For Canadian provinces and territories, use these abbreviations after the name of a community:

Alta.	N.B.	N.S.	Que.
B.C.	Nfld.	Ont.	Sask.
Man.	N.W.T.	P.E.I.	

Note: After the name of a community, use **Yukon** rather than Y.T. When standing alone, make it **the Yukon**.

2. For American states, use these abbreviations after the name of a community.

Ala.	Kan.	Neb.	R.I.
Ariz.	Ky.	Nev.	S.C.
Ark.	La.	N.H.	S.D.
Calif.	Me.	N.J.	Tenn.
Colo.	Md.	N.M.	Tex.
Conn.	Mass.	N.Y.	Vt.
Del.	Mich.	N.C.	Va.
Fla.	Minn.	N.D.	Wash.
Ga.	Miss.	Okla.	W.Va.
Ill.	Mo.	Ore.	Wis.
Ind.	Mont.	Pa.	Wyo.

Note: Do not abbreviate **Alaska, Hawaii, Idaho, Iowa, Ohio, Utah**; or **Puerto Rico, Virgin Islands**.

3. A placeline should refer to the province or territory a community is in. Exceptions are stories from territorial and provincial capitals other than **St. John's, Nfld.**, and these cities: **Montreal, Ottawa, Hamilton, Saskatoon, Calgary** and **Vancouver**.

GLACE BAY, N.S., PRINCE GEORGE, B.C., but YELLOWKNIFE.

➤ See **Placelines**, page 278; **Place names**, page 282; and **People, places**, page 270.

4. Generally do not abbreviate the names of countries, provinces or states when standing alone or used adjectivally.

The United States (not U.S.) declared war. The Nova Scotia (not N.S.) cabinet met. The United Kingdom (not U.K.) consists of Britain and Northern Ireland.

Note: The abbreviations U.K., U.S., B.C. and P.E.I. may be used adjectivally to reflect spoken usage.

the B.C. legislature, a U.K. bank holiday, rival U.S. teams

5. In numbered addresses, write **Ave., Blvd., Cir., Cres., Dr., Hwy., Rd., Rte., Sq., St., Ter.**

36 King St. E., 111 Sutherland Dr., 9 Binkley Ter.

Note 1: Spell out general locations.

on King Street, down Portage Avenue, the Yonge Street subway

Note 2: Spell out these official residences:

24 Sussex Drive, 10 Downing Street.

6. In general, abbreviate Saint and Sainte in place names.

St. John's, Nfld., Sault Ste. Marie

But **Saint John, N.B.**

Note: Use a hyphen instead of a period after **St** and **Ste** in Quebec place names.

Ste-Agathe, St-Eustache

➤ See **French**, page 207.

7. Do not abbreviate **county, fort, mount, point** and **port** as part of a proper name.

Fort McMurray, Mount Everest, Port Stanley, Ont.

Titles

1. Abbreviate **Gov. Gen.** and **Lt.-Gov.** before names on first reference.

Gov. Gen. Pamela King, Lt.-Govs. Joan Pappas and Alan Bucyk.

Note: Lowercase **former governor general** (not **former Gov. Gen.**), **former governors general** Georges Vanier and Jules Leger, the **late lieutenant-governor** Pat Filippo, the **then-president** John Redway (but prefer a more graceful construction: **John Redway, who was president at the time,** or some such).

2. Do not abbreviate **attorney general, auditor general, district attorney, postmaster general, representative, secretary, secretary general, senator** or **treasurer.**

3. Abbreviate **Dr., Msgr., Prof., Rev., Sgt.** and the like before full names on first reference.

Dr. Pamela Gucci, Msgr. Brian Doyle, Profs. Eva Oberast and John Green, Rev. Freda Cernetig

Miscellaneous usages

1. Use this style for bracketed political affiliations in parliamentary and legislature copy:

Tom Arlee (NDP—Edmonton East), Senator Mary Atkins (PC—Man.), Representative John Whyte (R—Pa.), Senator Obie Black (Ind—Va.), state Senator Darleen Healey (D—Queens)

Note: In general, prefer a descriptive phrase to the bracketed style.

➤ See **Government**, page 211.

2. Abbreviate degrees, awards, honors and orders after a name.

BA, LLD, MA, OBE, PhD, SJ, VC; Louis Buncak Jr., PhD, P.Eng.

3. Abbreviate ship and plane designations.

HMCS Restigouche, USS Johnson, SST (but spell out on first reference: **supersonic transport**)

4. Do not abbreviate books of the Bible.

Genesis, Leviticus

5. In general, spell out serial terms, but **article (Art.)**, **number (No.)**, **page (p.)**, **section (Sec.)** and **volume (Vol.)** may be abbreviated before a number.

Block 1, Chapter 2, page 3, p. 3, Vol. 9

➤ See **Numbers**, page 219.

6. Do not use periods with clipped forms that have become accepted as complete words.

ad, disco, exam, gym, hi-tech, lab, math, polio, porn

7. Do not use periods with shortened forms of first names if they are pronounced as spelled.

Al, Alex, Barb, Ben, Ed, Fred, Marj, Pat, Sam, Will

But **Danl.**, **Geo.**, **Thos.** when such terms appear in textual matter.

8. Do not use periods when letters designate persons or things.

the spy chief Z, exhibit A, the mysterious Madame X

But use a period if the letter is an abbreviation.

Mrs. G., (shortened from **Gamp**)

9. In general, do not use such shortenings as **Penetang** (for **Penetanguishene**), **Peterboro** (for **Peterborough**), **Soo** (for **Sault Ste. Marie**) and **Xmas** (for **Christmas**).

Note: Write **Soo Greyhounds**, the official name of the Ontario Hockey League team.

Capitalization

General

1. The Canadian Press follows a modified down style. That is, where a reasonable choice exists, CP uses lowercase. This is the basic rule:

Capitalize all proper names, trade names, government departments and agencies of government, names of associations, companies, clubs, religions, languages, nations, races, places, addresses. Otherwise lowercase is favored where a reasonable option exists.

Here are some guidelines:

2. Capitalize common nouns — base, drive, ocean — when they are part of a formal name: **Canadian Forces Base Comox, Sussex Drive, Atlantic Ocean.** Lowercase them when standing alone in subsequent references: **the Canadian Forces base, the drive, the ocean.**

Note: In sports references the words **Games** (as in **Olympic** or **Commonwealth Games**), **Plate** (as in **Queen's Plate**), **Series** (as in **World Series**) and so on are capitalized when standing alone in subsequent references. This is to avoid confusion with the generic use of the words (as in **a series of rained-out games**).

3. Lowercase the common-noun elements of names in plural uses: **the Atlantic and Pacific oceans, prime ministers Marie Leclair and James Dunn.** But retain capitalization for the plurals of abbreviations: **Lt.-Govs. Michael O'Hara and Robert Bernard, Drs. (Revs., Profs., Sgts.) Fraser Douglas and Berthe Lucas.**

4. Capitalize formal titles directly preceding a name: **Energy Minister Marc Edmond.** Lowercase them when standing alone or set off from the name with commas: **the energy minister; the energy minister, Marc Edmond; Marc Edmond, the minister of energy.**

5. As a rule of thumb, formal titles are those that could be used with the surname alone: **Bishop Vardy.** These embrace government titles (**Prime Minister Brown, Ald. Chester**), professional titles (**Dr. Masse, Prof. Seguin**), military and paramilitary titles (**Pte. Kirkup, Insp. Low**) and religious titles (**Rabbi Dubuc, Brother Agnew**).

6. Lowercase occupational titles and job descriptions: **GM president Andre Lefort, general manager Sid James, news editor Agathe Simard, author Susan Sontag, nurse Tom Atfield.**

Note: Such descriptions usually read better preceded by *the*.

➤ See **Titles**, page 292.

7. The instruction *capitalize* refers only to the first letter of a word. If other letters are to be capitalized, *all-caps* or other specific instructions are given.

8.   In sections dealing with the capitalization of book, film, music and other such titles, the term *principal words* means nouns, pronouns, adjectives, adverbs, verbs, the first and last word of the title, as well as prepositions and conjunctions of four letters or more.

9.   In The Canadian Press and many other organizations, internal documents capitalize staff titles (even when standing alone), department names and the like.

the President; Vice-President, Marketing; Head Office; Personnel

Alliances

1.   Capitalize alliances and similar groupings.

Confederation, the British Empire, Commonwealth, NATO allies, Warsaw Pact, East and West (ideological groupings), **Allies** (in world wars), **Group of Seven** (industrial countries)

2.   Write **western allies, imperial ambitions, the coalition against Iraq**.

Animals and birds

1.   Generally lowercase the names of animals, birds, fish and so on.

collie, dachshund, grizzly bear, palomino, pinto, quarter horse, shorthorn, blue jay, herring gull, mallard, phoebe, robin, snowy owl, eastern cottontail rabbit, brown trout, snapping turtle, western rattlesnake, red admiral, hawk moth, dragonfly

2.   Capitalize names derived from proper nouns except where usage has established the lowercase.

angora (cat, goat, rabbit), **Angus cattle, Baltimore oriole, Canada goose, Cheviot sheep, Clydesdale horse, German shepherd, Great Dane, Guernsey cow, Holstein-Friesian, Irish terrier, Kodiak bear, mandarin duck, Newfoundland dog, Percheron, St. Bernard, Shetland pony, Siamese cat, spaniel**

Note: Unless the sex has been established, refer to an animal as *it*.

The dog wolfed its dinner. Toby, who was famished, wolfed his dinner. A bull gored his tormentor. The doe licked her leg.

3.   In scientific names, capitalize only the first word.

Orcinus orca (killer whale), **Ovis canadensis** (Rocky Mountain bighorn sheep), **Ursus arctos horribilis** (grizzly bear), **Branta canadensis** (Canada goose), **Cyanocitta cristata** (blue jay), **Grus americana** (whooping crane)

Awards

1. Capitalize awards, honors and decorations.

Order of Canada, Order of Merit, Knight Commander of the Bath, Governor General's Awards, National Newspaper Awards, Southam Fellowship, Nobel Peace Prize, Nobel Prize for chemistry, a Nobel Prize winner, Pulitzer Prize for international reporting, a Pulitzer Prize-winning writer, Victoria Cross, Bronze Star.

Note: French awards follow French style: **Croix de guerre.**

2. Lowercase common-noun references standing alone.

the order, the awards, the prize, the cross

Buildings

1. Capitalize the proper names of well-known buildings, bridges, canals, parks, roads, rooms and other manufactured features.

Parliament Buildings, East Block, White House, Oval Office, Buckingham Palace, U.S. Capitol, Archambault Penitentiary, Calgary City Hall, Lions Gate Bridge, St. Lawrence Seaway, Welland Canal, Laurentian Autoroute, Vancouver International Airport, Union Station, War Memorial, CN Tower, Maple Leaf Gardens (the Gardens), Montreal Neurological Institute, Ottawa General Hospital, Berlin Wall, Square of Heavenly Peace, Hall of Mirrors, Sistine Chapel, Fundy National Park, French Embassy

2. Lowercase general terms standing alone, in plurals or in descriptive uses.

the palace, the international airport, the capitol, the city hall, the hospital, the Panama and Suez canals, a St. Lawrence bridge, Banff and Jasper national parks

Compositions

1. Capitalize the principal words in the titles of books, broadcast programs, films, plays, poems, songs, speeches, works of art and other compositions.

The Watch That Ends the Night, The Sheep Look Up, CBC's World at Six, Gone With the Wind, The Taming of the Shrew, In Flanders Fields, Gettysburg Address, The Laughing Cavalier

Note: Composition titles are not enclosed in quotation marks.

2.   Do not capitalize *the* at the start of names of almanacs, the Bible, dictionaries, directories, encyclopedias, gazetteers, handbooks and the like.

the Canadian Almanac, the Concise Oxford Dictionary, the Encyclopedia Britannica

3.   **Volume, chapter, section, act, scene,** etc., are capitalized when they precede a number. But **page, paragraph, verse** and **line** are lowercase in keeping with widespread practice: **page 20, line 7.**

➤   See **Numbers** below.

4.   Use this style for references:

Act 1, Scene 2; 1 Kings 15:5-7 (i.e. First Book of Kings, Chapter 15, verses 5-7); Henry IV, Part 2 or 2 Henry IV

5.   Capitalize the names of artistic movements, groups and styles, but lowercase terms used in a general sense.

Romanesque, the Renaissance, Gothic, Impressionism, the Impressionists, the Bloomsbury Group, Art Nouveau, Op Art, Art Deco

But a gothic novel, a renaissance of painting, a rococo air

➤   See **Music** below.

Courts

1.   Capitalize superior courts.

Privy Council, Supreme Court, Federal Court, Court of Queen's Bench, Superior Court (Quebec), Appeal Court, International Court of Justice (the World Court), European Court of Justice, High Court of Justice (the High Court)

Lowercase divisions.

the appeal division (or trial division) of the Supreme Court

2.   Lowercase lower courts.

family court, youth court

3.   Capitalize **Crown** when referring to the supreme governing power.

The Crown dropped the charge. The matter was in the hands of the Crown attorney.

CP, PC, AP, AFP, Reuters

1.   Capitalize **The Canadian Press** and **The Associated Press** when the full names are used. On second reference, write **CP** and **AP** or **the AP** (lowercase *the*).

Note: Where the use is possessive, the *The* is capitalized: **The Canadian Press's membership, The Associated Press's reporter**. But where the use is adjectival rather than possessive, the article is lowercased and the apostrophe omitted: **the Canadian Press membership, the Associated Press reporter**.

2.   The name of CP's French-language operation is **La Presse Canadienne**. The abbreviation **PC** is acceptable in second reference.

3.   **Agence France-Presse** is so spelled. **AFP** is acceptable in second reference.

4.   **Reuters** is spelled with the *s* except when bracketed in placelines, as **(CP-Reuter)**.

➤   See **Newspapers and magazines** below.

Derivatives

1.   Lowercase proper names that have acquired independent meaning.

arabic numerals, bohemian, brussels sprouts, cardigan, chinese red, draconian, duffel coat, dutch oven, french fries, mackintosh, manhattan, manila paper, morocco leather, oxford cloth, plaster of paris, portland cement, roman type, sandwich, scotch whisky, spartan, venetian blind, watt

2.   Medical terms tend to retain the capital longer than commoner words.

Achilles tendon, Fallopian tube, Pap smear, Freudian slip

But **caesarean section, siamese twins**

Note: When in doubt, capitalize.

Food and drink

1.   Brand names of foods and drinks are capitalized.

Post Toasties	Mars bar
Lee-Perrin sauce	Pepsi-Cola

2.   In the names of food, most proper nouns are capitalized.

beef Stroganoff	oysters Rockefeller
Bing cherries	quiche Lorraine
Boston baked beans	Smithfield ham
Cheshire cheese	Swiss cheese
McIntosh apple	

3. Names that have acquired independent common meaning are lowercased.

baked alaska	hamburger
cheddar cheese	melba toast
caesar salad	napoleon
danish	peach melba
french fries	russian dressing
graham crackers	spanish omelette

4. The names of drinks are generally lowercased.

brandy	Madeira
burgundy	manhattan
champagne	Sauterne
claret	scotch
cognac	vermouth

Note: Follow Oxford's style for capitalizing the names of foods and drinks unless *(CP) Caps and Spelling* shows otherwise.

5. At the start of a recipe list, capitalize the name of the dish being made:

Apple Oatmeal Squares
250 mL (1 cup) all-purpose flour
250 mL (1 cup) quick-cooking rolled oats, etc.

➤ See **Metric**, page 259, for more on recipes.

Foreign personal names

Such particles as **de, des, di, du, le, la, lo, van** and **von** are usually lowercase except when they begin a sentence.

Charles de Gaulle. De Gaulle said no. Manfred von Richthofen was nicknamed the Red Baron. Von Richthofen was a flying ace.

Note 1: Observe personal preferences.

Pierre De Bane, S. S. Van Dine, Martin Van Buren, Jean de La Fontaine

Note 2: Particles are sometimes dropped on second reference.

Ludwig van Beethoven, Beethoven; Guy de Maupassant, Maupassant; Jean de La Fontaine, La Fontaine; Joachim von Ribbentrop, Ribbentrop; Lorenzo de Medici, the Medici

Geography

1. Capitalize geographic and widely recognized descriptive regions.

the North, Far North, Northern Canada, High Arctic, Western Canada, Central Canada, East Coast (region, not shoreline), Maritime provinces, Prairies, Barrens, the Front, Niagara Peninsula, Nile Delta, Alaska Panhandle, West End (London), Upstate New York, Southern California, Far East, Orient, North Atlantic, Central Asia, Western Europe, Western Hemisphere, North Pole, the Pole, Tropic of Cancer

Note 1: Write eastern Quebec, southern Ontario but **Northern Ontario** (an administrative division).

Note 2: The **Atlantic provinces** are New Brunswick, Newfoundland, Nova Scotia and Prince Edward Island. The **Maritimes** consist of New Brunswick, Nova Scotia and Prince Edward Island.

Note 3: Write **English Canada** and **French Canada** but **English-Canadian** and **French-Canadian**.

➤ See **Political divisions** below.

2. Capitalize specific natural features.

Canadian Shield, Gulf Stream, Rocky Mountains, Mackenzie River, Yellowhead Pass, Atlantic Ocean, Lake Winnipeg, Great Lakes

3. Capitalize fanciful or imaginative terms.

Down East, Deep South, Down Under, Bible Belt, Cow States, Ho Chi Minh Trail, Promised Land, Eternal City, Silicon Valley

4. Lowercase points of the compass, mere direction and location, and descriptive regions not widely recognized as such.

north, to the west of Newfoundland, rain sweeping south, east coast (shoreline, not region), southern Saskatchewan, northwestern Ontario, eastern Newfoundland, downtown Calgary, north-end Toronto

5. Lowercase **northern, southern, eastern** and **western** in terms derived from regions.

a northern custom, southern hospitality, southern Californians, an easterner, eastern provinces, a western Canadian, a westerner, western armies, far eastern peoples

Note: In Western Canada, Ontario people are referred to as **easterners**. In Ontario, Maritimers are referred to as **easterners**.

6. Lowercase **parallel** and the like.

48th parallel, international date line, equator

7. Lowercase generic terms standing alone except when they are conventionally used as a short form of the proper noun.

Lake Erie, the lake; Rocky Mountains, the mountains; Grand Canyon, the canyon

But the **Interior** (for instance, British Columbia), **the Island** (for instance, Prince Edward Island), **the States** (the United States), **the Continent** (Europe), **the Channel** (English Channel), **the Lakes** (Great Lakes)

8. Lowercase the common-noun element in plurals.

lakes Superior and Erie, Red and Assiniboine rivers, the Northern and Southern hemispheres, King and Front streets

9. Lowercase **province** and **state** used in a geographic sense.

Quebec province, New York state

But capitalize as part of the corporate name.

Province of Quebec bonds, New York State vs. Smith

➤ See **Political divisions** below.

Government departments

1. Capitalize specific international, national, provincial and state government departments, ministries, agencies, boards, etc., including short forms of the proper name.

World Health Organization, United Nations Children's Fund, Department of Agriculture, Agriculture Department, Canada Post Corp., Canada Post, St. Lawrence Seaway Authority, National Parole Service, Library of Parliament, Revenue Canada, Canada Labor Relations Board, Pensions Appeal Board, Census Bureau (U.S.), **War Office** (Britain), **Ukrainian Embassy, Italian Consulate, Secret Service, Office of the Commissioner of Official Languages, Ontario Ministry of Labor, Ontario Labor Ministry, B.C. Highways Ministry, Georgia Department of Human Resources**

2. Capitalize cabinet portfolios only as part of a title directly preceding a name: **Finance Minister June Atkins.** But June Atkins, minister of finance. John Lee is in charge of transport.

Note: The line between capitalization and lowercase is the line between the actual ministry and its function. The sentence **John Lee is in charge of transport** is intended to suggest he's responsible for policy on rail lines, airports and other elements of national transportation. **John Lee is in charge of Transport Canada** signifies he runs the ministry itself.

3. Capitalize proper-name elements of a department or ministry when they stand alone.

The cuts will affect Justice and Communications. In those 25 years, she worked in the Archives, Housing and Natural Resources.

4. Lowercase common-noun elements standing alone and in plurals.

the department, a ministry spokeswoman, board figures, the authority, the service's record, departments of Justice and Defence

5. Lowercase local government councils, departments, boards, etc.

Peel regional council, Edmonton city council, Saskatoon board of education, Moncton development department

Historical terms

Capitalize the names of historic periods and events.

Stone Age, Dark Ages, Middle Ages, Crusades, Norman Conquest, Reformation, Age of Discovery, Industrial Revolution, the Depression or the Great Depression, Dirty '30s, Cultural Revolution, Me Decade, Creation, Exodus, the Flood, Civil War (American), Battle of the Plains of Abraham, War of 1812, Reign of Terror, Riel Rebellion, First World War, Prohibition, Holocaust, Battle of Britain, Vietnam War, Quiet Revolution

But medieval, a reformation, a renaissance in painting, 19th century, ice age (no single period)

Note: Capitalize **Confederation** in references to Canada: **Fathers of Confederation.**

Holidays

Capitalize holidays, religious feasts and all special times.

New Year's Eve (but in the new year), Ash Wednesday, April Fool's Day, Mother's Day, Canada Day, St-Jean-Baptiste Day, July Fourth, Fourth of July, Halloween, Christmas Day, Hanukkah, Yom Kippur, Passover, Ramadan, D-Day, Education Week

Note: Write election day.

Laws and documents

1. Capitalize proclaimed laws, treaties, important legal codes and historic documents.

British North America Act, Constitution (Canada), **Charter of Rights, Colombo Plan, UN Charter, Criminal Code, Declaration of Independence, Magna Carta**

Note: Constitution is capitalized in all references when the Canadian Constitution is meant. Otherwise it is capitalized only when preceded by a name: **the U.S. Constitution, the constitution.** Also lowercase **constitutional: the constitutional crisis.**

2. Lowercase proposed and defeated legislation, general references and plurals.

the proposed charter of rights, the Meech Lake accord, the free trade agreement, a disarmament treaty, the code, the BNA and human rights acts

3. Lowercase **speech from the throne, royal assent, third reading, the president's state of the union message, white paper, green paper.**

Legislative bodies

1. Capitalize international and national legislative bodies and their equivalents, including some short forms.

UN Security Council (Security Council), UN General Assembly (General Assembly), Parliament (national), **House of Commons, the House, the Commons, the Senate, House of Lords (the Lords), House of Representatives (the House), Chamber of Deputies (the Chamber), Bundestag, Cortes, Diet, Knesset, National Assembly** (French)

Note: Generic uses of parliament are lowercase: **the Knesset, Israel's parliament; the Sjem (parliament).**

2. Lowercase general terms, informal terms (except short forms listed above), plurals and derivatives.

the administration, the council, an assembly motion, government, cabinet, lower house, the Canadian and British parliaments, parliamentary, senatorial

But the Commons motion

3.   Lowercase provincial, state and regional legislatures and local councils.

Quebec national assembly, Ontario legislature, Ontario provincial parliament (but avoid), **Newfoundland house of assembly, New South Wales parliament, the Virginia senate, the Northwest Territories council, Peel regional council, Victoria city council**

4.   Lowercase committees and subcommittees.

the committee on communications and culture

5.   Capitalize the full name of royal commissions.

the Royal Commission on Corporate Concentration, the Royal Commission on Bilingualism and Biculturalism

But the royal commission, the bilingualism commission

➤   See **Laws and documents** above.

Military

1.   Capitalize **Canadian Armed Forces, Canadian Forces, Armed Forces** (Canada only).

2.   Capitalize **Canadian Army, (Royal) Canadian Navy** and **(Royal) Canadian Air Force** in references to pre-unification forces (before 1968).

3.   The general terms **army, navy** and **air force**, written lowercase, may be used of the appropriate branches of the unified Canadian Forces: **a Canadian navy boat**.

4.   For foreign forces, lowercase **army, navy** and **air force** when they are preceded by the name of a country.

Lebanese army, U.S. air force, Russian navy

Note: This style is intended for consistency. Many countries do not use **army, navy** or **air force** as the proper name.

5.   Otherwise capitalize full, specific names of formations, both military and paramilitary.

Royal Navy, U.S. 8th Air Force, the 27th Army, French Foreign Legion, Royal Marines, Canadian Coast Guard, U.S. National Guard

But the army, the navy, the air force, the legion, the marines, a marine, the coast guard, a coast guard plane, the national guard, a national guardsman

6. Capitalize specific bases, commands, schools and ships.

Canadian Forces Headquarters, Canadian Forces Base Comox, the Citadel (Quebec City), Joint Chiefs of Staff, French General Staff, 6th Fleet, Royal Military College, HMCS Restigouche, HMS Antelope, USS Iowa

But a Canadian Forces base

➤ See **Aircraft, ships, guns**, page 249.

7. Capitalize official names of units.

Royal 22nd Regiment, 3rd Battalion, B Company, 3rd Infantry Division, 10 Armored Brigade, 126 Squadron

8. Capitalize nicknames of units.

Van Doo, Desert Rats, Green Berets

9. Capitalize major armed conflicts and rebellions.

Battle of Marathon, Wars of the Roses, French Revolution, U.S. Civil War, Boxer Rebellion, Bolshevik Revolution, Battle of Britain, Battle of the Bulge, Six-Day War, Cultural Revolution

10. Capitalize fronts and important positions.

Western Front, Maginot Line

➤ See **Abbreviations**, page 169; **Military**, page 260.

Music

1. In general, capitalize the principal words in the English titles of musical compositions.

Tchaikovsky's Symphony No. 4 in F minor, Tchaikovsky's Fourth Symphony, Light My Fire by the Doors, Michael Jackson's Beat It

Note: The words **major, minor, sharp** and **flat** are written lowercase in keeping with widespread practice.

2. Informal names don't need quotation marks.

Beethoven's Sonata in E flat, Les Adieux (not "Les Adieux"), Mozart's Coronation Mass (not "Coronation")

3. When the opus number is given, set it off with a comma.

Handel's Concerti Grossi Nos. 4-6, op. 6; Mozart's Exultate, Jubilate, K. 165; Bach's St. Matthew Passion, BWV 244

4. Translate a foreign title into English unless the work is commonly known by its foreign name.

La Bohème, L'Après-midi d'un faune, Eine kleine Nachtmusik

5. For non-English titles the style varies.

In French titles, capitalize the first word, and the second word too when the first word is an article, and proper nouns: **Mon rêve, Le Rêve passé**.

In Italian, capitalize the first word and proper nouns: **La donna e mobile, La clemenza di Tito**.

In German, capitalize the first word and every noun: **Du bist mein ganzes Sehnen**.

In Latin, capitalize each word: **Te Deum**.

Names

1. For all-caps corporate and promotional names, capitalize only the first letters of words.

Amtrak (not **AMTRAK**), **Band-Aid** (not **BAND-AID**), **Oxfam** (not **OXFAM**), **Scrabble** (not **SCRABBLE**), **Via Rail** (not **VIA Rail**), **Visa** (not **VISA**)

Note: Initials are capitalized: IBM, CTV, EMI.

2. For names consisting of two or more words written solid, follow the organization's capitalization.

SkyDome, TransCanada PipeLines, PepsiCo, MuchMusic

3. For names of people or performing groups, follow their preference, as long as it doesn't excessively hamper readability.

k.d. lang (not **K.D. Lang**); **bp Nichol** (not **B.P. Nichol**); **hHead** (not **HHead**); **e.e. cummings** (not **E.E. Cummings**)

But for other names, follow normal style:

Adidas (not **adidas**); **5th Estate** (not **5th estate**); **Presstime magazine** (not **presstime**); **Sex, Lies and Videotape** (not **sex, lies and videotape**); **Thirtysomething** (not **thirtysomething**)

Nationalities and race

1. Capitalize the proper names of nationalities, peoples, races, tribes and the like.

Aborginal Peoples, Arab, Arabic, African, African-American, Asian, Caucasian, Chipewyan, Chinese, English-Canadian, Gypsy, Hispanic, Indian, Inuk, Inuit, Jew, Jewish, Latin, Negro, Nordic, Oriental (but prefer **Asian**), **Pygmy**

2. Write **aborigine** (but **Aborigine** for the Australian race), **black, brown, caucasoid, colored** (but **Cape Colored**), **red, white, yellow**.

Newspapers and magazines

1.   Lowercase **the** in names of newspapers.

the Toronto Star, the Star; the New York Times, the Times

2.   For French-language papers, write **Montreal La Presse** rather than the Montreal La Presse in first reference. In subsequent references avoid sentence constructions that juxtapose **the** and **le** or **la**: the La Presse editorial. Alternatives include La Presse's editorial, an editorial in La Presse, La Presse said in an editorial.

3.   For consistency, CP practice is to drop descriptions like **daily, evening** and **Sunday** from the formal title of a paper: the Fredericton Gleaner, not Daily Gleaner.

4.   Capitalize **magazine** only when it is part of the title.

Maclean's magazine, Harper's Magazine

➤   See **CP, PC, AP, AFP, Reuters** above.

Nicknames

Capitalize fanciful names and nicknames.

Iron Curtain, Third World, Boat People, Red Power, Little Italy, Golden Horseshoe, Old Guard, Big Three, Grits, Big Blue Machine, Just Society, Grand Old Party (GOP, but avoid), Tiger Williams, Herman (Babe) Ruth, Mack the Knife, Ethelred the Unready, Coeur de Lion, the Sun King, the Swedish Nightingale

➤   See also **Names, nicknames, initials**, page 215.

Note: Father, Mother, Mom, Uncle and the like are capitalized when used as a name: The doctor told Father that Aunt Jane is worse. After a personal pronoun, they are lowercased: The doctor told my father that my aunt Jane is worse.

Numbers

1.   In general, capitalize a noun followed by a number denoting place in a numbered series.

Act 1, Article 29, Book 3, Channel 2, Chapter 10, Cloud 9, Cosmos 150, Figure 13, Grade 3, Part 2, Pershing 2, Phase 1, Room 125, Square 1, Volume 12, Ward 7

Note: Avoid roman numerals except in personal sequences and in proper names where specified. Henry Ford III, Bluenose II, Rocky IV

2. Lowercase such words in plural use.

acts 3 and 5, chapters 1-3, grades 9 through 11

3. Lowercase **page, paragraph, sentence, size, verse, line.**

page 36, paragraph 2, line 3

Organizations

1. Capitalize the full names of organizations and institutions, but lowercase general references, with the exceptions noted below.

Canadian Airlines International, the Canadian Auto Workers, the B'nai Brith, the National Organization for Women, the airline, the autoworkers, the organization

Note 1: Company, Limited, Incorporated, Brothers and similar words are abbreviated as part of a name, **T. Eaton Co.**, except in cultural references: **Canadian Opera Company, Clancy Brothers**.

Note 2: For consistency, lowercase **the** in the names of organizations, except for those noted in *(CP) Caps and Spelling*.

➤ See **The** below.

2. Capitalize the names of major subdivisions of an organization.

the General Council of the United Church of Canada, the Cadillac Division of General Motors

3. Lowercase ordinary internal elements of an organization.

the United Church's division of mission, the board of directors of General Motors, the fire management centre of the Ministry of Natural Resources

4. Retain capitalization when the short form of a name is a household word. But use lowercase when referring to members of an organization.

Scouts Canada, the Scouts but two boy scouts; International Brotherhood of Teamsters, Chauffeurs, Warehousemen and Helpers of America, Teamsters union, the Teamsters; Ku Klux Klan, the Klan, a klansman; Odd Fellows and an Odd Fellow (capped to avoid ambiguity)

5. Retain capitalization when popular usage has reversed a name and eliminated **of, of the** and the like.

Department of Justice, Justice Department; Ministry of the Interior, Interior Ministry

➤ See **Abbreviations and acronyms**, page 172.

Plants

1. In plant names, capitalize proper nouns and adjectives derived from proper nouns.

Scotch pine, Kentucky blue grass, Douglas fir, white Dutch clover

2. In botanical names, capitalize the first word, lowercase others.

Primula japonica (Japanese primrose), **Taraxacum officinale** (dandelion), **Acer rubrum** (red maple), **Cornus florida** (dogwood)

3. Capitalize the names of fruit and vegetable varieties.

McIntosh, Delicious (apples); **Red Pontiac** (potatoes)

➤ See **Technical terms**, page 285.

Political divisions

1. Capitalize political and administrative divisions.

British Empire, Dominion (Canada), **United Kingdom, French Republic, Northern Ontario, Greater Vancouver Regional District, Montreal Urban Community, Metropolitan Toronto, Ward 2, 11th Congressional District, Precinct 2**

Note: Write **Niagara Region, Metropolitan Toronto** (government regions) but **Niagara region, the metropolitan area** (geographical descriptions).

2. Lowercase such words as **city, county, province** and **state** except when they are part of the incorporated name.

in the city of Halifax, the City of Halifax's credit rating; in Quebec province, the Province of Quebec vs. Smithers; the California state capital, the State of California's damage suit

Quebec City, New York City, Kansas City, Greenwich Village

Politics

1. Capitalize the full names of political parties and movements, but lowercase **party** in short forms.

Liberal Party of Canada, Liberal party, Progressive Conservative Party of Canada, Progressive Conservative party, Reform Party of Canada, Reform party, Pacific party, Green party, Christian Heritage party, Communist party, Young Liberals, National Liberation Front, IRA Provisional wing

But **New Democratic Party, Bloc Quebecois, Parti Quebecois**

2. Capitalize **Communist, Conservative, Democrat, Fascist, Liberal, Nazi, New Democrat, Socialist** and the like when they refer to a specific party or its members.

3. Lowercase these words when they refer to a political philosophy, except when they are derived from a proper name.

communism, democracy, fascism, socialism, separatism, democratic rights, conservative principles, independent nations, republican system, the left, right-wing group, liberals, communists, social democrats

But **Marxism, Marxists, Nazism, Nazis**

4. Capitalize fanciful names and nicknames.

Grits, Tories, Grand Old Party (GOP, but avoid), Just Society, Old Guard, Young Turks, Black Power, Reds, Big Blue Machine

5. Capitalize **Leader, Chairman** or **Secretary** when used with the name of a party and directly preceding a name, but lowercase as the title for others.

Reform (party) **Leader Preston Manning** (but **party leader Preston Manning**); **Communist party General Secretary Do Muoi** (but prefer **Do Muoi, the Communist party general secretary**)

But **Libyan leader Moammar Gadhafi, PLO leader Yasser Arafat, NDP chairman Roy Brown, party secretary Ann Rogers**

6. Capitalize **Politburo** and **Central Committee**, but lowercase other principal political bodies as well as political conventions.

the government, the administration, the cabinet, Liberal leadership convention, Republican platform committee

➤ See **Legislative bodies** above.

Quotations

1. Capitalize the first word of a complete quotation.

Pickets yelling "Scab!" deterred 200 men from entering.

McCabe replied to the lawyer's "Ah, Mr. McCabe" with an "Oh, hello, Mr. Trout."

Poirier asked, "Did you expect to hear shouts of 'Well done' and 'Good luck'?"

2.   Do not capitalize a word or phrase that is quoted merely for discussion or because it is controversial or used ironically or oddly.

What does "gating" mean?

One of the words used was "scab."

The "gift" cost $10.

➤ See **Punctuation**, page 242.

Religion

1.   Capitalize sacred names.

Adonai	Lord of Lords
Allah	the Madonna
the Almighty	the Messiah
the Angel Gabriel	Mother Mary
the Apostle Paul,	the Omnipotent
Paul the Apostle	the One Great Spirit
the Baptist	our Lady
Blessed Virgin	Prince of Peace
Buddha	the Prophet (Mohammed)
the Child Jesus	the Savior
Divine Providence	Siva
Father	the Son
God	the Son of Man
the Godhead	the Twelve Apostles
the Guru	the Virgin
the Holy Family	Vishnu
the Holy Spirit	the Word
Jehovah	Yahweh
King of Kings	

Note: Lowercase **fatherhood, providence** (in a general sense), **messianic, a savior** (in a non-religious sense), **the angel, an apostle.**

2.   Capitalize personal pronouns referring to God: **He, Him, His, Me, My, Mine, Thou, Thee, Thine** and so on. Lowercase relative pronouns: **who, whom, whose.**

3.   Capitalize the proper names and nicknames of the devil.

Satan, Lucifer, Father of Lies, Old Nick, the Antichrist

Note: Lowercase **satanic**, capitalize **Satanism**.

4.   Lowercase **god** and **goddess** in references to pagan gods but capitalize their proper names.

the sun god, the gods of Olympus, the goddess Venus, the god Thor

5. Capitalize the names of religions, faiths, their current heads and their adherents.

the Baha'i faith	Islam	Parsee
Buddhist	Jain	the Pope
Christianity	Jew	Shintoist
the Dalai Lama	Muslim	the Sikh religion
Hinduism	Neo-Confucianism	Zen-Buddhism

Note: Lowercase pagan, atheist, agnostic (in a general sense), gentile, spiritualist, theosophist.

6. Capitalize the names of religious denominations, movements, orders and their adherents.

Catholicism	Oxford Movement
Eastern Orthodoxy	High, Low Church
Protestantism	an Anglican
Sephardism	Baptist
Mormonism	Papists
Christian Science,	Reform Jews
a Scientist	Sons of Freedom,
Jehovah's Witness,	a Freedomite
a Witness	Franciscans
Seventh-day Adventist,	Grey Nuns
an Adventist	Essenes
Salvation Army,	Pharisees
the Army	

7. Capitalize sacred writings and their parts.

the Bible	Laws of Manu	the Talmud
Book of Genesis	New, Old Testament	the Upanishads
the Epistles	Romans	the Vedas
the Koran	Scripture	

Note: Lowercase fisherman's bible, biblical, the gospel truth, a parable, an epistle, apocryphal, talmudic, koranic, vedic.

8. Capitalize such familar references as the following.

Garden of Eden	Holy Week	the Shroud of Turin
the Chosen People	Good Friday	Diet of Worms
Tower of Babel	the Crucifixion	the Hegira
Noah's Ark	the Resurrection	(Mohammed's)
Ten Commandments	the Prodigal Son	Ramadan
City of David	Three Wise Men	Festival of Sacrifice
Day of Atonement	Good Samaritan	the Second Coming
Yom Kippur	Council of Trent	the Last Day

Note: Lowercase heaven, hell, paradise, purgatory, nirvana.

9. Lowercase sacraments, rituals and the like.

aqiqa	confession	holy communion
baptism	eucharist	kaddish
bar mitzvah	evensong	mass
christening	high mass	seder

10. Capitalize **church** as part of the name of a building, a congregation or a denomination.

St. Paul's United Church, the Anglican Church

Note: Write **an Anglican church, the Roman Catholic and Anglican churches, church and state.**

➤ See **Titles**, page 294.

Schools

1. Capitalize universities and colleges but not their departments.

Simon Fraser University, Macdonald College, McGill medical school, department of dentistry, English department, faculty of education

2. In general, lowercase schools.

York collegiate institute, York collegiate, Banff high school, Rolph Road elementary school, St. John's separate school

Note: Write **London School of Economics, Harvard Graduate School of Business, University of Toronto Schools.**

Slogans and headlines

1. Capitalize the principal words of written slogans and newspaper headlines, but do not use quotation marks.

On one placard was written Restraint — Practise What You Preach. Another sign read Help the Economy.

The editorial appeared under the heading Show Some Leadership.

➤ See **No. 8**, page 178, for a definition of principal words.

2. Capitalize only the first word of rules and mottoes.

Another rule suggests Think before you write.

There's much truth in the saying Too many cooks spoil the broth.

Space

1. Capitalize the proper names of asteroids, comets, constellations, planets, stars and other unique celestial objects.

Ceres, Andromeda, Great Bear, Ursa Major, Charles's Wain, Big Dipper, Milky Way, Solar System

2. In general, lowercase the common-noun element of the names of celestial objects.

Ceres asteroids, the constellation of Andromeda, Halley's comet, Crab nebula, Barnard's star

But the North Star (Polaris)

3. Lowercase **earth** except when referred to as an astronomical body. Lowercase **sun** and **moon** in all instances.

down to earth, move heaven and earth, returned to Earth from Mars, Earth's atmosphere, the new moon

4. Lowercase the names of meteorological phenomena.

northern lights, aurora borealis

5. Lowercase nouns and adjectives derived from proper names.

martian, jovian, venusian

Sports

1. Capitalize major sports events and trophies.

Olympic Games, Winter Olympics, World Series, World Cup, Canadian Open, Canada Cup, Grey Cup, Queen's Plate, Stanley Cup playoffs, Super Bowl, Vezina Trophy

2. In second references, capitalize **Games, Series, Cup, Open, Plate, Stakes** and the like: **the Series' leading batter, the Plate also-rans.** This is an exception to the rule that common nouns standing alone are lowercased.

➤ See **Sports**, page 80.

The

1. The word **the** (or its non-English equivalent) is capitalized at the start of titles of books, magazines, movies, TV programs, songs, paintings and other compositions.

The Last Spike, The New Yorker, L'Amour masqué, The Journal, The Holly and the Ivy, The Artist and His Model

2. **The** is not capitalized at the start of the names of such works as almanacs, the Bible, directories, encyclopedias, gazetteers and handbooks.

the Canadian Almanac, the Reader's Encyclopedia, the Concise Oxford Dictionary, the Canadian Press Stylebook

3. When the is capitalized in a geographical name, retain the capitalization.

The Pas, The Hague, El Salvador

But the Yukon, the Netherlands, the Congo, the City (London financial district), **the** Front (sealing ground off Labrador), **the** Barrens

4. In rare instances, **the** can be capitalized when it is used to give a singular meaning to an ordinary word.

The Change (menopause), **The Show** (baseball's major leagues)

5. For consistency, lowercase **the** in all other names: companies, associations, institutions, newspapers, awards, ships, trains, nicknames, rock groups and so on.

the T. Eaton Co., the Bay, the Royal Canadian Legion, the House of Commons, the External Affairs Department, the Anglican Church, the Air Defence Command, the Gazette, the Juno Awards, the Queen Elizabeth, the Transcontinental, the Royal York Hotel, Mack the Knife, the Beatles, the Prince of Wales

Note: Capitalize the definite article in the names of French-language newspapers in accordance with French style: **Le Droit.**

➤ See **Newspapers and magazines** above.

Times and seasons

Lowercase the seasons and spelled-out references to time.

spring, winter
mountain standard time, eastern daylight time,
Atlantic daylight time

But MST, EDT, ADT

Titles

1. Capitalize formal titles — those that are almost an integral part of a person's identity — when they directly precede the name.

Pope Pius, Queen Elizabeth, Prime Minister John Major, Dr. Hans Selye, Prof. Harold Smith, Sgt. Ann Rutherford, Brother Marcus

Note: With few exceptions, a title more than two words long should be set off from the name with commas: **Arnold Schaur, trade and commerce minister, . . .**

2. A title set off from a name by commas is lowercased. **The prime minister, John Major, will represent Britain at the talks.**

3. Lowercase occupational titles and descriptions. Titles of officials of companies, unions, political organizations and the like are also lowercased.

Widget president Barbara Sansom, UAW secretary Margaret Wilson, defenceman Ted Green, general manager Art Simpson, coach Guy Lebrun, contralto Maureen Forrester, astronaut John Young

Note 1: Avoid the inelegant practice of invariably affixing the description to a person's name as a false title: **rock star Bill Glass, bus driver Mary Owens, Niagara Falls businessman Mario Gucci.** Offer occasional relief by using a **the** phrase: **the contralto Maureen Forrester, the English historian Arnold Toynbee.** Or use a comma construction: **Violet Haynes, a Liberal member, disagreed. The spokesman, Tom Jameson, refused to comment. Eaton's president, Fredrik S. Eaton; a truck driver, Mary Owens.**

Note 2: Avoid such pileups as **public relations director John O'Connor's department; best-selling Canadian mystery writer Eric Wright.**

4. Capitalize all references to the current Pope, Canada's reigning monarch and the current Canadian Governor General. But lowercase most formal titles standing alone.

the Pope's visit, the Queen's family, wrote to the Governor General

But the king of Denmark, the prime minister, the president, the Communist party chairman

5. Capitalize **Royal Family** when referring to the British Royal Family. Also **Queen Mother, Her** or **His Majesty** and **Her** or **His Royal Highness**, whether standing alone or with names. For former and future British monarchs, capitalize the title: **the former King.** With foreign royalty, capitalize all current titles used with a proper name and lowercase others: **Queen Astrid, former king Farouk.**

6. **Royal** — as in **royal visit, royal assent** — is lowercase.

7. **Crown** is capitalized when it refers to the state.

the Crown corporation, the Crown alleged, the Crown jewels; but the Queen's crown

8. Capitalize titles of nobility, religion and such that are commonly used instead of the personal name. Lowercase on subsequent references.

the Prince of Wales, the prince; the Earl of Snowden, the earl; the Archbishop of Canterbury, the archbishop; the Bishop of Toronto, the bishop

9. Capitalize terms of honor, nobility and respect.

His Excellency, His Honor, Your Honor, Hon. John Jones, Her Worship, His Grace, My Lord

Note: Use such terms only when they appear in direct quotations.

10. To avoid ambiguity, all references to legislative **Speakers** are capped.

11. Lowercase titles preceded by **former, acting** and so on.

prime minister-designate Mary Brown, acting prime minister John Burgess, president-elect Tony Leech, the onetime president Gerald Ford, former mayor Joanne Lesniak

But Deputy Prime Minister Oskar Arendt

Note 1: Abbreviated titles are capped: the late Dr. Jean Savard.

Note 2: In references to past events, titles are capped when words like **former** and **the late** are dropped:

The official opening of the St. Lawrence Seaway — on June 26, 1959 — was attended by Prime Minister John Diefenbaker and U.S. President Dwight Eisenhower.

12. Lowercase plural uses of titles.

premiers Jean Martineau and Gerry Germain, popes John Paul II and John XXIII

Note: Capitalize the plural use of abbreviations: **Profs. Giuseppe Gucci and Helen Bruno.**

13. Lowercase derivatives.

presidential, papal, ministerial, senatorial, mayoral

14. Variations on the titles of cabinet ministers are not capitalized.

junior finance minister Robert Jack; acting health minister Kim Shen

Note: Titles of government officials below cabinet rank are lowercased: deputy minister Eva Swartz, House leader Ian Loy (federal), house leader Ian Loy (provincial).

15. Following titles are in CP style:

Prime Minister Jean Chrétien
Deputy Prime Minister Sheila Copps
the prime minister, Jean Chrétien
former prime minister John Turner
junior finance minister Jean Fortin
deputy trade minister Aldo Conti
Bloc Québécois Leader Lucien Bouchard
the Speaker
the Governor General
Gov. Gen. Romeo LeBlanc
lieutenant-governor
Lt.-Gov. Hal Jackman
Senator John Buchanan

➤ See **Government**, page 210; **Titles**, page 292. Also, **Government departments**, **Military** and **Religion** above. For composition titles, see **Compositions** and **Music** above.

Trade names

1. Capitalize all trade names but use them only when they give point, color or impact to a story.

The doctor refused to prescribe Laetrile or Essiac.
She blew the inheritance on a Rolls-Royce.
Jim Jones gave Kool-Aid laced with poison to 900 members of the People's Temple.

2. A generic term can often be used instead.

headache pill (Aspirin); adhesive bandage (Band-Aid); cola drink (Coca-Cola); fibreglass or glass fibre (Fiberglas); jelly dessert (Jell-O); tissues or paper handkerchiefs (Kleenex); hardboard (Masonite); heat-resistant glass (Pyrex); cotton swabs (Q-Tips); sticky tape (Scotch Tape); plastic foam (Styrofoam); petroleum jelly (Vaseline); photocopier (Xerox)

Note: Trade names subject to protection in Canada are normally listed in the *Canadian Trade Index*. Do not follow the capitalization in the *Concise Oxford Dictionary*.

➤ See **Trade names**, page 296.

Compounds

General

1. In the absence of widely agreed rules, writers and editors sometimes have to decide whether a compound word should be written open (**knuckle ball**), hyphenated (**knuckle-ball**) or solid (**knuckleball**).

2. In practice, a new compound is normally written at first as two or more words (**street car**), becomes increasingly hyphenated (**street-car**) and is then combined into a single word (**streetcar**).

3. In North America, the tendency is to drop the hyphen as soon as a new compound becomes familiar.

Guidelines

1. Hyphens are used to unravel meaning.

an old-book collector, an old book-collector; a white-slave racket, a white slave-racket; a light-blue coat; a dry-ice machine

2. Compound adjectives are often hyphenated before the noun they modify.

a world-class athlete, up-to-the-minute fashion, a 12-year-old child

3. When the words forming a compound adjective stand alone in a sentence, they are usually not hyphenated.

an athlete of world class, fashion that's up to the minute, the child is 12 years old

Note: In the sentence **The 12-year-old is from Vancouver, 12-year-old** is properly hyphenated as a noun. Similarly: **a race for three-year-olds**.

4. When Oxford and *(CP) Caps and Spelling* offer no help, write a compound noun as separate words or one word rather than with a hyphen.

Note: Compound nouns are not necessarily created from nouns but may be combinations of verbs, adverbs and so on.

teeter-totter, know-how, the down-at-heel, letdown

5. Compound verbs are usually either hyphenated or written as one word.

hand-picked, babysit, dry-clean, whitewash, deep-six

6. Compound verbs ending in an adverb or a preposition are not hyphenated.

break away, hold up, shoot out, run in, lean to, clip on

Note: The same two words used as nouns or adjectives are written solid. But if the solid form would be hard to grasp, use a hyphen.

breakaway, holdup, shootout
But **run-in** (not **runin**), **lean-to** (not **leanto**),
a clip-on lid (not **clipon**)

7. Keep in mind the advice of the Oxford University Press stylebook:

"If you take hyphens seriously, you will surely go mad."

➤ See **Punctuation**, page 238.

French

The Canadian Press delivers its news report in English for an audience that is not necessarily bilingual. Stories peppered with French break the flow and make reading difficult. At the same time, it is not always possible to avoid the use of French in the names of organizations or movie and book titles. In that case, a translation that remains as faithful as possible to the French should be provided. If a precise translation is impossible, an explanation or description can be used.

The aim is always ease of understanding without sacrificing the meaning of the French text.

Names of organizations

1. Prefer the English form for the names of organizations.

Quebec Liquor Corp. (not **Société des alcools du Québec**); **University of Montreal** (not **Université de Montréal**); **the Montreal campus of the University of Quebec** (not **Université du Québec à Montréal** or **University of Quebec in Montreal**); **Montreal Transit Corp.** (not **Société de transport de la communauté urbaine de Montréal**); **Quebec Labor Federation** (not **Fédération des travailleurs du Québec**); **Quebec provincial police** (not **Sûreté du Québec**); **Museum of Fine Arts** (not **Musée des beaux-arts**); **Great Whale hydro project** (not **the Grande baleine project**)

2. The names of some organizations cannot readily be translated. Others become familiar in their French version, or have no official English version. In such cases, the French name should be accompanied by an explanation.

Conseil du patronat, the largest employers group in Quebec; **Centrale de l'enseignement du Québec**, the teachers federation; **Société pour vaincre la pollution**, an environmental group; **Union des producteurs agricoles**, the farmers union; **Ecole polytechnique**, the engineering school affiliated with the University of Montreal

Note: Be careful with the following agencies set up in conjunction with Quebec's French-language law *(Law 101)*.

Office de la langue française, the agency that administers the provisions of the provincial language law; **Conseil de la langue française**, a research and advisory body on language issues.

3. For some organizations, known even to English speakers in Quebec by their initials, prefer a substitute rather than the full name or initials.

CEGEP (Collège d'enseignement général et professionel): junior college; CLSC (Centre local de services communautaires): community health centre

4. Some Quebec titles have equivalents in other provinces. Prefer a similar form for the Quebec version even if that means the translation is not identical to the French.

Corporation professionnelle des médecins du Québec: Quebec College of Physicians rather than the **Professional Corporation of Quebec Doctors; Directeur général des élections: chief returning officer**

5. A few organizations, titles and the like are commonly known by their French names and need not be followed by a translation.

Le Droit, Société St-Jean-Baptiste, Notre Dame

Books, movies, etc.

1. Prefer the English form for the titles of books, movies and the like if the English name is widely known.

Remembrance of Things Past (not **A la recherche du temps perdu**); **Jesus of Montreal** (not **Jésus de Montréal**); **The Decline of the American Empire** (not **Le Declin de l'empire américain**)

2. When a French name or title is used in a quotation, a list of awards or a review, it should be followed by the official translation, if available, in parentheses.

Le Malade imaginaire (The Imaginary Invalid); Le Matou (The Alley Cat); Dans l'oeil de l'aigle (In the Eye of the Eagle); Dans le ventre du dragon (In the Belly of the Dragon)

3. When there is no official translation — for example, if the movie or book has not been issued in English — provide a translation in parentheses that accurately conveys the meaning of the French title.

Au revoir, les enfants (Goodbye Children); Les Belles-soeurs (The Sisters-in-Law)

4. When there is no official or simple English title of a novel, TV program, movie or the like, or when the English translation conveys a different meaning from the French, an explanation is in order.

Les Fous de Bassan, the novel by Anne Hebert which was issued in English as In the Shadow of the Wind. Fous de Bassan refers to gannets, a type of seabird.

Bonheur d'occasion by Gabrielle Roy, which translates as Second-Hand Happiness but was issued in English as The Tin Flute

Un Train d'enfer, a movie whose title translates as A Train From Hell, but which also carries the meaning of breakneck speed

René Lévesque's Memoirs, whose original title, Attendez que je me rappelle, had a typically offhand suggestion of Hang On, It'll Come to Me — with a hint of Quebec's official motto

Capitalization

1. For most names in French, capitalize the first word, the second word too when the first is an article, and proper nouns.

This applies to:

a)   Titles of books, songs, movies and the like.

De la terre à la lune, Sur le pont d'Avignon, Les Liaisons dangereuses

b)   Names of newspapers and magazines.

Le Journal de Montréal, L'Actualité, Le Courrier du peuple, L'Acadie nouvelle, La Voix de l'Est (l'Est, meaning the East, is capitalized as the name of a region)

Note: When referring to a French newspaper, avoid repetition of the article. **La Presse reported today** (not **the La Presse report said today**).

c)   A variety of other kinds of names.

Fête nationale (a holiday), L'Auberge bonne nuit (a hotel), La Petite marmite (a restaurant), L'Académie canadienne-française (an association), Place d'armes (a city square), Conseil du patronat (employers' organization), Office de la langue française (government agency)

2. For names of corporate organizations, CP uses the English article preceding the name. Otherwise, capitalize the first word and proper nouns, lowercase other words.

the Service de perception, Emballages St-Laurent ltée, the Caisse de dépôt et placement

3. The main exception to the basic rule is for place names, which follow normal CP capitalization.

La Tuque, Pointe-aux-Trembles, St-Basile-le-Grand

4. **Franco-Albertan** and **Anglo-Quebecer** take capital letters; **francophone** and **anglophone** do not. Generally, prefer **French-speaking** and **English-speaking**. The word **allophone** is also entering the vocabulary to describe someone who is neither French- nor English-speaking, but it should be avoided.

5. **Fleur-de-lis** is capitalized when it refers to Quebec's flag.

Hyphens in place names

In CP copy, French place names follow the French style of punctuation, with hyphens instead of periods (St-Hyacinthe) or spaces (Riviere-du-Loup).

1. Most multiple-word place names in Quebec and other French-speaking areas of the world are hyphenated.

Trois-Rivières, St-Georges-de-Beauce, Stanstead-Est, Que.; Petit-Rocher, N.B.; Val-d'Isère, France

Note: In names preceded by the definite article, do not put a hyphen after the article.

La Malbaie, La Pocatière

2. Hyphens are omitted from purely English place names.

Stanstead Plain, East Broughton, Otterburn Park

3. Hyphens are omitted if the first word is not a place name but refers to a natural feature (*lake, river, mountain* etc.).

Lac Barrière, Baie des Chaleurs, Rivière des Prairies

Note: A natural feature can be part of the corporate name of some municipalities. They are hyphenated: **Baie-Comeau, Lac-Beauport, Mont-Laurier.**

4.   Street names take hyphens.

Ste-Catherine Street, 136 René-Lévesque Blvd.

Saint

1.   Family and place names that include *saint* or a variant are tricky, needing the same care in checking as *Mac* and *Mc* names.

2.   In Quebec place names, *saint* and *sainte* are abbreviated to *St* and *Ste* (no periods) and joined to the next word by a hyphen. Elsewhere in Canada, practice varies. Check the *Canadian Almanac.*

St-Jean-Port-Joli, Que; Ste-Anne-des-Monts, Que.

But St. Boniface, Man.; Sault Ste. Marie, Ont.; Saint John, N.B.; St. John's, Nfld.; St. Brieux, Sask.; Saint-Antoine, N.B.; St. Jacques, Nfld.

Note: It is not always obvious that a name is feminine or masculine (e.g. St-Hyacinthe); check if in doubt.

3.   Quebec family names may be written either with **saint** and **sainte** spelled out (**Louise Saint-Pierre, Marcel Sainte-Marie**) or in abbreviated form (**Chantal St-Amour** or **Pierre Ste-Croix**). Check with the person for a preferred spelling; if that is not possible, prefer the long form.

4.   For the names of saints, follow normal English practice and use St. for female as well as male saints and do not hyphenate.

St. Jean de Brébeuf, St. Marguerite Bourgeoys

Translation

1.   CP avoids double translation. The risk of error is compounded when a quotation moves from one language into another and then back again. Paraphrasing a quotation reduces the risk.

2.   When translating from an interview or from a French text, avoid awkward literal translations. Translate to convey the meaning of the quote or French text while remaining as true as possible to the original. If that requires too many contortions, paraphrase.

"Il a réussit à sauver les meubles": not "He managed to save the furniture" but "He was able to salvage the essentials."

3. Be alert to words that look alike in French and English but have different meanings.

amateur (in sports, fan); bulletin d'information (news report); circulation (traffic); commission parlementaire (legislature committee); déception (disappointment), déçu (disappointed); éditeur (publisher), rédacteur-en-chef (editor); exploiter (operate); formation (training, education); ignorer (be unaware of, not know); impliquer (involve); militant (member of a political party); nomination (appointment); populaire (popular, but more often of or for the people); sécurité (safety); sensibiliser (educate), sensible (sensitive to)

4. **Business terminology:** The business world uses some terms that present translation problems.

actif (assets); action (share); administrateur (director); bénéfice net (profit); chef de l'exploitation (chief operating officer); chiffres d'affaires (income); membre de la direction (officer); obligation (bond, debenture); passif (liabilities); président-directeur-général — pdg (president and chief executive officer — CEO); président du conseil (chairman of the board); société (company or corporation); société fermée (private company); société ouverte (public company)

5. **Legal terminology:**

effraction (break and enter); homicide involontaire (manslaughter); mandat de perquisition (search warrant); outrage au tribunal (contempt of court); voies de fait (assault)

Note: In Quebec, the Civil Code based on the French Napoleonic Code is used in civil litigation. The Canadian Criminal Code applies in criminal cases.

As a result, many procedures differ from elsewhere in Canada.

➤ See **Legal** section, page 95.

Government

Introduction

Question period shouting matches and hallway scrums offer only a small glimpse of what government does. Good reporting goes farther. It humanizes statistics, puts issues into perspective, illustrates the effects of new regulations and penetrates the silent bureaucracies that shape the lives of Canadians.

Most people connect with government through taxes, schools, police, hospitals, highways, jobs and the price of beer. These are tangible elements. They should appear in stories. That means putting real people looking for jobs in a report on unemployment statistics. It means showing how car owners and trout anglers will be affected by new environmental laws.

Corruption and waste are pursued, where they exist, but reporters must not become another official Opposition, looking only for something — *anything* — to criticize. The best reporting is concerned with more than quick hits from mock-indignant politicians. Time is better spent exploring how little-known regulatory agencies affect everyday concerns like food quality, aircraft safety or personal privacy.

The relationship between issues raised in the political arena and the concerns of the reader at home is often obscure. The reporter works to make that connection clear.

Capitalization

➤ For questions of capitalization on government, parliaments, laws, royalty, etc., see the chapter **Capitalization**, starting page 177.

National and provincial legislatures

1. Ministers with more than one portfolio should be referred to by the title most appropriate to the story. **Sergio Marchi, minister of citizenship and immigration**, becomes **Immigration Minister Sergio Marchi** in stories about immigration levels.

2. The **official Opposition** is the opposition party with most seats: **the Opposition Liberals, the two opposition parties**.

3. **MP** is always acceptable for member of Parliament. Don't use an abbreviation for members of provincial legislatures, since the title varies from province to province.

4. Write **Senate, Senator Nate Nurgitz, a senator, former senator Robert de Cotret**.

5. Make it **Parliament Hill, the Hill, Parliament Buildings, East Block, Peace Tower, lower chamber, upper chamber, lower house, upper house.**

6. The official residence of the Canadian prime minister is **24 Sussex Drive**; that of the Opposition leader is **Stornoway.**

7. Write **prime minister-designate** Jean Chrétien, not **prime minister-elect** Jean Chrétien, because the Canadian electorate does not vote for a prime minister or premier as such. But **president-elect** Bill Clinton is correct in U.S. contexts.

8. The forms **Progressive Conservative** and **Conservative** are equally acceptable in casual reference to the federal party. Some provincial parties prefer the full title. Check.

Political affiliations and designations

1. The political affiliation of elected members and the names of their constituencies are specified when they are relevant. For members of Parliament and provincial legislatures, give the party and constituency; for senators, party and province.

2. Streamlined abbreviations for party designations are fine in routine parliamentary and legislature copy, or in stories where many members are named. They are avoided otherwise, except for **NDP** and **PQ.**

The abbreviations are: **BQ** (Bloc Quebecois), **CoR** (Confederation of Regions), **EP** (Equality), **Ind** (Independent), **L** (Liberal), **NDP** (New Democratic Party), **PC** (Progressive Conservative), **PQ** (Parti Quebecois), **Ref** (Reform), **SC** (Social Credit).

Style is **(L—Winnipeg North Centre)**. The abbreviation is separated from the constituency by a dash with no spaces on either side.

Usually, a descriptive phrase reads better than a streamlined style: **George Baker, the longtime Liberal member for Gander-Grand Falls.** Sometimes a fuller description is desirable. For example, in a debate about federal transfer payments to Newfoundland: **George Baker, Liberal member for Gander-Grand Falls, is a politically well-connected Newfoundlander whose brother, Winston, is the province's deputy premier and finance minister.**

3. In the bracketed style, the names of federal constituencies not easily identified are followed by the name of the province: **(L— Egmont, P.E.I.).**

4. The names of cities are given when they have more than one seat: **Toronto Broadview-Greenwood** (city first). Similarly, the name of a subdivided constituency precedes that of the subdivision: **York West.**

5. When used in lists or tabulations, the abbreviations for parties change slightly and become **BQ, CoR., EP, Ind., Lib., NDP, Prog. Con., PQ, Ref, SC.**

First minister

Where the choice is between **prime minister** and **premier**, use **prime minister** for the heads of national governments in general but **premier** for the heads of government in France and its former colonies, Canadian provinces and Australian states. Some West Indies governments also have premiers; follow individual preferences.

Monarchy

The Queen and members of the Royal Family deserve normal respect for their constitutional role in Canada, but coverage of their visits to this country and other activities is governed by basic news standards.

In particular, that means stories should not gush (**looking radiant**). Nor should they pretend the visitor's casual asides are profound or witty, nor quote meaningless exclamations from bystanders (**"It's the most thrilling day of my life,"** said 11-year-old Melanie Simpson), nor be littered with royal this's and that's (the **royal breakfast**, the **royal limousine**, etc.).

It is no more acceptable to write condescendingly about ordinary people's responses to a royal tour. The fact that someone puts on hat and gloves to watch royalty pass, or belongs to the Monarchist League, is a matter of personal choice, not an occasion for fun.

The best stories tend to focus on one or two events in the visitor's day, stressing human elements that are genuinely newsworthy and describing them fully and frankly. The organization is also worth a story at times: in Halifax, they once used green paint on a bald stretch of the common as part of their spruce-up.

Such coverage excludes the kind of social-page filler that lists every hand shaken, royal guard inspected, memorial book inscribed and ribbon cut.

1.   The Queen is Canada's **head of state**; the prime minister is **head of government**. Officially, the **Governor General** acts as head of state when the Queen isn't in Canada, but avoid referring to the Governor General in such terms.

2.   Unless there are problems with identification — for instance, in a story dealing with a number of monarchs — the preferred term for Queen Elizabeth is **the Queen**, rather than **Queen Elizabeth. Queen of England** is wrong.

3.   Don't refer to the Princess of Wales as **Princess Diana**, since she isn't a princess by birth. In subsequent references, she is **the princess** or **Diana**.

Succession

Order of succession to the throne:

1. Prince Charles, Prince of Wales (Queen's eldest son)
2. Prince William (elder son of Charles)
3. Prince Henry (second son of Charles)
4. Prince Andrew (second son of the Queen)
5. Princess Beatrice (elder daughter of Andrew)
6. Princess Eugenie (second daughter of Andrew)
7. Prince Edward (third son of the Queen)
8. Princess Anne (only daughter of the Queen)
9. Peter Phillips (only son of Anne)
10. Zara Phillips (only daughter of Anne)
11. Princess Margaret (only sister of the Queen)

Ceremonies

1. The Queen and other members of the Royal Family receive a **royal salute** — the playing of *God Save the Queen* by a royal guard.

2. The Governor General and lieutenant-governors are accorded a **vice-regal salute** — part *God Save the Queen,* part *O Canada.*

3. The prime minister, visiting heads of state and political leaders, etc., are greeted with a **general salute** — a few bars of music other than *God Save the Queen* or *O Canada.*

➤ See **Military**, page 264.

First Lady

The Americanism **First Lady** refers to the wife of a U.S. president and is capitalized as a fanciful term. Prefer **Hillary Rodham Clinton** and the like. Do not apply the term to the Queen or to the wives of Canadian governors general, lieutenant-governors or prime ministers.

Nationhood

Nation means the people of a country; **country** is the territory of a nation. Hence avoid **nationwide** when used in a geographical sense, **the nation's capital** (for Ottawa), etc.

Canada

1. The national flag is the Maple Leaf.

2. The national anthem is *O Canada;* the royal anthem, *God Save the Queen.* The patriotic song *The Maple Leaf Forever* enjoys semi-anthem status outside Quebec.

3. The national emblem is the maple leaf. The beaver is a semi-official emblem.

4.   Canada's coat of arms bears the inscription *A Mari Usque Ad Mare* (From Sea Even Unto Sea).

5.   Canada's patron saint is St. Joseph (March 19).

Government jargon

1.   Avoid using the jargon that often flows so freely from government news releases or officials' mouths. Jargon fails to convey information to those unfamiliar with the term and can even mislead.

2.   Some words or phrases may be used sparingly. For example, **committee** can usually be substituted for **task force**. But **the Task Force on National Unity** may be referred to as **the task force**, because it is part of the official name.

3.   Avoid new verbs ending in *ize*, such as **priorize** or **prioritize**.

4.   Steer clear of pompous or awkward phrasing. Not **government initiative**. Initiative means **personal drive**. Use **government program** or **plan**. Not **referenced** (use **refer to**), not **impact on** (use **affect**), not **negatively impact on** (use **hurt**).

5.   Government budgets are rife with specialized terms. Keep it simple. A **negative growth in revenues** means government took in less money. A **surplus on the ordinary account** should not find its way into copy. Explain it instead: **The government showed a modest $10-million surplus on day-to-day operations, but once money spent on capital projects was taken into account — such as road repairs and a new court building — it ran a deficit of $500 million for the year.**

Names, nicknames, initials

1. In general, the names of people should be given in the form they normally use: **Ed Schreyer**, not **Edward Schreyer**; **Joe Clark**; **Kenneth Thomson**, not **Lord Thomson** (except when he is in the United Kingdom); **John F. Kennedy** or **J. F. Kennedy**; **P. G. Wodehouse**.

2. Follow personal preference for lowercased names: **k.d. lang** (not K.D. Lang), **bp Nichol** (not B.P. Nichol).

➤ For the names of organizations, see **Capitalization**, page 191.

3. In obituaries, try to spell out initials at some point but not in the lead where the unfamiliar name might confuse readers: **Pelham Grenville Wodehouse**.

4. A given name reads better than a single initial: **Robin Hood**, not **R. Hood**.

5. First and middle initials are used if that is a person's preference: **W. O. Mitchell**, **Ernest C. Manning**. And they are important in identifying a person charged with a crime and in listing accident victims.

6. Insert a *thin* space between initials — **E. P. Taylor, Sir John J. C. Abbott** — except when a person is referred to by initials only: **J.R., P.G.**

Note: Occasionally a public figure becomes known by initials without periods: **GBS, PET**.

7. Use **Sr.** and **Jr.** only with the full name and do not set them off with commas: **John Smith Jr.** But **John Smith Jr., PhD, B.Comm., was the name on the card.**

Note: In general, reserve **Sr.** and **Jr.** for cases where father and son are alive and known: **Edgar Bronfman Jr.**

8. Retain the designation **II** or **2nd** and the like if it is a person's preference: **Henry Ford III, Eric Van Husen 2nd**.

9. When necessary to distinguish between father and son in second reference, write **the elder** or **the younger Talbot**.

10. If confusion with another person is possible, include clarifying information: **O'Brien is not related to the businessman of the same name.**

11. When common names like **Mary Smith** and **Jean Dupont** get into the news, ages and occupations are needed to ensure proper identification, especially in police stories and if middle initials are not known.

12. People with first names applicable to either sex — **Beverley, Chris, Jean, Lee, Leslie, Terry, Tony** — should be identified as man or woman. Not **the accused, Pat O'Brien**, but **the woman accused, Pat O'Brien**. Often a pronoun introduced quickly — **he** or **she, him** or **her** — suffices.

13. A nickname is essential if it helps identify the subject: **Joseph (Joey) Smallwood**. Use a nickname instead of a given name only when a person is best known by the nickname: **Magic Johnson** (given name Earvin).

➤ See **Sports**, page 81.

14. To enclose nicknames, use parentheses, not quotation marks: **Gen. Norman (the Bear) Schwarzkopf**, not **Gen. Norman "the Bear" Schwarzkopf**.

15. If the relationship of a married couple is unclear, explain: **Joanne Woodward and her husband, Paul Newman**.

16. In non-English names, **de, di, la, ter, van, von** and the like are usually lowercase except at the start of a sentence: **Charles de Gaulle, the de Gaulle era**. But: **She said, "De Gaulle lived to retire."** And respect an individual's preference: **Robert de Cotret, Bill Vander Zalm**.

17. In transliterating a Russian name, use the English phonetic equivalent where one exists: **Alexander Solzhenitsyn**, not **Aleksandr**. Prefer **-ov** and **-ev** endings: **Khrushchev**, not **Khrushchyov**. But with Russian emigre names, follow the individual's preference: **Ignatieff, Rachmaninoff**.

18. In Chinese, Korean and many other Asian names, the family name comes first: **Roh** in **Roh Tae-Woo**. But westernized people often put the given name first: **Morris Lee**.

19. For Spanish and Portuguese names, the only safe guide is the way the individuals use them.

20. After first reference, it is often useful to include in important stories the pronunciation of unfamiliar, difficult names of people and places breaking into the news: **Gennady Yanayev (pronounced ghen-AH-dee yah-NYE-ev)**. Check Broadcast News as a source.

21. First names may be used on second reference for children and youths under 18, except in sports stories; they may also be used for adults for deliberate informality.

22. Plurals of proper names are usually formed by adding *s* or *es:* **Alexes, Burnses, Charleses, Henrys, Joneses, Marys, Perrys, Rubys**. But **Tommies, Johnnies**.

➤ See **Capitalization**, page 189; **Government**, page 210; **Plurals of nouns**, page 223; and **Titles**, page 292.

Numbers

General

1. In general, spell out whole numbers below 10 and use figures for 10 and above.

three batters, the fifth inning, nine minutes, 10 guests, the 16th hole, the 22nd day, the sixth Earl of Hodderston

2. In a series there will often be a mixture.

There are 27 trees: two beeches, 10 chestnuts, three elms and 12 maples. The dealer sold 10 four-cylinder cars, three sixes and 12 eights.

3. For numbers in official names, follow the organization's spelling style even when it is at odds with CP practice.

the TV show Thirtysomething, the film 7 Fathers

Note: Follow CP style on capitalization, however: **5th Estate** (not **5th estate**).

4. Use arabic numerals unless roman numerals are specified below.

5. Do not use commas with dimensions, measurements and weights consisting of two or more elements.

a woman five feet 11 inches tall; the baby weighs seven pounds six ounces; a trip of six months three weeks two days; in two hours 21 minutes 45 seconds (but the six-foot-three, 250-pound tackle)

6. To avoid ambiguity, write **increased to 15 per cent from 10** (not **increased from 10 to 15 per cent**).

7. To be meaningful, a percentage loss or gain should normally be accompanied by a dollar or some other amount.

Sales fell 10 per cent to $10,000. Sophie Dukakis, a hairdresser, said she now had 10 customers, a 20 per cent increase.

When to use figures

1. In addresses:

2 Newgate St., 3A Western Ave.

Note: Spell out **First** through **Ninth** as street names.

37 Fifth Ave., 23 59th St.

2.   In ages standing alone after a name:

Melanie, 2, has two brothers, eight and nine. Tim, two months old, had typhoid.

Note: When the context does not require **years** or **years old**, the reader presumes the number is years: **He was 21. One girl is five.**

3.   In dates and years:

3 BC, AD 5; Dec. 8, 8th of December; 1983, '83; the 1920s, the '20s; the Dirty '30s; the mid-1940s, the mid-'40s; he's in his late 50s.

Note: Write **the second century, the 20th century, the fifth century BC**.

4.   In decimals and in numbers larger than 1 with fractions:

0.25 centimetre, a .30-calibre rifle, pressures of 0.45 and 3.25, 2½ days, 99 and 44-100ths

But two-fifths, two-thirds finished

Note 1: Unless precision is essential, keep decimals to two places: **12.25 metres** (not **12.254 metres**).

Note 2: If there is no unit before a decimal point, use a cipher: **0.25.** But write **.30 calibre** and the like in keeping with common practice.

5.   In decisions, rulings, scores, votes and odds:

The court ruled 6-3, a 6-3 ruling. Montreal beat Vancouver 3-1 (but a two-goal margin). The bill was passed by a vote of 35-6, with one abstention; or a 35-6 vote. Of the 35 ballots, two were spoiled. It was a majority of nine.

odds of 5-2, a 10-1 longshot

6.   In heights expressed informally:

He stands 6-11.

7.   In highlights at the start of an item:

— 156 tanks and armored personnel carriers.

— $1.8 billion for new aircraft engines.

8.   In military and paramilitary terms:

2nd Lieut. Esther White (but White is a second lieutenant), U.S. Petty Officer 3rd Class Mike Kenny (but prefer Mike Kenny, a U.S. petty officer third class), a 6-pounder, 8 mm, M-16 rifle, 8th Army, 6th Fleet, 1st Canadian Division

9.   In monetary units preceded by a symbol:

$2 (not $2.00), two dollars; two francs, 2.5 francs; $1 million (but one million people); $2 billion, the $2-billion project; but the two-million-member federation and the 2.2-million-member CLC

10. In designations of aircraft, ships, spacecraft and vehicles:

Dash 7, A-4 Skyhawk, the liner Queen Elizabeth 2, QE2, the yachts Australia II and Canada 1, Apollo 8, Alouette 2

Note: Use a hyphen before the numeral but not after it: DC-8B.

11. In sequential designations:

Act 1 (but the first act), Article 3, Channel 2, Chapter 9, Grade 7, Highway 6, in No. 2 position, Room 4, RR 2, Section 5, back to Square 1

Note: The common nouns line, page, paragraph and size followed by figures are not capitalized: page 3, line 9, size 8 shoes.

12. In temperatures:

5 C, –6 C (tight dash, not hyphen)

But when Celsius or Fahrenheit is not specified spell out: five degrees.

13. In times:

1 a.m. (not 1:00 a.m.), 9 at night, 2 o'clock, 10:15 p.m., a 2:09 run, 3:20:15 but a time of three hours 20 minutes 15 seconds

When to spell out

1.   At the start of a sentence, if you must start with a number:

Twenty to 30 escaped unharmed, as well as 10 horses.

Note 1: Do not spell out the year at the start, but avoid: 1972 was a leap year.

Note 2: Do not spell out a street address at the start: 221 had a discreet sign: Oceano Palms.

Note 3: When numbers from 21 through 99 must be written out, use a hyphen: Thirty-five or 36 may have died.

2.   In informal or casual usage:

Letters poured in by hundreds and thousands. Damage was in the millions. a thousand and one delights

3. In formal usage:

in the year nineteen hundred fourteen

Note: Do not put commas or *and* between words forming a number:
one million thirty-three thousand two hundred ninety-eight.

4. In figures of speech and the like:

Twelve Apostles, Ten Commandments, Big Ten, wouldn't touch it with a ten-foot pole, a ten-gallon hat

Note: Write **the Dirty '30s, the Roaring '20s, the No. 1 or number 1 choice.**

5. In common fractions below 1 standing alone:

one-half, one-quarter inch, five-eighths

Note: In casual use, write **a half, half a loaf, a quarter share.**

Roman numerals

Use roman numerals to indicate sequence for people and animals and in proper names where specified. Otherwise avoid them as hard to grasp.

Queen Elizabeth II (rarely needed); **Pope John XXIII; Henry Ford III; Nijinsky II; Bluenose II** (but **Canada 1**); **The Godfather, Part II; Superman III**

Note 1: For the ship, write **Queen Elizabeth 2** or **QE2.**

Note 2: Write **SALT II, Vatican II** and the like to conform to widespread practice.

Large numbers

1. Round numbers in the thousands are usually given in figures.

They took 2,000 prisoners. $3,500, 375,000 francs

Note: Spell out for casual usage: **There were thousands of mosquitoes.**

2. Express large numbers in millions and billions instead of the less familiar **trillion, quadrillion** and the like.

a million billion (instead of **quadrillion**), **a billion billion** (instead of **quintillion**)

Note: In Canada and the United States, a billion is a thousand million; in the United Kingdom and some other places, it is a million million.

3.   Except for monetary units preceded by a symbol, round numbers in the millions and billions generally follow the rule of spelling out below 10.

two million bushels, 2.5 million bushels, 10 billion cubic metres, five billion marks, $1 billion

Note: Spell out for casual usage: What's a billion? I've told you a million times. a billion and a half

4.   In expressing a range, repeat million or billion.

25 million to 30 million

Note: The adjectival form may be written a $2- to $3-million loss, but prefer a loss of $2 million to $3 million.

5.   Hyphenate adjectival forms before nouns.

a two-million-bushel crop, a $10-billion gap, the 2.2-million-member CLC

6.   Use commas to set off numbers of four or more figures except house, telephone, page, year and other serial numbers.

2,500; 100,000 billion; 1265 Yonge St.; 364-0321; p. 1025; the year 2000

7.   Use figures for numbers up to 999,999. Above that, switch to words – if absolute precision is not required.

a loss of $100,000, a $1.2-million project

Plurals of nouns

In general, form the plural of a noun by adding *s* to the singular; add *es* if the singular ends in *s, x, ch, sh* or *z*.

taxis, lenses, complexes, stitches, lashes, topazes

The plurals of the following words often cause problems.

Nouns ending in *f, fe* and *ff*

1. Most nouns in this category have a plural in *s*.

beliefs, briefs, chiefs, griefs, mischiefs, roofs, safes, skiffs, tariffs, tiffs

2. Some have a plural in *ves*.

calves, elves, halves, knives, leaves, loaves, selves, shelves, thieves, wives, wolves

3. A few have two plurals; CP style is shown.

dwarfs, handkerchiefs, hoofs, scarves, still lifes, wharfs

Write **staffs** (poles), **staves** (music).

Nouns ending in *o*

1. Nouns ending with an *o* preceded by another vowel usually have a plural in *s* (not *es*).

cameos, folios, kangaroos, patios, portfolios, radios, ratios, rodeos, studios, tattoos, zoos

2. Nouns ending in *o* preceded by a consonant have a variety of plurals.

a) Some end in *es*.

dominoes, echoes, embargoes, heroes, mementoes, mosquitoes, mottoes, Negroes, noes, potatoes, tomatoes, tornadoes, volcanoes

b) Some end in *s*.

albinos, avocados, cantos, contraltos, dittos, dynamos, Filipinos, gauchos, ghettos, gigolos, octavos, pianos, piccolos, provisos, quartos, silos, solos, tangelos, tobaccos, twos, tyros, zeros

c) Some have two forms; CP style is shown.

banjos, buffaloes, cargoes, concertos, Eskimos, frescoes, innuendoes, lassos, salvoes, sopranos

Nouns ending in *y*

1. Nouns ending in *y* preceded by a vowel have a plural in *s*.

alloys, attorneys, chimneys, days, forays, keys, monkeys, storeys
But soliloquies; prefer moneys to monies.

2. Nouns ending in *y* preceded by a consonant have a plural in *ies*.

armies, authorities, beauties, bodies, caddies, categories, cherries, cities, communities, companies, cries, flies, ladies, parodies, skies

But drys (prohibitionists), standbys

Nouns ending in *ics*

Nouns of this type are singular or plural depending on use. They are singular when denoting the science or a course of study, plural when denoting an activity or quality.

Classics means Latin and Greek. The classics are neglected nowadays. Ethics is defined as a moral philosophy. His ethics are questionable.

➤ See **Singular or plural**, page 246.

Proper nouns

1. Proper nouns usually form the plural by adding *s*.

Drapeaus, Elizabeths, Germanys, Kansas Citys, Kennedys, Little Italys, Marys

Note: Some follow the *ies* rule: Johnnies, Tommies, the Alleghenies (Allegheny Mountains), the Rockies (Rocky Mountains)

2. Proper nouns ending in *ch, s, x* and *z* have a plural in *es*.

Finches, Joneses, Foxes, Heinzes

Compound words

1. Most compounds form the plural by changing the principal word to its plural form.

ambassadors at large, assistant surgeons general, attorneys general, chiefs of staff, commanders-in-chief, consuls general, courts martial, editors-in-chief, fathers-in-law, goings-on, governors general, lieutenant-governors, ministers-designate, ministers without portfolio, notaries public, secretaries general, solicitors general, trade unions

But Trades Union Congress

2. If both nouns are of about equal weight, both take the plural.

men employees, menservants, women writers

3. If no word is significant, the final word usually takes *s* or *es*.

forget-me-nots, hand-me-downs, no man's lands, pick-me-ups, will-o'-the-wisps, Johnny-come-latelies

4. Compounds ending in *ful* add *s*.

armfuls, cupfuls, handfuls, spoonfuls

Foreign nouns

Nouns of this type sometimes have an English as well as a foreign plural. CP style is shown.

addendum, addenda
adieu, adieus
alga, algae
alumna, alumnae (fem.)
alumnus, alumni (masc.)
analysis, analyses
antenna, antennas (aerials),
    antennae (feelers)
apparatus, apparatuses
appendix, appendixes
aquarium, aquariums
automaton, automatons
axis, axes
bacterium, bacteria
basis, bases
beau, beaus
bureau, bureaus
cactus, cactuses
census, censuses
cherub, cherubs
coccus, cocci
crisis, crises
criterion, criteria
curriculum, curricula
datum, data
dilettante, dilettantes
dogma, dogmas
ellipsis, ellipses
erratum, errata
focus, focuses
formula, formulas
fungus, fungi
genius, geniuses
genus, genera
gladiolus, gladioli
helix, helixes
hypothesis, hypotheses
impetus, impetuses

index, indexes
larva, larvae
larynx, larynxes
madam, mesdames
    (madams for
    brothel-keepers)
matrix, matrixes
maximum, maximums
medium, media
    (mediums in
    spiritualism)
memorandum,
    memorandums
minimum, minimums
minutia, minutiae
monsieur, messieurs
nucleus, nuclei
oasis, oases
opus, opuses
parenthesis, parentheses
phenomenon, phenomena
plateau, plateaus
prospectus, prospectuses
radius, radii
sanatorium, sanatoriums
seraph, seraphs
sinus, sinuses
stadium, stadiums
stimulus, stimuli
stratum, strata
syllabus, syllabuses
symposium, symposiums
tableau, tableaus
terminus, terminuses
thesis, theses
vertebra, vertebrae
virtuoso, virtuosos

Nouns with the same singular and plural

aircraft, alms, amends, bellows, bison, chassis, corps, counsel, deer, fish, forceps, goods, grouse, head (of cattle, etc.), headquarters, insignia, means, moose, offspring, pains, precis, proceeds, rendezvous, remains, series, salmon, shambles, sheep, species, sweepstakes, swine, trout, United States, wheat, whereabouts

Note: But when more than one kind or species is referred to, a regularly formed plural is sometimes used.

Many fishes, ranging from salmon to eel, are netted. New wheats — crosses of Thatcher and Selkirk — continue to be developed.

Nouns plural in form, singular in meaning

checkers, dominoes, measles, mews, mumps, news, rickets, shingles (disease), **works** (factory)

Dos and don'ts

Such expressions form their plurals normally.

no ifs, ands or buts; yeses and noes; all the ins and outs

But words being discussed as words form the plural by adding '*s*.

Some writers mistakenly leave out the the's. He filled his speech with like's and you know's.

➤ See **Punctuation**, page 228.

Possessives

1.   Singular and plural nouns not ending in *s* take an apostrophe and *s* to form the possessive case.

father's pipe, women's lib, people's food, the kibbutzim's leaders, alumni's donations

Note: It looks careless to err on words like **children's** (not **childrens'**) shoes, **women's** (not **womens'**) issues, **men's** (not **mens'**) salaries.

2.   Plural nouns ending in *s* take an apostrophe alone.

teachers' apples, the two peoples' history, the Joneses' daughter

3.   Singular nouns ending in *s* (or an *s* sound) normally take an *'s* to indicate a *sis* or *siz* sound. But if adding the extra *s* would make the word hard to say or grate on the ear, use an apostrophe alone.

Chris's sandwich, Burgess's novel, Butz's statement, the press's responsibility, Strauss's opera, the witness's testimony, Zeus's laws

But: **Moses' laws, Euripides' plays, Jesus' followers, Ulysses' wanderings, Silvers' cat, Ann Landers' column**

4.   Names ending in a silent *s* or *x* take an apostrophe and *s*.

Duplessis's cabinet, Delibes's Coppelia, Malraux's paintings, Francaix's symphony

Note: A few French names end in an *s* sound and follow normal rules for the possessive.

Saint-Saens' music, de Lesseps' canal

5.   For company and institutional names, follow the organization's preference.

Eaton's, Professional Golfers' Association, Canadian Forces Headquarters

Note: The possessive is an English form. In Quebec, corporate names and outdoor signs must follow the French form: **Eaton, Birk.**

6.   Where the usage is more descriptive than possessive, omit the apostrophe.

an autoworkers spokesman, a board of directors meeting, the carpenters union, citizens band radio, a Leafs defenceman

7. Use a single apostrophe for joint possession, separate apostrophes for separate possession.

Smith and Cusak's pharmacy, Pierre and Marie's children, Pierre's and Marie's shoes

8. A group of words used to express a single idea takes an apostrophe on the last word only, although many such phrasings can and should be avoided.

the mayor of Calgary's speech; the government of Canada's policy; her mother-in-law's car; Dodd, Mead's latest books

➤ For plurals of compound words, see **Plurals of nouns**, page 223.

9. In general, inanimate objects take an *of* phrase rather than an apostrophe.

the color of the coat, not **the coat's color**
the incidence of flu, not **the flu's incidence**

Note 1: But many idioms, particularly expressions of time and measure, take an apostrophe even though there is no actual ownership.

a stone's throw, the law's delay, a couple of dollars' worth

Note 2: To test whether an apostrophe is needed in such expressions as **two weeks(') pay** and **six months(') pregnant**, mentally substitute the singular and the correct answer will appear: **a week's pay, one month pregnant**.

10. Compound nouns with built-in apostrophes are generally singular.

arm's length, baker's dozen, confectioner's sugar, cow's milk, debtor's prison, farmer's market, fool's paradise, fuller's earth, printer's ink, traveller's cheques, writer's cramp

11. Most pronouns are written without an apostrophe.

hers, its, ours, yours, theirs, whose

But **anyone's guess, another's hopes, others' feelings, each other's view, nobody's fool, anyone else's house, no one else's**

Note: Beware the careless confusion of **its** and **it's** (it is), **theirs** and **there's** (there is), **your** and **you're** (you are), **whose** and **who's** (who is).

Punctuation

General

Punctuation brings order to writing. It helps make the message of a sentence immediately clear. But don't overdo it. A sentence littered with clauses set off by commas, dashes and semicolons can look like a word jungle and chase the reader away.

Apostrophe

1.   Use an apostrophe to denote possession.

Davis's car, the Davises' house, Marx's Capital, children's toys, the media's problem, Jesus' name

➤   See **Possessives**, page 226.

2.   Use an apostrophe to indicate the omission of letters or figures.

she'd, it's (for it is), couldn't, rock 'n' roll, fo'c's'le, Where E'er You Walk, "Give 'em hell!", the early '30s, the class of '80, "We'll 'elp 'im for 'is mother, an' 'e'll 'elp us by-an'-by." — *Rudyard Kipling*

Note: Contractions are acceptable, but avoid such forced contractions as it'd, should've, Tom'll go; use only readily recognized forms: **won't, shouldn't, he'd.**

3.   Use an apostrophe with verbs formed from capitals.

OK's, OK'ing, KO'd, MC'ing, X'd out

4.   Use an apostrophe in plurals of lowercase letters.

Mind your p's and q's. Dot your i's and cross your t's.

5.   In general, do not use an apostrophe with plurals of capital letters or numbers.

She graduated with straight As, the three Rs, the ABCs, two VIPs, a formation of F-18s, the Dirty '30s

Note 1: Use an apostrophe with plurals of capital letters if necessary to avoid ambiguity.

A's in math and physics are hard to come by.

Note 2: Whether to write a single letter as a capital or lowercase in a particular context depends somewhat on personal taste; logic favors **with a capital S** and **with a small s.**

6.   Do not use an apostrophe to form the plurals in expressions like **the whys and wherefores.**

Here are a few dos, don'ts and maybes. I don't want any ifs, ands or buts. Just give us straight yeses or noes.

Note: Use the apostrophe to form the plurals of words being discussed as words.

three as's, too many is's, not enough the's

7.   Do not use an apostrophe with shortened forms that have become accepted as complete words.

cello, copter, flu, gym, phone

Brackets   (parentheses)

1.   In general, try to use brackets sparingly, when other punctuation won't do the job.

Their biggest difficulties were the heat (temperatures were in the high 20s) and clouds of blackflies.

2.   Use brackets to insert fuller identification in proper names, direct quotation and such.

the Moose Jaw (Sask.) Times-Herald. Use commas when no proper name is involved: **the Moose Jaw, Sask., daily.** But prefer **the daily in Moose Jaw, Sask.,** or some such.

"When you ask how (Finance Minister Ellen) McFadden can survive, you are asking the wrong question."

3.   Use brackets to enclose a nickname within a name.

William (Bible Bill) Aberhart

➤ See **Names, nicknames, initials**, page 216.

4.   Use full brackets in numbering or lettering a series within a sentence.

The union pressed for (a) more pay, (b) a shorter work week and (c) better pensions.

➤ See **Period**, paragraph 6 note, below.

5.   Use brackets to enclose political affiliations.

Senator Iva Villman (PC—Man.)

6.   Use brackets to enclose equivalents and translations.

"We can expect two more inches (five centimetres) of rain." The measure now goes to the Bundestag (the lower house of parliament).

7.   If a punctuation mark applies to the whole sentence, put the mark after the closing bracket.

Words must be reputable (not socially frowned on). "I tell you this" (turning to the jury): "I am innocent."

8.   If a punctuation mark applies only to the words inside the parenthetical section, put the mark inside the closing bracket.

Most employees learned the new system quickly. (It helped to have supervisors on hand.)

"After I gave the alarm (by shouting 'Fire!'), I slid down the rope."

9.   In general, a parenthetical sentence takes a capital only if it is a direct quotation.

"We couldn't meet today (she had an appointment), but arranged to have lunch tomorrow."

His comment ("Wow, you're not exactly tall") had annoyed her.

Colon

1.   Use a colon, rather than a comma, to introduce a direct quotation longer than a short sentence.

Winston Churchill said in 1942: "This is not the end. It is not even the beginning of the end. But it is, perhaps, the end of the beginning."

2.   Use a colon in lines introducing lists, texts and tables.

VICTORIA (CP) — Highlights of the throne speech:
— The creation of 10,000 jobs . . .

3.   Use a colon to introduce an amplification, an example or a formal question or quotation. It takes the place of **for example, namely, that is**.

It was a mixed cargo: iron ore, wheat and coal. Various solutions were possible: sell the herd, try to renew the loan, take a partner.

4.   Generally do not capitalize the first letter of a sentence that follows a colon; but a capital may be used if emphasis is desirable.

Their learning is like bread in a besieged city: every man gets a little, but no man gets a full meal. — *Samuel Johnson*. This is the rule: Write in easy, conversational English. Verdict: Not guilty.

Note: Capitalize the first word of a quoted sentence: The prince cried: "Too late! Help came too late."

5.   Use a colon to mark a strong contrast.

Man proposes: God disposes. Eating isn't just a necessity: it's a pleasure.

6.   Use colons in question-and-answer formats and for interviews. Quotation marks are not used.

Q: When do you expect an agreement?
A: Before Christmas.

Tatje: Why are you a critic?
Papadakos: One must live.

7.   Use a colon to separate hours, minutes and seconds in clock and elapsed times, and periods before fractions of a second.

7:30 p.m.   a record time of 1:25:15.4

Note: Write 8 a.m., not 8:00 a.m.

8.   Use a colon after a formal salutation.

Madam Speaker: Gentlemen: Dear Mrs. Odisho:

Note: Informal salutations may take a comma.

Dear Jack, My dear Puran,

9.   Use a colon to indicate chapter and verse, act and scene and other citations.

A soft answer turneth away wrath. — *Proverbs 15:1*
There's daggers in men's smiles. — *Macbeth 2:3.147*

10. Use colons to separate titles and subtitles unless the author's or publisher's form differs.

The Chinese: Portrait of a People

11. Put colons outside closing quotation marks.

Paisley said of the charge of "bigot": "It's a lie."

She was referring to "the most serious of all charges": murder.

Comma

1. Put commas between the elements of a series but not before the final **and, or** or **nor** unless that avoids confusion.

men, women, children and pets

The major decided he must either attack at once, await fresh troops or withdraw.

Breakfast consisted of oatmeal, fried eggs, and bread and butter.

2. Use commas before clauses introduced by the conjunctions **and, but, for, or, nor** or **yet** if the subject changes.

We are all in the gutter, but some of us are looking at the stars. — *Oscar Wilde*

Note: The comma may be omitted when the clauses are short or the subject of both is the same.

The gun boomed and the race was on. The twins shouted and waved and finally managed to attract the driver's attention.

3. Use commas to set off an introductory clause or long phrase that precedes the main clause.

If God did not exist, it would be necessary to invent Him. — *Voltaire*

Note: Even if the introductory clause or phrase is short, a comma may be used for emphasis: **Even so, the vote was close.**

4. Put a comma after the main clause only if the clause that follows is parenthetical.

I'm selling you this gold brick because I like your face. The doctor bought a ticket, though she didn't expect to win.

5. Use commas to separate adjectives before a noun when the commas represent **and**.

a frank, open face; a vigorous, genial, popular man; well-meaning, enthusiastic, immature novices

6. Omit commas if the adjectives could not be separated by **and** and still make sense.

a cold marble floor; Tom's new 10-speed racing bike; her old brown winter coat; an aristocratic French family

Note 1: As another rule of thumb, if the order of the adjectives could not be changed (as in these examples), omit the commas.

Note 2: When in doubt, err on the side of too few commas.

7.   Do not put commas around an identifying word, phrase or clause if it is essential to the meaning of the sentence.

Margaret Atwood's novel Lady Oracle won.
But: One of Margaret Atwood's novels, Lady Oracle, won.

The Queen was accompanied by her son Prince Edward.
But: The Queen was accompanied by her youngest son, Prince Edward.

The girl who is singing is my daughter.
But: The girl, who was alone, got into the cab.

They drove to a village where they had seen bandits.
But: They drove to a village, where they bought bread.

8.   Use a comma to separate an introductory clause from a short, complete sentence in quotations.

The prime minister replied, "I have nothing to add to what I said in the House."

Note: Do not use a comma if a quotation is extremely short or is an integral part of the clause.

Stop saying "I told you so."

She heard a voice yelling "Baby needs new shoes!" and there was her husband shooting craps.

"A guy comes up to me and says 'Oh, yeah?' and I say 'Oh, yeah?' and slap his face."

9.   Use a comma to set off a paraphrased question or statement.

The question is, How can it be done? She said, No, she hadn't seen the boy.
But: She said no.

10. Use commas to set off parenthetical expressions, direct address and the like.

That's right, isn't it? Come into the garden, Maud.
Madam Speaker, I deny that.

Note: Commas are used with transition words like **besides, meanwhile, indeed, of course, too, in fact, as a result** and **consequently** if the sentence reads better with a pause.

11. Use a comma to separate words and numbers when confusion might otherwise result.

He who can, does. He who cannot, teaches. — *G.B. Shaw.* Ralph waxed the floor, and his sister dusted. All day, workers had been preparing the field. Some time before, the Plateans had surrendered. Instead of 20, 50 came.

12. When words readily understood are omitted for brevity, use commas to mark the omission, unless the sentence reads smoothly without them.

To Rolf he gave $5; to Mohammed, $2; to Darrin, nothing.
One child received $5, another $2 but the third nothing.
Let your yea be yea and your nay, nay.

13. Use commas to separate geographical elements.

The tour bus runs from Basel, Switzerland, to Milan, Italy, with frequent stops.

Note 1: Do not omit the second comma.

The runner left St. John's, Nfld. (comma) last week.

Note 2: Do not put a comma before of, indicating place.

Tom Stoddard (no comma) of Mission, B.C., was first.

Note 3: Avoid this clumsy construction: a Prince George, B.C., lawyer.

Prefer: A lawyer from (or in) Prince George, B.C.

14. Use commas to set off the year from the month plus day.

March 31, 1949, was the date that Newfoundland joined Confederation.

Note: Do not use commas when the day is not included.

January 1980 was mild in Victoria. Clark died at Easter 1835.

15. In general, use commas to set off thousands but not in years, street addresses or page, phone or serial numbers.

13,250 kilometres $1,450,250
the year 2000   1530 Rose St.   page 1235
(416) 364-0321   serial 76543

16. Use commas to set off a person's age, degrees, awards and affiliations.

Jean Tateyama, 48, Brandon, Man.; René Tremblay, PhD, faced Alex Dodd, VC, in the debate.

17. Do not use commas with **Sr.** or **Jr.**, or with numerals that can similarly be regarded as an integral part of a name.

Maurice Leblanc Sr. spoke first. Pope John XXIII was popular. Albatross II finally reached port.

18. Do not use commas with multi-unit dimensions, measures, weights or times.

two feet four inches by three feet 10 inches, 10 pounds 12 ounces, two hours 30 minutes 25 seconds

But: a four-foot-11, 90-pound youngster

19. Put commas inside closing quotation marks.

Barb said, "I don't want any," but the pedlar only smiled. The clue consisted of four words: "spinner," "blackbird," "watchman" and "maple." "It sounded like 'gorp,'" he said.

Note: Occasionally, such punctuation is not needed. More than 1,600 protesters chanting "We're anti-violent people" marched along Portage Avenue.

20. A comma follows a bracket if sentence structure requires it.

The speech was long, hard to hear (people were coughing), uninspired and uninspiring.

21. Use a comma or a dash but not both.

Not: Wilfred was, — like all the Clutterbucks, — a man of striking personal charm.

Dash

1.   The dash is an effective tool but can easily be overused. Many times it can be avoided by breaking a long sentence into two shorter ones.

2.   Use dashes to set off mid-sentence lists punctuated by commas.

The ministers will discuss common problems — trade, tourism, immigration and defence — before going to the summit talks.

3.   Use dashes when commas (generally preferable) would create confusion.

The pies — meat and fruit — were cheap.

4.   Use a dash in placelines after the service logo.

   HALIFAX (CP) — An oil . . .

5.   Use a tight boldface dash to introduce sections of a list.

   OTTAWA (CP) — Highlights of the federal budget Tuesday:
      —About 12,500 homeowners are expected to qualify for mortgage assistance.
      —Employee benefits . . .

6.   Use a tight dash for the minus sign in temperatures and with bracketed political affiliations.

—10 degrees, Joan Singh (PC—Man.)

7.   Use a dash to mark a sharp break in a word or sentence.

"I've been laughed at, ignored — but I'm boring you."

Note 1: When a sentence breaks off, no period is used after the dash.

"Really, Madam Speaker, I must —"
"Order!" the Speaker shouted.

Note 2: When a quotation simply trails away, use three spaced periods.

"Maybe if I had tried harder . . . "

8.   Use dashes to mark off interpolations.

"Besides" — he tapped me on the knee — "you're wrong."

9.   Use a dash to introduce a phrase or clause that summarizes, emphasizes or contrasts what has gone before.

Quiet, respectful, deferential, even obsequious — those were Mulliner's chief characteristics.

Our army is composed of the scum of the earth — the mere scum of the earth. — *Duke of Wellington*

The English country gentleman galloping after a fox — the unspeakable in full pursuit of the uneatable. — *Oscar Wilde*

10. Use a dash to attribute a quotation.

Pedantry is a misplaced attention to trifles which then prides itself on its poor judgment. — *Jacques Barzun*

11. Do not use dashes with colons, semicolons and commas.

12. Write dashes with spaces before and after but not with agate sports summaries and the exceptions noted above.

Ellipsis (. . .)

1.   Use three spaced periods to indicate an omission from a text or quotation.

The decision . . . rests solely with your elected representatives, not with pollsters or the news media.

Note: Put spaces before, between and after the periods. On news circuits, use a *thin space* between the periods so typesetting computers don't split them on two lines.

2.   In condensing a text, use an ellipsis at the beginning, inside or at the end of a sentence.

The decision . . . rests solely with your elected representatives. . . .

. . . But the government won't ignore thoughtful suggestions, no matter what their origin.

3.   In news stories, use an ellipsis only inside a sentence, not at the beginning or end.

"The decision . . . rests solely with your elected representatives," the prime minister said.

After a reference to comments of delegates, he added, "But the government won't ignore thoughtful suggestions."

➤ But see **Dash, No. 7**, above for one exception.

4.   When condensing texts, put other required punctuation before the ellipsis. Thus four periods end a sentence.

But the government won't ignore thoughtful suggestions. . . .

Similarly: **What is the answer?** . . . **We must strive harder,** . . . **produce more,** . . . **lower our expectations.** . . .

Note: Guard against distortion that might result from putting together statements that were not together in the original. The solution may be to interrupt the sequence by starting a new paragraph or renewing the attribution.

5.   Ellipses may be used to separate entries in the *Notes* section at the bottom of sports game copy.

Jays Notes — The roof at SkyDome was open to start the game but was closed during the third inning with rain threatening. . . . Pitcher Ken Dayley, sent to Florida on a 30-day rehabilitation stint after overcoming a problem with dizziness, returned Thursday with a sore left forearm. . . . Roberto Alomar extended his consecutive-game hit streak to eight with a seventh-inning single.

Exclamation mark

1.   Do not overuse this strong mark of punctuation. Use it to denote great surprise, a command, deep emotion, emphasis and sarcasm.

We won!   "Take aim! Fire!"   Ouch!   Never!   Oh, sure!

Note: If a one-word exclamation rates heavy emphasis, put it in a separate sentence; otherwise treat it as part of another sentence.

"Oh! She almost fell." "Oh! you frightened me!" or "Oh, you frightened me!"

2. Use an exclamation mark with questions that are exclamatory in form.

"You mean we won!"

"How could she do that to him!"

3. Do not use an exclamation mark to end a mildly exclamatory sentence.

Hurry along, please. Have your tickets ready.

4. Do not use a comma or period after an exclamation mark.

"Fire! Fire!" the janitor shouted.

Someone cried "She's drowning!"

5. Put an exclamation mark inside quotation marks when it is part of the quoted material, outside when it is not.

"That's a lie!" a backbencher shouted.

Imagine calling a cabinet minister a "liar"!

Hyphen

1. Compound words may be written solid (**sweatshirt**), open (**oil rig**) or hyphenated (**white-haired**).

➤ See **Compounds**, page 202.

2. Write words as compounds to ease reading, to avoid ambiguity and to join words that when used together form a separate concept.

a once-in-a-lifetime chance, a hit-and-run driver, a big-car lover, a used-car dealer, a small-business tax, an extra-high collar, light-year, first-fruits, man-hour, blackbird, streetcar, airbrush

3. In general, hyphenate compound modifiers preceding a noun, but not if the meaning is instantly clear because of common usage of the term.

the third-period goal, three-under-par 69, a 5-4 vote, multimillion-dollar projects, 40-cent coffee

But the acid rain threat, the United States dollar, a savings bank deposit, a sales tax increase, the task force landing

4. Adverbs ending in -ly are not followed by a hyphen. The -ly alerts readers that the word that follows is modified: a brightly lit room, an eagerly awaited speech.

5. Hyphens are seldom needed with proper nouns (a United Kingdom custom), established foreign terms (a 10 per cent drop) or established compound nouns (a high school principal).

6.   Certain word combinations are often hyphenated even when standing alone.

noun plus adjective (**fire-resistant, fancy-free**), noun plus participle (**blood-stained, thought-provoking**), adjective plus participle (**sweet-smelling, hard-earned**), adjective plus noun plus *-ed* (**open-handed, red-faced**)

7.   Use a hyphen to indicate joint titles and to join conflicting or repetitive elements.

secretary-treasurer, writer-editor, musician-painter, comedy-tragedy, drip-drop, walkie-talkie

8.   Hyphenate most well-known compounds of three or more words.

happy-go-lucky, good-for-nothing, Johnny-come-lately, forget-me-not, mother-in-law, a two-year-old

But **coat of arms, next of kin, no man's land**

9.   Use a hyphen with certain compounds containing an apostrophe.

bull's-eye, mare's-nest, cat's-paw

10. Use a hyphen to avoid doubling a vowel, tripling a consonant or duplicating a prefix.

co-operate, re-emerge, anti-intellectual, doll-like, brass-smith, re-redesign, sub-subcommittee

But **readjust, reaffirm, reinstate, reopen**, etc.

11. Use a hyphen to join prefixes to proper names.

anti-Trudeau, pro-Communist, French-Canadian

But **transatlantic, transpacific**

12. Use a hyphen to join an initial capital with a word.

T-shirt, V-necked, X-ray, S-bend, H-bomb

13. Use a hyphen with fractions standing alone and with the written numbers 21 to 99.

two-thirds, three-quarters, fifty-five, ninety-nine

Note: Omit the hyphen between numerator and denominator when one or the other already contains a hyphen.

one twenty-fifth, three ten-thousandths

14. Use hyphens with a successive compound adjective (note spacing).

18th- and 19th-century fashions; 10-, 20- and 30-second intervals

15. Use a hyphen in aircraft identification and such, between the symbols for make or type and model number, but not after the number.

DC-10, DC-8L, MiG-25

But **Boeing 767**

16. Use a hyphen to connect dates except when preceded by **from** or **between.**

the 1982-83 tax year, from January to May (not **from January-May**), **between 1970 and 1976** (not **between 1970-76**)

17. Use a hyphen to differentiate between words of different meanings but the same or similar spellings.

correspondent (letter writer), **co-respondent** (in divorce); **resign** (quit), **re-sign** (sign again); **recover** (regain health), **re-cover** (cover again); **recreate** (entertain), **re-create** (create again)

18. Use a hyphen to avoid awkward combinations of letters.

cave-in, not **cavein; co-star,** not **costar; de-ice,** not **deice; non-native,** not **nonnative; re-ink,** not **reink; set-to,** not **setto; sit-in,** not **sitin**

Parentheses ➤ See **Brackets**

Period

1. Use a period to end a declarative or a mildly imperative sentence.

The wind blew and the ground began to dry. Give me the book. Let them have their say.

Note: For greater emphasis, use an exclamation mark, advisedly.

"Stick 'em up!"

2. Use a period to end an indirect question, a request phrased as a question, or a rhetorical question.

The reporter asked how many were killed. Would someone answer my question. What do I care.

3. Use a period with decimals, including decimal currencies.

3.25 $9.50

4. Use a period after certain abbreviations.

➤ See **Abbreviations and acronyms**, page 170.

5. Put periods inside quotation marks.

The writer said, "This is the end." Her brother said, "I don't know why she said 'This is the end.'"

6. Omit periods after headings, figures, roman numerals, single letters (except initials) and scientific and metric symbols.

POPE, UNIONIST MEET; $52; Chapter 2; Albatross II; E flat; Au (for gold); 15 cm; 20 C

Note: But use periods, as an alternative to brackets, after a letter or number denoting a series.

To improve readability: 1. Don't be too formal. 2. Organize before you start to write. 3. Be active, positive, concrete.

7. Omit periods after letters used as names without specific designation.

Suppose A takes B to court for damages.

➤ For the use of periods to indicate omission, see **Ellipsis** above.

Question mark

1. Use a question mark after a direct question, but not after an indirect one.

What day is this? The nurse asked what he wanted.

Note: When a question occurs within a question, both ending at the same time, use only one question mark.

Who asked "Why?"

2. Use question marks to express more than one query in the same sentence.

Reporters must ask themselves, How does it look? sound? feel? taste? smell?

Note: If a question is not complete until the end of the sentence, use a question mark there.

Do you want coffee, tea or milk?

3. Use a question mark to express doubt or uncertainty.

The dates of the English dramatist John Heywood are given as 1497(?)-1580(?).

4. Do not use a question mark if the person addressed is expected to act rather than answer.

Would you mind spelling the second name.

5. Question marks go inside or outside quotation marks, depending on meaning.

The Speaker asked, "What was the question?" Did the prime minister say "fuddle-duddle"? He asked, "Did the prime minister say 'fuddle-duddle'?"

6. A question mark supersedes the comma or period that usually ends a quotation.

"Who goes there?" the sentry shouted.

Quotation marks

1. Use quotation marks to enclose direct quotations.

The lawyer said, "I don't think the police should be paying suspects for information."

2. Use quotation marks to begin and end each part of an interrupted quotation.

"We can't hear you," the girl said. "The radio is on."

Note: Capitalize the first word of the second part of an interrupted quotation only if the second part begins a new sentence.

3. Alternate double and single marks in quotes within quotes.

"I heard her say, 'I only hit him when he sneered and said "Never."'"

4. Capitalize the first word of any mid-sentence quote that constitutes a sentence.

The woman said, "He sneered and said 'Never.'"

This has the same effect as the brush-off used in theatrical circles of "Don't call us. We'll call you."

The trainmaster gave the order to "Get the hell out!"

5. Put each speaker's words in a separate paragraph to make it immediately clear that the speaker has changed.

Vilmik laughed. "Who gave him the quarter?"

"Not me," said his wife. "I'm broke."

"I know," said Vilmik. "Let's ask your mother."

6. When a quote by a single speaker extends more than one paragraph, put quotation marks at the beginning of each paragraph but at the end of only the last.

"As I said earlier, my father was always reasonable about things like that.
"But when it came to money, he could be totally unreasonable. An out-and-out miser.
"Still, on the whole, he was fair-minded."

7. Provide the speaker's identity quickly if a quotation is unusually long. It should either precede the quotation, follow the first sentence (or the second if it is short and closely linked to the first), or be interpolated.

"This is the best time to call an election," Lumie said. "There is a tremendous momentum going to us. Waiting can only cost us votes. It's now or never."

"We've lost. We've lost," wailed another bystander. "The British have won. Our army has been lying to us."

"The Puritan hated bear-baiting," Macaulay adds, "not because it gave pain to the bear, but because it gave pleasure to the spectators."

8. Use quotation marks to set off a pungent or significant word or phrase but not around routine words or phrases.

His first ship was an old "rustbucket."

Not: The minister replied that the economy is "improving."

Note: Fragmented quotes are justifiable only when the words are controversial, add color or give the flavor of an event or the style of a speaker.

9. Use quotation marks around unfamiliar terms on first reference.

The fluid was named "protoplasm" by a Czechoslovak.

10. Put quotation marks around words used ironically.

The "friendly" soccer game ended with two players booked.

11. In partial quotes, do not put quotation marks around words the speaker could not have used.

Not: Ali boasted "he was rarin' to go."

12. Do not use quotation marks to enclose slang, colloquialisms or specialized words. Use such words only when the context is right; in an interview with a pop musician, for example, it would be proper to write **groove, rap** and **gig** in senses that make the meaning clear.

13. Do not use quotation marks to enclose titles of compositions.

➤ See **Capitalization**, sections **Compositions**, page 179, **Music**, page 188, **Quotations**, page 193.

14. Do not use quotation marks to enclose slogans and headlines.

The pickets carried signs that read Cut Taxes, Not Jobs and Cut Government Spending. The article was headed Drug Squad Flouts Gun Rules.

15. Do not use quotation marks in question-and-answer formats.

Q: Do you recognize this man?
A: Yes.

16. Do not use quotation marks on texts or editorial excerpts in symposiums.

OTTAWA (CP) — Text of Gov. Gen. Rhoda Mann's New Year's message:
The mood at the dawn of a new year . . .

St. John's (Nfld.) Telegram: The real needs of Canadians . . .

Note: In editorial symposiums, the name of the paper is in boldface, followed by a colon, not a dash.

17. Periods and commas always go inside closing quote marks; colons and semicolons outside. The question mark and exclamation mark go inside the quote marks when they apply to the quoted matter only; outside when they apply to the entire sentence.

18. When a sentence ends with single and double quotation marks, separate them by a thin space.

Semicolon

1. Use the semicolon sparingly. Overused, it gives writing an old-fashioned, musty flavor.

2. Use a semicolon to separate statements too closely related to stand as separate sentences.

"I never read a book before reviewing it; it prejudices a man so." — *Sidney Smith*

3. Use a semicolon to separate phrases that contain commas.

Best actor, Robert De Niro, Raging Bull; best actress, Sissy Spacek, Coal Miner's Daughter; best film, Ordinary People.

4. Use a semicolon to precede explanatory phrases introduced by **for example, namely, that is** and the like when a comma seems too weak.

Some pleasures cost next to nothing; for example, reading.

5. Semicolons go outside quotation marks.

Police finally cornered the "bear"; it was a poodle.

Singular or plural?

1. In general, a subject singular in form takes a singular verb; a subject plural in form takes a plural verb.

An outbreak of bombing and shelling was heard. On each side of the road were drifts of trilliums.

2. Collective nouns (groups of people and things) take a singular verb unless the individuals are to be emphasized.

The audience was silent. The audience were stamping their feet. Her family is sending money. Her family are all ill.

3. When two parts of a compound subject are separated by **with, together with, including, besides, no less than, in addition to, plus, as well as** or **likewise**, the verb agrees with the first part.

The ship with all its crew was lost. Gray as well as his wife and son was in the car. The meat plus packaging weighs about a kilogram.

4. **All, a lot, any, half, majority, more, most, per cent, remainder, rest** and **some** take either a singular or plural verb depending on whether the noun is singular or plural.

Is all the money accounted for? All the cars are new. The government's majority makes it safe from defeat. A majority of Canadians favor wage control.

5. **Anybody, anyone, another, anything, each, either, every, everybody, everyone, many a, neither, no one, nobody, somebody** and **someone** take a singular verb.

Everyone wants his money back. No one knows the future. Neither of the teams stands a chance. Each of the three students comes from a different country.

6. When a sentence contains **not only . . . but also, either . . . or** or **neither . . . nor**, the verb agrees with the nearer subject.

Either the sergeant or the troops are out of step. Either the troops or the sergeant is out of step. Not only the children but also the babysitter was asleep.

7. **None** takes a plural verb when it stands for *not any;* it takes a singular verb when it is followed by a singular noun or when the idea of *not one* is to be emphasized.

None of the passengers were Canadian. None of the furniture was dusted. Ten climbers have tried but none (preferably not one) has succeeded.

8. In general, **acoustics, economics, gymnastics, politics, mathematics** and other words ending in *-ics* are singular when they are referred to as a science or course of study and plural when referred to as a practical activity or a quality.

The acoustics are bad. Acoustics is on the curriculum. Her politics are left wing. Politics is a dirty business. My mathematics are weak. Mathematics, rightly viewed, possesses not only truth, but also supreme beauty. — *Bertrand Russell*

Note: When in doubt, use the singular.

9. When **number, total** and **variety** are preceded by *the*, they take a singular verb. Preceded by *a*, they take a plural verb.

The number of unemployed rises monthly. A number of unemployed have found jobs. The total stolen has topped $1 million. A total of 21 people were involved.

10. When **couple** is used in the sense of two persons, it almost always takes a plural verb and plural pronouns.

The couple were hurt when their car crashed.

Note: Couple in this sense is singular on the rare occasion when it is treated as a unit.

A couple pays $5 a ticket.

11. A numerical statement may be singular or plural depending on whether the number is thought of as a unit or as a collection of items.

Three weeks is a long time. Six feet of earth is enough for any man. There was two minutes left in the game. Two days of spring make winter seem almost worth while.

12. Subjects plural in form but singular in effect take a singular verb.

Great Expectations has been made into a movie. Jarndyce and Jarndyce is literature's most famous lawsuit.

13. When two subjects form one idea, the verb is singular.

Bread and butter is included. The tumult and the shouting dies. — *Rudyard Kipling*

14. **Data** and **media** are plural. Treat **agenda** as singular.

The media were blamed. The data support this theory. The agenda was short.

Note: Data is sometimes treated as a collective noun: **This is vital data,** a use disliked by conservative writers, who prefer **These are vital data.**

15. When a sentence begins with an introductory **there**, the number of the verb is determined by the delayed subject.

There is much to be seen. There are many beautiful sights.

16. **One of those** takes a plural verb when the phrase introduces a clause.

The clerk is one of those people who are always right. It must be one of the longest sentences that have ever been written.

Note: To confirm that the verb must be plural, reverse the sentence: **Of the longest sentences that have (not has) ever been written, it must be one.**

Spelling

1. CP's authority for spelling is the *Concise Oxford Dictionary,* with exceptions listed in *(CP) Caps and Spelling.*

2. Where Oxford gives alternative spellings — **amok/amuck, judgement/judgment** — CP style is the first, unless shown otherwise in *Caps and Spelling:* **judgment.**

3. CP's main departure from Oxford is in spelling words ending in *-our/-or:* **colour/color, labour/labor, valour/valor.** CP uses the *-or* ending, the form favored by Henry Fowler in *Modern English Usage.*

4. When the spelling of the common-noun element of a proper name differs from CP style — **Canadian Labour Congress, Lincoln Center, U.S. Defense Department, Travelers Canada, Harbour Castle Hilton Hotel** — CP style prevails: **Canadian Labor Congress, Lincoln Centre, U.S. Defence Department, Travellers Canada, Harbor Castle Hilton Hotel.** The exception is geographical names: **Honey Harbour, Ont.,** not **Honey Harbor, Ont.**

5. Unless Oxford shows otherwise, the plural of a noun is formed normally, by adding *-s* or *-es:* **shaman/shamans, box/boxes.** If the plural is irregular, it is given in parentheses: **man (men).** Where there is a choice — **mango (-es** or **-s), virtuoso (-i** or **-os)** — CP uses the first spelling: **mangoes,** except when *Caps and Spelling* says otherwise: **virtuosos.**

6. When a verb has two forms for the past tense — **kneeled/knelt, leaped/leapt** — CP uses either one without preference.

7. CP prefers the *sh-* spelling for Yiddish words: **shlemiel, shlock, shmatte.** This is a departure from Oxford's *sch-.*

8. Some troublesome spellings:

abscess	dilemma	instalment	privilege
accommodate	diphtheria	iridescent	propeller
allotted	disappoint	jodhpurs	questionnaire
anoint	drunkenness	judgment	rarefy
battalion	ecstasy	khaki	reconnaissance
benefited	embarrass	lavender	restaurateur
buoy	gauge	liaison	resuscitate
caffeine	guttural	liquefy	rhythm
carburetor	harass	mayonnaise	sacrilegious
cemetery	hemorrhage	mileage	shepherd
cirrhosis	hygiene	millennium	siege
compatible	hypocrisy	moccasin	supersede
confectionery	idiosyncrasy	occurrence	tendinitis
connoisseur	impostor	paralleled	weird
consensus	impresario	paraphernalia	wiener
deductible	infallible	pavilion	
delicatessen	innocuous	perseverance	
deterrent	inoculate	prerogative	

➤ See **Plurals of nouns,** page 222; see also *(CP) Caps and Spelling.*

Aircraft, ships, guns

Style for names

1. For the names of aircraft, guns, tanks, rockets, satellites and the like, use a hyphen when a figure follows a letter.

a DC-10 jetliner, a CF-18 fighter, an M-16 rifle, an M-60 tank, a Russian SSN-8 rocket

2. Do not use a hyphen when a letter follows a figure.

an FA-18A fighter, a 727-100C cargo plane, the JT-15D fan-jet engine

3. Do not put a hyphen between a spelled-out name and a number.

a Dash 8-300, an F-4 Phantom 2 fighter, a Leopard 2 tank, a Polaris A-3 rocket, a Cosmos 650 satellite

4. Form plurals by adding *s* without an apostrophe.

two Dash 7s, a shipment of AK-47s, 15 M-60s

Aircraft

1. Refer to an aircraft with or without the name of the maker or designer.

Lockheed L-1011 TriStar, Lockheed L-1011, L-1011, TriStar

2. North American military aircraft carry a prefixed letter to indicate the basic function: *A* for *attack*, *B* for *bomber*, *C* for *cargo* or transport, *F* for *fighter*, *H* for *helicopter*, *S* for *anti-submarine*, *T* for *trainer*.

Note: Do not confuse the prefix *C* for *Canadian* (**a CF-18 fighter**) with the *C* for *cargo* (**a CC-130 Hercules**).

3. Russian aircraft carry a prefix that is an abbreviation of the maker's or designer's name: *Il* for *Ilyushin*, *M* for *Myasishchev*, *MiG* for *Mikoyan and Gurevich*, *Su* for *Sukhoi*, *Tu* for *Tupolev*, *Yak* for *Yakovlev*.

4. The NATO name for a Russian plane may be used or omitted as desired.

Tu-144 Charger, MiG-25 Foxbat, M-4 Bison, Il-76 Candid

5. A jumbo jet is any very large jet aircraft, such as a *DC-10, Boeing 747, L-1011* or *C-5A*.

Ships

1. The terms **ship** and **boat** are less than precise. A good general rule is to use **boat** for smaller inshore or lake craft, **ship** for larger ocean-going craft. **Vessel** is a handy catch-all for anything bigger than a rowboat. Deepsea freighters, tankers, bulk carriers, container ships, ocean-going passenger liners and most naval ships should never be called boats. (Naval exceptions: motor torpedo boats and submarines.)

2. Words to describe boats and ships vary from region to region. **Laker** is a common term for Great Lakes vessels but may be unfamiliar to readers in some areas of the country. **Fish boat** is an everyday term on the West Coast but unheard of on the East Coast, where such craft are called **fishing boats**.

3. Avoid *nauticalese* that is indecipherable to the average reader — or be prepared to translate it: **fo'c's'le** (forward part of a ship where crew live); **bottom** (a freighter or tanker); **hawser** (cable or heavy rope used to secure a ship to a wharf); **dead-reckoning** (fixing a ship's position by instruments when observation of stars is not possible); **"She's going down by the head."** (A ship is sinking bow-first.)

4. For numbers in ships' names, use the vessel's own style: **Queen Elizabeth 2, Bluenose II**.

5. The familiar abbreviations **HMCS, USS** or **HMS** may be used before the name of a military ship: **HMCS Terra Nova, USS Coral Sea**, etc.

Note: Do not put *the* in front of HMCS or HMS for reasons that are obvious when the abbreviation is written out: *(the)* **Her Majesty's Canadian Ship Halifax**, etc. Naval tradition also drops *the* on second reference to military ships: **The damaged tanker was escorted by Terra Nova into port at Vancouver.** But use the article *the* before names of non-military ships: **The Titanic sank off Cape Race, Nfld.**

6. Avoid or spell out less familiar, cumbersome or archaic abbreviations: **MV** (for motor vessel) **Lollipop**; **CCGS** (for Canadian Coast Guard Ship) **Louis S. St. Laurent**; **RMS** (for Royal Mail Ship) **Titanic**, etc.

7. Avoid terms like **seamen** and **fishermen** unless the sex is important and known to be male. **Crew members** and **crew** are always serviceable.

8. Ships have been referred to in the feminine form — **she** and **her** — for generations and the practice shows no sign of waning. Use either **she** or **it** but be consistent in the same story. Beware of chatty nautical language (**she's temperamental**) that can appear blatantly sexist in print.

9. Ships' tonnage is measured and expressed in several ways, all of them complex and rarely in need of explanation in news stories. If tonnage must be noted, use the **gross register tonnage** as listed in large boldface type in column No. 3 of each ship's entry in *Lloyd's Register of Shipping*. Never write that a ship **weighs** such-and-such. The tonnage figures relate to the capacity of a ship, which means little to the non-nautical reader. Better to check Lloyd's for such dimensions as length and try to express these in everyday terms to provide a sense of size: **The tanker is about as long as 40 typical transit buses parked bumper to bumper.**

10. A ship's country and port of registration may have nothing to do with the vessel's ownership or the nationality of its crew. Many ships sail under what is known as a **flag of convenience**, meaning they are registered in countries with lower registry charges and wage rates than the owners would pay in their home countries. Hence, a ship identified as **Panamanian-registered** may in fact be owned in a country halfway around the world from Panama. Check Lloyd's for the name and nationality of the ship's owners. Shipping agents may be able to help with such details as the nationality of the crew, the nature of the cargo, last port of call, etc.

11. Some marine measures:

nautical mile   1.853 kilometres (6,080 feet)
knot   one nautical mile an hour
fathom   six feet (slightly under two metres)

Guns

1. A **rifle** has a grooved bore and fires bullets from cartridges. A **shotgun** has a smooth bore, may be double-barrelled and fires shot from shells. A **pistol** may be a revolver, which holds cartridges in a revolving cylinder, or an automatic, which holds cartridges in a magazine. A **cartridge** is a case consisting of an explosive charge and a bullet or shot. Shotgun **shells** are filled with powder and shot made of lead or steel.

2. When reporting crime stories, avoid the casual use of the term **hunting rifle**, which wildlife and hunting organizations argue is accurate only when used in context with a hunter legally pursuing game. Try to get a precise description of weapons from police and other authorities.

3. Rifles, pistols, revolvers and other small arms are usually described in **calibre**, which is a measurement of the diameter of the inside of the barrel and is expressed in decimal fractions of an inch or in metric. The word calibre is not used in metric measurements. Write a **.22-calibre rifle, a 9-mm pistol**.

4. More precise description of calibre is expressed by an added set of figures (after a hyphen) to designate load, speed of bullet or year of adoption: **.30-30, .250-3000, .30-06**. Often such precision is necessary to differentiate among .30-calibre guns.

5. Shotguns are measured in **gauge**. Gauge refers to the number of balls, with a diameter the size of the inside of the barrel, that can be made from a pound of lead. For a shotgun with a barrel 0.729 inches in diameter, for instance, a pound of lead yields 12 balls, so the gun is called a **12 gauge**. The .410 is a calibre but is commonly called a gauge. Other gauges have no decimal point.

6. **Gun** is an acceptable term for any firearm; it may also be used to describe larger weapons, such as artillery pieces.

7. Large naval and artillery guns fire **shells**; mortars fire **bombs**. A **round** is one shot, whether from a handgun, a rifle or a cannon.

8.   The **magazine** of a firearm simply refers to the reservoir or device holding extra rounds of ammunition to be fed into the chamber through spring, bolt or some other action. The magazine can take various forms, such as the **rotary** (as found on the Thompson machine-gun or **tommy-gun**), **tubular** (in some bolt action, semi-automatic, lever and pump-action rifles), **belt** (which feeds ammunition into rapid-fire automatic weapons) or **box** (either a fixed or detachable compartment).

The term **clip** describes a detachable magazine used with bolt-action, semi-automatic and automatic rifles, as well as some shotguns and handguns (usually semi-automatic or fully automatic) holding a varying number of cartridges, from two up. Note that a magazine is not always a clip.

➤   See **Military**, page 260.

Metric

General

Metric, eh?

It was a typical Canadian compromise: the country would join most of the rest of the world in using metric measurements — but gradually.

That was in the 1970s. Since then Canadians of all ages have become accustomed to charting winter freezes in Celsius, family drives in kilometres and milk in litres.

But it will be a long time before Canada looks as metric as Europe. Old habits die hard, especially among Canadians educated in the imperial system. Then there is the daily bombardment of feet and Fahrenheit, pounds and miles-an-hour from the United States.

In Canada, the media have largely adopted metric, with a dwindling number of exceptions.

CP's position from the beginning has been: **Metric, yes,** but even more important, **Be clear**. Specific descriptions are often needed, but comparative examples from everyday life can be even more helpful: **big as a truck, small as a thimble, knee-deep snow** and the like.

When metric?

1. In general, report measurements in metric. Among the lingering exceptions are cases where some other measurement remains conventional — personal weights and heights, sections of land on the Prairies, precious metals in troy ounces, two-by-fours, quarter-inch screws and the like.

2. The number of exceptions is limited. Many farmers in Canada may still think in acres and grocery shoppers in pounds, but CP uses metric when figures are needed and descriptions when they're not (**a dusty patch of Saskatchewan grain field, a bag full of turnips**).

3. Metric measurements are not put into the mouths of those who speak in the inch-pound system, either in direct quotes or in indirect speech. Rephrasing can be used to limit such occasions.

4. In most other cases when imperial must be used, it should be accompanied by a metric equivalent. For example, Canada's 200-nautical-mile (**370-kilometre**) fishing limit, or the number of litres in a 35-gallon barrel of oil (**about 159**).

5. But when repeated use of bracketed equivalents may slow down or annoy the reader, consider a separate line or paragraph giving the metric equivalent. Thereafter let the specialists speak in their own tongue.

6.   Speed and distances are expressed in metric, including very great distances such as the number of kilometres between planets in the solar system. Certain astronomical distances, such as those between stars or galaxies, are often measured in light-years — the distance light travels in one year moving at almost 300,000 kilometres a second, or about 9.46 trillion kilometres.

7.   The altitude of airplanes and the height of mountains are expressed in metres, not feet, and distances at sea are expressed in kilometres, not miles or nautical miles. Measure speeds in kilometres an hour, not knots.

8.   The size of animals is expressed in kilograms and metres (centimetres and the like for extremely small animals). Meat on the store shelf is in kilograms.

Let logic be your guide

1.   In handling material from U.S. sources, it is usually possible to make a straight conversion from imperial. **The plane crashed about 90 metres from a home for the elderly.** (The source material reads **100 yards**.)

2.   But tend to use round figures. Most of the world uses metric and material routed through the United States from abroad has possibly gone through one conversion already.

3.   In converting to metric, do not use figures that imply greater accuracy than justified by the original data. For instance, using 2.54 centimetres to the inch, convert 35 inches to 89 or even 90 centimetres, not 88.9.

4.   Don't leave the impression people spoke in metric when they did not, even in indirect quotations. A bracketed equivalent may be necessary. Example: **The survivors said they rowed more than five miles (eight kilometres) to safety.**

5.   Don't needlessly mix imperial and metric in comparisons in the same sentence. Make it **the 60-pound boy was attacked by a dog almost twice his weight.** Save the exact weight of the dog (50 kilograms in this case) for another sentence.

6.   And, of course, it's axiomatic that a writer doesn't meddle with the idiomatic: **The crowd inched forward.**

Sports

1.   Most Olympic and many non-Olympic sports are contested and reported in metric. But others, such as golf, horse racing and North American football, continue to use imperial.

2.   Where figures are appropriate in descriptions of imperial-measure sports, CP increasingly uses metric: **a 10-metre slapshot, a 120-metre homer to left field.** And use of imperial is kept to essentials in stories and results. Often a descriptive phrase will do instead: **won by three car lengths.**

3.   Different types of motor racing use different measures. Grand Prix racing is in metric, but motorcycle, U.S. stock car and Indy-type racing are in imperial.

4.   A race for 12-metre yachts should be described as such. But include an explanatory note that the vessels themselves are about 20 metres long and that the classification of 12 metres is determined through a complicated formula involving length, sail area and displacement.

➤ For details, see **Sports**, page 86.

Odds and ends

1.   The names of metric units are usually spelled out: **a 20-kilogram sack**, not **a 20-kg sack**; **covering 50 hectares**, not **covering 50 ha**; **ran 10 kilometres**, not **ran 10 km**.

2.   There are no abbreviations in metric, only symbols. These symbols take periods only at the end of a sentence, never take *s* in the plural and are separated from a number by a space. In adjectival uses, the space is replaced by a hyphen.

3.   *C* (for Celsius) is now well enough understood to be used on first reference. Other common symbols such as **km-h** and **mm** may be used on second reference when preceded by a number: **at 70 km-h, a 105-mm cannon**.

4.   A number less than one has a zero before the decimal: **0.25 ha**, not **.25 ha**; but prefer **a quarter hectare** and the like when common fractions are involved.

5.   Treat the names of metric units as singular when the number preceding them is less than one: **0.25 litre** but **2.5 litres**.

6.   For temperatures less than 0 C do not write **below zero**; use a minus sign as in **−5 C**. The minus sign is a dash preceding a number with no space between.

7.   The clipped form **kilo** is not acceptable for **kilogram** or **kilometre** since kilo simply means a thousand and is not a specific unit.

8.   The preferred metric symbol for kilometres an hour is **km/h**, but the slash is not available on many keyboards and **km-h** is used. Similarly, superior numbers are not available for the preferred symbols for square metres (m^2), cubic centimetres (cm^3) and such. Instead write **sq. me, cu. cm**, etc. The symbol for degree (°) is unavailable; for **15°C** write **15 C**, or **15 degrees C**.

9.   Symbols may be used in tabular matter and certain sports and financial routine.

10. Metric units named after people have capitalized symbols (**A** for Andrew Marie Ampere, **C** for Anders Celsius, **Pa** for Blaise Pascal and **W** for James Watt); but when the name of a unit is written in full, only Celsius is capitalized. Otherwise write ampere, pascal, watt, etc. Litre is not named after a person, but its symbol is L to avoid confusion with the figure 1.

11. A few symbols for metric prefixes are capped, including **M** for **mega** (one million) and **G** for **giga** (one billion); for example, **MPa** (megapascal), **GJ** (gigajoule). But avoid prefixes denoting extremely large multiples and such small fractions as **pico** (one-trillionth), **nano** (one-billionth), **micro** (one-millionth).

Metric conversion table

Into Metric

If you know	multiply by	to get
Length		
inches	25.4	millimetres
inches	2.54	centimetres
inches	.0254	metres
feet	0.3	metres
yards	0.91	metres
miles	1.61	kilometres
Area		
sq. inches	6.45	sq. centimetres
sq. feet	0.09	sq. metres
sq. yards	0.84	sq. metres
sq. miles	2.59	sq. kilometres
acres	0.4	hectares
Mass (weight)		
ounces	28.35	grams
pounds	0.45	kilograms
tons (short)	0.907	tonnes/metric tons
Volume		
Imp. — not U.S.		
fluid ounces	28.41	millilitres (cu. cm)
pints	0.57	litres
quarts	1.13	litres
gallons	4.54	litres
cubic inches	16.39	cubic centimetres
cubic feet	0.03	cubic metres
cubic yards	0.76	cubic metres
Temperature		
Fahrenheit	Subtract 32, then multiply by 5/9ths	Celsius
Temperature variations		
Fahrenheit	.555	Celsius

Out of Metric

If you know	multiply by	to get
Length		
millimetres	0.04	inches
centimetres	0.39	inches
metres	3.28	feet
metres	1.09	yards
kilometres	0.62	miles
Area		
sq. centimetres	0.15	sq. inches
sq. metres	10.76	sq. feet
sq. metres	1.19	sq. yards
sq. kilometres	0.4	sq. miles
hectares	2.47	acres
Mass (weight)		
grams	0.035	ounces
kilograms	2.2	pounds
tonnes/metric tons	1.1	tons (short)
Volume		
		Imp. — not U.S.
millilitres (cu. cm)	0.03	fluid ounces
litres	1.76	pints
litres	0.88	quarts
litres	0.22	gallons
cubic centimetres	0.06	cubic inches
cubic metres	35.31	cubic feet
cubic metres	1.31	cubic yards
Temperature		
Celsius	Multiply by 9/5ths, then add 32	Fahrenheit
Temperature variations		
Celsius	1.8	Fahrenheit

Common metric units

	CP style for symbol		CP style for symbol
Length			
millimetre	mm	metre	m
centimetre	cm	kilometre	km
Area			
square millimetre	sq. mm	hectare (10,000 sq. m)	ha
square centimetre	sq. cm	square kilometre	sq. km
square metre	sq. m		
Volume			
millilitre	mL		
litre	L		
cubic centimetre	cu. cm		
cubic metre	cu. m		
Mass (weight)			
milligram	mg	kilogram	kg
gram	g	tonne/metric ton (1,000 kg)	t
Electricity			
volt	V	ohm	ohm
ampere	A	hertz	Hz
Energy		**Power**	
joule	J	watt	W
kilojoule	kJ	kilowatt	kW
megajoule	MJ	megawatt	MW
kilowatt hour	kW-h		
Pressure		**Temperature**	
pascal	Pa	Celsius	C
kilopascal	kPa		
megapascal	MPa		
Speed		**Rotation**	
metres a second	m-s	revolutions a minute	r-min
kilometres an hour	km-h		

Different strokes

1.   In much of the world, spaces are used to separate long numbers into blocks of three digits (**25 353 425**) and a comma is used as a decimal mark (**245,3**). CP style is to separate figures with commas rather than spaces (**25,353,425**) and to use a period rather than a comma in decimals (**245.3**).

2.   In Quebec, French-language media have adopted the international style: a space instead of a comma in long numbers, a comma instead of a decimal point and a currency symbol after an amount instead of before. Thus **12,24$** is used for **$12.24**.

Converting

1.   Fuel consumption of automobiles is given in number of litres per hundred kilometres, written **L per 100 km**. The lower the figure, the lower the rate of consumption. To convert, use these formulas:

from U.S. gallons

$$\text{L per 100 km} = \frac{234.2146}{\text{m.p.g.}}$$

from Canadian gallons

$$\text{L per 100 km} = \frac{282.48}{\text{m.p.g.}}$$

2.   To change Fahrenheit to Celsius, subtract 32, then multiply by five and divide by nine. To convert Celsius to Fahrenheit, multiply by nine, divide by five, then add 32.

Recipes

Follow this style for recipes, where imperial continues to be in wide use:

Apple Oatmeal Squares

250 mL (1 cup) all-purpose flour
250 mL (1 cup) quick-cooking rolled oats
125 mL (½ cup) firmly packed brown sugar
5 mL (1 tsp.) nutmeg
2 mL (½ tsp.) salt
175 mL (¾ cup) butter
6 medium cooking apples
50 mL (¼ cup) sunflower seeds

Combine flour, oats, sugar, nutmeg and salt. Cut in butter until mixture is crumbly. Measure out 125 mL (half a cup) and set aside for topping. Press remaining oatmeal mixture evenly in bottom of greased 23-cm-square (nine-inch-square) pan.

Peel and core apples, cut in halves lengthwise. Place cut side down on oatmeal base. Add sunflower seeds to reserved crumb mixture and sprinkle over top. Bake at 190 C (375 F) for 40 to 45 minutes. Cut into squares and serve warm or cooled. Makes 12 squares.

Military

General

1. All Canadian servicemen and servicewomen are members of the **Canadian Armed Forces**, often shortened to the **Canadian Forces**, the **Armed Forces** or simply **the Forces.**

Note: Uppercase **Armed Forces** applies only to Canadian forces; all others are down.

2. The Canadian Forces are headed by the **chief of the defence staff,** responsible to the minister of defence.

3. There are five commands: **Maritime, Mobile, Air, Communications** and **Canadian Forces Europe**.

4. Units making up land, sea and air formations go by a variety of names. The main field units are **division, brigade, regiment, battalion, squadron, company, troop** and **platoon**; naval units are **fleet, squadron** and **ship**; air units are **division, group, wing, squadron** and **flight.**

5. One rank structure, based on army grades, is used for army and air force personnel, another for navy personnel.

➤ See **Ranks**, page 261.

6. The terms **army, navy** and **air force** are acceptable, and personnel may be referred to as **soldiers, sailors** and **airmen** or **airwomen.**

Bases

1. National Defence Headquarters in Ottawa is the headquarters of the Canadian Forces and the Defence Department.

2. Major service establishments include **Canadian Forces bases: Canadian Forces Base Comox, B.C.,** or **CFB Comox** in second reference. There are smaller establishments called **Canadian Forces stations** and specialist installations such as **Canadian Forces ammunition depots**.

3. Canada's four **rescue co-ordination centres** — at Halifax, Trenton Ont., Edmonton and Victoria — are controlled and staffed by the Canadian Forces. In addition, a Canadian Coast Guard officer is on duty at each of the rescue centres in Halifax, Trenton and Victoria.

4. Avoid the abbreviations **CFS, CFAD** and **RCC** as being unfamiliar to readers.

Units

1.   To help readers evaluate a military action, put the numbers and types of troops and their support high in the story. Because **battalion, brigade, army** and other formations vary in size and makeup from country to country, the terms mean little unless qualified.

2.   These are some Canadian land units and their approximate sizes: **section**, 10 soldiers; **platoon**, three sections totalling 35; **company**, three platoons totalling 125-150; **battalion**, three or four companies totalling 375-600. A **brigade** consists of three battalions, but a **brigade group** — an infantry brigade supported by armor and artillery — numbers about 4,500 troops.

Note: The figures do not add up because, in addition to fighting personnel, each unit includes a varying number of commanders, signallers, etc.

3.   A **regiment** is a unit with a proper name — **the Grey and Simcoe Foresters**, for example — and usually consists of three battalions. It remains a regiment whether it has 20 or 2,000 members.

Capitalization

➤   See chapter **Capitalization**, page 187.

Ranks

1.   The Canadian Forces modify British tradition in the use of ranks and appointment titles, particularly for land forces. In an artillery regiment, for example, a private is a gunner, and a corporal is a bombardier. In an engineer regiment, a private is a sapper; in an armored unit, a trooper; in a communications unit, a signalman; in a guards regiment, a guardsman; in a rifle regiment, a rifleman.

2.   Plurals of military ranks and appointments add *s* to the principal rank category, not to the qualifying word: **major-generals, lieutenant-colonels, sergeants major**.

3.   Since ranks were reorganized at the time of Armed Forces unification, the rank of **corporal** has signified a person with four years of service who has achieved certain technical qualifications. In effect, it is equivalent to a senior private rather than a rank indicating leadership responsibility. The first level requiring leadership and special qualifications is the rank of **master corporal**.

Titles

The Canadian Forces use such titles as guardsman and master seaman for both males and females. Following are listed by descending order of rank.

Use these titles for army and air force personnel:

Rank	Before a name
general	Gen.
lieutenant-general	Lt.-Gen.
major-general	Maj.-Gen.
brigadier-general	Brig.-Gen.
colonel	Col.
lieutenant-colonel	Lt.-Col.
major	Maj.
captain	Capt.
lieutenant	Lieut.
second lieutenant	2nd Lieut.
officer cadet	Officer Cadet
chief warrant officer	Chief Warrant Officer
master warrant officer	Master Warrant Officer
warrant officer	Warrant Officer
sergeant	Sgt.
master corporal	Master Cpl.
corporal	Cpl.
bombardier	Bombardier
private	Pte.
guardsman	Guardsman
gunner	Gunner
rifleman	Rifleman
sapper	Sapper
signalman	Signalman
trooper	Trooper

Use these titles for navy personnel:

Rank	Before a name
admiral	Admiral
vice-admiral	Vice-Admiral
rear admiral	Rear Admiral
commodore	Commodore
captain	Capt.
commander	Cmdr.
lieutenant-commander	Lt.-Cmdr.
lieutenant	Lieut.
sub-lieutenant	Sub-Lieut.
acting sub-lieutenant	Acting Sub-Lieut.
chief petty officer	Chief Petty Officer
first class, second class	1st Class, 2nd Class
master seaman	Master Seaman
leading seaman	Leading Seaman
able seaman	Able Seaman
ordinary seaman	Ordinary Seaman

Usage for some foreign ranks and old Canadian ranks that may appear in copy periodically. They are listed alphabetically, not by descending order of rank:

Rank	Before a name
air commodore	Air Commodore
aircraftman first class	Aircraftman 1st Class
airman	Airman
airman first class	Airman 1st Class
air marshal	Air Marshal
air vice-marshal	Air Vice-Marshal
chief master sergeant	Chief Master Sgt.
commissioned warrant officer	Commissioned Warrant Officer
craftman	Craftman
ensign	Ensign
field marshal	Field Marshal
first lieutenant	1st Lieut.
first sergeant	1st Sgt.
flying officer	Flying Officer
fusilier	Fusilier
group captain	Group Capt.
gunnery sergeant	Gunnery Sgt.
lance-corporal	Lance-Cpl.
leading aircraftman	Leading Aircraftman
master chief petty officer	Master Chief Petty Officer
master gunnery sergeant	Master Gunnery Sgt.
master sergeant	Master Sgt.
midshipman	Midshipman
pilot officer	Pilot Officer
platoon sergeant	Platoon Sgt.
private first class	Pte. 1st Class
regimental sergeant major	Regimental Sgt. Maj.
seaman apprentice	Seaman Apprentice
seaman recruit	Seaman Recruit
senior chief petty officer	Senior Chief Petty Officer
sergeant first class	Sgt. 1st Class
sergeant major of the army	Army Sgt. Maj.
technical sergeant	Tech. Sgt.
wing commander	Wing Cmdr.

Retired officers

1. In certain circumstances, a military rank may be used in first reference before the name of an officer who has retired. Do not use the abbreviation **Ret.** but put **retired** before the lowercase rank: **retired brigadier Pat Turner.**

2. In stories involving military activities, former majors, lieutenant-commanders, squadron leaders and other high officers may be referred to by their old rank.

3. Even in stories involving purely civilian matters, brigadiers and higher may be referred to by rank, if the officers prefer.

4.   When rank is used, decorations may at times be added. In civilian stories, decorations need not be mentioned except for the Victoria Cross, Cross of Valor or other outstanding awards normally pertinent to the story.

Courts martial

1.   Military courts martial are properly open to the media, though in many instances the media are not advised they are in progress. Their decisions are privileged.

2.   Keep in mind that a court martial's decision must be reviewed by the commander of the unit that convened it and by other military authorities. The decision may be overruled by the federal cabinet or the court martial appeal board upon the person aggrieved presenting a petition. In either case the further ruling merits equal prominence.

Ceremonies

1.   **Guards**

a)   A **royal guard** is paraded for visiting royalty, governors general and lieutenant-governors. It consists of 100 men and women with arms, a band and colors (regimental flags). A **guard of honor** is turned out for any other dignitary: 50 troops with arms and usually a band. A **mounted escort** accompanies the dignitary's vehicle, the riders armed, often with lances, and drawn from the RCMP or a regiment.

b)   In Canada, a dignitary **inspects** the guard by walking up and down the ranks. In the United States, a dignitary **reviews** it.

2.   **Colors**

a)   In Canada, the colors are carried by a **color party**, an officer bearer escorted by non-commissioned officers. The American equivalent is called a **color guard**.

b)   Regimental colors are dipped only to the sovereign or a member of the Royal Family. In the ceremony of **trooping the color** — carrying the regimental flag along ranks of soldiers — only one color is trooped, hence the name.

c)   Flags are always raised to the top of the mast or pole. Then, if required, they are **lowered to half-mast**. If tangled with the rope, they are **fouled**.

3.   **Military funerals**

a)   A **gun carriage** consists of a towed gun, with a platform fixed above the barrel, on which the coffin is fastened. The six who carry the coffin are the **bearer party**; the 12 who fire volleys at the graveside are the **firing party**.

b)   Wreaths are **laid** or **placed**, trumpets **sounded** and bugles **blown** or **sounded**.

Miscellaneous

1.   Write **promoted major-general**, not **promoted to major-general**. But **promoted to the rank of major-general** is correct.

2.   Distinguish between **rank** (position within the military hierarchy) and **appointment** (specific duty). A person with the **rank** of master warrant officer may be given the **duties** of regimental quartermaster sergeant, a non-commissioned officer in charge of a regiment's quarters, supplies, etc.

Master Warrant Officer Pat Smith has been named regimental quartermaster sergeant.

Regimental Quartermaster Sergeant John Smith holds the rank of master warrant officer.

3.   When locating a Canadian regiment, be sure to use the *official* home town or towns.

4.   Do not refer to the Princess Patricia's Canadian Light Infantry as **the Pats**, a term disliked by its members. But **the Patricias** (no apostrophe) is acceptable for the unit or a group of individuals.

5.   The nickname of Quebec's Royal 22nd Regiment is **the Van Doo** (from vingt-deux). Personnel of the regiment may be referred to as **the Van Doos** and one of them as **a Van Doo**.

6.   Write **Mobile Command**; avoid the bilingual designation **Force Mobile Command** except in direct quotation.

7.   The term **Snowbirds** is officially used to designate the Canadian Forces aerobatic team. The full complement including support personnel is designated 431 Air Demonstration Squadron.

8.   The **Skyhawks** parachuting performers are formally known as the Canadian Forces Parachute Team.

9.   **CF-18** is the designation for the Canadian version of the U.S. fighter aircraft F-18.

10. Avoid Americanisms. Canadian usage is **Last Post, guard of honor** and **AWL** (absent without leave). American usage is **Taps, honor guard** and **AWOL**. And Canadians take **basic military training**; they do not attend **boot camp**.

11. Do not refer to the Royal Military College at Kingston, Ont., as the **West Point of Canada** or **Canada's Sandhurst** in stories for Canadian consumption.

12. A **volley** is one shot from each of several weapons fired simultaneously; a **fusillade** is several shots fired from one weapon sequentially. One gunman can fire a fusillade but not a volley. Artillery fires in **salvos**.

13. A **sniper** fires shots from hiding, usually at long range, into the enemy's camp or at individuals.

14. In flying, a **sortie** is one mission by one plane.

15. While the term **troops** can be used to refer to a body of soldiers —
100 troops advanced — it should not be used in the singular as a
substitute for **soldier**. A troop is a military unit.

➤ See **Aircraft, ships, guns**, page 249.

Native peoples

Indians, Métis, Inuit

Canada's Aboriginal Peoples comprise three distinct groups: Indians, Inuit and Métis. Their numbers are estimated at about 1.2 million, about 4.3 per cent of the Canadian population.

About 570,000 of these are status Indians registered with the federal government. The term means they qualify as Indians under the Indian Act and can take advantage of certain rights reserved for them, such as tax breaks and special hunting and fishing rights.

By agreeing to treaties most Canadian Indians exchanged some interests in their ancestral lands in return for various payments and promises from Crown officials. About 60 per cent of registered Indians live on reserves. They do not pay income tax and qualify for education, housing and other grants.

There are 607 Indian bands and about 2,400 reserves across Canada, comprising over 2.8 million hectares of land – an area almost as large as Belgium. The largest band is the Six Nations group of about 15,000 near Brantford, Ont.

The remaining registered Indians, as well as most non-status Indians, live off reserves. A larger proportion of the overall Indian population now live in urban centres than anywhere else.

Indian languages

Algonquian is the most prevalent language family, with versions being spoken by about two-thirds of Canadian Indians — including Ojibwas and Algonquin of Central Canada, Prairie Cree, Micmacs of the Maritimes and Montagnais and Naskapi of northeastern Quebec and Labrador.

(Note the difference in spelling: **Algonquian** is the overall term for the language group. **Algonquin** is classified as an Ojibwa dialect, one of the languages of the Algonquian family. The Algonquin live along the Ottawa River in Quebec and Ontario.)

Iroquois languages are spoken by such groups as the Six Nations, including Mohawks and Oneidas.

Many northern Indians speak **Athapaskan** languages, while those in British Columbia speak languages from several families — the most common being **Salishan**.

Canada's Indians speak about 52 languages from 10 language families. About two-thirds speak some form of the Algonquian language. Traditional language-family areas are shown here.

(CP—Sylvie Caron)

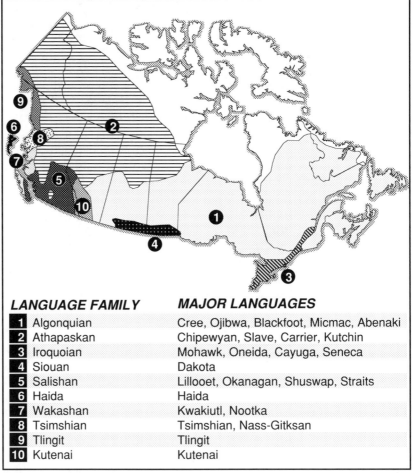

LANGUAGE FAMILY   **MAJOR LANGUAGES**

1	Algonquian	Cree, Ojibwa, Blackfoot, Micmac, Abenaki
2	Athapaskan	Chipewyan, Slave, Carrier, Kutchin
3	Iroquoian	Mohawk, Oneida, Cayuga, Seneca
4	Siouan	Dakota
5	Salishan	Lillooet, Okanagan, Shuswap, Straits
6	Haida	Haida
7	Wakashan	Kwakiutl, Nootka
8	Tsimshian	Tsimshian, Nass-Gitksan
9	Tlingit	Tlingit
10	Kutenai	Kutenai

Source: The Canadian Encyclopedia   **(CP)**

Writing about Indians

Canada's Indians are not a homogeneous group with a standard set of interests and grievances. An effort should be made to reflect their diversity in stories specifically dealing with Indians and native groups.

Saying someone is **an Alberta native** is unhelpful. Try to identify the tribal affiliation or the reserve.

Milton Born With a Tooth, an Alberta Peigan; Cameron Kerley, a former resident of Sioux Valley reserve in Manitoba; MP Ethel Blondin, a Dene from the Western Arctic; Neil Sterritt, hereditary chief of the Gitksan Nation in British Columbia; Mike Mitchell, chief of the Mohawk council at Akwesasne reserve near Cornwall, Ont.

If a language other than English or French is spoken, include it in the body of the story: **Ellen Gabriel, who addressed the forum in Mohawk**.

Métis

The meaning of the word **Métis** is elusive and subject to argument.

Originally, the word was applied to descendants of French traders and trappers and Indian women in the Canadian northwest. Now it is usually taken to mean anyone of mixed Indian and European blood, although there are Métis communities on the Prairies where French is spoken.

There were 75,000 Métis in the 1991 census. However, many status Indians are in fact Métis and many whites have Indian blood but do not consider themselves Métis.

Inuit

There are about 30,000 Inuit (never Eskimo) in Canada, strung out in small settlements from Labrador to Alaska. Their language is Inuktitut.

The Inuit of the Western Arctic call themselves Inuvialuit.

The singular of Inuit is Inuk.

People, places

(Numbers refer to notes at end, page 276.)

Country/ Region	Noun	Adjective	Capital	Currency
Afghanistan	Afghan(s)	Afghani	Kabul	afghani
Albania	Albanian(s)	Albanian	Tirana	lek
Algeria	Algerian(s)	Algerian	Algiers	dinar
American Samoa	American Samoan(s)	American Samoan	Pago Pago	dollar
Andorra	Andorran(s)	Andorran	Andorra La Vella	franc/ peseta
Angola	Angolan(s)	Angolan	Luanda	kwanza
Antigua	Antiguan(s)	Antiguan	St. John's	dollar
Argentina	Argentine(s)	Argentine	Buenos Aires	austral
Armenia	Armenian(s)	Armenian	Yerevan	ruble
Aruba	Aruban(s)	Aruban	Oranjestad	guilder
Australia	Australian(s)	Australian	Canberra	dollar
Austria	Austrian(s)	Austrian	Vienna	schilling
Azerbaijan	Azerbaijani(s)	Azerbaijani	Baku	ruble
Azores	Azorean(s)	Azorean	Ponta Delgada	escudo
Bahamas	Bahamian(s)	Bahamian	Nassau	dollar
Bahrain	Bahraini(s)	Bahraini	Manama	dinar
Bangladesh	Bangladeshi(s)	Bangladesh	Dhaka	taka
Barbados	Barbadian(s)	Barbadian	Bridgetown	dollar
Belarus	Belarussian(s)	Belarus	Minsk	ruble
Belgium	Belgian(s)	Belgian	Brussels	franc
Belize	Belizean(s)	Belizean	Belmopan	dollar
Benin	Beninese (sing. and pl.)	Beninese	Porto-Novo	franc
Bermuda	Bermudian(s)	Bermudian	Hamilton	dollar
Bhutan	Bhutanese (sing., pl.)	Bhutanese	Thimphu	ngultrum/ rupee
Bolivia	Bolivian(s)	Bolivian	La Paz	boliviano
Bosnia-Herzegovina	Bosnian(s)	Bosnian	Sarajevo	dinar
Botswana	Motswana (sing.) Batswana (pl.)	Botswana	Gaborone	pula
Brazil	Brazilian(s)	Brazilian	Brasilia	cruzado
Brunei	Bruneian(s)	Bruneian	Bandar Seri Begawan	dollar
Bulgaria	Bulgarian(s)	Bulgarian	Sofia	lev
Burkina Faso	Burkina Fasan(s)	Burkina Fasan	Ouagadougou	franc
Burma❶	Burmese (sing. and pl.)	Burmese	Rangoon	kyat

Country/ Region	Noun	Adjective	Capital	Currency
Burundi	Burundian(s)	Burundi	Bujumbura	franc
Cambodia	Cambodian(s)	Cambodian	Phnom Penh	riel
Cameroon	Cameroonian(s)	Cameroonian	Yaounde	franc
Canary Islands	Canary Islander(s)	Canary Island	Las Palmas	peseta
Cape Verde	Cape Verdean(s)	Cape Verdean	Praia	escudo
Cayman Islands	Cayman Islander(s)	Cayman	Georgetown	dollar
Central African Republic	Central African(s)	Central African	Bangui	franc
Chad	Chadian(s)	Chadian	N'djamena	franc
Chile	Chilean(s)	Chilean	Santiago	peso
China	Chinese (sing., pl.)	Chinese	Beijing	renminbi/ yuan
Colombia	Colombian(s)	Colombian	Bogota	peso
Comoros	Comoran(s)	Comoran	Moroni	franc
Congo	Congolese (sing., pl.)	Congolese	Brazzaville	franc
Cook Islands	Cook Islander(s)	Cook Islands	Avarua	dollar
Costa Rica	Costa Rican(s)	Costa Rican	San Jose	colon
Croatia	Croat(s)	Croatian	Zagreb	dinar
Cuba	Cuban(s)	Cuban	Havana	peso
Cyprus	Cypriot(s)	Cypriot	Nicosia	pound
Czech Republic	Czech(s)	Czech	Prague	koruna
Denmark	Dane(s)	Danish	Copenhagen	krone
Djibouti	Afar(s), Issa(s)	Afar, Issa	Djibouti	franc
Dominica	Dominican(s)	Dominican	Roseau	dollar
Dominican Republic	Dominican(s)	Dominican	Santo Domingo	peso
Ecuador	Ecuadoran(s)	Ecuadoran	Quito	sucre
Egypt	Egyptian(s)	Egyptian	Cairo	pound
El Salvador	Salvadoran(s)	Salvadoran	San Salvador	colon
Equatorial Guinea	Equatorial Guinean(s)	Equatorial Guinean	Malabo	franc
Eritrea	Eritrean(s)	Eritrean	Asmara	birr
Estonia	Estonian(s)	Estonian	Tallinn	kroon
Ethiopia	Ethiopian(s)	Ethiopian	Addis Ababa	birr
Falkland Islands	Falkland Islander(s)	Falkland Island	Stanley	pound
Faroe Islands	Faroe Islander(s)	Faroe Islands	Thorshavn	krone
Fiji	Fijian(s)	Fijian	Suva	dollar
Finland	Finn(s)	Finnish	Helsinki	markka
France	French(wo)man	French	Paris	franc
French Guiana	French Guianese (sing., pl.)	French Guianese	Cayenne	franc
French Polynesia	French Polynesian(s)	French Polynesian	Papeete	franc
Gabon	Gabonese (sing., pl.)	Gabonese	Libreville	franc
Gambia	Gambian(s)	Gambian	Banjul	dalasi

Country/ Region	Noun	Adjective	Capital	Currency
Georgia	Georgian(s)	Georgian	Tbilisi	ruble
Germany	German(s)	German	Bonn❷	mark
Ghana	Ghanaian(s)	Ghanaian	Accra	cedi
Gibraltar	Gibraltan(s)	Gibraltan	Gibraltar	pound
Gilbert Islands	Gilbert Islander(s)	Gilbert Island	Tarawa	dollar
Greece	Greek(s)	Greek	Athens	drachma
Greenland	Greenlander(s)	Greenlandic	Godthab	krone
Grenada	Grenadian(s)	Grenadian	St. George's	dollar
Guadeloupe	Guadeloupian(s)	Guadeloupe	Basse-Terre	franc
Guam	Guamanian(s)	Guamanian	Agana	dollar
Guatemala	Guatemalan(s)	Guatemalan	Guatemala City	quetzal
Guinea	Guinean(s)	Guinea	Conakry	franc
Guinea-Bissau	Guinean(s)	Guinean	Bissau	peso
Guyana	Guyanese (sing., pl.)	Guyanese	Georgetown	dollar
Haiti	Haitian(s)	Haitian	Port-au-Prince	gourde
Honduras	Honduran(s)	Honduran	Tegucigalpa	lempira
Hong Kong		Hong Kong	Victoria	dollar
Hungary	Hungarian(s)	Hungarian	Budapest	forint
Iceland	Icelander(s)	Icelandic	Reykjavik	krona
India	Indian(s)	Indian	New Delhi	rupee
Indonesia	Indonesian(s)	Indonesian	Jakarta	rupiah
Iran	Iranian(s)	Iranian	Tehran	rial
Iraq	Iraqi(s)	Iraqi	Baghdad	dinar
Ireland	Irish(wo)man	Irish	Dublin	pound
Israel	Israeli(s)	Israeli	Jerusalem❸	shekel
Italy	Italian(s)	Italian	Rome	lira
Ivory Coast	Ivorian(s)	Ivorian	Abidjan	franc
Jamaica	Jamaican(s)	Jamaican	Kingston	dollar
Japan	Japanese (sing., pl.)	Japanese	Tokyo	yen
Jordan	Jordanian(s)	Jordanian	Amman	dinar
Kazakhstan	Kazakh(s)	Kazakh	Alma-Ata	ruble
Kenya	Kenyan(s)	Kenyan	Nairobi	shilling
Kiribati	Kiribatan(s)	Kiribatan	Bairiki❹	dollar
Kuwait	Kuwaiti(s)	Kuwaiti	Kuwait	dinar
Kyrgyzstan	Kyrgyz	Kyrgyz	Bishkek	ruble
Laos	Laotian(s)	Laotian	Vientiane	kip
Latvia	Latvian(s)	Latvian	Riga	ruble
Lebanon	Lebanese (sing., pl.)	Lebanese	Beirut	pound
Lesotho	Masotho (sing.) Basotho (pl.)	Basotho	Maseru	loti
Liberia	Liberian(s)	Liberian	Monrovia	dollar
Libya	Libyan(s)	Libyan	Tripoli	dinar
Liechtenstein	Liechtensteiner(s)	Liechtenstein	Vaduz	franc
Lithuania	Lithuanian(s)	Lithuanian	Vilnius	ruble
Luxembourg	Luxembourger(s)	Luxembourg	Luxembourg	franc

Country/ Region	Noun	Adjective	Capital	Currency
Macao	Macanese (sing., pl.)	Macanese	Macao	pataca
Macedonia	Macedonian(s)	Macedonian	Skopje	dinar
Madagascar	Malagasy (sing., pl.)	Malagasy	Antananarivo	franc
Malawi	Malawian(s)	Malawian	Lilongwe	kwacha
Malaysia	Malaysian(s)	Malaysian	Kuala Lumpur	dollar/ ringgit
Maldives	Maldivian(s)	Maldivian	Male	rufiyaa
Mali	Malian(s)	Malian	Bamako	franc
Malta	Maltese (sing., pl.)	Maltese	Valletta	lira
Mariana, Caroline and Marshall Islands	Mariana, etc., Islander(s)	Mariana, etc., Island	Saipan	dollar
Martinique	Martinican(s)	Martinican	Fort-de-France	franc
Mauritania	Mauritanian(s)	Mauritanian	Nouakchott	ouguiya
Mauritius	Mauritian(s)	Mauritian	Port Louis	rupee
Mexico	Mexican(s)	Mexican	Mexico City	peso
Micronesia, Federated States of	Micronesian(s)	Micronesian	Kolonia	dollar
Moldova	Moldovan(s)	Moldovan	Kishinev	ruble
Monaco	Monacan(s)	Monacan	Monaco	franc
Mongolia	Mongolian(s)	Mongolian	Ulan Bator	tugrik
Montserrat	Montserratan(s)	Montserratan	Plymouth	dollar
Morocco	Moroccan(s)	Moroccan	Rabat	dirham
Mozambique	Mozambican(s)	Mozambican	Maputo	metical
Namibia	Namibian(s)	Namibian	Windhoek	rand
Nauru	Nauruan(s)	Nauruan	Yaren	dollar
Nepal	Nepalese (sing., pl.)	Nepalese	Katmandu	rupee
Netherlands❺	Netherlander(s)/ Dutch(wo)man	Netherlander/ Dutch	Amsterdam❻	guilder
Netherlands Antilles	Netherlands Antillean(s)	Netherlands Antillean	Willemstad	guilder
New Caledonia	New Caledonian(s)	New Caledonian	Noumea	franc
New Zealand	New Zealander(s)	New Zealand	Wellington	dollar
Nicaragua	Nicaraguan(s)	Nicaraguan	Managua	cordoba
Niger	Nigerois (sing., pl.)	Niger	Niamey	franc
Nigeria	Nigerian(s)	Nigerian	Lagos	naira
Niue	Niuean(s)	Niuean	Alofi	dollar
Norfolk Island	Norfolk Islander(s)	Norfolk Island	Kingston	dollar
North Korea	North Korean(s)	North Korean	Pyongyang	won
Norway	Norwegian(s)	Norwegian	Oslo	krone

Country/Region	Noun	Adjective	Capital	Currency
Oman	Omani(s)	Omani	Muscat	rial
Pakistan	Pakistani(s)	Pakistani	Islamabad	rupee
Panama	Panamanian(s)	Panamanian	Panama City	balboa
Papua New Guinea	Papua New Guinean(s)	Papua New Guinean	Port Moresby	kina
Paraguay	Paraguayan(s)	Paraguayan	Asuncion	guarani
Peru	Peruvian(s)	Peruvian	Lima	inti
Philippines	Filipino(s), Filipina(s)	Philippine	Manila	peso
Pitcairn Island	Pitcairn Islander(s)	Pitcairn Island	Adamstown	dollar
Poland	Pole(s)	Polish	Warsaw	zloty
Portugal	Portuguese (sing., pl.)	Portuguese	Lisbon	escudo
Puerto Rico	Puerto Rican(s)	Puerto Rican	San Juan	dollar
Qatar	Qatari(s)	Qatari	Doha	riyal
Reunion	Reunionese (sing., pl.)	Reunionese	Saint-Denis	franc
Romania	Romanian(s)	Romanian	Bucharest	leu
Russia	Russian(s)	Russian	Moscow	ruble
Rwanda	Rwandan(s)	Rwandan	Kigali	franc
St. Helena	St. Helenan(s)	St. Helenan	Jamestown	pound
St. Kitts-Nevis	Kittsian(s), Nevisian(s)	Kittsian, Nevisian	Basseterre	dollar
St. Lucia	St. Lucian(s)	St. Lucian	Castries	dollar
St-Pierre-Miquelon	St-Pierrais (sing., pl.)	St-Pierrais	St-Pierre	franc
St. Vincent, Grenadines	St. Vincentian(s), Grenadinian(s)	St. Vincentian, Grenadinian	Kingstown	dollar
Samoa	Samoan(s)	Samoan	Apia	tala
San Marino	San Marinese (sing., pl.)	San Marinese	San Marino	lira
Sao Tome, Principe	Sao Tomean(s), Principian(s)	Sao Tomean, Principian	Sao Tome	dobra
Saudi Arabia	Saudi(s)	Saudi Arabian, Saudi	Riyadh	riyal
Senegal	Senegalese (sing., pl.)	Senegalese	Dakar	franc
Seychelles	Seychellois (sing., pl.)	Seychellois	Victoria	rupee
Sierra Leone	Sierra Leonean(s)	Sierra Leonean	Freetown	leone
Sikkim	Sikkimese (sing., pl.)	Sikkimese	Gangtok	rupee
Singapore	Singaporean(s)	Singaporean	Singapore	dollar
Slovakia	Slovak(s)	Slovak	Bratislava	koruna
Slovenia	Slovene(s)	Slovenian	Ljubljana	dinar
Solomon Islands	Solomon Islander(s)	Solomon Island	Honiara	dollar
Somalia	Somali(s)	Somalian	Mogadishu	shilling

Country/ Region	Noun	Adjective	Capital	Currency
South Africa	South African(s)	South African	Pretoria❼	rand
South Korea	South Korean(s)	South Korean	Seoul	won
Spain	Spaniard(s)	Spanish	Madrid	peseta
Sri Lanka	Sri Lankan(s)	Sri Lankan	Colombo	rupee
Sudan	Sudanese (sing., pl.)	Sudanese	Khartoum	pound
Suriname	Surinamer(s)	Surinamese	Paramaribo	guilder
Swaziland	Swazi (sing., pl.)	Swazi	Mbabane	lilageni (emalangeni, pl.)
Sweden	Swede(s)	Swedish	Stockholm	krona
Switzerland	Swiss (sing., pl.)	Swiss	Bern	franc
Syria	Syrian(s)	Syrian	Damascus	pound
Taiwan	Taiwanese (sing., pl.)	Taiwanese	Taipei	dollar
Tajikistan	Tajik(s)	Tajik	Dushanbe	ruble
Tanzania	Tanzanian(s)	Tanzanian	Dar es Salaam	shilling
Thailand	Thai(s)	Thai	Bangkok	baht
Togo	Togolese (sing., pl.)	Togolese	Lome	franc
Tokelau Islands	Tokelau Islander(s)	Tokelau Islands	Fakaofo	dollar
Tonga	Tongan(s)	Tongan	Nuku'alofa	pa'anga
Trinidad and Tobago	Trinidadian(s), Tobagan(s)	Trinidadian, Tobagan	Port-of-Spain	dollar
Tunisia	Tunisian(s)	Tunisian	Tunis	dinar
Turkey	Turk(s)	Turkish	Ankara	lira
Turkmenistan	Turkmen (sing., pl.)	Turkmen	Ashkhabad	ruble
Turks and Caicos Is.	Turks/Caicos Islander(s)	Turks/Caicos Islands	Grand Turk	dollar
Tuvalu	Tuvaluan(s)	Tuvaluan	Fongafale❽	dollar
Uganda	Ugandan(s)	Ugandan	Kampala	shilling
Ukraine (not *the*)	Ukrainian(s)	Ukrainian	Kiev	grivna
United Arab Emirates	Emirian(s)	Emirian	Abu Dhabi	dirham
United Kingdom	Briton(s)	British	London	pound
United States	American(s)	American/U.S.	Washington	dollar
Uruguay	Uruguayan(s)	Uruguayan	Montevideo	peso
Uzbekistan	Uzbek(s)	Uzbek	Tashkent	ruble
Vanuatu	Vanuatuan(s)	Vanuatuan	Vila	vatu
Vatican City		Vatican	Vatican City	lira
Venezuela	Venezuelan(s)	Venezuelan	Caracas	bolivar
Vietnam	Vietnamese (sing., pl.)	Vietnamese	Hanoi	dong
Virgin Islands (Br.)	Virgin Islander(s)	Virgin Island	Road Town	dollar

Country/ Region	Noun	Adjective	Capital	Currency
Virgin Islands (U.S.)	Virgin Islander(s)	Virgin Island	Charlotte Amalie	dollar
Western Sahara	Western Saharan(s)	Western Saharan	Laayoune	dirham
Yemen	Yemeni(s)	Yemeni	San'a	rial/dinar
Yugoslavia	Yugoslav(s)	Yugoslav	Belgrade	dinar
Zaire	Zairese (sing., pl.)	Zairese	Kinshasa	zaire
Zambia	Zambian(s)	Zambian	Lusaka	kwacha
Zimbabwe	Zimbabwean(s)	Zimbabwean	Harare	dollar

❶ The regime in Burma uses the name Myanmar for the country and Yangon for the capital.

❷ Bonn is the capital of unified Germany but legislators decided in June 1991 to return the capital to Berlin. The Bundestag, the decision-making lower house of parliament, and most of the ministries will move to Berlin by early in the next decade. The Bundesrat, or upper house, will remain in Bonn.

❸ Recognition withheld by many countries over the Palestinian question. Tel Aviv is the administrative capital.

❹ Bairiki on Tarawa Atoll.

❺ Holland may be used in casual contexts.

❻ The seat of government is The Hague.

❼ Pretoria is the executive capital, site of the president's office and of foreign embassies. The legislature sits in Cape Town.

❽ Fongafale on Funafuti Atoll.

Provincial descriptive terms

Albertan
British Columbian
Manitoban
New Brunswicker
Newfoundlander

Nova Scotian
Ontarian
Prince Edward Islander, Islander
Quebecer
Saskatchewanian (rare; prefer *a resident of Saskatchewan*)

U.S. state descriptives

Alabamian	Louisianian	Ohioan
Alaskan	Mainer	Oklahoman
Arizonan	Marylander	Oregonian
Arkansan	Massachusettsan	Pennsylvanian
Californian	Michiganite	Rhode Islander
Coloradan	Minnesotan	South Carolinian
Connecticuter	Mississippian	South Dakotan
Delawarean	Missourian	Tennessean
Floridian	Montanan	Texan
Georgian	Nebraskan	Utahn (Utahan, adj.)
Hawaiian	Nevadan	Vermonter
Idahoan	New Hampshirite	Virginian
Illinoisan	New Jerseyite	Washingtonian
Indianian	New Mexican	West Virginian
Iowan	New Yorker	Wisconsinite
Kansan	North Carolinian	Wyomingite
Kentuckian	North Dakotan	

Placelines

General

1. Most stories carry a placeline as their first piece of information. The placeline tells a reader where most of the story took place. Whenever possible, place stories where the main event occurred. The community is written in lightface capitals and any other designation (country, province, state) is in upper and lower. On news agency copy, the agency logo and a heavy dash follow.

Avoid **here** in copy, since it may force the reader to check the placeline a second time. Do the reader a favor by repeating the name of the community at app ropriate times in the story (**the mayor of Ste. Agathe, south of Winnipeg**).

2. Although the placeline normally tells the reader where the event occurred, there are exceptions. On a credited pickup from a newspaper, the placeline is usually the city where the paper is based, even if the event took place elsewhere.

> **WINNIPEG (CP)** — The Conservatives plan a leadership convention in March, the Winnipeg Free Press said today in a report from Ottawa.

But use the placeline given by a newspaper to a story when the material is not exclusive or is readily available, and the newspaper has granted permission for it to be used.

> **MONTREAL (CP)** — As much as 20 per cent of Canada's 10 million tonnes of annual newsprint capacity could disappear over the next two years as producers close aging and unproductive mills.
> "It's a disaster out there," consultant Jim Rowland told the Toronto Globe and Mail in an interview.

Note: It is often necessary to obtain permission from the newspaper to pick up a story from outside the paper's Return News district. If the story is voluntarily filed to CP, that implies permission for it to be picked up.

3. A story that rounds up events or developments in several centres does not have a placeline, but instead is slugged **Roundup**.

> **AM-Budget-Rxn-Rdp, Bgt**
> code:3
> **Roundup Budget**
> **By Stephen Ewart**
> **The Canadian Press**

Note: Many member papers prefer a placeline on all stories, so use one whenever possible. The **Roundup** slug should be reserved for those stories that are true roundups, not stories with most of the elements from one centre and a couple of elements from another. In that case, placeline the story in the first centre and specify in the body of the story where the secondary material came from.

4. Other items that don't carry a placeline include stories and Quicks that don't have or need a geographic focus, and columns for sports, entertainment or other inside sections. These types of stories do not need an UNDATED slug.

AM-Video-Views
code:3

By Jane Stevenson
The Canadian Press

Use an UNDATED slug on an exceptional story from a specific community where the reporter deserves a byline, but was not in the community. This will alert editors not to put a placeline on the story if they are using the byline.

5. A byline is used on a placelined story only when the reporter has been in the community to collect information. In a story obtained by phone but carrying the placeline of the event, it is sometimes worth explaining how the information was gathered.

The masked gunman disrupted the meeting just as city council was to vote on the Sunday shopping proposal, Mayor Shirley Millson said in a phone interview.

➤ See **Bylines**, page 382.

6. Stories based on news releases in Canada reporting incidents abroad should be placelined where the release is issued.

7. Avoid contrived novelty placelines, for example: IN THE CAB OF A SEMI-TRAILER TRUCK SOMEWHERE ON HIGHWAY 97. Unconventional placelines are occasionally legitimate when copy is written and filed from that point, for example: HMCS ATHABASKAN (not ON BOARD HMCS ATHABASKAN). Ensure the approximate position of the ship is described early in the text.

8. Stories that take place on Armed Forces bases can carry the short form CFB – for example, CFB TRENTON. Or they can be placelined in a nearby civilian community – for example, HALIFAX – with an explanation in the body of the story that the event took place on an Armed Forces base.

9. Prefer placelines that would fit in one line of body type in a newspaper column. Most domestic and foreign news is reported from capitals or major cities; those listed below under Canadian, U.S. and foreign placelines require no other identification in the placeline.

10. It saves readers the trouble of guessing if stories from lesser-known placelines outside Canada and the United States name the country in the placeline or the first paragraph.

Canadian placelines

1. The community is followed by the province or territory with the exceptions of these well-known cities:

CALGARY	MONTREAL	VANCOUVER
CHARLOTTETOWN	OTTAWA	VICTORIA
EDMONTON	QUEBEC	WHITEHORSE
FREDERICTON	REGINA	WINNIPEG
HALIFAX	SASKATOON	YELLOWKNIFE
HAMILTON	TORONTO	

Note 1: WHITEHORSE and YELLOWKNIFE stand alone as placelines, but *the Northwest Territories* or *the Yukon* should be mentioned in the opening paragraph.

Note 2: QUEBEC stands alone as a placeline; use *Quebec City* in the body of a story.

Note 3: Write ST. JOHN'S, Nfld., and SAINT JOHN, N.B., to avoid confusion.

2. Most multiple-word place names in Quebec are hyphenated: **Trois-Rivieres, Notre-Dame-de-la-Merci**. Names preceded by the definite article do not need a hyphen after the article: **La Malbaie, La Pocatiere**. Hyphens are omitted from purely English place names: **Otterburn Park, Stanstead Plain**.

➤ See **French**, page 207.

3. Use TORONTO as a placeline instead of the component Metro municipalities of *Scarborough, Etobicoke, York, East York* and *North York*. Specify the community in the body of the story if it is relevant. All other near-Toronto communities carry their own placelines.

The 28 municipalities on the Island of Montreal are part of the Montreal Urban Community and carry a MONTREAL placeline. Communities off the island carry their own placelines.

Vancouver does not have a regional government, so communities such as *West Vancouver* and *North Vancouver* carry their own placelines.

U.S. placelines

1. The community is followed by the state abbreviation with these exceptions:

ATLANTA	HONOLULU	OKLAHOMA CITY
BALTIMORE	HOUSTON	PHILADELPHIA
BOSTON	INDIANAPOLIS	PITTSBURGH
CHICAGO	LOS ANGELES	ST. LOUIS
CINCINNATI	MIAMI	SALT LAKE CITY
CLEVELAND	MILWAUKEE	SAN DIEGO
DALLAS	MINNEAPOLIS	SAN FRANCISCO
DENVER	NEW ORLEANS	SEATTLE
DETROIT	NEW YORK	WASHINGTON

➤ For state abbreviations, see **Abbreviations**, page 173.

2. Use the commonly accepted **United States**, not United States of America.

Other foreign placelines

1. The community is followed by the country in the placeline with these exceptions:

ADDIS ABABA	DAMASCUS	MEXICO CITY
ALGIERS	DUBLIN	MONACO
AMSTERDAM	EDINBURGH	MOSCOW
ATHENS	FRANKFURT	MUNICH
AUCKLAND	GENEVA	NAIROBI
BAGHDAD	GIBRALTAR	NAPLES
BANGKOK	GLASGOW	NEW DELHI
BARCELONA	GUATEMALA CITY	PANAMA
BEIJING	HAGUE, THE	PRAGUE
BEIRUT	HAMBURG	RIO DE JANEIRO
BELFAST	HANOI	ROME
BERLIN	HAVANA	ST. PETERSBURG
BERN	HELSINKI	SAN SALVADOR
BOGOTA	HO CHI MINH CITY	SEOUL
BONN	HONG KONG	SHANGHAI
BRASILIA	ISTANBUL	SINGAPORE
BRUSSELS	JERUSALEM	STOCKHOLM
BUCHAREST	JOHANNESBURG	TEHRAN
BUDAPEST	KUWAIT	TEL AVIV
BUENOS AIRES	LIMA	TOKYO
CAIRO	LISBON	TUNIS
CANBERRA	LONDON	VATICAN CITY
CANTON	LUXEMBOURG	VENICE
CAPE TOWN	MACAO	WARSAW
CARACAS	MADRID	WELLINGTON
COPENHAGEN	MARSEILLE	ZURICH

Note: Write HAMILTON, Bermuda and SYDNEY, Australia to avoid confusion with the Canadian cities.

2. Use the commonly accepted short version of a country's name.

Argentina, not Republic of Argentina
Bahamas, not Commonwealth of the Bahamas
China, not People's Republic of China
Kuwait, not State of Kuwait
Sikkim, not Kingdom of Sikkim
Taiwan, not Republic of China

3. Do not use *The* with the name of a country in placelines.

Bahamas	Gambia	Philippines
Congo	Netherlands	

Note: Do use El Salvador.

4. Use UNITED NATIONS alone in placelines.

Place names

General

1. The style authority for Canadian place names is the *Canadian Almanac and Directory*. In Quebec place names, retain hyphens: **St-Georges-de-Beauce**. Do not hyphenate English place names in Quebec: **East Broughton, Otterburn Park**.

➤ See **French**, page 207.

2. National Geographic Society spellings are style for place names outside Canada with exceptions listed below.

3. The umlaut in German names is indicated by placing the letter *e* after the vowel affected. *Düsseldorf* becomes *Duesseldorf.*

Exceptions

The following are exceptions to National Geographic Society spellings:

Algiers	Dubai	Padua
Antioch	Dunkirk	Pescadores Island
Antwerp	Florence	Port Arthur
Aral Sea	Foochow	Prague
Archangel	Geneva	Rhodes
Athens	Genoa	Riga, Gulf of
Azov, Sea of	Hague, The	Rome
Bangkok	Hamelin	Salonika
Belgrade	Havana	Sinai, Mount
Benares	Hook of Holland	Sofia
Black Forest	Ithaca	Sparta
Blue Nile River	Kingstown (Ireland)	Tadzhikistan
Brest Litovsk	Lions, Gulf of	Taipei
Brunswick	Lisbon	Tiber River
Brussels	Lucerne	Tibet
Bucharest	Macao	Tiflis
Canton	Majorca	Turin
Cape Horn	Marcus Island	Tyre
Coblenz	Milan	Venice
Cologne	Moscow	Vesuvius, Mount
Constance, Lake	Mukden	Vienna
Copenhagen	Munich	Vistula (Wislo)
Corfu	Nansei Island	Warsaw
Corinth	Naples	Wenchow
Damascus	New Siberian Islands	White Sea
Danube	North Cape	Wrangel Island
Dardanelles	Nuremberg	Yellow River
Devil's Island	Olympus	Zuider Zee
Doha, Qatar	Ostend	

Regions

1. In the broadest sense, *America* refers to North and South America, and *American* to any resident of the continents. But the narrower meanings of the words — the United States and its citizens — are acceptable in informal and unambiguous contexts.

2. **North America**: Canada, the United States, Mexico, Greenland, Central America, the tiny French islands of St-Pierre-Miquelon and, in broad contexts, the islands of the Caribbean.

Central America: Belize, Costa Rica, El Salvador, Guatemala, Honduras, Nicaragua and Panama.

Note: Some definitions of North America exclude Central America.

3. **South America**: Argentina, Bolivia, Brazil, Chile, Colombia, Ecuador, Paraguay, Peru, Uruguay, Venezuela, plus French Guiana, Guyana and Suriname on the northeastern coast which regard themselves as Caribbean countries.

4. **Latin America**: the parts of Central and South America where Spanish or Portuguese is the dominant language. Most countries south of the United States are included. Exceptions are French Guiana, Suriname and areas with a British background: the Bahamas, Barbados, Belize, Grenada, Guyana, Jamaica, Trinidad and Tobago and the smaller islands in the West Indies.

5. **British Isles**: Britain and all Ireland and the islands near their coasts.

United Kingdom: England, Scotland, Wales and Northern Ireland.

Britain: England, Scotland and Wales, but *British* encompasses the United Kingdom.

Ireland: The island is divided into Northern Ireland (part of the United Kingdom) and the independent republic of Ireland.

6. **Middle East** or, less desirably, **Mideast**: usually taken to include Afghanistan, Bahrain, Egypt, Iran, Iraq, Israel, Jordan, Kuwait, Lebanon, Oman, Qatar, Sudan, Saudi Arabia, Syria, Turkey, the United Arab Emirates and Yemen. Do not use *Near East*.

7. **Far East**: China, Japan, Macao, North and South Korea, Taiwan, Hong Kong and the eastern Soviet Union.

8. **Southeast Asia**: Burma, Cambodia, Indonesia, Laos, Malaysia, New Guinea, the Philippines, Singapore, Thailand and Vietnam.

People and places

1. Shorten *Great Britain* to *Britain* in news stories. Write *Briton*, not *Britisher*.

2. Refer to the British capital, both in placelines and the body of a story, simply as *London*. Use *London, England,* only if ambiguity would otherwise result; for example, if two Londons appear in the same story.

3. For the people, prefer *Scot, Scots(wo)man,* not *Scotch(wo)man.* Use *Scottish* as the usual adjective, meaning pertaining to Scotland: **Scottish Highlands, Scottish thrift.** Use *Scotch* of food, drink, plants, animals and things originating in Scotland: **Scotch broth, Scotch tweed, Scotch thistle, Scotch terrier.** But **scotch** (whisky).

4. Where necessary, specify *the republic of Ireland* or *Northern Ireland.*

5. *Ulster* is acceptable as an informal name for Northern Ireland, though the original Ulster comprised the present Northern Ireland and the counties of Cavan, Donegal and Monaghan, now part of the republic of Ireland.

6. *Eire* is the former name of the republic of Ireland.

7. Israel declared Jerusalem its capital in 1950 despite Arab protest. Many countries, including Canada, do not recognize it as such. They maintain their ambassadors in Tel Aviv, which may be referred to as the administrative capital.

Place names to watch

Abidjan	Mackenzie River
Aklavik	Marseille
Aqaba, Gulf of	Mediterranean
Athabasca	Mississauga, Ont.
Bahrain	N'djamena
Basel	Northwest Territories (*but* N.W.T.)
Battle Harbour, Nfld.	Nunassiaq, N.W.T.
Bern	Philippines
Burk's Falls, Ont.	Portage la Prairie, Man.
Cap-aux-Meules, Que.	Port aux Basques, Nfld.
Caribbean	Qatar
Coral Harbour, N.W.T.	Riyadh
Corner Brook, Nfld.	Sa'na
Crowsnest, B.C.	St. Catharines, Ont.
Dar es Salaam	St-Jean, Que.
Duesseldorf	Saint John, N.B.
Esquimalt	St. John's, Nfld.
Gods Lake, Man.	St. Marys, Ont.
Goteborg	St-Pierre-Miquelon
Greenly Island	*(never as placeline)*
Harbour Grace, Nfld.	Smiths Falls, Ont.
Headingley, Man.	Stoney Creek, Ont. *and* N.B.
Honey Harbour, Ont.	Stony Mountain, Man.
Hudson Bay (Hudson's Bay Co.)	Suriname
Jidda	Tehran
Kejimkujik National Park	Témiscamingue
Klondike	*(Quebec county, electoral district)*
Kootenai River *(U.S.)*	Timiskaming *(Ontario district)*
Kootenay River *(B.C.)*	Trois-Rivières, Que.
Krakow	Val-d'Isère
Lac la Biche, Alta.	Vermilion, Alta.
L'Orignal, Ont.	Whitehorse, Yukon

➤ See **Placelines**, page 278; **People, places**, page 270.

Technical terms

General

1. Avoid unfamiliar scientific, medical and technical terms. When they must be used, give a simple, accurate explanation.

She acted oddly because she had Tourette's syndrome, a nervous disorder characterized by involuntary movements and vocal sounds.

2. Explain the unfamiliar in terms of the familiar.

A centrifuge acts like a cake mixer or merry-go-round, forcing objects outward from the centre.

Keratin is the main protein in fingernails, tiger claws, alligator scales, rhinoceros horns and feather quills.

3. Technical language can be less intimidating if the explanation is given first.

The medical team said a study of the mammoths' white blood cells, called leucocytes, shows them to be perfectly preserved.

4. An everyday term is generally preferable to a scientific one. For example, use **evergreen** instead of **coniferous**, **marijuana** instead of **cannabis**.

Scientific names

1. The name of a family or genus is capitalized: **Branta**. Use lower case for the species, even when derived from a proper name like Canada: **Branta canadensis** (Canada goose).

2. The genus may be shortened on second reference:

Brucella abortus (aborts cows, causes undulant fever in people)	Br. abortus
Escherichia coli (intestinal bacterium)	E. coli
Staphylococcus aureus (causes boils)	S. aureus

Drugs

1. In general, refer to a drug by its generic name, not its brand name: a tranquillizer, diazepam; a pain reliever, ASA.

2. If a brand name has to be used, follow it with the generic name: Antabuse, a brand of disulfiram used to discourage the drinking of alcohol; Valium, a brand of the mild tranquillizer diazepam; Aspirin, a brand of the pain reliever ASA (acetylsalicylic acid).

When allied news agencies use the term **aspirin**, change it to **ASA** in most cases. In Canada, Sterling Winthrop Inc. owns the Aspirin trademark and it must be capitalized.

➤ See **Capitalization**, page 201; **Trade names**, page 296; **Business terms**, page 44.

Medical

1. Prefer a common term to a medical one:

bleed to **hemorrhage**	chickenpox to **varicella**
broke to **fractured**	whooping cough to **pertussis**
clot to **embolism**	German measles to **rubella**
indigestion to **dyspepsia**	bad breath to **halitosis**
cut to **laceration**	scarlet fever to **scarlatina**
scrape to **abrasion**	shingles to **herpes zoster**
injury to **lesion**	stitch to **suture**

2. In general, don't capitalize diseases, conditions, symptoms, tests and treatments:

legionnaire's disease, scarlet fever, infarction, barium X-ray, cobalt therapy.

But capitalize proper names that are part of the term:

Alzheimer's disease, German measles, Parkinson's disease, Down's syndrome, Lassa fever, Pap smear, Heimlich manoeuvre.

3. Unless there's a compelling reason to give the precise cause of death, it's usually enough to say a person died, say, of **a stroke, a heart attack** or **in childbirth**, rather than of **cerebral hemorrhage, coronary thrombosis** or **puerperal fever.**

4. Similarly, say **Gruber sprained his right thumb**, instead of **Stress X-rays taken on Gruber, under local anesthetic, showed a tear of the ulnar collateral ligament of the metacarpal-phalangeal joint of the right thumb.**

In most cases, **arthroscopic surgery** can simply be referred to as **surgery**. If use of the term can't be avoided, say **The doctor inserts a tiny telescope into the body joint and uses thin instruments to do repairs.**

5. Widespread interest justifies giving more details in reporting the illness or death of a prime minister, president, pope, movie star or other major figure.

➤ See **Obituaries**, page 69.

Condition

1. Descriptions used by hospitals to report a patient's condition are often vague. It helps if a story explains that a patient is **conscious, allowed to sit up** or **receive visitors, is being fed intravenously**, and so on.

2. Here are four common descriptions of conditions, with the meanings some hospitals attach to them:

Good: The pulse, breathing and other vital signs are normal and stable. The patient is comfortable and conscious, and the outlook for recovery is good.

Fair: The pulse, breathing and other vital signs are near normal and the patient is conscious, but he or she is uncomfortable or may have minor complications. The outlook for recovery is favorable.

Serious: The patient is acutely ill and the chance of recovery is uncertain. The pulse, breathing and other vital signs may be abnormal or unstable.

Critical: Death may be imminent. The pulse, breathing and other vital signs are abnormal and unstable and there are major complications.

Burns

There are four degrees of burns, but most hospitals refer to only three: *first, second* and *third* — the third being the most severe.

First degree means the skin is red; *second*, it's blistering; *third*, skin has been destroyed along with underlying tissue and won't heal without grafting.

In a *fourth*-degree burn, muscle and bone have also been damaged.

Hospitals may also refer to partial and full burns. Ask specifically about the extent of tissue damage and the need for skin grafts and other measures.

AIDS

Acquired immune deficiency syndrome (or acquired immunodeficiency syndrome) is a breakdown of a person's immunological system, the body's natural defences against disease.

Someone is said to have AIDS if a life-threatening infection or cancer results from failure of the defence system.

It's inaccurate to say someone has died of AIDS. Give the actual cause of death — pneumonia, perhaps — and add that it was complicated by AIDS or was AIDS-related.

AIDS is believed to be spread through the exchange of blood, semen and vaginal secretions in the following ways: through sexual activity; use of HIV-infected syringes; transfusion of HIV-infected blood; and from an infected mother to her fetus.

AIDS was first diagnosed in the early 1980s and most of the early victims were homosexual males. The disease has since spread among male and female heterosexuals, intravenous drug users and hemophiliacs who received tainted blood before a proper screening system for donations was set up.

Although much research is still being conducted into the onset of AIDS, researchers generally agree that HIV, the human immunodeficiency virus must be present. Therefore, it is permissible to say that **HIV causes AIDS**.

Remember, however, that HIV can cause several infections or diseases, not just AIDS. In some contexts, it may be better to use the more inclusive **HIV**, rather than **the AIDS virus**.

The onset of AIDS has understandably led to a public tolerance of much greater frankness in discussing risky sexual behavior. CP stories must not shy away from plain language, where warranted, to inform readers.

➤ See **Obituaries**, page 69; **Disabilities**, page 19.

Richter scale

The Richter scale is an open-ended gauge of ground motion recorded on a seismograph during an earthquake. Every increase of one number means that the ground motion is 10 times greater.

However, science has refined the art of comparing earthquakes since 1935 when Charles Richter helped develop a scale that measured quakes in southern California. Modern seismology equipment is more sensitive and can measure a wider range of quakes than the original Richter scale, although newer scales have been designed to meld with Richter's model. Don't automatically use the phrase **on the Richter scale** when writing about earthquake magnitudes. General references, such as **a quake of 5.2 magnitude**, are usually sufficient.

A quake with a magnitude of 2 is the smallest normally felt by humans. One of magnitude 4 can cause moderate damage in a populated area, one of 5 considerable damage, one of 6 severe damage, and one of 7 widespread heavy damage. A quake of magnitude 8, a "great" earthquake, is capable of tremendous damage.

Time

Introduction

The Canadian Press divides its day into two news cycles.

The **PMs** cycle runs from 2 a.m. to 2 p.m. for papers that publish in the afternoon-evening. Copy carries a **PM** slug.

The **AMs** cycle runs from 2 p.m. to 2 a.m. for morning papers. Copy carries an **AM** slug.

The goal is to provide fresh stories for papers in each cycle.

Sometimes copy will carry a **BC** (**both cycles**) slug to identify stories that might straddle the cycles or that stand up in either cycle.

What day is it?

1. In copy for afternoon papers, write **today** to mean the current day. A lead sent after 2 p.m. for PMs papers will sometimes still say **today** for the current day.

2. In copy for morning papers, write **today** and **tonight** to mean the date of publication. If it's very early in the cycle (say 3 p.m.) consider a note to editors to clarify: **EDs: Today in para 2 is Thursday.**

3. CP doesn't use **yesterday** or **tomorrow**. To avoid confusion, the day is named.

4. Name the day if it falls within seven days of the current date: **on Tuesday** or **next Sunday** or **last Friday**.

5. For more distant dates, use the date: **May 5**.

6. For significant events and in sports schedules, give the day and the date: **The budget will be presented Friday, Nov. 4**; or **Dec. 22 (Sat.) Edmonton at Calgary**.

7. Place the day in a sentence where it would fall normally in conversation: not **The premier Thursday announced** but **The premier announced Thursday**.

8. Use **on** when it helps readability or to break up a series of capitalized words:

The measure passed in the House of Commons on Monday. The Quebec Nordiques defeated the Vancouver Canucks on Friday.

9. Don't wrench a lead out of shape trying for a weak or phoney **today** angle. Bury the time element if necessary, and get the news in the lead.

10. For afternoon-evening papers, especially, avoid putting an obsolescent angle in a lead: **The vote was expected today**. The event will have occurred by the time the newspaper is read. Instead, concentrate on getting the latest information in the lead and bury the time element so it can be dumped if necessary. Get a new lead out as soon as possible after events overtake the story.

11. Don't write that an event has taken place if the story is written beforehand in anticipation of the event.

➤ See **Advances,** page 378.

What time is it?

1. The exact time of an event is usually unnecessary. Instead, give the reader a sense of the time by describing the scene.

Not: A spectacular collision between two commuter trains occurred at 9 a.m. today.

But: A spectacular collision between two commuter trains caused chaos in downtown Montreal during the morning rush hour.

2. But give a specific time for important announcements, key votes, space launches, ransom deadlines or other events in which the time is a vital component. Give the time in the placelined community, with the equivalent in eastern time in brackets if necessary: **The volcano erupted at 8 a.m. local time (4 p.m. EDT).**

3. Specify the time zone in undated stories.

4. Specify time zones in stories involving the time of live radio and TV programs broadcast nationally. In cases of recorded or delayed broadcasts, provide the eastern time. Each newspaper can provide information on local broadcasts if need be.

5. Time is written in figures. However, write **noon** or **midnight**, not **12 noon** or **12 midnight**.

6. Write **5 a.m.**, not **5:00 a.m.**

7. A colon separates hours, minutes and seconds when figures are used. A period separates seconds from hundredths of seconds: **7:32 p.m.** or **Her time was 3:45:20.6.** When written out it would be: **Her time was three hours 45 minutes 20.6 seconds.**

What zone is it?

1. Use abbreviations for time zones with a clock reading: **11 a.m. MST** or **midnight Sunday night PST**. Spell out time zones when they are not accompanied by a clock reading: **Newfoundland daylight time**.

2. Capitalize Newfoundland, Atlantic and Pacific time zones when spelled out. Other time zones — eastern, mountain and central — are lowercase: **Atlantic daylight time**, but **eastern standard time**.

3. Write **daylight time,** not **daylight saving time.**

4. Greenwich mean time is five hours ahead of eastern standard time and four hours ahead of eastern daylight time. From April through October, when Britain is on **summer time** — their equivalent of **daylight time** — London is one hour ahead of GMT.

➤ See **Abbreviations and acronyms,** pages 169 and 171.

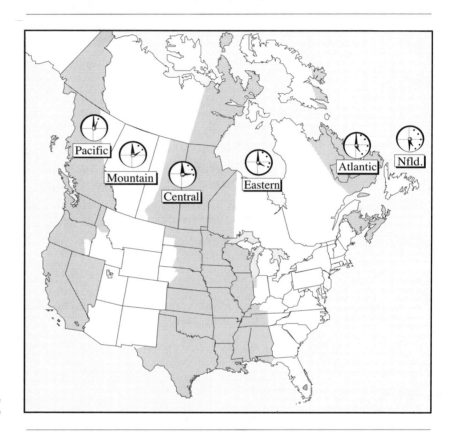

(CP—**Andrée** Lachapelle)

Titles

General

1. For rules on capitalization of titles, ➤ see **Capitalization**, page 177.

2. With few exceptions, a person's given name is used with surname on first reference.

Note: Famous authors, composers and the like may be referred to by surname only: **Dickens's Bleak House, Beethoven's Fifth, Darwin's theory of evolution.**

3. Front-loading — piling nouns in front of a name — is hard on the reader. Instead, use *of, the* and *a*, and set off long titles with commas.

Not: RPM Records of Canada president Gerry Lacoursiere . . .

But: The president of RPM Records of Canada, Gerry Lacoursiere, attended the news conference.

Not: Deputy external affairs minister Jacques Martin was the main architect of the program.

But: Jacques Martin, the deputy external affairs minister, was the main architect of the program.

4. False titles are best avoided.

U.S. modern dance innovator Margaret Mason, retired Yukon judge Roger Kimmerly

A phrase in apposition, preceded by *the*, is proper English.

the U.S. modern dance innovator Margaret Mason, the retired Yukon judge Roger Kimmerly

5. Use titles on first reference but seldom after that.

Ambrozic (not Archbishop Ambrozic) also attended the mass.
The size of the deficit startled Bourassa (not Premier Bourassa).
Berger (not Sgt. Berger) was first ashore.
The next in line is William (not Prince William).

But when a story is long or filled with names, repeat a title rather than risk losing a reader.

6. Use such titles as **Dr.** and **Rev.** only when those named are dealing with their speciality. A doctor in the Commons speaking about the environment is simply **Martha Singer, the Regina Conservative.** Speaking about medicare, she becomes **Dr. Martha Singer, the Regina pediatrician and Conservative.**

7. Use **chairman** or **chairwoman, spokesman** or **spokeswoman** as appropriate. Avoid artificial constructions like **alderperson**, or the awkward **chair** (noun or verb) for a person presiding at a meeting. If a person or organization insists on an artificial title, reword the reference to emphasize the activity (**presiding at Tuesday's meeting**) rather than the title.

Courtesy titles

1. In general, do not use the courtesy titles **Mr., Mrs., Miss** or **Ms.**

Justice (not **Mr. Justice**) **John Sopinka wrote the ruling. Murray said she enjoys singing. Campbell said abortion should be illegal.**

When it is necessary to use **Mrs., Miss** or **Ms.**, follow the woman's preference.

2. When possible, refer to a couple on first reference by their first names and their common last name: **William and Jane Levinski**. If their relationship is not that of husband and wife, explain: **Wayne Gretzky and his sister, Kim.**

3. When married people do not use a common surname, an explanation is needed.

Anne Murray and her husband, Bill Langstroth

4. To distinguish between persons of the same last name on second reference, repeat first names or use a courtesy title.

Kim Gretzky, Miss Gretzky

Professional titles

1. In general, use **Dr.** for licensed health care professionals. Where pertinent specify.

Dr. John Lucyk; Lucyk, an orthodontist. Dr. Sonya Chong; Chong, a chiropractor. Dr. Bert Clifford; Clifford, a veterinarian

Note: Each province decides which of its health care practitioners may use **Dr.** If in doubt, check.

2. Do not use **Dr.** for people with doctorates outside the health-care field. If pertinent, say a person has an earned or an honorary degree and give the discipline.

Chretien, a doctor of divinity. Callaghan received an honorary doctorate of letters from the University of Moncton

Religious titles

1.   Use a religious title before a person's name on first reference. Subsequently use either the surname alone (in most instances), the title preceded by *the*, or a general description.

Archbishop Adam Exner; Exner, the archbishop. Rabbi David Silverstein; Silverstein, the rabbi. Rev. Keith Wallace; Wallace, the priest

Note: Write **Rev.**, not **the Rev.** Never write **Rev. Wallace**.

2.   All popes and some Eastern Orthodox archbishops and bishops, as well as some Roman Catholic and Anglican nuns and brothers, are known by a title and given name only. In such instances, the title is usually retained in subsequent use of the name.

Pope John Paul, Metropolitan Andrew, Archbishop Volodymyr, Mother Mary, Sister Agatha, Brother Jude

Note: The convention of referring to **Pope John Paul** in subsequent references as **John Paul** is acceptable.

3.   The name of the office (**Bishop, Canon, Deacon**, etc.) is preferred as the title before the name: **Archbishop T.D. Somerville**. But such forms as **Most Rev. T.D. Somerville, Archbishop of New Westminster, B.C.**, are acceptable on occasion.

4.   Write **John Cardinal Brown**, not **Cardinal John Brown**.

5.   Some of the more common identifying titles that apply to various levels of Christian religious office include:

Roman Catholic:
The Pope - **His Holiness**
Cardinal - **His Eminence**
Archbishop - **Most Rev.**
Bishop - **Most Rev.**
Monsignor - **Right Rev.** (but usually **Msgr.**)

Anglican:
Primate - **Most Rev.**
Archbishop - **Most Rev.**
Bishop - **Right Rev.**
Dean - **Very Rev.**
Canon - **Rev.** (**Rev. Terry Scott** or **Canon Scott**)

United Church:
Moderator - **Right Rev.**
Ex-Moderator - **Very Rev.**

Presbyterian:
Moderator - **Rev.**

6.   Some religions lack a formal hierarchy, with leaders chosen by the congregation or community. In such cases use descriptive terms such as **holy man** or **priest**, as in **Hindu priest Sharad Rao** or **Sikh priest Satinder Singh**.

7.   Forms of address familiar to the clergy but not to others should be avoided except when in direct quotation:

His Holiness, His Eminence, His Grace, Lord Bishop, His Lordship, His Excellency

8.   Unfamiliar titles should be explained.

Primate Michael Peers, the head of the Anglican Church of Canada; Imam Mohammad Nasim, minister of the Jami Mosque; Kazi Mohammad Abdul, a Muslim religious judge.

9.   **Rev.** precedes the full name of most ministers and priests, including Buddhists. It is not used by Christian Scientists, Mormons, Jehovah's Witnesses or Seventh-day Adventists, among others. Muslims use the title **Imam** for leaders of their mosques.

Note: Do not use **Rev.** as a noun meaning clergyman: **The reverend reads murder mysteries**.

10. Unless it is immediately obvious from the context, do not use **Catholic Church** on first mention for the **Roman Catholic Church**. Several other communions maintain the Catholic tradition in varying degrees while rejecting papal infallibility and other dogmas. These include Eastern Orthodox, Anglican, Old Catholic, Polish National Catholic, Lusitanian (Portugal), Spanish Reformed Episcopal and Philippine Independent Catholic.

Honorable, Lady, Lord

1.   The honorary titles **right honorable** and **honorable** are used only when they appear in direct quotation.

2.   **Right Hon.** applies for life to the Governor General, prime minister, chief justice of Canada, and members of the British Privy Council.

3.   **Hon.** is applied for life to members of the Canadian Privy Council and lieutenant-governors. With royal assent, it may be used **for life** by retired judges of superior courts and some others. It is applied **during office** to senators, Speakers of the Commons and legislatures, judges of the Supreme and Federal courts of Canada and corresponding courts in the provinces, and members of provincial cabinets. Also applied to most peers' children.

4.   **Lady**, as in **Lady Anne** or **Lady Jane**, is applied only to the daughters of dukes, marquesses and earls. Wives of baronets or knights are simply **Lady Simpson**. Life peeresses select a title. The wife of the British wartime prime minister became **Baroness Spencer-Churchill of Chartwell**, addressed as **Lady Spencer-Churchill**.

5.   **Lord** is a conventional term for any nobleman from baron to marquess (whose wife is marchioness). Life peers are barons; but some baronies are hereditary.

Trade names

1. Capitalize trademarks: names (and symbols) used by organizations and protected by law.

Frigidaire, Hostess potato chips, Baggies

Note: Brand name is a non-legal term for **trademark** or **service mark**.

2. Variety names and names of market grades are capitalized.

Golden Delicious apples, Choice lamb

3. Common-noun elements of trademarks are generally lowercased.

Pears soap, Harris tweed, White Owl cigars, Spancore spandex yarn, Spic and Span cleaner

4. In general, follow an organization's capitalization. But for readability, capitalize all-lowercase names.

iNet, TelePrompTer, SkyDome but **the program Fifth Estate** (not fifth estate), **Adidas** (not adidas) sportswear, **the American movie Sex, Lies and Videotape** (not sex, lies and videotape)

5. For all-caps promotional names, capitalize only the first letters.

Scrabble (not **SCRABBLE**), **Via Rail** (not **VIA Rail**), **Oxfam** (not **OXFAM**)

6. The use of a trademark is easily avoided by substituting a general term.

soft drink/pop for **Coke, adhesive bandage** for **Band-Aid, flying disc** for **Frisbee**

7. Use a trademark when it gives point, color or impact to a story.

She wore an Yves Saint Laurent gown that had seen better days.

The children were playing a board game using Smarties as counters.

The robbers escaped in a red Cadillac convertible.

➤ See **Capitalization**, page 201.

8. Although it is a generic term abroad, **Aspirin** is a trademark in Canada owned by Sterling Winthrop Inc. Generic alternatives include **acetylsalicylic acid, ASA pills** and **a painkiller**.

9. Trademarks not guarded by their owners from being used as generics may lose the protection of the law.

cellophane	kerosene	nylon
corn flakes	lanolin	raisin bran
cube steak	linoleum	shredded wheat
dry ice	milk of magnesia	trampoline
escalator	mimeograph	yo-yo

10. Sources of information about trademarks include the *Canadian Trade Index* and reference books on drugs. Do not follow the capitalization in the *Concise Oxford Dictionary*.

11. Here are trademarks often encountered in news stories, with generic alternatives.

Baggies plastic bags
Band-Aid adhesive bandage
Benzedrine pep pill
Bic ballpoint pen
Brillo soap pads
Caterpillar tractor
Celanese acetate, nylon
  polyester, rayon
Chiclets chewing gum
Coca-Cola, Coke cola drink
Cream of Wheat cereal
Crisco shortening
Dacron polyester fibre
Deepfreeze food freezer
Dictaphone dictating machine
Diet Coke, Diet Pepsi low-
  calorie soft drink
Ditto duplicator, copier
Dramamine travel-sickness
  medicine
Fiberglas glass fibre, fibreglass
Fig Newton cakes
Formica laminated plastic
Frigidaire appliances
Frisbee flying disc
Fritos corn chips
Fudgsicle ice cream on a stick
Hamburger Helper dinner
Hawaiian Punch fruit drink
Hush Puppies casual shoes
Jacuzzi whirlpool tub
Javex bleach
Jeep vehicles, but **jeep** for the
  military vehicle
Jell-O gelatin dessert
Kleenex tissues

Lastex elastic yarns
Laundromat laundry
Levi's jeans
Linotype typesetting machine
Lycra spandex fibre
Lysol disinfectant
Mace tear gas
Masonite hardboard
Mercurochrome antiseptic
Minute rice rice
Mixmaster food mixer
Multigraph duplicator
Muzak background music
Novocain anesthetic, but
  novocaine
Orange Crush soft drink
Orlon acrylic fibre
Ouija seance board
Pablum baby cereal, but
  pabulum
Pampers disposable diapers
Pepsi-Cola, Pepsi cola drink
Photostat photocopier
Plexiglas acrylic plastic
Polaroid camera, sunglasses
Popsicle flavored ice on a stick
Post Toasties cereal
Postum cereal drink
Pyrex oven glassware
Q-Tips cotton swabs
Realtor (a member of the
  National Association of
  Realtors, prefer **real estate
  agent**)
Sanforized pre-shrunk
Scotch tape adhesive tape

Scrabble word game
Seven-Up or 7Up soft drink
Stetson hat
Styrofoam plastic foam
Tabasco pepper sauce
Technicolor colored movies
Teflon non-stick coating
TelePrompTer cueing device
Teletype teleprinter
Telex telegraphic exchange
  system
Terramycin antibiotic

Touch-Tone push-button
  dialling
Trivial Pursuit board game
TV Dinner frozen dinner
Valium tranquillizer
Vaseline petroleum jelly
Velcro tape fasteners
Videoscan document reader
Videotape recording tape
Walkman headset stereo
Xerox photocopier

12. For sponsored sports events, concerts and the like, use the sponsor's name for the event in first reference and a generic term in later references: the Labatt Brier, the Canadian men's curling championship.

➤ See **Sports**, page 86.

Weather

Introduction

Weather affects everyone. It's almost impossible to write too much about the weather. But write about it in human terms.

The heavy snowfall that is commonplace in Northern Ontario during the winter months — closing schools, stranding motorists, generally disrupting life — is news to Vancouver residents basking in 20 degree C sunshine. It is certainly news to anyone planning to travel through the region.

Endless rainfall on the Prairies while farmers are trying to bring in their fall harvest not only causes the farmers major concern but affects the commodity markets as well.

Write about weather in terms of its effects on people. Numbers help but prefer descriptions: **ankle-deep puddles, knee-deep snow, winds turning umbrellas inside out and bending small trees, a downpour causing wading pools to overflow and soaking through clothing**.

Weather knows no boundaries. A storm in Halifax affects those in Truro to the northeast and fishermen off the Atlantic coast. Did the storm originate in Maine and sweep through New Brunswick? Are Prince Edward Island and Newfoundland in the storm's path?

Add Canadian content to any story about weather problems in the northern United States.

Where warranted, use comparisons of other recent storms or those that caused major damage.

Consider a regional weather roundup to provide a proper perspective of what the weather pattern has done.

National weather stories should be considered whenever there is a thread to tie everything together.

Weather in metric

Temperatures are expressed in degrees Celsius, with **0 C** the freezing point of water and **100 C** the boiling point. Do not use **below zero**; use **−5 C** (minus five degrees C). **Degrees C** is commonplace; it is not necessary to write out Celsius each time.

For everyday comparison: **30 C** is swimming weather, **20 C** room temperature, **−10 C** skating weather.

Wind speed is measured in kilometres an hour: **light**, up to 20 km-h; **moderate**, 21-40 km-h; **strong**, 41-60 km-h; **gale**, 61-90 km-h; **whole gale**, 91-116 km-h; **hurricane**, over 117 km-h.

Rainfall is given in millimetres and **snowfall** in centimetres. A centimetre of snow equals a millimetre of rain.

Light shower   2.5 mm-h rainfall.

Heavy downpour   25 mm-h rainfall.

Good base for skiing   100 cm of snow

Atmospheric (barometric) pressure is measured in kilopascals. Normal pressure ranges from 98 to 103 kPa.

Terminology

Following are terms that may appear in weather forecasts from Environment Canada. Temperatures are Celsius.

acid rain: Rain mixed with sulphur dioxide, nitrogen oxide and other industrial and automobile pollutants to form acids, at times as strong as lemon juice or vinegar.

air mass: A large body of air with uniform temperature and moisture in a horizontal plane. The transition zone between different air masses is called a **front**. In a **cold front**, cold air is replacing warm; in a **warm front**, warm air is replacing cold.

atmospheric (or **barometric) pressure:** The pressure exerted by the atmosphere as a result of gravity. A rapidly falling barometer generally heralds a storm; when the barometer is rising, fair weather can usually be expected.

blizzard: A fierce storm with winds of more than 40 kilometres an hour, temperatures of less than –10, visibility less than half a kilometre.

chinook: A warm, dry wind which mainly affects the foothills of the Rockies. Can raise temperatures 20 degrees within minutes.

cyclone: A wind system rotating counterclockwise around a calm central area. In North America the term is sometimes used for a tornado or storm, in the Indian Ocean region for a hurricane.

flash flood: A sudden flood caused by heavy rain or the rapid melting of snow. A **flood crest** is the highest level reached before the water recedes.

freezing rain, freezing drizzle, ice storm: Rain or drizzle that freezes on impact with objects.

gale warning: Issued when winds are expected to be 34 to 48 knots (about 63 to 89 km-h) over water.

heavy snow: The definition varies from region to region. Heavy snow in Vancouver may be five centimetres, in Montreal 15.

high: An area of high pressure with winds moving clockwise, which often brings fine weather. Used interchangeably with anticyclone (a term not widely understood, however).

humidex: An index that combines the effects of summer temperatures and humidities:

Humidex	Degree of comfort
20-29	Comfortable
30-39	Varying degrees of discomfort
40-45	Most people uncomfortable
46 and over	Some outdoor work must be restricted

humidity, relative: The amount of water vapor in the air expressed as a percentage of the maximum amount the air can hold at that temperature and pressure.

hurricane or **typhoon:** A tropical storm with wind speeds of over 117 kilometres an hour. The hurricane eye is the relatively calm centre. Hurricanes develop east of the international date line. Typhoons develop west of the line; in the Indian Ocean they are called cyclones.

inversion: Instead of decreasing with height as is normal, the temperature remains constant or increases.

knot: A unit of speed: one nautical mile (6,080 feet) an hour is about 1.85 km-h.

low: An area of low atmospheric pressure that has an air circulation counter-clockwise in the Northern Hemisphere.

marine warning: Alerts mariners and shoreline residents of dangerous winds or freezing spray.

nearshore waters, coastal waters: Within five to 10 kilometres of shore.

offshore waters: Up to 400 kilometres from shore.

probability of precipitation: The chance of rain, snow and so on for a specified period, expressed in increments of 10 per cent, from zero (none expected) to 100 (a certainty).

ridge: An elongated area of relatively high pressure extending from the centre of a high-pressure region.

severe thunderstorm: Damaging winds usually with gusts to more than 60-80 kilometres an hour, heavy rain and possibly hailstones, frequent lightning and occasionally a tornado.

small craft warning: A warning issued for pleasure boaters when winds are expected to maintain speeds of 20-35 knots (37-63 km-h).

snow pellets: Tiny balls of snow that rebound on striking hard ground.

thundershower: Rain lasting 10-15 minutes, associated with a thunderstorm.

tornado: A destructive rotating column of air with a funnel shape touching the ground and accompanied by a loud roar. Sometimes called a twister.

tropical storm: A weather system one step below a hurricane; winds from 62 to 117 km-h.

trough: An elongated area of relatively low pressure extending from the centre of a low-pressure region.

typhoon: ➤ See **hurricane**.

weather advisory: Alerts the public that weather conditions, though not dangerous, may cause general inconvenience.

weather warning: Alerts the public to conditions that may endanger life, property and the public welfare.

whiteout: Dense snowcloud and total obscurity of physical features. Commonest in the Arctic and on the Prairies.

wind chill factor: An index of the effects of wind velocity and low temperature.

Factor	Degree of discomfort
700	Comfortable when dressed for skiing
1200	Conditions unpleasant on overcast days
1400	Conditions unpleasant on sunny days
1600	Exposed skin may freeze depending on the degree of activity and amount of sunshine
2300	Outdoor travel such as walking is dangerous; the exposed face may freeze in less than a minute
2700	Exposed flesh freezes within half a minute

Note: While Environment Canada uses a factor expressed in watts per square metre, there is a move toward using a temperature equivalency to express the wind chill factor.

wind direction: The direction from which the wind blows: an east wind blows toward the west.

wind shear: A swirling current of air produced at the junction of two horizontal air streams of greatly differing speed or direction. A possible hazard to aircraft landing or taking off.

Access to information

The federal and many provincial governments have laws that allow access to their information by reporters, researchers, businesses, academics and the general public. Other governments are bound to follow suit.

The federal law is the Access to Information Act; provinces tend to use variations on the name of the U.S. law, the Freedom of Information Act. Only Prince Edward Island lacks such a law.

But the concept is the same: make records available so it's easier to understand how governments make decisions, carry out public business, spend money and make history.

To an extent. With exceptions. Under many conditions.

General

The following is aimed mainly at users of the federal law, but many points are applicable to all such access acts.

1.   The acts are better tools of history than of journalism. Expect to wait at least 30 days for an answer to a request, no matter what the law says. Access laws should be a last resort for reporters. Use them only after asking for information to be released publicly and informally. Challenge a government employee to find reasons why the material shouldn't be disclosed immediately.

2. Access is often costly, but the initial application fee is cheap, or even free (in the case of Ontario, Quebec, British Columbia, Alberta, Saskatchewan and Manitoba acts). The main costs come from searching for records. The more detailed the request, the greater the search time and the greater the fees. In the federal case, a $5 application fee gets five hours of search time; after that, it's $10 an hour to search. Other jurisdictions have limits on free search time. In Quebec and New Brunswick, there are no search fees.

3.   There are Mack Truck-sized holes through which the bureaucracy can legally manoeuvre to deny information. Governments can use some 500 reasons to keep their records from view. The most common categories:

•   Cabinet confidences, meaning any record brought to the cabinet table for discussion; this provision expires after a certain number of years, 20 in Ottawa's case.

•   National security, a catch-all for such things as police records and controversial human rights matters.

•   International relations, a far-reaching exemption that avoids many embarrassing diplomatic episodes.

•   Information involving a person or a business.

•   Legal advice, a category that governments usually think means anything written by a lawyer (though the courts don't always agree).

What you can get

There are some easy records to obtain.

1. What's going on: basic facts on just about anything the government does.

2. Who's telling governments what: public opinion research, including surveys of the public, focus groups or experts.

3. How well the money and effort was spent: audits, the details of spending practices and assessments of the effectiveness of departments and programs.

4. Who went where and did what: bureaucratic expenses covering such items as the costs and contractual details for consultants, hospitality, travel and conferences.

5. Who wrote what and when: memos and reports, some of which may have crucial information deleted. These records have to be in the control of a department or agency subject to the act. They can't be owned by someone else. Crown corporations like the CBC and CN Rail are exempt from the purview of the act. The government considers them businesses. Also exempt are records held by ministerial offices and political party operations.

Tips

1. Every department or ministry has at least one person designated to handle information requests. Those people can help — in confidence — to phrase a request so it has the best chance of producing the records sought.

2. Information-seekers must know what they want. They should not be on a fishing expedition. The acts are not set up to do someone's research, so specify the subject matter. Don't ask for *all records on refugees* — mountains of material, millions of dollars to obtain — when what is wanted are *all records on Ethiopian refugees*.

3. Narrow the time-frame of requests. Don't ask for *all records on Ethiopian refugees*, when what is wanted are *records from 1991 on Ethiopian refugees*. The application fee covers a certain number of hours of research by a government employee for the records. It's a bargain, so divide requests chronologically or by small categories to keep costs down.

4. Askers should not be so precise that they outsmart themselves. For instance, always ask for *records*, not for *reports, analyses, documents* or anything as specific. The records wanted may be on computer disk, or may be a tiny element of a large report. Ask for anything other than *records* and the government may say no actual reports or analyses or documents on the specific request exist — technically correct — and the chase is over.

5.   Records won't be created for requesters. If a *list* of things is requested and no list exists, the government is under no obligation to create a list. If the aim is to see all records on Ethiopian refugees in 1991 — but it's a tall order to ask for all this material in one request — start by asking for the *title pages* of records. After those pages are received, go to a second round of requesting and ask for what is wanted among those records.

6.   Ask to look at the disclosed records in a government office to avoid costly photocopying. The acts allow a review of the material in any branch office of a department.

When you feel cheated

People dissatisfied with the outcome of the request can complain within one year to the information commissioner, whose office will review what was disclosed. The office cannot force the disclosure of records, but it can use moral suasion.

It can also, at its expense, take the government to court on a requester's behalf. It is also possible for a requester to pursue the matter through the courts.

Good news

There is an ever-improving chance of getting material. The courts have generally ruled in favor of wider access to records, and all sorts of precedents have been set within departments and ministries to pave the way for similar requests.

Bear in mind that the acts are less than 20 years old. In other countries where there are similar laws, they have taken a generation to become effective.

There is no doubt the acts have yielded information that would have otherwise been kept secret. Despite their many shortcomings, there is good reason to see the laws as a positive force for public policy journalism.

Words

This chapter is designed to demonstrate some tricky distinctions in the meanings of words and some rulings on correct or preferred usage in the CP news report.

according to	Avoid in attributions if it seems to cast doubt on the source's credibility.
adventuresome **adventurous**	ready to take risks fond of adventure
adverse **averse**	unfavorable opposed
affect (verb) **effect** (noun or verb)	influence, have an effect on a result; bring about, accomplish
aggravate **irritate**	make worse annoy, exasperate
allude to **refer to**	suggest without naming name
allusion **illusion**	a casual or indirect reference a false impression
altercation	a noisy dispute or quarrel (not a fistfight)
alternate, an	a person who substitutes
alternate(ly) **alternative(ly)**	in turns, first one and then the other: **The raiders lay alternately watching and sleeping.** providing a choice (usually the word wanted): **an alternative route.**
ambiguous **ambivalent**	having two or more meanings: **The large lady's hat** is ambiguous. having mixed feelings: **He was ambivalent about arms spending, recognizing the need for defence but wishing the money better spent.**
amiable **amicable**	friendly, of people friendly, of situations and agreements
among **between**	introduces three or more items. introduces two items; or three or more considered a pair at a time; **the difference between borrow, lend and loan.**

amount	How much? (weight and money)
number	How many? (individual items)
antagonist	➤ See protagonist.
apparent	Write He died apparently of a heart attack, not He died of an apparent heart attack.
apparently	seemingly, presumably
obviously	plainly, unmistakably
apt	customarily inclined; naturally fit
liable	open to something unpleasant
likely	probable, expected
arbitrate	render a binding decision in a dispute
mediate	help settle a dispute
as	meaning *since* or *because* should be used with care. It can sometimes be mistaken for *while* or *during the time that*: As he was going out, she asked him to buy a paper.
as	introduces clauses: It tastes good as a cigarette should.
like	introduces a noun or pronoun not directly followed by a verb: He smokes like a chimney.
as if, as though	may be used interchangeably to connect clauses.
assume	accept for the sake of argument
presume	take for granted
assure	➤ See ensure.
at present	➤ See presently.
audience	watches or listens.
spectators	watch.
avenge	retaliate for another
revenge	retaliate for oneself
averse	➤ See adverse.
avocation	a hobby, diversion
vocation	a career, occupation
awhile	➤ See while.

bait	lure (a **baited hook**); torment
bate	hold in (**bated breath**)
barely	➤ See **hardly**.
beg the question	assume the truth, usually unjustifiably, of the thing to be proved: **The worthless Senate should be abolished.** Beg the question doesn't mean evade a straight answer.
begin	is the general word.
commence	sounds formal.
start	usually applies to physical motion.
beside	at the side of
besides	in addition to
between	➤ See **among**.
bi-	is ambiguous in **biweekly, bimonthly, biennial,** etc. Prefer **twice a week, every two weeks, semi-weekly, semi-annual, half-yearly,** etc.
blatant	offensively noisy, obtrusive
flagrant	shameless, brazen
bloc	a combination of people, countries or organizations to foster a shared interest
block	a group of things: shares, seats, tickets
blond (adjective)	She has blond hair.
blond (noun)	a male or female
boat	a small craft propelled by oars, sails or motor; also a submarine, motor torpedo boat, ferry
ship	a large craft with sails or engine
vessel	a ship or a boat bigger than a rowboat
born	come into being by birth
borne	carried, endured
breach	break a contract or a wall
broach	open a barrel or a topic
breech birth	baby born buttocks first
bring	carry here
take	carry there
can (could)	denotes ability or power to do something.
may (might)	suggests doubt; also expresses permission to do something.

cannon	a gun
canon	a church decree; a clergyman
canvas	coarse cloth
canvass	solicit
careen	heel over, lean, sway
career	move at high speed
catch-22	a dilemma from which there is no escape. Note the lowercase.
celebrator	one who celebrates, a partygoer
celebrant	an officiating priest
cement	powder used in making concrete
concrete	rocklike material for roads, buildings, etc.
centre (verb)	is followed by **on** or **in**.
revolve (verb)	is followed by **round** or **around**.
childish	silly, puerile
childlike	innocent, confiding
chord	used in musical and mathematical senses: **The name struck a chord.**
cord	used in anatomical senses: **spinal cord, vocal cord, umbilical cord**; also: **nylon cord, cord of wood.**
client	uses the services of a professional person other than a doctor, or of a business.
customer	buys goods from a shop or a business.
climactic	of a climax
climatic	of climate
climax	➤ See **crescendo**.
collide	strike a moving object
commence	➤ See **begin**.
communique	Use for official communications, not for terrorists' threatening notes and the like.
compare to	liken to: **The staff compared (likened) him to Hitler.**
compare with	show similarities and differences (the term usually wanted): **He cannot compare with Ruth Rendell as a writer of mysteries.**
contrast with	show differences

complementary completing; supplying needs
  complimentary praising; free

comprise (no of) contain all the parts
  include contain some of the parts

concrete ➤ See **cement.**

connotation ➤ See **denotation.**

consensus agreement, majority view (**general consensus of opinion** is redundant)

contagious passed on by contact
  infectious passed on by contact or some other means

contemptible despicable
  contemptuous scornful, insolent

continual frequently repeated (a dripping tap)
  continuous uninterrupted (Niagara Falls)

controversial is not needed when it is clear from the context that the subject is contentious: **The Opposition let the legislature bells ring for three hours Monday in its fight against a (controversial) housing bill.**

convict ➤ See **inmate.**

convince is followed by **of** or **that**, but not **to.**
  persuade is followed by **of**, **that** or **to.**

cord ➤ See **chord.**

council (noun) an assembly
  counsel (n. or v.) advice, a legal adviser; to advise

country ➤ See **nation.**

couple almost invariably plural in reference to people: **The couple were hurt when their plane crashed.** But **A couple pays $5.**

credible believable
  creditable praiseworthy
  credulous gullible

crescendo increasing in strength or loudness
  climax highest point, top of a crescendo

customer	➤ See **client**.
debate	Write debate **something**, not **someone**.
decimate	destroy a tenth of, much of; not destroy most of
defective **deficient**	faulty lacking, incomplete
definite **definitive**	firm, clear final, absolute
defuse (verb) **diffuse** (adjective)	to render harmless scattered
demolish, destroy	**completely** is redundant. (Avoid as synonym for **defeat** in sports stories.)
denotation **connotation**	what a word specifically means: **Pig denotes a swine.** what a word suggests: **Pig connotes dirt, greed, the little pig who went to market and other storybook characters.**
deny	➤ See **rebut, refute**.
dependant (noun) **dependent** (adj.)	one who depends on another depending on
deprecate **depreciate**	express disapproval of lose in value; belittle: **a self-depreciating smile**
desert **dessert**	barren; something deserved; to abandon a sweet
different from **different than**	is used with a noun or pronoun. introduces a clause.
dilemma	a choice between two equally pleasant or unpleasant things (not a synonym for **difficulty**)
disc **disk**	in all references except for computers: **a compact disc, a disc jockey, a slipped disc** of computers only: **disk drive, a floppy disk**
discomfort **discomfit**	make uncomfortable, uneasy embarrass, thwart
disinterested **uninterested**	impartial not interested
dissatisfied	➤ See **unsatisfied**.

dove	Make it **dived**.
draft	current of air, sum of money, rough plan, military service, hauling, beer drawn from a barrel (never **draught**)
due to	Use only if *caused by* or *ascribed to* could be substituted: **The crash was due to ice.** Not: **Due to ice, the plane crashed.** Try **because of, owing to**.
each other **one another**	refers to two. refers to three or more.
eatable **edible**	can be eaten because not revolting can be safely eaten
economic **economical**	relating to economics thrifty
-ee, -er	In general, *-ee* denotes the recipient of an action: **employee, examinee, trainee**; *-er* denotes the doer of the action: **employer, examiner, trainer**. But *-ee* sometimes applies to a person who behaves in a certain way: **absentee, debauchee, escapee, refugee**.
effect	➤ See **affect**.
effective **effectual**	having an effect; coming into operation answering its purpose
elder, eldest	used to denote seniority in a family
elicit (verb) **illicit** (adjective)	to draw out, evoke not legal

emigrant
  immigrant
  migrant
	leaves the country.
	enters the country.
	moves from one place to another.

eminent **imminent**	prominent near at hand
ended **ending**	Use of past: **week ended (last) Jan. 1.** Use of future: **week ending (next) May 1.**
enormity **enormousness**	monstrous wickedness, serious error great size

ensure
  insure
  assure
	to make sure
	to provide insurance
	to remove worry or uncertainty

especially	➤ See specially.
execute	describes judicial killings, not gangland or terrorist murders.
exhausting **exhaustive**	causing exhaustion complete
expedient **expeditious**	suitable for a particular purpose; advantageous quick
extradite **extricate**	hand person to another country; obtain such person for trial disentangle, release
farther **further**	denotes physical distance: **farther down the road**. everything else: **to slip further into debt.**
female **feminine**	refers to sex of human beings, animals or plants: **female servants**. applies to qualities said to be characteristic of girls and women: **feminine charm**. ➤ See gender.
fewer **less**	Use with plurals: **fewer bills**. Use with singulars: **less sugar, a man less.**
figuratively **literally**	means in an allied but not exact sense: **She (figuratively) broke his heart.** means exactly as stated. Wrong: **She literally broke his heart.**
find	➤ See locate.
first, firstly	Write either **first, second, third** or **firstly, secondly, thirdly**, but not a mixture.
flagrant	➤ See blatant.
flair **flare**	aptitude, knack a flame; a widening
flaunt **flout**	show off mock, scoff at
flounder **founder**	move clumsily fill with water and sink; fail
following	Prefer **after** as a preposition.

foot, feet	In compounds before a noun, use **foot: a six-foot pass**. In more formal and precise contexts, use **feet: six feet three inches**. In informal usage, **inches** is omitted and **foot** is usual: **six foot three**.
forbid	is followed by **to: The captain forbade them to go ashore.**
prohibit	is followed by **from: Government workers were prohibited from striking.**
forego	precede
forgo	abstain from
fortuitous	by chance
fortunate	lucky
fulsome	disgusting, loathsome, excessive
gambit	a chess opening in which a player sacrifices a piece to secure an advantage; any opening move
gamut	a whole series or scope of anything
gas	may be used for **gasoline** if there is no confusion with manufactured or natural gas.
gender	refers to words: **A noun or pronoun that denotes a male is in the masculine gender: boy, brother, he, him.**
sex	refers to humans, plants and animals: **athletes of both sexes** (not **genders**).
generation	about 30 years
genius	➤ See **talent**.
gibe	➤ See **jibe**.
Gothic	of architecture: **a Gothic cathedral**
gothic	all other uses: **a gothic novel**
gourmand	a heavy eater
gourmet	a connoisseur of food
greeted by	used with people
greeted with	used with things
grill	a metal frame for cooking; question closely
grille	grating, screen
grisly	gruesome, horrible
grizzly	greyish, of bears and beards

hail	greet, call to
hale	take forcibly (as to court). **But avoid.**
hanged	killed by hanging
hung	suspended
happen	➤ See transpire.
hardly, barely, scarcely	1. These are used without a negative: I can (not can't) hardly read the small print. 2. They are followed by when, not than: Scarcely had they got home when (not than) the phone rang.
healthful	promoting good health
healthy	in good health
historic	important or famous in history
historical	about or based on history
hoard	a store
horde	a crowd
homosexual	either male or female
lesbian	a female homosexual (lowercase *l*)
human (adjective)	used for both good and bad traits of humanity
humane	merciful, kind
humans	used in contrast to animals. In other cases, **human beings** is more appropriate.
hurting	normally requires object. **Poor sales hurt the company** (not **The company was hurting**); **Guy Carbonneau has been playing with knee problems** (not **Guy Carbonneau has been hurting**).
if and when	Use one, not both.
if, whether	are interchangeable when they make sense and are not ambiguous.
illusion	➤ See allusion.
immigrant	➤ See emigrant.
imminent	➤ See eminent.
imply	suggest or hint at; speakers or writers imply.
infer	deduce or conclude; hearers or readers infer.

inapt	unsuitable
inept	clumsy
individual	used of a person when contrasted with a society or a group
infectious	➤ See **contagious**.
inflammable, flammable	Used interchangeably to mean capable of being set on fire. Prefer **flammable**.
inmate	occupant of a hospital, home, prison or other institution
prisoner, convict	occupant of a prison
insure	➤ See **ensure**.
irritate	➤ See **aggravate**.
it's	abbreviation for **it is** (or **it has**)
its	belonging to it (**held its own**)
jibe	agree or be in accord with
gibe	jeer, mock
judicial	of a judge or law court
judicious	sound of judgment
jurist	a person versed in law (not necessarily a lawyer or a judge)
laden	**a truck laden with melons** implies it is weighed down.
loaded	**a truck loaded with melons** is simply carrying melons.
lay (laying, laid, laid)	to lay something down (takes a direct object): **The boy laid the towel on the sand.**
lie (lying, lay, lain)	to recline (does not take a direct object): **Then he lay on the towel.**
lead (noun and verb)	metal; present tense of **to lead**
led (verb)	past tense of **to lead**
leading question	a question so worded that it prompts a person to give the desired answer: **"You weren't in the house at the time of the murder, were you?"**
lectern	➤ See **podium**.

lend (lent, not **loaned)** **loan**	Use as the verb: **Lend me your ears. Lend me** **$10.** Use as the noun: **a $100 loan**
lesbian	➤ See **homosexual.**
less	➤ See **fewer.**
lighted, lit	Used interchangeably in the past tense, though **lit** is more common: **The lamps were lighted/lit.** As an adjective before a noun, **lighted** is preferable: **a lighted cigarette**; except when the adjective is preceded by an adverb: **a brightly lit room.**
like **such as**	Normal usage for comparisons is **Mother Teresa helped rescue people like the poor, the sick and the abandoned.** is often used to introduce examples set off with commas: **Several famous composers, such as Mozart and Schubert, died young.**
like - as	➤ See **as - like.**
likely, liable	➤ See **apt.**
linage **lineage**	number of lines ancestry, descent
lit	➤ See **lighted.**
literally	➤ See **figuratively.**
loaded	➤ See **laden.**
loath **loathe**	reluctant to detest
locate **find**	fix the position of (a downed aircraft) discover without reference to a particular setting (a missing child)
luxuriant **luxurious**	lush costly, rich
madam **madame**	a polite form of address: **"No, madam"**; a brothel-keeper a French title of respect: **Madame Jules Benoit**
male	refers to sex of humans, animals or plants: **a male lion.**

masterful	domineering
masterly	expert, skilful
may (might)	➤ See can (could).
me, I	To, with, from and other prepositions are followed by me, him, her, us and them, not I, he, she, we or they: Mother gave it to Jack and me (not I). Put your trust in him (not he) who knows best. Many of us (not we) voters are tired of promises.
media	takes a plural verb: The media are blamed.
mediate	➤ See arbitrate.
meter	a measuring machine
metre	a measure of distance; a verse rhythm
meticulous	careful about small details
scrupulous	conscientious, thorough
migrant	➤ See emigrant.
momentarily	➤ See presently.
momentary	short-lived, for a moment
momentous	important
moral	virtuous; a lesson from a story
morale	mental attitude
more than	is followed by a singular verb when the noun is singular: More than one tank was hit. ➤ See over.
myself	is properly used to intensify: I myself wouldn't have gone. Do not use it instead of I or me: Gord and myself (I) weren't invited. The bride didn't invite Gord or myself (me).
naked	the general word meaning without clothing or covering
nude	often a synonym for naked; otherwise usually restricted to artistic or pornographic contexts
nation	the people of a country
country	a nation's territory
nauseous	causing nausea
nauseated	feeling nausea, inclined to vomit
noxious	harmful, unpleasant

negligent	careless
negligible	small, unimportant
noisome	harmful, foul-smelling
no sooner	is followed by **than**, not **when**.
notable	worth noting
noticeable	easy to see, prominent
nude	➤ See **naked**.
number	➤ See **amount**.
O	is usually restricted to invocations: **O God, help me**. It is always capitalized and is written without a comma.
oh	is an exclamation: **Oh God, he's back. Oh, did he?** It is capitalized only at the start of a sentence. Write **oh-oh**, not **oh, oh**.
observance	obeying, paying heed to
observation	noting, looking at
obsolete	no longer in use
obsolescent	becoming obsolete
obviously	➤ See **apparently**.
official	connected with an office; authorized
officious	meddlesome, bossy
oh	➤ See **O**.
one another	➤ See **each other**.
one of those who	is followed by a plural verb.
oral	spoken
verbal	spoken or written
over	In the sense of *in excess of,* used interchangeably with **more than**: **Creasey and Simenon have each published over (more than) 500 books.**
overall	total, all-inclusive
overalls	protective clothing
pair	generally plural: **The pair were seen with their son.** But **A pair receives a smaller pension.**

paramount	supreme
tantamount	equal to
parliamentarian	an expert in parliamentary procedure; a skilled debater; not a synonym for **MP**
peddle	sell; a **pedlar** sells.
pedal	cycle; a **pedaller** pushes pedals; to **softpedal** is to play music with the soft pedal down.
people	In general, use **people**, even if the number is small or precise: **Two people died.** Better: **A man and a woman died.**
persons	Use for formality or occasional variety: **Persons over 21 are eligible.**
perquisite	special privilege, advantage (a perk)
prerequisite	a necessary condition
persuade	➤ See **convince**.
podium	the platform a speaker stands on
lectern	the reading desk a speaker stands behind
pompon	ornamental tuft
pompom	rapid-firing gun
practicable	able to be done
practical	useful, sensible, functional
precede	to go before
proceed	to go along, continue
prerequisite	➤ See **perquisite**.
presently	soon, in a moment (**avoid**: usually misunderstood)
at present	now
momentarily	for a moment
presume	➤ See **assume**.
principal	chief, most important; capital sum; school head
principle	basic truth or rule; code of conduct
prior to	Use **before**.
prisoner	➤ See **inmate**.
prohibit	➤ See **forbid**.
prone	➤ See **supine**.

protagonist	chief actor, champion of a cause
antagonist	opponent
punctilious	attentive to detail
punctual	prompt
quartet	➤ See trio.
rack (noun)	framework: **hat-rack**
rack (verb)	to trouble, torture, destroy: **nerve-racking**
wrack (noun)	wreckage, seaweed
rampage	➤ See spree.
rankle	A thing **rankles**; it does not **rankle someone**.
	Right: **The insult rankled.**
	Wrong: **The insult rankled Joe.**
ravage	damage badly, devastate
ravish	delight, enrapture; rape
reason	is followed by **that** or **why**, not **because**: **The reason for the loss was that taxes rose.**
rebut, refute	prove to be false: **She refuted the charge of theft by producing a sales receipt.**
deny	declare to be false: **He denied the charge but had no alibi.**
regretful	full of regret
regrettable	the cause of regret
reign	monarch's rule
rein	harness
reluctant	unwilling, grudging
reticent	sparing of words, reserved
repetitive	characterized by repetition: **a repetitive beat**
repetitious	characterized by unnecessary or tedious repetition: **repetitious arguments**
revenge	➤ See avenge.
revolve	➤ See centre.
rob	A person or place is robbed, not the thing stolen: **A company was robbed of a payroll.** Not: **A company's payroll was robbed.**

rush	Do not use when the idea of speed is implicit, as in stories involving ambulances, fire trucks and police cruisers. Not: **She was rushed to hospital.** Write **taken** or some such.
scarce **rare**	of things normally available of things seldom found at any time
scarcely	➤ See **hardly.**
scrupulous	➤ See **meticulous.**
seasonable **seasonal**	suitable to the occasion or season occurring at a particular season
sensual **sensuous**	arousing or satisfying bodily appetites or sexual desire: **the sensual pleasures of eating; a sensual striptease** appealing to the senses, sometimes the mind: **a ballet dancer's sensuous movements; a sensuous passage of Mozart**
sex	➤ See **gender.**
ship	➤ See **boat.**
shot	Use the specific **shot and wounded** or **shot and killed** as appropriate.
situation	Avoid the practice of putting other nouns or phrases before **situation: a crisis situation, a classroom situation, a bad-debt situation.**
some	meaning *about* is proper: **some 20 years later, some 500 troops.**
spare **sparse**	scanty, frugal; thin: **a spare diet, a spare style of writing; a spare man** thinly scattered, not thick: **a sparse population, a sparse beard**
specially **especially**	for a particular purpose to a great degree, outstanding
spectators	➤ See **audience.**
spree **rampage**	a frolic; a drinking or shopping bout; not violent behavior violent behavior, a bout of violence
start	➤ See **begin.**

stationary	unmoving
stationery	writing material
stimulant	drug, etc. (not alcohol, a depressant)
stimulus	incentive, spur
strait	narrow, confined (**straitjacket, Davis Strait**)
straight	unbent, direct
strategy	refers to the overall campaign.
tactics	the art of moving forces; adroit management
such as	➤ See like.
supine	face upward (but **avoid**)
prone	face downward
tack	course of action or policy
tact	ability to deal sensitively with others; sensitivity
tactics	➤ See strategy.
talent	special ability
genius	exceptionally great talent
tantamount	➤ See paramount.

that — As a conjunction, *that* may be omitted if no confusion results: **King said** (that) **she would go.** It is often needed after such verbs as **assert, declare, estimate, make clear, point out, propose, state, warn: She warned** that **the committee would oppose the plan.** It may be needed with time elements (**White said that in 1950 he was destitute**) and before such conjunctions as **after, although, as, because, before, in addition to, when: Green said** that **when she heard the shot, she was asleep.**

that — often introduces an essential clause — one that defines the noun it is attached to and cannot be omitted: **The house that is painted white is mine.**

which — introduces a non-essential or parenthetical clause — one that adds information that could be omitted without changing meaning: **The house, which was built in 1940, is white.**

that-who — ➤ See which-who-that.

the	Do not drop *the* from the beginning of sentences or wherever idiom or grammar demands it. Not: **Terms of the contract were secret; Police would not reveal names of the injured.**
then	Avoid putting *then* as an adjective before a noun if it sounds equally well or better in its normal position. Not: **the then prime minister, Lester Pearson.** But: **the prime minister then, Lester Pearson.**
transpire **happen**	become known occur
trio, quartet	Use only in the musical sense, not of any casual grouping of three or four.
troops	In general, **troops** describes a body of soldiers: **The troops were flown in by helicopter.** It is not used of small numbers of individuals: **30 troops.** But idiom permits its use with large numbers, say in the hundreds: **Some 250 troops surrounded the prison.**
try to	try to (not **and**) understand
uninterested	➤ See **disinterested.**
unsatisfied **dissatisfied**	falling short of satisfaction discontented
upcoming	Write **coming, approaching** or **forthcoming** if an adjective is needed.
urban **urbane**	of a town or city well-bred, suave
usage	a manner of use established by custom
verbal	➤ See **oral.**
vessel	➤ See **boat.**
veteran	one who served in the military; person of long experience. Avoid such as **five-year police veteran** and **a veteran of four NHL seasons.**
virtual	means in effect though not in fact: **The slowdown was a virtual strike.** Not **She's a virtual angel.**
vocation	➤ See **avocation.**

waive	give up, forgo
waver	falter, move to and fro
-ward, -wards	Americans prefer the -ward form: **toward, backward, afterward**; Britons prefer -wards: **towards, backwards, afterwards**; Canadians use both forms.
was	simple past tense
were	Use **were** when expressing a wish or a condition contrary to fact, and after **as if** and **as though**: **I wish I were you. She spoke to him as if he were a fool.**
whether, if	➤ See **if, whether.**
whether or not	Retain the *or not* when an alternative is emphasized: **I will go whether you like it or not.**
which-that	➤ See **that-which.**
which	normally refers to things but may be used of people in a body: **She spoke to the crowd, which grew silent.**
who	usually refers to people but sometimes to animals, especially those with names: **Snip, who is 14, is a toy poodle.**
that	refers to people or things: **It was the pilot that** (or **who**) **spoke.**
while (noun)	They had to wait for a while (note the **for**).
awhile (adverb)	They had to wait awhile (no preposition).
who-whom	Who stands for **he-she-they, whom** for **him-her-them.** When in doubt, break the sentence in two: **She met a man** who **she thought was her brother.** (She thought **he** was her brother, so **who** is correct.) **She met a man** whom **she took for her brother.** (She took **him** for her brother, so **whom** is correct.)
wove	the normal past tense of **weave: His daughter wove him a scarf.**
weaved	the past tense of **weave** means to avoid hitting something: **The forward weaved through the defence**; or to tell an involved story: **The old man weaved a chilling plot.**
wrack	➤ See **rack.**
yoke	wooden crosspiece
yolk	yellow of an egg

Illustrating the news

Pictures
  Good illustrations
  Content
  Quality
  Composition
  Photo manipulation
  PhotoNet
  Sending photos
  Captions
  Kills and corrections
  Pictures and the law
  Copyright photos
  Picturing money
  Specials
  Cartoons
Graphics
  Information please

Pictures

Pictures sell stories.

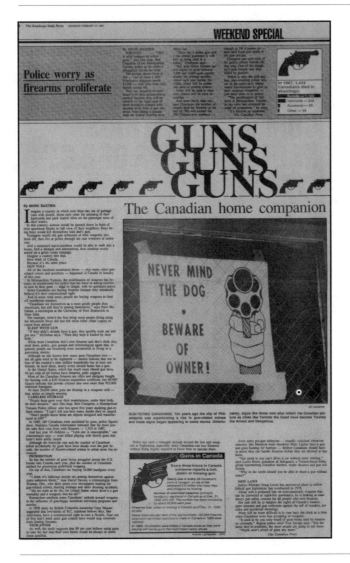

A good picture can carry a story on to page 1; lack of a picture can take a good story off the front page — and right out of the paper. CP aims to illustrate every worthwhile story with color or black-and-white photos, maps or graphics.

Having that happen depends on awareness. All CP staff need to be alert to illustrating the story, whether it is a rewrite or the germ of an idea for a staff-written series. The story without pictures and graphics won't get the play it deserves.

Effective CP work involves developing an understanding of what makes a good illustration and the mechanics of getting it from the photographer or artist to the network of receiving newspapers.

CP Picture Service began in 1948 as an exchange of mailed photos. The first Wirephoto network based on an analogue or sound signal transmitted over telephone wires began in Ontario and Quebec in 1954 and 10 years later was coast-to-coast. Wirephoto became LaserPhoto in 1978, when new transmission equipment using a laser beam was introduced. The network name was changed to PhotoNet in 1991 after digital transmission by satellite began.

CP uses the electronic picture desk to send and receive photos. Newspapers use it to crop and enhance photos before sending them directly to print.

PhotoNet delivers an average of 160 photos a day, half in color, to Canadian daily newspapers. Almost half the photos originate in Canada — split about equally between those from newspaper photographers and those from CP staff photographers and freelances hired by CP. The international content, about 90 photos a day, is provided by The Associated Press and its photographers around the world.

Every newspaper subscribing to the photo network — three-quarters of the CP membership — is obligated to provide its local photos to CP. With the introduction of the electronic picture desk in 1990-91, and the CP computer bulletin board (Canadian Press BBS) in 1994, each newspaper subscriber has the capacity to transmit directly to CP.

A separate network called **GraphicsNet** delivers CP and Associated Press graphics directly to Macintosh computers in the newsrooms, providing original graphic quality in either French or English. CP graphics are also transmitted on PhotoNet.

Good illustrations

Good photos have similarities to good stories. They:

1.   Are new and in some way unusual.

2.   Show action the instant it happens.

3.   Portray people and appeal to the emotions.

4.   Relate to some important person, event or place.

5. Wrap up a story or provide an overall view of it.

6. Tie in with a current story, the season, the weather, a fad.

A good illustration will be marked by attention to content, quality and composition.

Content

Content

A soldier home from the Persian Gulf War holds his son for the first time as his family meets him at Halifax. Human interest, reader appeal and the happy ending to a major story are all rolled into one picture. Tight cropping and the uniform help promote the photo.

(CP—Doug Ives)

1. Does the photo tell a story?

2. Is its subject important?

3. Is it appealing?

4. Is there outstanding human interest or some other quality that overrides minor news value?

Any news break that is visually either important or interesting makes the good-quality photo worth distributing. A window cleaner suspended in mid-air by his braces makes a good shot; a minor auto wreck usually doesn't because all wrecks tend to look much the same. A 20-car pileup, multiple deaths or trapped passengers can give an accident photo the news value needed to get it on the network.

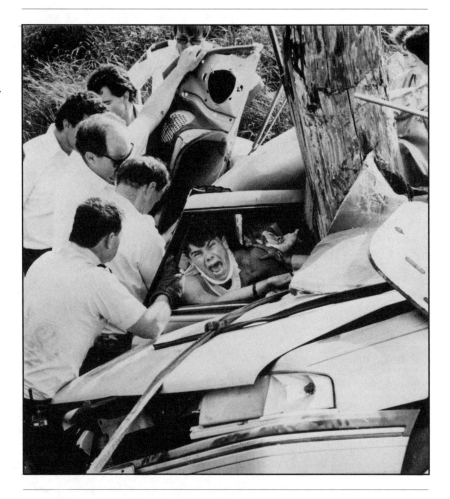

Picture judgment is partly personal and partly a matter of experience. A photo is almost certainly worth while if an editor experienced in handling news finds it eye-catching. A newspaper photo editor's recommendation is always a valid reason for selecting a picture.

Quality

1.　The main subject has clear, sharp details.

2.　There are bright colors or a gradual range of grey tones between black and white.

3.　Skin tones for light-skinned people are a natural color or light grey against a white shirt. There must be definition in the facial shading of people with darker skins.

A poor-quality picture might be slightly out of focus — look at the eyes. It might have heavy blacks and brilliant whites, or have an overall grey cast with no blacks and whites. Colors may be washed out or too dark.

The sole exception to these demands for quality is a shot of such outstanding news value it will get into print despite poor quality.

Quality

An elderly woman sobs after she and her husband were evicted from their Winnipeg home, about to be torn down to make way for a sewage treatment plant. The details of her face are sharp, and shading makes the face stand out from the wall.

(Winnipeg Tribune—
Frank Chalmers)

Composition

Composition

A policeman stands waist-deep in flood waters to guard against looting in downtown Cambridge, Ont. The sign on the right both tells the story and balances the photo as bystanders who could be looters stand in the shadowy centre.

(Hamilton Spectator—
Robert Hanley)

1.   Are the main subject and its surroundings arranged so as to be attractive and cohesive?

2.   Is the picture cropped to make the subject stand out clearly?

Standup group shots are not wanted, although sometimes the personalities involved create exceptions. The Queen with Commonwealth prime ministers or a new cabinet are usually newsworthy. In the best such photos, the group's attention is not centred on the camera.

Be careful that the *arranged* photo does not turn into a picture that is contrived or set up by the photographer. There is no objection to cleaning up a cluttered background or moving the company president from behind his desk to stand in front of his widget-stamping machine.

The photo becomes contrived when elements or interpretations are added or subtracted to make a point that would not normally be there.

Photo manipulation

CP does not alter the content of photos. Our pictures must always tell the truth — tell what the photographer saw happen. Nothing can damage our credibility more quickly than deliberate untruthfulness. The integrity of our photo report is our highest priority.

The electronic picture desk is a sophisticated editing tool that allows photographic images to be manipulated easily. It's technically possible to change their content and their impact on the reader, whether by accident or design.

Use of this tool must follow the long-established chemical darkroom standards of photo printing. Simple *burning* (making light portions of a print darker), *dodging* (making dark portions lighter), black-and-white *toning* and *cropping* are acceptable. Exaggerated use of these features to add, remove or give prominence to details in the photo is not acceptable.

Retouching is limited to removal of dust spots, film scratches or abnormal marks and patterns introduced during PhotoNet transmission.

Color adjustment is to be minimal. Adjustments can be made to ensure honest reproduction of the original when the scanning and transmission processes alter colors. Cases of abnormal color or tonality in the original must remain, pointed out clearly in the caption.

Consult the Picture Editor first on any question of photo manipulation.

PhotoNet

CP PhotoNet facilities can get a picture across Canada in time to illustrate any breaking story in the same publishing cycle if newspapers and CP bureaus move fast.

Pictures that don't move in the same cycle with the story they illustrate will likely not be used, unless the content is exceptional or they illustrate a continuing story.

When a story breaks:

1.   Immediately ask the nearest newspaper what its plans are and when pictures will be available.

2.   Explain CP's needs.

3.   Advise the Toronto Picture Desk immediately. They will watch for the picture and make follow-up calls if the pictures don't arrive.

Every paper illustrates local stories with photos that could have wider interest. To get these on the network in the same cycle for use by others, papers should be checked well before publication time. Ask the photo editor or the city editor:

1.   What local stories are you illustrating today?

2.   Are there any photos now being worked on that you expect to get into the next edition?

3.   Any good feature pictures coming up?

Ideally, when the newspaper arrives on the CP bureau's desk, the editor should have known about and tipped the Toronto Picture Desk of the available pictures.

But what to pick up and what to reject?

1. Ask yourself whether you would be interested in printing it if you were the editor of a newspaper 100 kilometres away. If the answer is yes, pick it up.

2. Pick it up if CP picked up the related story.

3. Pick it up if it piques your interest in any way.

4. The most frequent request from newspaper editors is for more news photos that can be used on their inside **national** and **regional** pages. On a slow day for spot-news photos, even pictorially interesting weather and feature photos will help fill this demand. Watch for them.

5. Rely on the expertise of the CP Toronto photo editor. If you're not sure, tell the Toronto desk about it. They can decide whether to request it.

Weekends are often exceptionally slow for news shots on PhotoNet. Sunday and Monday papers often have to scratch to find enough Canadian news photos to meet their needs. Approach newspaper photo desks on Fridays to discuss their weekend coverage plans. Then tip the Toronto Picture Desk. If the paper has no plans to cover a scheduled event, CP may decide that a freelance photographer should be assigned.

Sending photos

Most newspapers deliver their photos by telephone directly to Toronto, where they are uplinked to a satellite and broadcast to CP receiving dishes. There are two methods of sending photos to the Toronto Picture Desk: through a computer bulletin board and through transmitters.

The Canadian Press BBS

Introduced in 1994, this computer bulletin board has quickly become the transmission method of choice by most members. The system allows members and staff photographers to send scanned pictures directly from their computers via modem to the CP bulletin board. These pictures are then transferred to the computer at the Toronto Picture Desk, which relays them on PhotoNet.

To use the bulletin board:

1. Contact the Toronto Picture Desk to arrange for CP supplied user software and a user account.

2. Install the software into a computer that is equipped with Adobe Photoshop and a modem (a Hayes-compatible 14,400-baud or higher modem is recommended).

3. Create a folder or directory dedicated to CP pictures on the hard drive where the scanned photographs can be stored.

4. Run the CP user software (TFUSER is the program name). In the dial window that automatically appears, choose the modem model being used. Type in the name, password and telephone number supplied by the CP Toronto Picture Desk and press the dial button.

5. Once connected to the bulletin board, open the folder or directory where the picture (JPEG) is stored and drag it to the send icon. Windows users choose the *Upload* command from the file menu. The picture will begin transferring.

A few guidelines should be followed to ensure top quality pictures are sent to the CP wire:

• The scan of a photograph should be between six and nine megs before saving it as a compressed JPEG file.

• Keep enhancements to a minimum. Using excessive sharpen or unsharp mask settings in Photoshop will cause quality problems as it is transferred to the CP Picture Desk and out on the network to other members. Adjusting the color balance and setting the levels is often necessary. Keep the photograph in the RGB mode.

• Before saving the photograph as a JPEG ensure that a full caption has been written.

• Save the file as a JPEG using the midpoint of the quality scale. A six- to nine-megs file should be about 300 to 500k when compressed and take from three to six minutes to transmit to the CP bulletin board.

Transmitters

Negative transmitter: CP photographers and many newspapers use a transmitter that reads 35-millimetre negative or positive film, eliminating the need for a print. It is computer-based and can be operated by following the instructions and answering the questions as they show on its small operator screen. However, a short course from a photographer in how to operate it and reference to the operator's manual are necessary initially.

Portable color transmitter: Uses a revolving drum to rotate a print in front of a scanning light.

1. Mount an 8x10 black-and-white or color print on the drum by sliding the edges under two clamping bars. One bar is adjustable – it slides – to accommodate a short print.

2. If color is to be sent, pull up the vertical color post to the first of the three separator positions, cyan, indicated by a blue ring. After transmitting it, pull up again for the magenta or red separator and send the picture a second time. Yellow is the third transmission.

3. If it's not color, push the post all the way down so only the black ring shows. Also use the black ring position to send black-and-white from a color print.

Laser transmitter: Takes a black-and-white print fed on its widest side into a slot on the top.

1. Face the 8x10 picture away from you with either the top or the left side (whichever is longer) going in first.

2. Align the picture with the guide on the left of the slot.

Internal rollers grab the print when the *Transmit* button is pushed and haul it down in front of the scanning laser beam. You can check that it is going down by drawing a line across the back of the print.

Smaller prints can be used, but always put the longer edge – top or left side – in first. A color print cannot be transmitted.

All three transmitter types are connected to a telephone through a switching box, which allows you to either talk on the phone or, by throwing a switch, to send the photo from the transmitter. You can't talk during the transmission.

How to transmit:

1. Use the phone beside the transmitter to call the Toronto Picture Desk (**416-363-2790**), putting the connector box switch to the phone position.

2. Give a very brief description of the picture.

3. Say if it's color, or available in color.

4. Say if there is a priority. The editor needs to know if it illustrates a hot story or is highly competitive – a Reuters photographer was at the event. If so, it can be moved ahead of other less interesting photos.

5. Advise about **Locals Out** or other stipulations, such as holding the picture to go with a story moving several days later.

6. When the editor asks you to start sending, throw the connector box switch to *Transmit*, then push the *Start* button on the transmitter.

The transmitter will turn off automatically when transmission is complete. Put the connector box switch back to *Phone* and hang up. The photo editor will call back if there is a reception problem.

The photo editor receives the picture directly into an electronic picture desk and is able to check quality, content, cropping and caption before sending it on the network. Ask that it be checked immediately if the print won't be available later on.

Captions

Handle captions with the same care for accuracy and style as you would any CP story. Send them to a dump printer with a good-quality ribbon.

Photo captions are typed single-spaced in this style:

❶ WINNIPEG OUT
❷ SEE STORY-Selkirk AM-Hay-Fever
❸ (WPG104) ❹ SELKIRK, Man., ❺ March 10— ❻ HIGH FLYER—Keltie Johnson, 22 months, dozes as mother Elaine (left) and aunt Anne tend her in an aircraft 3,000 metres above Selkirk, Man., on Monday. Her father, Darrell Johnson of Winnipeg, arranged the flight in the hope the rarefied air might cure Keltie's hay fever. It didn't. ❼ (CP PHOTO) ❽ 1992 ❾(Winnipeg Free Press—Phil Hossack) ❿ rpz

❶ An **OUT** slug tops the caption to prevent distribution of a newspaper photo to other papers in the same city.

❷ This slug is used whenever there is or will be a story. It helps editors match picture and story by giving the story placeline, cycle designation and keyword field.

❸ The designation for the *transmitter* site, in this case the Winnipeg Free Press; and the number of the photo from that site, starting daily with 101 for color and 1 for black and white.

❹ The picture *placeline*, which is not necessarily the same as the transmitter location. The placeline must be repeated in the body of the caption.

❺ The *date* is the day of transmission. The body of the caption must contain the day, and date if relevant, on which the picture was actually taken.

❻ The *overline*, always in capitals, is a two- to four-word summary of the picture.

❼ The *CP credit*. Rarely, it may credit an important handout picture— (CP PHOTO FROM NATIONAL DEFENCE).

❽ The current *year*.

❾ The full *name* of the newspaper and the *byline* of the photographer who shot the picture. *Staff* or *Flnc* are used with the photographer's name where appropriate.

❿ The initials of the *caption writer*.

⓫ Captions are always written in the present tense. They tell the reader, briefly and clearly, the basic details of the picture and tie it to the story it illustrates. Remember that photos attract even the most casual reader, so captions are probably the best-read words in the paper, after headlines. Like headlines, captions must be crisp. Like stories, they must be readable and informative, interesting and lively.

Some reminders to make caption-writing easier:

1. Does the caption say when and where?

2. Does it identify, fully and clearly?

3. Are the names in the right order? List people in a group shot from the left, and specify position (**left** or **front row, second from right**).

4. Use at least two short, snappy sentences. One long, involved sentence is boring.

5. Stick primarily to explaining the action in the picture, but don't speculate. The prime minister's grin may be teeth-gritting anger. The dozing legislator may be reading a paper on his desk. Be sure — or leave it out.

6. Watch attribution and don't let libel creep in.

7. Read what you've written. Are all the questions answered? Count the people in the picture and the number of names. Are the left-to-right designations correct? Is the action mentioned in the caption really shown?

Credit the photographer in the body of the caption if the picture has exceptional merit or the circumstances in which it was shot were very unusual. Say so when abnormal techniques such as multiple exposures or time exposures were used.

Say in the caption what day the picture was taken. Avoid **today**. Bracket the date after the day when needed for clarity.

Captions on stock or library photos must always say when the photo was taken. Stating the year is usually enough.

Caption position

Place the caption on the top or left of long pictures with the type facing *towards* the image on short captions and *away* from the image on long captions.

Do not cover a vital part of the photo with the caption. Instead, make space for the caption by adding paper to one side of the print after removing unnecessary picture from the opposite side.

Leave half an inch of white border on unneeded picture material between the caption and edge of the print. This space will be eliminated in transmission and you don't want to lose the first line of the caption.

*Note the direction
in which the
caption type faces.*

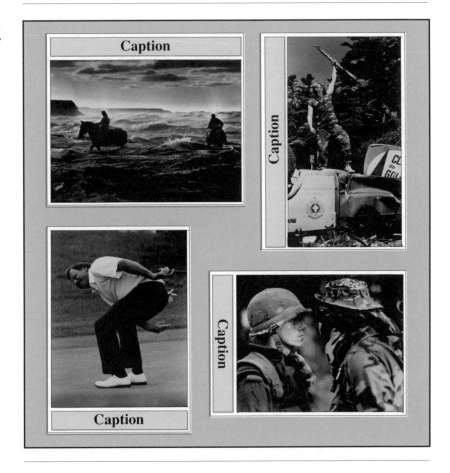

➤ See **Sending photos** section for feeding or mounting the picture into the transmitter.

Kills and corrections

All picture kills and corrections are handled by the Toronto Picture Desk, which alone knows the exact distribution of a picture.

If you see an error in a caption or a graphic, phone the Picture Desk immediately.

Kills and corrections are transmitted on the same photo networks that carried the orginal. The style differs slightly from the style on news circuits.

KILL KILL KILL
KILL VCR7 of July 27, VANCOUVER photo of man identified as former premier Vander Zalm. The person is not Vander Zalm. Destroy this photo. A correct photo of Vander Zalm will be transmitted shortly. CP Picture Service 27-07-91hdh1906

CAPTION CORRECTION CORRECTION CORRECTION
In HFX3 of Aug. 4, TRURO photo of horse race finish, read . . . won by pacer Queenie (NOT Myrtle) Hanover . . .(Corrects name.) CP Picture Service 04-08-91tjc1406

WITHHOLD WITHHOLD WITHHOLD
WITHHOLD from publication EDM2 of Dec. 11, EDMONTON photo of stripper Martha MacDonald on courthouse steps. Identity is questioned. A further advisory will move as soon as positive identity is made. CP Picture Service 12-12-91kc0910

Pictures and the law

The **Legal** section of the stylebook applies equally to the Picture Service. Ensure that neither the caption nor the content of a photo violates the law or individual rights.

A picture of a person accused of bank robbery could prejudice the outcome of the court hearing if there is a question of identity. And there usually is. Consult the Picture Editor or Main Desk before transmitting.

Withhold immediately any picture questioned after transmission, using a news-circuit advisory and a note on all photo networks that received the original. Send a follow-up advisory and note, killing or releasing the picture as soon as the question is resolved.

Copyright photos

CP owns the copyright of photos by its staff and made by freelance photographers working on direct assignment from CP. A freelance who shoots a picture before selling it to CP retains the copyright. CP can use it only for the purpose agreed to when it was bought — usually unlimited editorial use by CP and AP member newspapers and magazines.

Any unusual restrictions that the freelance demands must be noted by caption slug to avoid inadvertent violation of a copyright picture. These restrictions could include:

1. **One-time use only.** The photo can be used once with the current news story.

2. **Magazines out.** The photographer hopes to sell the picture separately to that market.

3. **Copyright photo, credit mandatory.** The newspaper must credit the photographer.

Photos provided by public relations firms or businesses may not be legally available for CP transmission other than at the time they illustrated a specific story. Always check with the photographer or the source before reissuing a picture of this type.

Remember that freelance photos are copyright whether or not that is marked on the back. The photographer must be checked before the photo is reused.

The CP Picture Service Plan requires newspapers who are members of the plan to include CP in copyright release of photos by their staff and regular freelances. Be especially careful of occasional freelance photos picked up from newspapers or borrowed later from their libraries. The libraries file every picture used, no matter what the source. Rights may not have been obtained for CP use and must be checked. Do not use a photo if the source is not indicated or cannot be determined from the newspaper's own publication.

Picturing money

It is against the law to picture in print any Canadian banknote or a recognizable portion of one. Such photos cannot be carried on PhotoNet.

A Bank of Canada employee loads up used dollar bills for destruction. On an overall basis, it's easily recognizable as Canadian money, yet there is no violation of the law against picturing money since no individual bill is clear enough to recognize and there is no complete word visible.

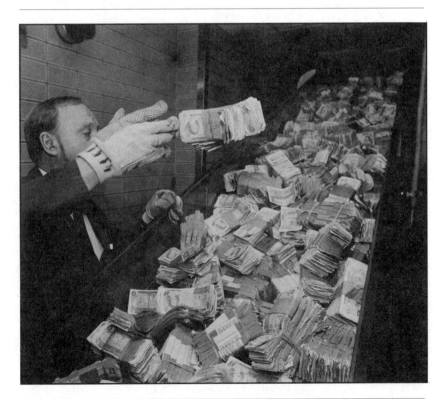

(CP Photo)

Stories about money can be illustrated without breaking the law. A photo of a person waving a sheaf of bills, his hand hiding words on them, gets the idea across. Be sure that no complete word shows since that would be a recognizable portion.

A carefully prepared graph can get the idea of money across and stay within the law by using distortions and blank spaces.

Occasionally the Bank of Canada will provide a replica of a banknote and agree to waive prosecution, usually to promote a newly issued note. These may be transmitted.

Specials

Newspapers regularly phone bureaus asking for specific pictures to illustrate their own stories. Usually these will come from the CP picture library in Toronto or will be shot by a CP or freelance photographer in another bureau. In passing on the request to the Picture Desk, the following information is necessary:

1.   The name of the requesting newspaper and its editor authorizing the extra expense involved. What is the expense limit?

2.   The date and time when it must be in the newspaper's hands to meet a deadline.

3.   The picture wanted. This includes the full name or complete description of the subject, and whether a head shot or action picture is needed.

4.   The date, time and location of the subject by street address as well as city if the picture is to be shot.

5.   The name and phone number of a contact, if possible.

6.   The type of film — black-and-white or color negative or positive.

7.   Does the member want a photographer assigned if the local newspaper isn't planning coverage?

8.   If it is strictly a file photo, say whether the newspaper authorizes a search of Associated Press files in New York. The CP and local newspaper libraries will be checked automatically.

Newspapers with the appropriate receivers may use CP transmitters on request. Usually the newspaper will have a picture delivered to a CP bureau and will supply caption information. Transmission will normally be by long-distance telephone. The Picture Desk has a list of most PhotoNet receiver phone numbers in the country if the person delivering the picture is unable to provide the number.

Where necessary, photo specials may also be delivered directly on PhotoNet during quiet periods. This is done for newspapers without receiver phones and for chains such as Southam and Thomson wishing to distribute a photo that CP is not interested in or is not entitled to.

There are two caption changes:

1. Change the credit to **(SOUTHAM PHOTO)** from **(CP PHOTO)**.

2. Spell out use limitations across the top of the caption: **SPECIAL FOR SOUTHAM SUBSCRIBERS ONLY.**

CP staff are expected to handle all member newspaper requests promptly and cheerfully, being as helpful as possible in getting the job done.

Cartoons

CP picks up cartoons for use with news stories in special circumstances, as when a cartoon becomes the subject of political or other controversy, or to illustrate a story about a cartoonist.

Cartoons may also make good illustrations for backgrounders or analyses if they offer fair comment. Where there is controversy, more than one cartoon may be needed to reflect opposing views.

Newspapers are not obligated to provide CP with their cartoons and most editorial cartoonists retain and syndicate the rights to their work. Permission for the use of each cartoon must be arranged in advance with the newspaper or the cartoonist.

The use of any cartoon must be approved in advance by the Chief of Picture Service or Vice-President, Editorial. Requests for such approval should include the name of the newspaper editor or cartoonist authorizing use.

Graphics

Reading habits are changing. Average readers are spending less time with the daily newspaper because of busier lives, shorter attention spans, and competition from television and other media that offer packaged information.

Newspapers are changing to meet the challenge. Some have been dramatically made over, with greater use of boxed information and striking makeup. Almost all papers have moved toward shorter stories and stronger illustrations.

One of the most noticeable changes is in the use of a relatively new page element, the information-filled graphic. Graphics artists have joined reporters and photographers in many newsrooms, helping to make clear the *how* and *what* of a story.

Newspapers are working hard to present stories in a way that wins a reader's attention. The Peterborough Examiner combined this CP story and graphic for a strong visual effect.

Computers have speeded up the production of a graphic. The artist can manipulate drawings, take them apart and store the elements in the computer memory for later use in another graphic, vary text styles and sizes, and apply color electronically. The slow mechanical work done in typesetting shops or separation labs is a thing of the past.

CP has met these changing needs with GraphicsNet, a service of graphics created by CP and Associated Press artists and delivered by satellite into a newspaper's newsroom computer. At the newspaper, the graphics can be further manipulated to change typefaces, color or size. GraphicsNet subscribers are also able to contribute their own work to a graphics exchange.

Staff everywhere should be alert for graphics ideas. They can be the best way to locate a manhunt in southern Manitoba, illustrate the impact of inflation on salaries or compare models of camper vans. A good graphic, like a good photo, can be a wedge for squeezing a story into tight news holes.

The average news day is full of material that can be made into a graphic. The letterhead on an application for press credentials might make a good standing logo for continuing stories on a coming sports tournament. The diagram in the back of a press kit that helps reporters understand a new computer product might be just as helpful for readers if it's used as a graphic.

Information please

The first element in producing any news graphic is always the same — information. Reporters need to gather this detail in their contact with news sources.

If the plane crashed on takeoff, find out what runway it was using. How are the runways configured? How far did it go past the runway? Did it crash in trees or a field? What buildings are in the area? Reporters can get this information on the phone. Often, those on the scene — reporters or sources — can do a rough sketch for the graphics artist. It's the kind of detail the artist needs, and it's the kind of detail readers are demanding.

Graphics can help readers see the story, even in cases where only a plan exists. The success of this type of graphic depends on good detail.

(CP—Andrée Lachapelle)

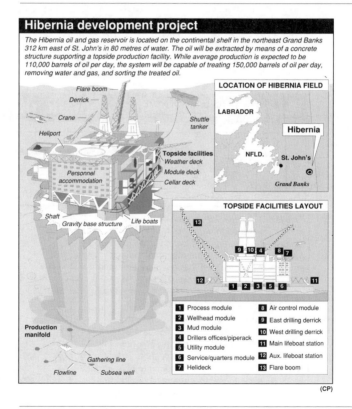

Hibernia development project

The Hibernia oil and gas reservoir is located on the continental shelf in the northeast Grand Banks 312 km east of St. John's in 80 metres of water. The oil will be extracted by means of a concrete structure supporting a topside production facility. While average production is expected to be 110,000 barrels of oil per day, the system will be capable of treating 150,000 barrels of oil per day, removing water and gas, and sorting the treated oil.

Flare boom
Derrick
Crane
Heliport
Shuttle tanker
Topside facilities
Weather deck
Module deck
Cellar deck
Personnel accommodation
Shaft
Gravity base structure
Life boats
Production manifold
Gathering line
Flowline
Subsea well

LOCATION OF HIBERNIA FIELD
LABRADOR
Hibernia
NFLD.
St. John's
Grand Banks

TOPSIDE FACILITIES LAYOUT

1 Process module
2 Wellhead module
3 Mud module
4 Drillers offices/piperack
5 Utility module
6 Service/quarters module
7 Helideck
8 Air control module
9 East drilling derrick
10 West drilling derrick
11 Main lifeboat station
12 Aux. lifeboat station
13 Flare boom

(CP)

From a Montreal massacre, a reporter learns that the gunman used a Ruger Mini-14 rifle. A graphics artist in Toronto, using that information, borrows a catalogue and a few bullets from a nearby sporting goods store. The result is a graphic description that brings the details of the rifle and size of the bullets home to the reader.

A business reporter who hears that a company's sales have been climbing steadily since 1982 can get a graphic going if the annual sales figures can be obtained. The numbers might show that sales are up from 1982, but there have been a number of ups and downs in the period. The fact-digging needed for a graphic is often important for getting an accurate understanding of the story.

Press kits, catalogues, guidebooks, instruction manuals and program books are often the source of material that can be turned into a news graphic.

The artist needs reference images. A graphic about a new offshore oil project requires a depiction of the rig as seen by the planners. Details are important and are known by somebody familiar with the story. Staff can help by finding that person.

If the jackknifed tractor trailer has four axles, the graphic is wrong if it shows only three. Sometimes a photographer's pictures will help with detail, but many times graphics are portraying action that can't be seen by photographers, like the inside of a mine that's collapsed. Help CP get it from an expert, just as you would the detail for a story.

Fax machines get source information to graphics artists quickly. A scientist at the other end of the country can sketch something fast, fax it to the artist and discuss the graphic as it develops.

The Picture Service fax number is **(416) 594-2168**.

Graphics can be used to highlight sidebar material and aid understanding with illustrations.

Ruger Mini-14 semi-automatic rifle

Ruger Mini-14

The Mini-14 semi-automatic used in the shootings at the University of Montreal is described by its maker, Sturm, Ruger & Co., as a compact, lightweight rifle ideal for small-game hunting. It is 95 centimetres long and weighs three kilograms. It fires .223-calibre ammunition and has an optional magazine which can hold 30 cartridges.

Semi-automatic rifles require pulling the trigger to fire each shot. Cartridges are automatically placed in the firing chamber and the casing is ejected after each shot. A fully automatic rifle would continue shooting as long as the trigger is squeezed. Fully automatic weapons are not legal in Canada.

.223 bullets are small (about half a centimetre wide) but are driven by a large charge of gunpowder in the cartridge.

.223   .22

(CP)

(CP—Andrée Lachapelle)

The CP news report

Main Desk and bureaus

Keeping editors advised
  Advisories
  Spot breaks
  Planned events
  Publishable and non-
    publishable notes
  Long-range advisories
  Other advisories
  Calendar and Look-Ahead
  Fronts advisories
  News Budgets

Packaging the news

  At-a-Glance, Highlights, Quicks
  Editorial symposiums
  Newspage copy
Dealing with members

The way we do things

Advances
  Speeches
  Broken embargoes
  Advance slugs
  Advance advisories
Bylines
  Basic guidelines
  Style
Completes
  Examples
Corrections
  Withhold, kill, sub
Correctives
  General guidelines
  Style
  Clarifications

Slugs and coding
  Coding
  Priorities
  Departmental designators
  Keyword slug line
  Version field
  Specific slugs
  Catchlines and pickup lines

Handling vital routine

Handling business news
  What designation
  Avoid duplication
  Illustrations
  Foreign currencies
  Precise figures
  Net earnings
  Dividends
Foreign filing
  Points to watch
  Language
  Place names
  Legal
Sports handling
  Slugs
  Agate
  Tabulation
  Results formats
  Alphabetical list of sports
Writing for cable, etc.
  Cable TV news
  Canadian Press Information
    Network

Main Desk and bureaus

Main Desk in Toronto is the minute-by-minute guardian of the overall quality of the CP news report. Quality originates in the skills of the duty editors at department desks and regional bureaus countrywide.

Main Desk

Main Desk is staffed round the clock weekdays by senior editors, with shifts overlapping during the afternoon copy crush of the AMs-cycle News Budget for morning papers.

Co-ordination of coverage and ensuring that copy meets CP standards sum up this position's prime duties.

Main Deskers:

• See that CP moves quickly and effectively on major breaking stories, tip deadlining members to important developments, consult with Broadcast News and CP Pictures and alert the General News Editor, Vice-President, Editorial or the President as warranted.

• Guard against, and act fast to remove, libel or other legal concerns in copy, usually by dealing personally with legal counsel and the bureau involved.

• Approve the content and format of Correctives and Clarifications before they are transmitted and later fill out a relay report confirming they have moved to all newspapers that received the erroneous original.

• Ensure that copy reads easily and is complete, interesting, well-written and properly edited.

• Suggest significant improvements in stories, perhaps asking a bureau to sharpen a lead by bringing key facts or interesting details higher.

• Watch for regional stories that can be developed for a national audience by a change of approach or addition of background detail — noting similar legislation in another province, for example.

• Consult bureaus by message or phone with a view to building the next-cycle News Budget (➤ See **Advisories**, page 363), suggesting story angles if necessary. Prepare and relay the News Budget advisories.

• Field requests, queries and problems from newspapers or the public, or direct them to the appropriate person or department.

• Proofread CRAFT stories — concerning the newspaper and broadcast industries — for style and content before they are transmitted at times when department or bureau supervisors are not available to OK them.

• Mark and relay nightly synopses of the CBC and CTV newscasts, indicating the status of CP coverage of each story.

- Oversee marking of the Toronto newspapers, chasing matchers to stories from outside their coverage areas. Scan the front-page advisories sent by bureaus, looking for prominently played stories that rate pickup or chasing.

- At change of shift, prepare for the incoming desker and for distribution to Head Office supervisors a Developing Sked, which details the status of major stories during the last cycle and plans for such stories in the cycle ahead.

- Assemble and relay the twice-daily Calendar and weekly Look-Ahead List from bureau contributions (➤ See **Advisories**, page 360).

Bureaus

The duty deskers at each bureau are charged with the overall goal of explaining their region to the rest of Canada.

Among other things, this demands that bureaus be alert to the kind of context, background information, local color or other news elements that make a regional story of interest to a broader audience.

The mark of a good bureau is development of its regional news.

Anticipating and planning for news is critical. This starts with a carefully kept datebook of future events; with thorough checks of regional newspapers for news and background information; and with intelligent guidance of newspaper and string correspondents on story development.

Each bureau is responsible for the copy it files, whether written by staff or by travelling staffers assigned to special events. Bureau deskers working alone, or inexperienced deskers, may call upon Main Desk or Toronto General Desk to proof important stories before relay.

Bureau staff is familiar with — and is collectively responsible for updating — the Desk Book. This is a loose-leaf record of news-handling tips and style directives, newspaper deadlines, return-news districts, staff and newspaper phone lists, etc.

Cultivating co-operation with the papers is a constant preoccupation. Politeness and helpfulness on the phone are where this starts, and it extends to notifying them promptly on major breaks, especially on Canadian stories that may merit staffing or picture orders.

Stories provided to meet a regional paper's request are pointed out in a bureau phone call to the person who asked.

Duties

Bureau duties include efficient dispatch of certain routine designed to keep members, fellow staffers and other bureaus abreast of coverage:

- Front-page advisories on major papers in the region (➤ See **Advisories**, page 361).

- Marking papers: At the end of each cycle, desk editors leave over for their reliever the latest editions of local papers with stories and pictures marked to indicate handling.

At the same time, staffers watch for major play of CP copy and pictures and follow bureau routine to make sure clips and tearsheets are exchanged.

These are the usual markings:

NO — Not carried by CP, with the reason briefly noted (e.g., LOCAL on stories of strictly local interest). Reasons for not carrying prominently played or controversial stories and pictures should be detailed on the inter-cycle Developing Sked. Rejected stories likely to attract other papers' interest may warrant an Advisory to spell out the reasons after consulting Main Desk.

NO ASKED — Not carried, CP checking (with arrangements made for matching spelled out in the Developing Sked).

OLD — Fully covered previously.

NCP — Not CP copy but covered by CP; ensure CP copy covers all significant and interesting points in the newspaper's version.

PU — Picked up for CP use.

PU for PMs (AMs) — Picked up for next-cycle use.

• Developing Sked: Essentially a memo from a desker going off shift at the end of a cycle to the desker who follows, although schedules are also sent on the message wire for the reference of Toronto Main Desk and other supervisors.

Format varies to reflect bureau needs but a DevSked's purpose remains the same: an essential at-a-glance guide to incoming deskers on the status of major stories in the past cycle and in the cycle ahead, on outstanding requests, and on staff assignments and coverage plans, with reminders of new standing orders and changes in routine.

A properly assembled DevSked will be the first thing a seasoned desker consults at the start of a shift and the last thing left at the end of a cycle. If the DevSked is just a time-consuming chore to all concerned, it's not being done properly.

Events in the region for the next day are listed at the bottom of each DevSked under the heading Calendar (➤ see **Advisories** for format). Each bureau's Calendar contribution is assembled by Main Desk into a national list for transmission to newspapers.

Keeping editors advised

"Extra! Extra! Triple Murder!" Like an oldtime newsboy hawking papers on the corner, CP knows that to move news, you have to get the paying customers' attention.

Newspaper editors want to know:

• About the news that's coming 10 minutes from now. In the cycle ahead.

• What's happening tomorrow? Next week? Next month?

• Will there be pictures and graphics?

• Anything special in the CP report that will be worth saving space for?

• How did other papers play the news?

These questions and others are answered by means of *advisories*— notes to editors transmitted along with the news copy.

Some are improvised, pounded out as a hot story breaks and develops. Some are routine — **Fronts**, the twice-daily **News Budgets** and **Calendar** items, the weekly **Look-Ahead List**. Others are issued in advance of major events such as elections to detail CP coverage plans. Still others commend editors' attention to special projects that CP has undertaken.

All are driven by the same rationale: the customers expect information from an information company.

Advisories

"Keep us posted." — Front-page editor to a CP desker as a major story breaks.

Newspapers say the most helpful thing CP can do is keep them fully and quickly informed. Not only when big news breaks but as it develops, situations change and deadlines approach.

If a story expected at 9:30 a.m. is going to be delayed, send an advisory. Explain the delay if possible.

Don't be shy with **Top Copy** notes. These give editors an early tip that major unbudgeted stories are coming.

But papers also need to know about CP's plans beyond the day's top news. They want advisories as early as possible on major long-range plans for Enterprise series, foreign assignments, advance stories leading up to a political leadership convention and the like.

And make no mistake: These advisories translate directly into play.

Note: Most advisories, including all routine ones, move with message — or **M**-type — designators. The exception is when the advisory concerns copy already sent. It takes the same designator as that on the story: **G** for General, **W** for Foreign, **S** for Sports, etc. This ensures the advisory is routed to the same newspaper desk that is handling the story.

Spot breaks

1. The phone rings. A major break seems to be in the making. But there is no immediate official confirmation. Remember: Newspapers somewhere are on deadline. They want a message like this:

PM-Tornado-Advisory
    Eds: CP is checking a report that a major tornado has touched down near Olds, Alta., about a 40-minute drive north of Calgary. Official word is expected from police shortly. There are no confirmed reports of injuries or damage at the moment.
    CP EDMONTON

Once the information has been confirmed and a story moved, send a follow-up advisory:

PM-Tornado-Advisory
    Eds: The town clerk at Olds, Alta., has confirmed a tornado has caused severe damage in the town north of Calgary. See 627 PM-Tornado 1st Lead at 9:59 MDT. CP-BN reporters Sylvia Strojek and Anna Geddes and photographer Dave Buston are en route to the scene and are expected to arrive at about 10:45 a.m. A 2nd Lead will move within 10 minutes.
    CP EDMONTON

---

2. Keep editors up to the minute as coverage plans take shape. Don't wait until an eyewitness account or other strong sidebar is fully written before sending a tip. Send fast word on the timing of a news conference or official police statement. Move an immediate advisory if a scheduled briefing is delayed or cancelled. Advisories take seconds to write and send. One advisory may save a dozen phone calls, crucial during a major breaking story.

PM-Tornado-Advisory
    Eds: The town clerk of Olds, Alta., will brief reporters on the tornado that struck today, killing at least seven people and causing severe damage throughout the area north of Calgary. The briefing will be held in the town office at 4911 51st Avenue at 11:45 a.m. CP is staffing.
    CP EDMONTON

---

3. Give editors as full a rundown as possible on plans for copy, CP Graphics and CP Photos in the next cycle. This can be done in either the AMs or PMs Budget message or with a separate advisory:

> Eds: Besides the budgeted stories **AM-Tornado, NL**, **AM-Tornado-Victims** and **AM-Tornado-Rebuild**, there will be separates on past tornadoes in the West (**Undated—AM-Tornado-Past**) and how tornadoes are formed (**Undated—AM-Tornado-Profile**), a first-person account by a man who saw the tornado strike (**AM-Tornado-Eyewitness**), a QuickSketch, QuickQuotes, CP Graphics and CP Photos.
> **CP EDMONTON**

Co-ordinate advisory handling with Head Office or another bureau when appropriate:

> Eds: An UNDATED list of major Canadian disasters this century will move shortly.
> **CP TORONTO**

> Eds: The prime minister is expected to comment on today's tornado in southern Alberta at 3:45 p.m. EDT. CP's Helen Branswell is covering.
> **CP OTTAWA**

Planned events

1. Expected timing of copy on staged events is vitally important as well. Editors want to know whether copy will move in time for final deadlines. Tell them:

> **PM-McKenna-Advisory**
> Eds: Premier Frank McKenna is to hold a media briefing on New Brunswick's new labor laws at the legislature in Fredericton at about 10:40 a.m. ADT. CP reporter Chris Morris is covering. First copy is expected by 11:05. Adds will move in short takes, followed by a 1st Lead for PMs and a QuickFacts and CP Graphic on the major changes in the law. There will a budgeted Night Lead, incorporating reaction.
> **CP HALIFAX**

2.   Give advance notice on major announcements whenever possible, even if details are sketchy:

PM-Mulroney-Economy
   Eds: Expected shortly — in advance for release by advisory — is an announcement by the prime minister on the economy. He is expected to start speaking in the Commons at 2:40 p.m. EDT but other business may cause a delay. An urgent release note will move as soon as he starts to speak. Guard against premature use.
   CP OTTAWA

Publishable and non-publishable notes

Advisories carried on the top of stories fall into two general categories: publishable and non-publishable. The former are aimed at the reader. The latter are for editors' information.

Publishable:

BC-NHL-Preview-Red-Wings, Bgt
code:2
See CP Photo CPT11, CP Graphics
Budget

   The following story is one in a series by Canadian Press sports writers previewing the new National Hockey League season. Alan Adams of Toronto reports on the "new-look" Detroit Red Wings and their chances of improving their strong finish in the Central Division last season.
                              By Alan Adams
   DETROIT (CP) — Gordie Howe may have put it best . . .

And at the end of the story:

   . . . nowhere to go but up."
   Next: Chris Cariou of Edmonton looks at the Dallas Stars.

Non-publishable:

   Eds: Petr (not Peter) in the following is correct. Macdonald is small d. Tonight refers to Tuesday.

Long-range advisories

1.   Advance billing on special projects, foreign travel and other major assignments means better play for CP stories. Editors will look for the copy and use the advance notice to block out space in editions days ahead of time. A CP advance advisory also gives papers a chance to plan local follows, often a key selling point.

An example:

BC-VE-Day-Advisory
code:8
MANAGING EDITORS
NEWS EDITORS
FEATURE EDITORS
SPECIAL SUPPLEMENT EDITORS
   The Canadian Press will mark the 50th anniversary of the Nazi surrender with a two-part package of stories. The main package will move April 5 and will feature stories focused on Canada's role in the end of the war and how the war changed the country.
   An added package of mostly international stories will move in mid-April.
   The April 5 package will be suitable for use as a special edition supplement. The stories will also be written so that each main feature can stand on its own and be run on daily newspages in the days leading to the anniversary. A graphic logo will be provided to run with stories used this way.
   The packages will be illustrated by graphics and photos.
   The lineup for the mid-April package will include items on Hitler, liberation of the concentration camps, and the liberation of the Netherlands by Canadian troops.
   If you have any questions or wish to offer any items for the package, call series co-ordinator Malcolm McNeil or Neil Davidson at 416-594-2150.
   CP TORONTO

Other advisories

The range of potential advisories is unbounded.

There is a simple test: If you as an editor were coming up to today's deadline or were in the early planning stages for open pages in next Wednesday's edition, would a CP advisory help?

By no means complete, here is a selection of other advisories:

AM-Copy-Advisory
   Eds: Top copy from Ottawa today includes: OTTAWA — A former Iraqi minister, Jawad Hashim, says he, Mohamed Al-Mashat and one other prominent defector have been sentenced to death in absentia by the Saddam Hussein regime. New 400. Will stand. By Gord McIntosh.
AM-Mashat-Death-Sentences
   CP OTTAWA

PM-Hibernia-Advisory

Eds: Newfoundland Premier Clyde Wells has called a news conference for 11 a.m. NDT (9:30 EDT) in St. John's to discuss the federal government's decision to expand the Hibernia offshore project. CP reporter Beth Gorham and a freelance photographer are covering.

CP HALIFAX

AM-Mulroney-Advisory

Eds: Please note 877 Insert in Tokyo NL Mulroney on Gary Filmon's reaction should have been slugged WINNIPEG OUT. Winnipeg papers: Please make no use of the material in the insert.

CP WINNIPEG

AM-Budget-Advisory

Eds: The sports story slugged AM-Expos-Wallach on tonight's news budget is delayed by technical problems at Olympic Stadium. It is not known immediately how long the problems will last. We will keep you informed.

CP MONTREAL

AM-Sinking-Advisory

Eds: Ladysmith, B.C., AM-Sinking, NL subs for the budgeted AM-Sinking-Yacht, NL placelined Nanaimo.

CP VANCOUVER

AM-Brownwich-Advisory

Eds: The trial of former P.E.I. cabinet minister Ethel Brownwich resumes this morning with testimony from her secretary. CP's Alan Jeffers is staffing and expects to file a PMs story by noon AST, depending on the testimony.

CP HALIFAX

AM-Budget-Advisory

Eds: The Kamloops, B.C., budget item AM-Loons will move Lifestyles and not Entertainment as listed.

CP VANCOUVER

AM-Peigan-Advisory

Eds: The Maycroft, Alta., budget item AM-Peigan will not be available. A news conference scheduled for 2 p.m. MDT was cancelled. An unbudgeted 250-word night lead will move by 5 p.m. MDT, and if there are further developments later in the day an advisory will be sent outlining coverage plans.

CP EDMONTON

AM-RCMP-Spy-Advisory
    Eds: Your attention is drawn to 815 AM-RCMP-Spy, an exclusive story by CP Ottawa's Jim Brown. The story reveals that a former RCMP counter-intelligence officer was identified in the mid-1980s as a Soviet agent who had compromised top-secret operations. Also note the sidebar: 814 AM-RCMP-Spy-History.
    CP OTTAWA

Calendar and Look-Ahead

Few features of journalism can match the exhilaration of covering a sudden, fast-breaking story. Few frustrations can match trying to catch up with a major story that could have been foreseen and planned for if it hadn't been for neglected datebooking.

Every CP bureau and department seeks out hints of news to come in the reams of news releases, newsletters, press kits and other material that are directed its way.

CP keeps track of coming events for its own coverage planning and to inform its newspaper and broadcast customers. There are two public advisories, the weekly **Look-Ahead List** and the twice-daily **Calendar**.

The Look-Ahead is assembled by Toronto Main Desk from bureau messages, usually prepared by News Editors or their designates and messaged by noon, Thursdays. It moves each Friday morning at about 5 a.m. eastern time.

Each Look-Ahead covers events, by date, from east to west, from the Sunday of the coming weekend through to the Saturday one full month ahead. The Calendar, also prepared by Main Desk, lists events for the following day and is transmitted at 4 p.m. and 6 a.m. eastern time. The Calendar sent Fridays covers events through the coming weekend.

The 4 p.m. Calendar is compiled from messages sent by bureau deskers each afternoon by 3:30 p.m. The 6 a.m. update is taken from the Calendar sections of each bureau's Day Developing Sked, messaged to Toronto.

Format for contributions to both these lists is the same: a brief description of the event, time, place and any other information useful to regional newspapers or broadcasters who may plan to cover. An **x-** in front of the placeline denotes that CP is staffing the event.

Examples:

    HALIFAX — Corrections Canada news conference on lack of prison facilities for women in the Atlantic region; offenders now serve sentences in Ontario, 3 p.m., Sheraton Hotel (EDS: Note news conference was rescheduled from Monday to today).

> x-MONTREAL — Canadian Medical Association executive meets to draft policy on physicians with AIDS, through Thursday, McGill Medical School (most sessions closed to media; CP staffing open symposiums 2 p.m. Tuesday and 9 a.m. Wednesday).

> FORT SMITH, N.W.T. — Dene National Assembly begins, registration only today, business sessions begin 9 a.m. Tuesday, continue through Sunday, Bell Rock Campsite.

• Specify when times, places are unavailable. But such detail, or an explanation for its absence, is essential when the event carries an **x-**. Newspapers and broadcasters find such information helpful and the stories they get are shared with CP.

• Description of the event should be brief but still spell out its news interest.

Not: Joe Saxon appears in court.

But: Joe Saxon, accused of attacking a neighbor with an electric weed trimmer, stands trial for first-degree murder.

• Include only events that are likely to produce copy. Routine court dates for secondary crimes are not needed. Include the nature of a court appearance — bail hearing, preliminary hearing, trial, appeal, etc.

• Placelines are capped but not boldfaced. Entries are in full — no in-house abvns. Follow format with care. Reworking entries to conform is time-wasting.

Fronts advisories

Editors are naturally interested in what other newspapers are doing with the major national and international stories of the day. And they like to know what local or regional stories are getting big play in papers elsewhere.

A routine item called a **Fronts Advisory** is CP's method of letting editors across the country know about the front-page picture and news choices of newspapers in most major cities. Each bureau is responsible for preparing and sending these advisories as soon as local papers are available.

As well, the advisories include brief notes on major play for CP's work — especially section fronts and op-ed pages — as a form of instant feedback on how staff's work is received.

Advisories follow these formats:

For a broadsheet:

BC-Advisory-Fronts-Edm-Jnl
Edmonton Journal Fronts, Wednesday, July 29
Above Fold:
  MOSCOW (CP, Jim Sheppard byline) — Mideast peace conference may result from Bush-Gorbachev summit.
  EDMONTON (Staff) — City proposes rotating schedule for garbage pickup. LOCAL, NOT MATCHING.
  OTTAWA (Southam) — Restless Tories show disenchantment with Mulroney amid rumors he will step down before next election. Backgrounder. SOME ELEMENTS CVD PREVIOUSLY; NOT IMMEDIATELY MATCHING SPECULATIVE ANGLES.
Below Fold:
  WASHINGTON (News Services) — U.S. may lift trade embargo to allow food sales to Iraq. MAIN ELEMENTS CVD.
  OTTAWA (Staff) — Unnamed Alberta MPs hint at federal aid for troubled oil-drilling sector. PICKED UP WITH CREDIT and CHECKING.
  VANCOUVER (Staff) _ Reform party Leader Manning suggests alliance between his federal party and B.C. provincial Socreds. MAIN ELEMENTS CVD MONDAY.
  NEW SAREPTA, Alta. (Staff) — Switch to organically grown ginseng brings bonanza to former beet farmer. Feature. PICKING UP FOR PMS BUDGET.
  Pictures: Gorbachev greets Bush (CP, Ron Poling); goat farmer poses with his stock (staff), PICKING UP.
  CP Major Play: Op-ed analysis on government cost-cutting by Clyde Graham, Ottawa; lifestyles section-page feature on Alzheimer's disease by Sylvia Strojek, Calgary; entertainment-page profile of Codco comedy troupe by Beth Gorham, St. John's, Nfld.
  CP Edmonton

For a tabloid:

BC-Advisory-Fronts-Ott-Sun
Ottawa Sun Fronts, Wednesday, July 29
  MAIN HEADLINE: TORONTO (Staff) — Parliament Hill janitors to split $13 million lottery jackpot. (CP STORY UPCOMING).
  MAIN PHOTO: OTTAWA (Staff) — Nine-year-old girl points to toilet where she found two-metre-long python; inset pic of herpetologist with snake (STORY AND PHOTOS PICKED UP).
TEASERS:
  OTTAWA (Staff) — Drought threatens trees. LOCAL, NOT MATCHING. HOLLYWOOD — Record sales for Mutant Turtles video (Reuter).
  CP Major Play: Winnipeg lawyer reaped most government work, access-to-info records show, by Kirk LaPointe, Ottawa; sports section photo feature of McNall, Candy, Gretzky at Toronto Argo practice, by Hans Deryk, Toronto; business-page Money Monitor by Allan Swift.
  CP Ottawa

- A scan of story queues in the computer usually reveals whether national or international stories are covered. If in doubt, consult Toronto Main Desk.

- Notations such as **CVD** are not needed on stories credited to CP, AP, AFP or Reuters.

- Some variation of **CVD PREVIOUSLY** is acceptable for backgrounders and features. But consult Newstex and include a day or date for hard-news stories that CP has covered before.

- Fronts advisories are sent with **M**-type message headers.

- Credits of syndicates or supplementary services are not abbreviated (e.g. **Knight-Ridder**, not **K-R**).

- Placelines are not boldfaced.

News Budgets

Putting together a newspaper without a clue of what will be available to fill the pages would be like ordering dinner without a menu. Surprises are certain but so is a sense of queasy uncertainty.

CP tells its editors what's cooking with a twice-daily advisory called the **News Budget**. It details the top stories in sight for the next publishing cycle listed by order of domestic, international, lifestyles, entertainment, business and sports news.

The budget is considered essential reading as papers across the country convene news meetings to plan the next edition. Each budget entry provides:

- A summary of the story's content and approach, phrased attractively.

- Expected wordage to help plot a paper's space needs.

- What developments are expected that could change the story.

- What illustrations are being provided.

- Whether sidebars are planned, whether other current stories are related.

- Whether the story might interest other newspaper departments.

- The keyword slug under which the story can be found in computer queues.

Putting together the budget starts with bureau desk staff, news editors and department editors, who consider the top stories of the day in their regions and specialties and how they can be presented to qualify for the budget.

Staff-written spot stories, analyses, backgrounders and features almost always rate a place. So do the best pickups from newspapers.

Breadth of interest and the quality of the copy are the major criteria. Good writing, background information and local color can elevate a story from strictly regional interest to a place on the News Budget.

Descriptive lines are messaged to Toronto Main Desk, grouped by category. Lines for the **Night Budget**, which moves each afternoon for morning papers (AMs) of the following day, should be received by 1:30 p.m. eastern time. Contributions for the **Day Budget**, transmitted early each morning for evening papers (PMs) of that day, are needed by 1:30 a.m. In addition to new contributions, the PMs budget includes a listing of AMs budget stories that will stand for afternoon-paper publication.

Main Desk should be notified by message or phone if late budget notes — commonly known as *skedlines* or *budget lines* in CP lingo — are expected. Those received after the main list is transmitted can be sent as an add, but this practice is generally reserved for hard news. If in doubt, consult Main on whether a top-copy advisory is in order.

The targets for transmission of budgeted stories is 6 p.m. for AMs and 6 a.m. for PMs. Updating advisories to editors are needed if copy is significantly delayed.

A typical budget line, with a description of its components:

BRUSSELS – Spain is still unhappy with the draft deal on the turbot dispute agreed to by Canada and the European Union earlier this week, Spanish sources said Friday. Sharing the turbot quota is the main sticking point. 450. Developing. By Helen Branswell. See CP Photo, Graphic. With AM-EU-Fishermen. AM-EU-Cda-Fish.

- Placeline is capped, boldface.

- Descriptive line requires at least as much care as composing the lead sentence of the story – both are intended to attract interest as well as convey information. Simply using the lead paragraph as a budget line doesn't always work.

- Wordage of the story or the best possible estimate.

- **Developing** indicates the story is still unfolding. This description would only be used if the developments are hard to anticipate. (A speech planned for later in the day is not a developing story, for instance.) **CP Backgrounder, CP News Analysis, Newsmaker** or **Roundup** can also be used here to signify the nature of the story.

- Byline.

- A CP Photo and CP Graphic are to be sent. Include the number (e.g. **CPT102**) if available.

- Related stories, or sidebars, QuickFacts or QuickQuotes are pointed out.

- Keyword slugline, which newspaper editors will look for when seeking the copy. It must be identical on the story.

More examples:

> **MONTREAL** – Expos president and part-owner Claude Brochu met with the media Friday to announce a corporate-sponsorship agreement, the first time he has publicly commented on his cash-strapped team's busy week on the trade market. 500. By Terry Scott. Business interest. AM-BBL-Expos.

• The absence of what Brochu had to say hints that this budget line was submitted before the meeting. But it takes care to include context on why the news conference is expected to be newsworthy. Something lame – **Expos owner holds news conference** – does nothing to encourage use of the story.

• The possible interest of this story to another newspaper department – business in this case – is noted. Variations include **Lifestyles interest**, **Entertainment interest**, **Sports interest**. Or **Newspage interest** for stories budgeted under any of those categories.

> **OTTAWA** – Parliament concludes a passionate debate about the death penalty with a vote. 500. By Wendy Cox. Will be Lead after vote expected at 10 a.m. EST. See CP Photos. With Vars PM-Death-Penalty. PM-Death-Penalty-Vote.

• Developments at a specific time that will result in an update to a budgeted story are noted, especially if copy is likely to be late or the developments fall when key newspaper deadlines are approaching.

> **TORONTO** – The Ontario government has reached a deal that will allow thousands of teachers to retire at an earlier age, clearing the way for the hiring of younger – and cheaper – replacements. 450. With QuickFacts and AM-Teachers-Pensions. TOR OUT. Moves REGIONAL (C). AM-Teachers.

• Pickups from newspapers that are subject to **locals OUT** codes – protection from a competitor's use of the story – are noted.

• Stories that will move with a regional designator are also noted.

Stories that are not worth budgeting but accompany other budgeted stories, as well as routine items such as basketball roundups, can be included in the budget lines under a **See also**: slug.

See also:
- AM-Budget-Seniors
- AM-Budget-Agriculture
- AM-Budget-QuickFacts

See also:
- PM-NBA-Rdp.

The budget is grouped according to the section of a newspaper the copy is destined for: Canadian, World, Sports, Business, Lifestyles, Entertainment.

A particularly important news event can produce a number of related stories for the budget. They should be grouped under an appropriate subhead: Federal Budget, Stanley Cup Final, Winnipeg Floods.

Sometimes stories just don't pan out as expected. When this happens, or copy for some reason is not available, an advisory is issued to delete the story from the budget.

For example:

AM-Budget-Advisory
EDS:
Please delete Edmonton-placelined AM-Getty from the Night News Budget. Speech cancelled due to minor illness.
CP Edmonton

At-a-Glance, Highlights, Quicks

Newspaper market surveys often agree: many readers feel pressed for time. Modern life leaves less time than in the past to devote to their daily paper. Non-subscribers frequently give lack of time as the main reason for not getting a paper regularly.

The response of many newspapers has been to add news summaries, capsules and other digests of information — often along with eye-catching graphics — that can be absorbed quickly. In many cases, these new features have been added without sacrificing the additional detail that devoted readers look for.

CP helps by offering three types of specialized editorial packaging: **At-a-Glance**, **Highlights** and **Quicks**. Each has a different look but each offers the same thing: fast access to information that is important, helpful or just plain interesting. Illustrations from the Graphics service of CP Photos round out the displays.

Packaging information makes the page more interesting but it also helps readers digest some of the facts and figures that give weight to the story. With boxed material like Quicks, At-a-Glances and Highlights, CP answers a need. This page is from the Toronto Sun.

At-a-Glance

When a major story is breaking here, there and everywhere, the occasion calls for an At-a-Glance:

AM-Cda-Fish-Glance ❶
code:5
EU-Fish-Dispute-at-a-Glance
                    By The Canadian Press ❷
    The feud over fishing rights in the northwest Atlantic took an ugly turn Thursday as the European Union and Canada hurled accusations at each other. The major developments: ❸
        – ❹ The captain of one Spanish trawler says Canadian patrol boats tried to cut his nets and board his ship. A captain on another trawler says his nets were destroyed.
                        — — —❺

    – Canada denies the charges, saying three patrol boats had sailed near six Spanish vessels to identify them and see if they were fishing with illegal nets for turbot.
                        — — —

    – In Dallas, Prime Minister **Jean Chrétien ❻** strongly defends Canada's position. "We had to do something."
                        — — —

    – The French EU presidency condemns ❼ Canada for what it calls continuing harassment of EU trawlers. ❽
                        — — —

    – In Madrid ❾ , several thousand angry Spanish fishermen ❿ . . .

---

❶ **Keyword** slug is variation of the slug on the main story the Glance accompanies (Soviet).

❷ Not bylined except for the **CP credit**, boldface, centred.

❸ Glances accompany rapidly developing stories. They are frequently **updated** to keep pace with events.

❹ Each paragraph is indented and preceded by a boldface **em dash** and a **space**. It ends with a period, not a semicolon.

❺ Each paragraph is separated by a **three-em dash**, boldface, centred.

❻ **Names** are boldfaced.

❼ Entries are written in the **present tense** whenever possible to lend immediacy. Avoid headline writing that drops articles and auxiliary verbs. Each paragraph should be constructed in the same pattern for ease of reading.

❽ Paragraphs should not exceed **30 words**. Sentences are kept concise but not to the point where reader understanding or significant detail is sacrificed.

❾ **Location** is noted where the entry concerns a development away from the centre of the action.

❿ An At-a-Glance includes material that is dealt with at least briefly in the **main story**. But a Glance of more than eight entries likely includes secondary material that should be trimmed.

Highlights

When complex elements of a story need summarizing, use Highlights.

BC-Bgt-Highlights
URGENT ❷
   ❸OTTAWA (CP) — Highlights of the federal budget presented Thursday: ❹
   — ❺ About 50,000 new home-buyers are eligible for loan guarantees of up to $3,000.
                              — — — ❻
   — Builders are offered❼ interest-free loans of up to $7,500 for each rental unit constructed in tight-market areas. ❽
                    — — —
   — One-third of Canada's 16 million income-tax payers will be taxed less but few will save more than $100. ❾
                    — — —
   — Farmers facing bankruptcy ❿ . . .

---

❶ **Keyword** slug is a variation of the slug on the main story the Highlights accompany (Bgt).

❷ **Not bylined.**

❸ Usually **placelined** because it pulls together the key points of a major story focused in a single centre.

❹ Usually accompanies fully developed stories. **Rarely requires updating.**

❺ Each paragraph is indented and preceded by a boldface **em dash** and a **space**. It ends with a **period**, not a semicolon.

❻ Each paragraph is separated by a **three-em dash**, boldface, centred.

Note: Short sections of Highlights included in the text of a story — often referred to as **bullets** — are not separated by dashes.

❼ Entries are written in the **present tense** whenever possible to lend immediacy. Avoid headline writing that drops articles and auxiliary verbs. Each paragraph should be constructed in the same pattern for ease of reading.
— Sales tax rises to eight per cent Sept. 1.
— Single parents get child-care deduction up to $2,000.

❽ Paragraphs should not exceed 25 words. Sentences are kept concise but not to the point where reader understanding or significant detail is sacrificed.

❾ Highlights emphasize the key points of a story most closely affecting readers' lives, give specific examples and avoid jargon.

Not: Benefit eligibility for involuntary job-seekers reduced by one week.

But: Laid-off workers get unemployment pay after two weeks instead of three.

❿ Highlights include material that is dealt with at least briefly in the main story. But Highlights of more than a half-dozen entries likely include secondary material that should be trimmed.

Quicks

Almost every good story presents an opportunity for a **QuickFacts**, **QuickSketch** or **QuickQuotes**, whether hard news or feature.

Quickly defined, Quicks are short, sharp collections of information — facts, figures, trivia, biographical snapshots, memorable quotations.

These features are boxed for display or brightened by an accompanying CP Graphic to break up fields of grey type and offer interesting highlights, sidelights or insights into the news.

There is no real limit on what can go in a Quick.

Among other things, Quicks can:

- Provide a tight summary of main points from a high-profile meeting.

- Explain technical language from any kind of specialized get-together.

- Provide a calendar of main events at a multiple-day conference.

- Recite a selection of worthwhile jokes from a comedy festival or one-liners from an entertainer's news conference.

And especially, never neglect a Quick when it can give readers news they can use:

- What a new innovation means to you.

- How to tell if you've got the problem.

- What you can do about it.

- How the program works.

- Where to go for information.

- Pitfalls to watch for.

A Quick should rarely consist only of information already reported in the main news story. It may blend elements of the story with supplementary material from reference works or other sources. Or it may be a collection of related snippets not found anywhere else.

Formats are highly adaptable. Informative, interesting and amusing are the main criteria. Question-and-answer formats are especially useful for complicated subjects.

Some guidelines:

- Quicks can be either placelined or undated. They are not bylined apart from CP credit.

- Quicks should be snappy. Bare-bones, not story form. Unlike At-a-Glances and Highlights, complete sentences not required. Nor detailed tie-ins to main story. **Here are** not a mandatory introduction.

Not: Here are some facts and figures about Yugoslavia, where civil war has claimed hundreds of lives in recent days:

But: Facts and figures on Yugoslavia, embroiled in civil war:

Not: Early career: Born in 1920 to vaudeville entertainers, Rooney made his first stage appearance at 15 months. He made his film debut in silent-era short subjects at six and went on to star as perpetual juvenile Andy Hardy in a popular MGM series that ran from 1936 to 1946.

But: Early career: Born 1920 to vaudevillians. Stage debut at 15 months, on screen from age six. Top box-office draw in Andy Hardy series 1936-46.

• Quicks should be brief; 100 to 250 words is ideal. Anything longer should be packaged as something else. On rare occasions — such as separate QuickSketches prepared in advance on four new Senate appointees — they can be transmitted as a group for ease of handling.

• As in regular news copy, prefer the specific to the general. In some circumstances, Quicks can be used to provide detail that would clutter up the main story, such as province-by-province comparisons or statistical data.

Not: Showed interest in politics from early age.

But: At nine, insisted on joining father at Mackenzie King campaign rally.

Not: Union seeks 11 per cent pay increase over two years.

But: Union wants 76 cents hourly in first year and 67 cents in second half of two-year contract, net rise of 11 per cent over average hourly wage of $12.79.

• Try to include something offbeat in each Quick. A funny or shocking statement is a good lead-in to a collection of otherwise sober QuickQuotes or a good kicker to close a straightforward QuickSketch. An oddball statistic can enliven a businesslike QuickFacts (e.g. **stacked in a pile, copies of the committee's reports would reach higher than the 100-metre Parliament Building Peace Tower**). Don't overlook colorful personal traits in QuickSketches (e.g. **Jean Chrétien's deliberately folksy English, George Burns's trademark cigar**).

• QuickQuotes can expand on statements that appear in the main story. They can offer more direct quotes on statements that are treated briefly, or actual words for paraphrased material, or new quotes that weren't essential to the story. Quotes are separated by **three-em dashes**, boldfaced, centred. Limit the selection to four or five, whether from a single person or several principals in an event. Where essential quotes run too long for the Quick format, adopt a different slug (**BC-Meech-Quotes**).

• QuickTips can offer practical information for readers: five steps to healthier meals, seven ways to organize cupboards, etc.

• Avoid all-caps for headings.

Some examples:

BC-Keep-Fit-QuickFacts
code:3
With BC-Keep-Fit, Bgt
By The Canadian Press
Fitness trainer Bob Delmonteque dispels some myths about aging and fitness:
Myth: You can't turn back the clock.
Fact: The average person can lead a longer, healthier and more productive life by exercising. Keeping active can slow down and reverse the signs typically associated with aging.
Myth: Older people can't build muscle and strength.
Fact: People past middle age can gain muscle and increase strength by as much as 200 per cent. Older exercisers increase their strength at about the same rate as younger people.

BC-TV-Gemini-QuickQuotes
code:8
With Hamilton AM-TV-Gemini
By The Canadian Press
Some of what was said at Sunday night's Gemini awards for Canadian television:
"I have to thank Paul Haggis for being clinically insane." – Paul Gross thanking Due South's producer after winning his best actor award.

—

"No matter how much time I'm forced to live in exile I'm always first, last and foremost a Canadian. This land is your land, this land is my land, from the big snowy part to the other big snowy part." – Stephen McHattie, who won a best actor award for Life With Billy.

—

"I was on an airplane today ...

Note: Prefer the quote, then the attribution and context, if appropriate.

BC-MUSIC-Lightfoot-QuickSketch
code:3
With Toronto AM-MUSIC-Lightfoot
By The Canadian Press
A sketch of Gordon Lightfoot's career:
Beginnings: Piano lessons. Sings in church choir at age eight.
First group: Swinging Singing Eight, on CBC-TV's Country Hoedown.
First album: Joined Terry Whelan in 1962 as the Two Tones on Chateau Records.
Life's work: Eighteen original albums; about 180 songs.
Breakthrough: If You Could Read My Mind, a smash hit in U.S. and Canada.
Greatest Hits: You Are What I Am (1973), Sundown (1974), The Wreck of the Edmund Fitzgerald (1976).
Quote: "If they (the songs) have stood the test of time, it makes me happy."
(Source: Encyclopedia of Canadian Rock, Pop and Folk Music.)

Editorial symposiums

Some cynic once defined editorial writers as bandits who descend from the hills when a battle is over to shoot the wounded.

But at their best, newspaper editorial pages are in the thick of the fray, armed with argument, reason, wit and not-so-common common sense.

A selection of excerpts from well-turned editorials can reflect the depth of debate and range of opinion at play on important national and world issues — federal elections, key developments in the constitutional arena and the like.

Such selections are provided by CP in an **Editorial Symposium**, a sampling of what newspapers countrywide have to say.

Symposiums are most often started by Head Office, via Toronto Main Desk, but bureaus and departments are welcome to suggest appropriate topics. Requests for symposiums from member newspapers should always be referred to Toronto.

Providing a truly national, representative selection is essential. Metropolitan newspapers aren't alone in having opinions worth reading; a small-town view of events can be equally provocative.

Bureaus should actively solicit contributions from newspapers in their region, delivered electronically or by fax. The timeliness of a symposium effectively ends about 24 hours after it starts, so waiting for mailed copies of papers is not practical.

The General Desk usually puts together symposiums from messaged editorial excerpts. Style for the first selection:

BC-Elxn-Symposium
code:4
Editorial Symposium
                    By The Canadian Press
    Selections from newspaper editorials and columnists, with headlines, following Monday's federal budget:
New budget misses mark
    Timmins Press: Finance Minister Paul Martin wanted to unite ...

For subsequent contributions:

BC-Elxn-Symposium, add
code:4
Add Editorial Symposium

Martin performs fiscal exorcism
    Toronto Star: Call it a budget of penance for 20 years ...

- Keep excerpts brief. They should rarely exceed 100 words. Choose sentences that fairly summarize the editorial position.

- Use *ellipses* (three periods, separated by *en* spaces) to indicate material omitted. But give preference to blocks of comment that can be run without ellipses, since too many of them can create a poor typographical effect.

- Any citations must be exactly as printed. Paraphrasing isn't allowed.

- Newspaper names are boldface, uppercase and lowercase and followed by a colon.

- Contributions take a G-type designator and are sent on the same circuits normally used for general news copy.

Newspage copy

1. Newspage copy or *the newspager* is most often tied to a major break in Sports or Business news. These stories fall into two main categories:

a) Short items that capture the key elements of the event and their impact. These items are written to whet the appetite for fuller coverage on sectional pages: for example, four paragraphs on the Montreal Expos winning the National League's Eastern Division title. In some cases, a longer add can be sent for papers wanting fuller newspage-type treatment. But in all circumstances, the top of the newspage story should be complete enough to flag fuller treatment inside.

b) Longer stories that take a non-specialist approach to a specialist event: how Edmonton celebrates a Grey Cup win; how employees in a small town react to a big-city decision by their only employer to go out of business after 80 years; how consumers will be affected by the merger of two meat-packing plants that have long been competitors. Strong human elements are essential in looking behind the game score, job-loss statistics and other hard-news angles.

2. In either case, plain English and the absence of jargon are essential. Sports-page copy on the Expos winning the pennant can talk about *RBIs* (runs batted in) and assume the reader knows all about Spike Owen and Tim Wallach, but newspage stories must go back to basics. Technical terms should be explained, issues presented in terms of their impact on the public or readers and leading figures in the story seen in human terms.

3. Advisories tipping editors that newspage copy is planned are essential and should be carried as early as possible. But even short notice about a newspager on a late-breaking development can help editors planning front and section pages.

Dealing with members

The 100 or so daily newspapers that own CP — the members — and the hundreds of radio and television stations that are clients of CP's subsidiary, Broadcast News, provide much of the CP-BN daily report.

Contributions can range from a two-paragraph story from the Truro News on a downtown fire to a bylined series from the Kitchener-Waterloo Record on the plight of Mennonites in an increasingly urbanized southern Ontario.

Newspaper copy is usually turned around as quickly as possible. Sometimes it is held to ensure good play — to be included on the daily News Budget of top stories, for example. Or it may be used as the seed of a national story. A report on increasing municipal taxes in Regina from the Leader-Post, for example, may become the basis of a provincewide — or even national — look at municipal tax increases. Other departmental items with no time element may be held to be included in a weekly package to ensure the story will not be missed by the appropriate editor at each newspaper. A brief from the Sudbury Star on French immersion courses for adults, for example, may be held to be included in a package of items for lifestyles pages.

Getting those contributions can be as easy as a CP editor picking up the phone and asking a night news editor at a newspaper to push a button that shuttles the story into CP's computer system. Or it can be as difficult as tracking down a newspaper reporter at the news scene — or at home — to fill in the essential details needed before a spot story can be distributed.

The best policy when dealing with newspapers and clients and their copy is a common-sense one: Be direct. Be polite. And don't waste their time.

CP needs quick tips from members when an urgent story breaks, even if that paper is hours away from deadline. Quick filing is also a necessity for any copy in the paper that is of more than local interest. To ensure CP gets that co-operation, editors should be prepared to offer the same goodwill in return.

Conscientious deskers should always:

• Tip a member newspaper — especially one on deadline — if a story has just broken that is of major interest to the newspaper.

• Ensure member requests for specific stories are dealt with quickly. If the request cannot be met, say so and explain why. Don't say maybe.

• Deal just as promptly with contributions from newspapers. If a story is offered over the phone and cannot be accepted, explain why. If a newspaper is regularly filing updates on a local situation and CP is not carrying them, call the paper to explain why.

• Pass along exceptional examples of member co-operation or lack of co-operation to a supervisor.

CP deskers should not:

• Make repeated phone calls to papers with questions about stories or coverage plans. Make a list of what is needed and phone once. Don't call papers several times to confirm they will file a story.

• Call editors on deadline, especially those in small newsrooms, unless the request is urgent.

• Make last-minute requests for stories. Give members as much warning as CP would want.

• Turn down copy that CP has requested. Don't request a story unless certain it will be needed.

Pickups

1. Stories developed from credited pickups must not give the impression that CP doubts the accuracy of a member's copy.

2. In most cases, denials of member pickups should be written for insert high in the story. They should always be messaged to Head Office for approval. No-comment follow-up stories, seldom required, should be handled similarly.

3. Permission should be sought from the originating newspaper and internal credit should be given (as in: **the Vancouver Province reported Tuesday**) if the story is exclusive enterprise material or involves significant material from outside the newspaper's regular coverage area.

Note: Exceptional stories that cannot be ignored should be briefly picked up, regardless of whether permission is given. CP should immediately attempt to match the story.

4. Bylines of newspaper reporters should be carried if the story is more than a routine item and requires few editing changes. The newspaper's name should follow the byline.

AM-Prison-Reform, Bgt
Budget
See CP Photo KGN2
                        By Leah Laverick
                    Kingston Whig-Standard
        KINGSTON, Ont. (CP) — . . .

➤ See **Copyright**, page 119; **Placelines**, page 278.

News from broadcasters

1. Do not credit radio and TV stations for routine pickups.

2. Credit a network or station when it has shown unusual initiative in obtaining information. As well, credit when the information is newsworthy but CP does not expect to confirm it quickly or cannot confirm it.

Advances

General

Texts of speeches, reports and other material are routinely provided to the media in advance of their delivery to the public. That allows reporters to treat the material more carefully and organize background or explanations as needed.

Some of this material can be distributed early by a news agency, embargoed for release when the speech or whatever is delivered. There's no reason to mislead readers in such cases into believing the stories were prepared in haste, on the spot. The stories should be candid about the fact material was prepared in advance.

Once such stories have been distributed with embargoes — or with internal phrasing that suggests the copy was prepared in advance — editors must be kept informed. Was the speech delivered or the report presented? Send advisories. If the stories need to be modified for any reason, do it promptly.

Speeches

1. Stories about speeches distributed before the speech is made need a phrase such as **in a speech prepared for delivery to**. A separate paragraph can say **A text of the governor's address was provided to the news media before delivery.** The paragraph can be easily deleted if a newspaper wishes; it should not include material essential to the story.

2. Divergences from the prepared speech, audience reaction and circumstances surrounding the event can give life to the bare text.

3. Corrections or additions to update a story moved in advance must be transmitted promptly. An important addition by the speaker is indicated by saying **Madhani digressed from her prepared speech and . . .** On occasion, the divergence may rate a new lead. If there is an important omission, say so and indicate in the story the wording of the original text.

4. When a speech has been checked and the advance stands, advise editors with a note.

AM-Madhani, Advisory
   EDS: See Ottawa Madhani. A check shows Madhani did not depart from the text released in advance.
   CP Ottawa

The paragraph referring to an advance text may be deleted and the reference to **prepared for delivery** changed to **in a speech to . . .**

5.   When a text contains controversial or spectacular statements, every effort should be made to confirm the statements were indeed delivered. If CP cannot staff the speech, arrangements should be made for a fast check with some assigned newspaper or broadcast reporter.

6.   When a speaker drops a controversial statement from a speech, this is sometimes more important than the speech itself if it indicates a change in policy or a moderation of tone. The speaker must always be questioned about the reason for the omission. As warranted, CP should also seek reaction from others involved in the issue.

Broken embargoes

1.   CP editors should tell the source of embargoed material that we will abide by the release time only as long as others do. We will release the material immediately if someone else is found to have broken the embargo.

2.   CP will take no account of the size or importance of the newspaper or broadcaster that broke the embargo.

PM-Royal, Release Advisory
   EDs: Toronto PM-Royal-Bank 748 on the Royal Bank of Canada's annual report, moved in advance for release at 10 a.m. EDT, is now available for publication. The embargo has been broken by other media.
   CP Toronto

Advance slugs

1.   The tops and bottoms of all advance items and their adds carry cautionary slugs. Style examples follow.

2.   In copy relay by Toronto deskers, embargo times are converted to eastern time. Specific times in the body of a story, however, are not changed to their eastern equivalent.

3.   To avoid misunderstanding, sources issuing important releases should be encouraged to provide specific release times. If a source specifies release in morning papers or evening papers, the item should be slugged for use at 6:30 p.m. or 6:30 a.m., respectively.

Style for Slugs

Follow these styles for advances. In examples 1-4, the ADVANCE slugline is the same at the top and bottom of each item.

1.   On copy for a specific time today:

PM-Prisons, Advance
ADVANCE — 12:30 p.m. EDT TODAY, June 11

2.   On copy for a specific time the following day:

PM-Prisons, Advance
ADVANCE — 10 a.m. EST THU Feb. 12

3.   On copy moved more than 24 hours in advance:

AM-Awards, Advance
ADVANCE — 9 p.m. EDT THU Oct. 12
NOTE FUTURE DATE

4.   On copy intended for a specific publishing cycle:

AM-Brothers, Advance
ADVANCE — 6:30 p.m. (or a.m.) EDT

Or

BC-Glover, Advance
ADVANCE — SAT June 15
NOTE FUTURE DATE

5.   On copy to be held for release by an advisory:

BC-Throne-General, Advance
ADVANCE — NOT TO BE USED UNTIL RELEASED BY
ADVISORY, POSSIBLY ABOUT 2:15 P.M. EDT TODAY JUNE
12. GUARD AGAINST PREMATURE USE

At end:

ADVANCE — NOT TO BE USED UNTIL RELEASED BY
ADVISORY

Use this form to release copy moved in advance for indefinite-time release:

BC-Advisory, Release
URGENT
    OTTAWA — Release all advance copy on federal budget.
    CP Ottawa

6.   On copy broken into takes; at end of each take:

MORE — ADVANCE or **MORE LATER — ADVANCE**

Adds are slugged:

PM-Prisons, Advance 1st add
ADVANCE
OTTAWA — 1st add 823 . . . again."

Advance advisories

1.   On major announcements, advance notice should be given by note to editors where possible.

BC-Economy, Advisory
   EDS: We expect to move shortly in advance for release by advisory an important announcement by the prime minister on the economy. She is expected to start speaking at 2:40 p.m. EDT but other Commons business may cause delay. An urgent release note will be sent immediately when she starts to speak. Guard against premature use.
   CP Ottawa

---

2.   Newspaper editors must be kept informed of changes in the prospects for release by advisory. If we have said a release is possible at 2:40 p.m. and it does not develop, a cautionary note slugged Urgent and accompanied by five unspaced bells must be carried at 2:40 p.m. or earlier.

BC-Economy, Advisory
URGENT
   EDS: The prime minister's statement about the economy, originally expected to be released about 2:40 p.m. EDT, is delayed by a procedural wrangle in the Commons. Meanwhile, the embargo on Ottawa Economy continues until the prime minister begins her announcement. Release will be by an urgent advisory.
   CP Ottawa.

---

3.   Use this form for the release:

BC-Economy, Release advisory
URGENT
   OTTAWA — Release the prime minister's statement about the economy.
   CP Ottawa

Bylines

General

Bylines recognize a reporter's original contribution and diligence on a story. When a CP byline is preserved by a newspaper, it sends a public signal of a job well done.

Bylines shouldn't be misused. They aren't normally warranted for a rewrite of someone's news release, the monitoring of a telecast or other task involving minimal imagination and enterprise. Solid original reporting and bright writing can rate a byline.

CP staff with full-time specialist beats should let editors and readers know about their expertise. Such identifications are used whenever department heads or specialist writers are reporting about their areas of speciality.

Newspapers are loath to credit more than two people for a single story. Multiple bylines can look awkward. Consult Toronto Main Desk before sending a story with more than two bylines.

Newspaper editors sometimes eliminate bylines when stripping sluglines from a story in their computer. A blank line inserted after the last slugline and just before the byline helps highlight the writer's name.

Basic Guidelines

1. Bylines are used on top stories, outstanding features and stories by specialist writers.

2. A byline may be removed at the request of a writer if extensive changes are made to the story. In the case of Analyses or first-person material, which should not be distributed without a byline, the writer may request that the story be ditched if a dispute over editing changes cannot be resolved.

3. Desk editors may remove the byline when a story requires exceptionally heavy editing and the writer's approval is not available for the changes.

4. Bylines are not used from placelines where the writer has not been to collect the information reported. Where a reporter's diligence with the phone and other resources has helped produce a story that deserves recognition, consider moving the story without a placeline.

5. Department heads and specialist writers drop their titles when their position or speciality is irrelevant; for instance, if the CP Business Editor covers an axe murder next door.

6. Aside from columns, first-person writing is normally reserved for a vivid, dramatic experience involving the writer: **As I watched, the avalanche roared down on the village, flinging trees and rocks aside.** The first person is also justified when a staffer is an expert on the subject in the news: as a former Olympic sculler commenting on a world record in the event, for instance.

7. Always obtain consent (written consent on major events) before using any non-staffer's byline on a first-person descriptive story.

8. Bylines are set uppercase and lowercase, boldface and centred. No other slug intrudes between them and the story.

Style

For staff of CP, AP and Reuters:

1. For most stories with a placeline:

By Sarah Binder

**By Christopher
Vaughan-Johnston**

**By Chris Cariou
and
Gwen Dambrofsky**

---

2. For most stories without a placeline:

**By Rob Russo
The Canadian Press**

**The Associated Press
Reuters**

---

3. For department heads and specialist writers with job titles:

**By Lee-Anne Goodman
CP Life-Entertainment Editor**

---

4. For reviews by staffers without job titles but with special knowledge of a particular field, use the byline and add a boldface note at the end of the review under a boldface three-em dash centred:

— — —

CP reporter Arlene Forbes studies opera and is a former freelance opera critic.

---

5. For Notes packages and other collections of material from a variety of sources, put together with originality, add a boldface note at the end under a boldface three-em dash centred: **Compiled by Judy Creighton.**

For non-staffers:

1. For string correspondents, use only the byline on stories with a placeline:

> **By Dennis Passa**

But on stories without a placeline, add the service:

> **By Dennis Passa**
> **Canadian Press Correspondent**

2. For stories picked up with few if any changes from member newspapers and used with the byline:

> **By Walter Smith**
> **Hamilton Spectator**

Note: On the rare occasion when a story from a member newspaper carrying a byline and newspaper credit must be Undated, use the boldface credit line **Distributed by CP** at the end of the story, on a separate line.

3. For experts writing about their speciality, use the byline alone and add the credentials in a boldface note, usually at the end of the story under a boldface three-em dash centred.

> — — —
>
> **Eleanor Shu is a professor of economics at the University of British Columbia.**

Note: If further detail is needed, the expanded note may go above the byline in boldface and above a boldface three-em dash centred.

4. For arts reviews from papers or freelance writers, use the byline alone and add the identification in a boldface note at the end of the review under a boldface three-em dash centred:

— — —

Michael Walsh is a theatre critic for the Calgary Herald.

Barbara Dumont, a graduate of the National Ballet School, is a freelance dance critic.

5. Similarly for travel stories and other material by freelances:

— — —

Joan Hanright is a freelance writer based in Darmouth, N.S.

6. For unplacelined copy by freelances, experts and so on, follow this style:

By Rosemary O'Connor
For The Canadian Press

Add the identification in a boldface note at the end under a boldface three-em dash centred:

— — —

Rosemary O'Connor is a freelance writer based in Vancouver.

7. For stories written especially for CP, such as a first-person account by an eyewitness, always preceded by a publishable editors note:

Jim Anderson was working in the fields of his 100-hectare farm Friday when a twin-engine jet crashed less than a kilometre away, killing 10 people. Here is his eyewitness account.
Written for CP
By Jim Anderson
BRADFORD, Ont. (CP) — It was the high-pitched whine of the engine that first caught my attention . . .

For unbylined stories:

1. For stories without placelines:

   a) From a single service:

   By The Canadian Press
   By The Associated Press
   By Reuters

   b) From two or more services:

   From AP-Reuters
   From CP-Reuters-AP

Note: It is *From,* not *By.*

2. For stories with placelines:

   a) From a single service, use an agency credit in the placeline:

   HALIFAX (CP) — Six . . .

   b) From two or more services, use a combined credit line above a CP-credit placeline:

   From AP-Reuters
   PARIS (CP) — Oil ministers . . .

   c) The placeline credit CP-AP or CP-Reuter indicates CP has extensively rewritten an ally's story.

   TOKYO (CP-Reuter) — Canada will gain . . .

Note: In placelines, it is *Reuter,* no *s.*

Completes

General

1. A Complete puts all components of a story — leads, adds, inserts and corrections — into a single edited file.

2. Completes move as soon as possible after any change to a story and are normally sent only on the full CP Datafile service. However, when there have been a number of revisions that would make a story cumbersome, a Complete should also be considered for other services.

3. Do not file a Complete simply to combine two parts or *takes* of a story. However, when a second add has been transmitted, consider doing a Complete.

4. A Complete carries the same log number as the item that made it necessary — a correction or a lead, for example — but with a *Z* header instead of an originating bureau header.

5. When a Complete includes Bulletin or Urgent material, with five bells, delete the bell characters. Unnecessary alarm signals at the newspapers diminish the overall value of the alarms.

➤ See **Slugs and coding**, page 398.

Examples

1. Halifax moves a budgeted Night Lead on a ship going down off Nova Scotia, assigning it the number *HG432*.

AM-Sinking, NL Bgt
Night Lead Budget

2. A Canadian Forces helicopter arrives on the scene and Halifax moves a 1st Lead, item *HG444*, picking up into the Night Lead.

AM-Sinking, 1st Ld
1st Lead-432 (Updates with rescue copter arriving)

3. Halifax now moves a Complete, item *ZG444*

AM-Sinking, 1st Ld Complete
Complete
1st Lead-432 (Updates with rescue copter arriving)

4. Later, the number of crew is revised, so a correction is moved as item *HG453*.

AM-Sinking, 1st Ld Cxn
!!!!CORRECTION
HALIFAX — 1st Ld 444 para 2 revises number of crew to 27 from 25 . . . reported.

5. Halifax now files a second Complete, slugged Complete 2, as item *ZG453.*

AM-Sinking, 1st Ld Cxn Complete
Complete 2
!!!!CORRECTION
HALIFAX — 1st Ld 444 para 2 revises number of crew to 27 from 25.

Corrections

CP uses the following forms to make important changes to stories:

CORRECTION — makes a change in fact or wording, including any error in the lead

WITHHOLD — puts a hold on publication of questionable or erroneous material

KILL — eliminates a story that is wrong, legally dangerous or damaging

SUB — replaces an earlier story in its entirety; particularly used for a story that has been killed

1. Explanations or information provided to justify the **CORRECTION**, **WITHHOLD**, **KILL** or **SUB** slugs must be clear and easily understood.

2. All stories carrying any of these slugs get top priority on news circuits where the erroneous or suspect copy was previously transmitted. The slugs are all-caps and boldface.

Note: Each such item carries the keyword field of the original story.

➤ See **Slugs and coding**, page 398.

3. CORRECTION — Used to alter an erroneous, unnecessary or superseded statement. Often used to update material. The slug is preceded by four exclamation marks: !!!!CORRECTION. The catchline always includes the story placeline, log number and paragraph, and it specifies the error.

Not: fixes name.

But: changes Eve to Eva.

Simple fixes to the first paragraph of a story are also handled with a Correction.

Corrections always replace entire paragraphs. Lines of copy processed at newspapers vary in length. Use of a full paragraph guarantees all erroneous material is eliminated.

The label **CORRECTION** and the catchline are sent flush left. The catchline for a first paragraph Correction has no pickup word. The pickup line, also boldface, is indented.

AM-Truck-Crash, Cxn
!!!!CORRECTION
REGINA — 631 para 4 changes location to city hall . . . truck.
   A police spokesman said the accident happened two blocks from city hall.
    AMBULANCES WERE . . . para 5-631

---

4. When correcting a story by deleting an erroneous paragraph or paragraphs for which no substituted material is needed, move a correction along these lines:

PM-Truck-Crash, Cxn
!!!!CORRECTION
    EDs: In Regina 631 PM-Truck-Crash, delete para 7, beginning "The highway was . . . " and ending ". . . were no injuries." The reference to a crash in the same area two years ago is erroneous. The paragraph will not be subbed.
    CP Edmonton

As usual, this would be followed by a **COMPLETE**, deleting the paragraph.

5. Important corrections, such as those which substantially change the lead of a story, are flagged with five unspaced bells. The slug !!!!**URGENT CORRECTION** or !!!!**BULLETIN CORRECTION** is sometimes used.

PM-Truck-Crash, URGENT Cxn
!!!!URGENT CORRECTION
REGINA—631 para 1 fixes criminal negligence charge
    REGINA (CP) — A Saskatoon driver was charged with dangerous driving and leaving the scene of an accident today after his pickup truck jumped a curb and demolished the fronts of two downtown stores.
    THE DRIVER . . . para 2-631

Note 1: The five bell characters, inserted directly after !!!!URGENT CORRECTION or !!!!BULLETIN CORRECTION and on the same line, must be unspaced to trigger alarms at some papers.

Note 2: When doing a Complete, delete the bell characters.

6. **WITHHOLD** — Used to warn editors that a story may be erroneous, dangerous or premature and that it must not be published pending a check.

Withhold notes are sent as bulletins. They identify the story by placeline, subject and log number, and detail the reason for the Withhold.

AM-Truck-Crash, BULLETIN WITHHOLD
BULLETIN WITHHOLD
    EDITORS: Withhold from publication Regina Truck-Crash — 638. The identity of the driver charged has been questioned.
    CP Edmonton

---

7. **RELEASE WITHHOLD** — Used to notify editors that a story previously withheld has been cleared for publication. Notes releasing a withheld story are sent as bulletins.

AM-Truck-Crash, BULLETIN RELEASE
BULLETIN RELEASE
    EDITORS: Release Regina Truck-Crash — 638 — previously withheld because identity of the driver was questioned. Police have confirmed the identity of the driver.
    CP Edmonton

---

8. **KILL** — Used to eliminate an erroneous or unnecessary story, whether or not it has been previously withheld. Kills are sent as bulletins. They identify the story by placeline, subject and log number, specify the reason and say whether a substitute story is planned.

AM-Truck-Crash, BULLETIN KILL
BULLETIN KILL
    EDITORS: KILL Regina Truck-Crash — 638 previously withheld, which identified the driver of the pickup truck. Legal counsel confirms it is possibly dangerous. Will be sub.
    CP Edmonton

---

9. **SUB** — Used on a story that completely supersedes an erroneous item. It rates an urgent slug.

A sub repeats the story but with the erroneous material corrected. It is flagged at the top with an explanatory note to editors.

AM-Truck-Crash, URGENT SUB
URGENT SUB Regina 638
EDITORS: Subs for Regina Truck-Crash — 638 previously killed. It eliminates the possibly dangerous identification of the driver.
    REGINA (CP) — A Saskatoon driver . . .

---

10. The bureau originating any correction, sub or kill that removes possibly dangerous matter from the CP report must send a note to editors at the start of the next publishing cycle, drawing attention to the elimination.

PM-Truck-Crash, Advisory
    EDITORS: Note the important SUB 640 night eliminating possibly dangerous identification of the driver from Regina Truck-Crash — 638.
    CP Edmonton

Correctives

Mistakes happen. Misinformation gets reported. When it does, the first priority is always to get it fixed, quickly and properly.

The CP Corrective is used to catch up with an error that has probably already been published. It is specifically designed to face the error head on and set the record straight frankly.

It deals *only* with information shown to be in error, when enough time has passed for the mistake to get into print. If the error is caught in the same news cycle in which it is made — within a few hours, in other words — move a *Correction* (see page 389).

Always go back to the original story when writing a Corrective. Focus on the precise words that are wrong and deal only with the erroneous information. But deal with it fully and openly. Never try to *interpret* the original. If it is wrong, it is wrong.

Here is a sample Corrective when the mistake is CP's alone:

> **BC-Bay-Simpsons, CCTV**
> **CORRECTIVE**
>   TORONTO (CP) — The Canadian Press erroneously reported Wednesday that Simpsons was once owned by Sears, Roebuck and Co. of Chicago.
>   In fact, Simpsons and Sears, Roebuck and Co. were partners in the formation of Simpsons-Sears stores in Canada in the early 1950s.

When the mistake originates with a newspaper story, the Corrective should say that CP *distributed* an erroneous report. In all but extreme cases (see No. 8 in the *General guidelines* below), consult the newspaper before carrying a Corrective based on a pickup. Put out a *Withhold* (see page 390) if the paper cannot be reached immediately. Advise a CP supervisor so that further steps may be taken to reach newspaper staff.

CP believes that readers should be given both the correct version and the erroneous version together, to make clear what was wrong. It is not enough to present the correct information while acknowledging only that *erroneous information was reported previously.*

When an error originates with a government announcement, a company news release or some other official source, a Corrective is not used.

Rather, the follow-up story should aim for a legitimate news angle.

For example, a follow-up to a story based on erroneous mortgage rates released by a bank might be tied to the angle that bank branches were flooded with calls. Failing that, the story simply quotes the bank as saying it gave the wrong information.

The *Clarification* (see page 394) is **not** a substitute for a Corrective. The Clarification deals with a story that is not so much wrong as it is incomplete or capable of leaving a wrong impression.

General guidelines

1.   When a mistake is discovered, send a proposed Corrective to Main Desk immediately, with a full explanation of how the error was made and who made it. Make sure it fully corrects what was wrong in the original. The Corrective *always* includes a reference to The Canadian Press erring or distributing an erroneous report. It also includes the date of the error. It carries a boldface **Corrective** slug.

2.   Once approved, move the Corrective immediately. Repeat Correctives or point them out by advisory in the next cycle:

PM-Ship-Corrective, Advisory
   Eds: Note the important corrective item BC-Ship, CCTV, moved in the previous cycle and intended for papers that published the Halifax ship-sinking story of Saturday, May 25.
   CP HALIFAX

3.   When facts and figures are involved, simply admit the error and give the correct information.

4.   Consult counsel if there is a chance libel or contempt may be involved. Seek advice also if a Corrective might hurt CP's legal position or aggravate the damage caused to a potential complainant.

5.   Add regrets or an apology where there has been obvious damage to the reputation of a person or corporation. Such a story should be approved by counsel. It must be headed by a boldface note asking newspapers that published the original error to give equal prominence to the Corrective. (See page 394.)

6.   Never try to fudge a mistake in a developing story by overtaking it with a 1st Lead that includes a clarifying statement or skates around the original error completely. A Correction is needed in the original cycle. If there was time for the error to be published, a Corrective is called for.

7.   If a member of the public with a vested interest disputes a story, and if CP itself or an originating newspaper stands by it, carry the person's denial along with a statement that CP or the paper stands by its report. Main Desk may need to check counsel on the appropriate wording.

8.   Consider an immediate Corrective if a complainant demands such or if the weight of evidence suggests the original was wrong, even when the originating newspaper cannot be reached. But report that senior editors from the newspaper were not available and keep pushing to reach them. Consult Main Desk.

9. Correctives carry a placeline, almost invariably that of the original story.

10. Correctives must go on all news circuits on which the original was sent. Main Desk compiles a relay report to make sure the Corrective reaches every newspaper that received the original. Specific checks must be made with CP Montreal to establish whether the original story was relayed by the French-language services. Circuit editors may discard a Corrective only when they are certain the error did not reach the papers they serve.

Style

The following forms are for the guidance of editors preparing Correctives for Main Desk approval:

1. Specific reference:

OTTAWA (CP) — The Canadian Press erroneously reported Nov. 28 that oil exports during the first eight months of 1991 declined by 17 per cent. In fact, oil exports fell by 27 per cent.

2. Correcting serious or legally dangerous errors:

Eds: Papers that published the St. John's, Nfld., Elwood Hatcher slaying story of Sunday, June 1, dealing with the arrest of two suspects, are asked to give equal prominence to the following CORRECTIVE.

3. Apology for serious error:

The Canadian Press regrets its error and apologizes for any embarrassment or inconvenience caused John Doe or Margaret Roe.

Clarifications

1. A Clarification is carried when a story is not essentially wrong but is incomplete or may have left room for a possible misunderstanding. It is a brief placelined item with the boldface slug **CLARIFICATION** and follows the handling steps set out for Correctives.

2. A Clarification should make clear that the original CP story — or in the case of a pickup, the story distributed by CP — left out important information or could be misinterpreted. The clarification would then provide a fuller version or straighten out the possible misunderstanding.

3. A Clarification would be appropriate, for example, if a CP story gave only one side of an issue, or if the wording could be read two ways, or if someone felt unfairly treated, even though there were no errors of fact.

An example:

BC-Suspensions, Clarification
CLARIFICATION

WINNIPEG (CP) — The Canadian Press reported July 15 that Winnipeg city council had ordered two municipal employees suspended from their jobs for going fishing when they should have been inspecting sewage lines.

The story may have left the impression that the suspended workers had not disputed council's action. In fact, both workers have been supported by their union and are contesting the suspensions.

They maintain they were on accumulated leave when they were spotted with fishing equipment on the banks of the Red River just outside Winnipeg.

Slugs and coding

The top of a story on the computer screen in a Canadian Press office looks slightly different from the version that shows up on the screen at a newspaper. The difference is in the coding: instructions to the CP computer system about what text to distribute to which receiving points. These codes are deleted by computer before they reach the newspaper editor's screen.

What the CP editor sees:

❶ *Coding*

❷ *Selector code field*

❸ *Cycle designator*

❹ *Keyword(s)*

❺ *Version field*

❻ *Ranking*

❼ *Slug lines*

❽ *Byline*

❾ *Story break*

cp:u❶
cpstf❷
AM❸-Legis-NS-Vote❹, URGENT Bgt NL❺
code:2❻
URGENT❼
Night Lead Budget
EDS: Will be lead
See CP Photo HFX10
                              By Alan Jeffers❽
   HALIFAX (CP) – Nova Scotia's one-seat majority government has survived a crucial budget vote in the legislature.
   Looking pale and drawn and still wearing a hospital bracelet, disgruntled Tory backbencher Colin Stewart stuck to party lines Tuesday and supported the government's $4.7-billion restraint budget even though he didn't like it. . . .

   And it means Cameron would have to face a summer election campaign. <BREAK>❾
   The government entered the spring session of the legislature on May 10 with a one-seat majority. But Cameron, who took over from former premier John Buchanan in February, insisted he wouldn't water down his policies to win approval from the opposition.

What the newspaper editor sees:

AM-Legis-NS-Vote,URGENT Bgt NL
URGENT
Night Lead Budget
EDS: Will be lead
See CP Photo HFX10
                              By Alan Jeffers
   HALIFAX (CP) – Nova Scotia's one-seat majority government has survived a crucial budget vote in the legislature.
   Looking pale and drawn and still wearing . . .

   And it means Cameron would have to face a summer election campaign.❿
   The government entered the spring session . . .

❿ *Only Datafile papers see from here on.*

Introduction

Editors at the newspapers are introduced to a CP story from the labelling lines at the top of the story that show up on their computer screens. These lines have the overall name of **slugs**.

Slugs say at a glance whether the story is for news or sports pages, what the topic is, whether this is a new story or a variation of an old one, whether there are illustrations to accompany the story, and other information editors should have.

Slugs should be terse, informative, logical — and do a selling job. An editor pressed for time is likely to skim past something labelled **AM-Statement**, but will stop to read through a story slugged **AM-Premier-Denies**.

Properly used, the CP system of labelling and coding stories puts the news into the hands of the right editors at the time they want it. Basic to its success is precise slugging so that various parts of the same story — leads, adds, inserts and so on — may be easily located and assembled in a newspaper's computer system.

Coding

Coded instructions to the computer determine what textual material goes where. Some coding is placed at the top of the screen. Another code can cut a text short to some receiving points. A final set of codes is used when the text is ready to be transmitted.

The first coding line (numbered ❶ in the first illustration, facing page) designates which service the text goes to – CP, Broadcast News or another outlet. It also assigns a priority to the text, telling the computer how urgent the material is (**see Priorities page 398**). The same line can be used to channel the text to printers at specific bureaus or desks within the CP network for their attention.

The second coding line (❷) is the selector code, a field in the copy which allows the editor to specify the origin of the material or where it is going. If it is being used to indicate the source of the story, it will read **cpstf** (created by CP staff), **cpmem** (CP member), or **apreu** (AP-Reuters). This allows computer sorting of copy to ensure clients receive, for example, only CP-originated material.

This line can also carry a code that allows an editor to direct the file to an individual newspaper. The code for a repeat for the daily paper in Sydney, N.S., is illustrated. The CP system also allows filing material to newspaper chains and other groupings through unique codes.

```
cp:u
SC930
```
AM-Legis-NS-Vote, REPEAT
```
code:2
```
REPEAT FOR CAPE BRETON POST
Night Lead Budget

The third coding line (**❻**), directly below the labels that identify the text, assigns a rank to it. The largest newspapers can receive everything CP distributes; this service is called Datafile. Smaller papers get a trimmed-down service called NewsStream. Bureau desk books provide details on the rankings in the code:# system.

CP editors can also embed a code within the body of a story – a Break code (**❾**) – to cut short a story for NewsStream subscribers. Datafile papers get the full story.

In addition, there is a system of coding instructions (not illustrated) that dispatches the text after it has been edited and stored in the CP computer. This final code assigns a file number to the text and a departmental designator (**see page 400**) which channels the story to a particular department at the newspaper.

Priorities

Priority coding in the first line on the CP editor's screen instructs the computer how to rank stories for delivery. (With all newspapers now receiving high-speed delivery, the practical value of the transmission priority is limited to periods of exceptionally heavy news flow.)

As with other CP codes, the first line is stripped from computer systems at the receiving newspapers.

The priority codes include:

f — Flash. The highest priority, only for news of overwhelming urgency. Breaks into news flow and into any other story being transmitted.

b — Bulletin. For one-paragraph items of hot news, Kill advisories or NewsAlerts. Supersedes all but a flash in the computer queue.

u — Urgent. Used on high-priority copy of more than one paragraph.

r — Regular priority. Used on the longer stories that are the backbone of the CP news report in each cycle, and stories of similar calibre. These include stories on the CP News Budget.

d — Deferred priority. Used for spot copy that can be delayed while more important material is transmitted.

a — For **weekday advances** designed for use more than 12 hours after transmission. Hold-for-release material sent for use in less than 12 hours carries a spot news priority.

s — For **weekend advances** designed for use more than 12 hours after transmission.

c — Cycle priority, transmits continuously. Used only for Cable TV service.

h — Hold priority. Stories are held from transmission until raised to a moving priority.

General

1. In order of appearance, the opening slugs say whether the story is for morning or evening papers, what the story is about, whether it's a core story or a new lead or insert, and whether it's urgent or not.

2. Each story is identified by a one-word or multiple-word keyword slug describing the contents. The exact same keyword should be used any time the story is to be changed by later developments, or when other stories are related to the same topic: **PM-Chretien**; **PM-Chretien, Cxn**; **PM-Chretien, 2nd Ld**; **PM-Chretien-Reaxn**.

3. Uniqueness in slugging is important to avoid confusing two or more stories: **Obit-Michener**, not **Died**.

4. Slugs go boldface and most are in upper and lowercase.

5. The all-caps exceptions include frequently used slugs identifying specific types of stories, such as **PEOPLE** (people news), **ENVIR** (for environmental interest), **CRAFT** (stories about the news industry), **CRIME, OUTDOOR, WKND** (for weekend publication) and others.

Departmental designators

Departmental designators help the papers sort copy into categories and into different queues in their computer systems.

The file name created at the originating point in the CP news network contains two (uppercase) letters and three or four numbers.

The first letter refers to the bureau or department of origin and is invisible to papers receiving the material.

The second letter is the departmental designator, based on the type of story: Canadian general news, foreign news, sports and so on.

These are the departmental designators:

A — **Atlantic** regional general news
B — **Business**
C — **Quebec-Ontario** regional general news
D — **Western** regional general news
E — **Entertainment**
F — **Financial** routine
G — National **general** news
H — Quebec-Ontario regional **sport**
I — Atlantic regional **sport**
J — **Travel**
K — **Agriculture**
L — **Lifestyles**
M — Service **messages** and advisories
Q — **Photo** service captions
R — **Sport scores**, summaries and other tabular sports copy
S — **Sports** in general
V — **Western** regional **sport**
W — **Foreign** general news
X — **Spare** category for **sport**, such as Olympics
Y — **Spare** category for **news**, such as elections
Z — **Spare** category

Keyword slug line

The line under the coding and priority line is the **keyword slug line**, consisting of the **cycle designator**, a **keyword** or keywords, and the **version field**.

PM-Michener   **PM-Obit-Michener**
PM-Obit-Michener, 1st add

The cycle designators used on CP copy:

AM — Used on stories intended primarily for morning papers.

PM — Primarily for evening papers.

BC (both cycles) — Stories that may be used in either cycle. An example would be a story delivered early in the night news cycle for next-day morning papers that is available for publication in late editions of evening papers in the West, or for use any time on the day of publication if the story has been delivered in advance.

The keyword field should not exceed 24 characters, including the cycle designator and punctuation. This is exclusive of the version field.

When more than one keyword is used, join the words with hyphens.

Version field

The **version field** provides more detailed information for editors using directory displays to search for copy. This information helps editors link the various components of a story.

The version field is separated from the keyword field by a comma and a space. Some examples:

PM-Michener, 1st add	**AM-Michener, Bgt NL 1st add**
PM-Michener, Cxn	**AM-Michener, Bgt Cxn**
PM-Michener, Insert	**AM-Michener, 2nd Ld Insert**
PM-Michener, 1st Ld	**AM-Michener, BULLETIN KILL**
PM-Michener, Complete 3	**BC-Clandestine, Advance**

Material in the version field is listed in the following order:

— Flash, Bulletin, Kill, Advisory, Withhold, Urgent, Bgt
— Lead status — DL, NL, 1st Ld, Precede, etc.
— Cxn, Insert, 1st add, Advance, etc.

Note that **Bgt** is not repeated in the version field when **1st Ld, 2nd Ld**, etc., are filed.

In the version field, **Budget, Day Lead, Night Lead, Lead** and **Correction** may be abbreviated to **Bgt, DL, NL, Ld** and **Cxn**. However, they should be written out in other slug lines.

Words within the version field are separated by spaces, not by commas or hyphens.

The combined keyword/version field should be kept to a maximum of 45 characters, including punctuation, to allow for proper display in newspaper computer systems.

Specific slugs

This section outlines the main story slugs and the forms in which they are written by CP editors and writers. Note that the code:# line is not included to save space.

1. FLASH — An emergency signal to editors that outstanding news is breaking. Limited to one sentence, a flash has transmission priority and can break into any other story being transmitted before it. It is extremely rare and must be followed immediately by a bulletin.

The word **FLASH** is sent all caps, centred and flagged with five unspaced bells. The text is indented and boldface. The item has a placeline but no service logo.

BC-Ship-Collision, Flash

FLASH

TORONTO — An iron ore carrier with 37 crew members has sunk in Lake Ontario.

---

2.   BULLETIN — Used on the first publishable paragraph — usually not more than 50 words — of important breaks. It should be followed almost immediately by an **URGENT** add. The word **BULLETIN** is sent all caps, centred and carries five unspaced bells. It is publishable and, except for a byline, immediately precedes the story.

PM-Ship-Collision, Bulletin

BULLETIN
By Betsy Powell

TORONTO (CP) — A bulk carrier loaded with iron ore collided with another vessel in a fierce storm on Lake Ontario early today and sank, with all 37 crew members apparently still aboard, the Canadian Coast Guard reported.

MORE

---

3.   URGENT — Used on the first add to a bulletin and on stories of bulletin or near-bulletin character running more than 50 words or so. Adds to bulletins are kept short for fast relay.

The word **URGENT** is sent all caps, flush left and carries five unspaced bells. It is not intended for publication and comes immediately after the keyword slug line.

PM-Ship-Collision, URGENT 1st add
URGENT
TORONTO — 1st add 712 . . . reported.

The Coast Guard reported that the second vessel, a general cargo freighter, suffered little damage and was returning to port in Hamilton. There were no serious injuries among its 21 crew members.

MORE

Note the number **712** in the catchline is the **log number** in the CP computer system and has no significance for newspapers.

4. **Night Lead New** and **Day Lead New** — Used when a story in the previous cycle has developed significantly or there has been substantial reaction to the original event. The slugs are upper and lowercase, flush left.

AM-Ship-Collision, Bgt NL
Night Lead New Budget
See CP Photo CPT12, CP Graphic CPT21

By Betsy Powell
TORONTO (CP) — Four crew members from a sunken iron ore carrier were found alive in a lifeboat during a fierce storm on Lake Ontario on Tuesday, 10 kilometres from the spot where their ship collided with a freighter and sank.
    The other 33 crew members . . .

---

5. **Night Lead** and **Day Lead** — Used when there have been few or no major developments in the story from the previous cycle. The slugs are upper and lower, flush left.

AM-Ship-Collision, Bgt NL
Night Lead Budget
See CP Photo CPT12, CP Graphic CPT21

By Betsy Powell
TORONTO (CP) — The iron ore carrier Lady Alexandria collided with a freighter in a fierce storm on Lake Ontario on Tuesday and sank. The Canadian Coast Guard said 37 crew members . . .

---

6. **1st Lead** — Used on a story superseding a previous story in the same cycle from the same point. When warranted, it is followed by **2nd Lead**, **3rd Lead** and so on.

A lead usually contains new information, more details or fresh quotes. Sometimes a lead simply reorganizes the same information, tightens it or improves the writing. A complete write-through of a story — simply to tighten to improve the writing, but offering no new information — is labelled a **recast**.

In a breaking story, a 1st or subsequent lead may correct earlier attributed information — the estimated death-toll in an earthquake, for instance.

Editors on deadline need to know quickly why they are getting a new lead — explain the reason in the slug line alongside the 1st Lead slug. Does the lead contain significant new information, for example?

A 1st Lead or subsequent lead is **not** a substitute for a correction of factual error. If a story is seriously wrong, it should be killed. Otherwise, it should be corrected. Never try to camouflage such a problem with a 1st Lead.

The slug is upper and lower, flush left. For style on picking up into the previous story, see **Catchlines** below. If the story stands on its own, it is slugged **NO PICKUP**.

See examples next page.

AM-Ship-Collision, URGENT 1st Ld
URGENT
1st Lead-712 (adds eyewitness comments)
See CP Photo CPT14, CP Graphic CPT23

By Betsy Powell

TORONTO (CP) — A lifeboat carrying the only four survivors of the sunken iron ore carrier Lady Alexandria was found late Tuesday, four kilometres from the spot where the ship collided with a freighter in a fierce storm on Lake Ontario.

"They were wet, cold and pretty scared . . . but basically all right," said James Chou, a crew member on the Canadian Coast Guard vessel that found the lifeboat about nine hours after the collision occurred.

The freighter sustained little damage and returned to dock in Hamilton, 20 kilometres west of where the ore carrier went down at about 7:30 a.m.

The Coast Guard reported that the ore carrier had a disabled navigation system and had been en route to dry dock in Port Weller when the collision occurred.

THE CREW OF . . . para 5 NL—710

AM-Ship-Collision, URGENT 2nd Ld
URGENT
2nd Lead-714 (adds details on crew members, debris found; NO PICKUP)
See CP Photo CPT14, CP Graphic CPT23

By Betsy Powell

TORONTO (CP) — An iron ore carrier, its navigation system disabled, collided with a cargo freighter in a fierce storm on Lake Ontario on Tuesday and sank with the loss of all but four of its 37 crew members.

A Canadian Coast Guard ship picked up the four surviving crew members in a lifeboat about 10 kilometres from the spot where the collision occurred.

"They were wet, cold and pretty scared . . . but basically all right," said James Chou, a crew member on the Canadian Coast Guard vessel that found the lifeboat about 20 hours after the collision occurred.

The nationality of the survivors was not immediately known.

Most of the crew were recruited in Asia. The officers were mainly from Greece.

The freighter, which sustained little damage, returned to dock in Hamilton, 20 kilometres west of where the Greek-registered Lady Alexandria went down at about 7:30 a.m.

Jaspal Singh, a crew member on the freighter, said: "It (the ore carrier) came out of nowhere . . . no warning."

The Canadian Coast Guard reported that the ore carrier had been en route to dry dock in Port Weller for repairs to the navigation system when the collision occurred. There was no initial indication of what caused the ore carrier to sink so quickly.

The 37 crew members aboard the Lady Alexandria had flown to Toronto and joined the vessel before it sailed. A spokesman for the ship's owners, Global Shipping of Athens, said most of the crew were from Taiwan.

Three empty lifeboats and other debris were spotted by helicopters searching the area where the collision occurred . . .

Note: Always relate a lead to the previous lead — **3rd Lead** to **2nd Lead**, **2nd Lead** to **1st Lead**, etc. Had the 2nd Lead above not been marked NO PICKUP, it would have picked up into the 1st Lead and not the Night Lead.

7. **Precede** — Used on a story in the same cycle that replaces an earlier story from another community. The slug is upper and lower, flush left.

Precedes are placelined and can stand alone, or they may pick up into an existing story in the same cycle.

AM-Ship-Collision, URGENT Precede
URGENT
Precede Toronto 2nd Lead-717 (Freighter captain said ore carrier ignored warnings of collision)

By Wendy McCann
HAMILTON (CP) — The iron ore carrier Lady Alexandria ignored a radioed warning that it was on a collision course before it struck a cargo freighter early Tuesday and sank in Lake Ontario with the loss of all but four of its 37 crew members.
The Canadian Coast Guard said radio traffic monitored by a ham radio operator indicated the captain of the freighter pleaded with the Greek-registered ore carrier to change course before the collision.
The Lady Alexandria was sailing with a disabled navigation system.
"IT CAME OUT . . . para 2 2nd Lead—717

---

8. **See** — Used on a story that follows in the next cycle but with a different placeline. While a Precede may pick up into the earlier story, a story with a See slug must be complete and cannot pick up into the previous cycle story. The slug is upper and lower.

PM-Ship-Collision, URGENT Bgt
URGENT
See Hamilton day

By Stephen Ewart
ST. CATHARINES, Ont. (CP) — "He was screaming, 'You're going to hit us, change course, now!'" a veteran ham radio operator said Wednesday, recalling the radio traffic he monitored early Tuesday as an iron ore carrier collided with a cargo freighter and sank in Lake Ontario.
Jeremy Duffy said the captain of the freighter repeatedly pleaded with the iron ore carrier Lady Alexandria to change course before the collision. Thirty-three of the 37 crew members on the ore carrier were lost when it sank at about 7:30 a.m. Tuesday. . . .

9. **With** — Used on a sidebar from another point in either news cycle. The slug is upper and lower.

BC-Ship-Collision-Others
With Hamilton Ship-Collision
UNDATED

By The Canadian Press
At least a dozen large ships have sunk in the Great Lakes . . .

---

10. **MORE** — Indicates that additional information will move within 10 minutes. The slug MORE is sent all caps, flush right at the bottom of copy.

11. **MORE LATER** — Indicates that an add will move within 20 minutes. The slug MORE LATER goes all caps, flush right.

If information is expected beyond 20 minutes, no slug is used on the bottom. Instead, an advisory is sent specifying when additional copy is expected.

Delays in the 10- or 20-minute relays must also be explained in a quick advisory to editors.

12. **INSERT** — Used on a paragraph or more of new matter for inclusion in a story already transmitted. It includes the specific reason for the insert.

AM-Ship-Collision, 2nd Ld Insert
TORONTO — 716 INSERT after para 2 (adds details on how quick ship sank) . . . 7:30 a.m.
   "The boat turned on its side fast," said Singh, who appeared shaken by the tragedy. "Then it was gone...down in three, maybe four minutes."
   THE COAST . . . para 3—716.

---

13. CORRECTION and KILL. ➤ See **Corrections**, page 389.

14. **Espy** — Used on a story aimed at a particular community or region. The slug is upper and lower, flush left. **Espy Mtl**, **Espy West**.

15. **Attn** — Used to draw a story to the attention of a CP bureau, usually for a follow. The slug is upper and lower, flush left. **Attn Hfx**.

16. **Note** — Used to draw a bureau's attention to a story that may be useful as background in future, but not demanding immediate attention. The slug is upper and lower, flush left. **Ottawa note**.

17. **Asked** — Used on a story delivered to meet a request. The slug is upper and lower, flush left. **Truro asked, CTV asked, AP asked**. The

slug should not be used when it will signal a paper's or subscriber's interest to its competition. Instead, send a message to the nearest CP bureau for relay to the asker. **Wpg Art-Theft is Tor Star asked.**

18. **Out** — Used on a story based on a pickup from a newspaper in a city with more than one paper. The slug includes a three-letter code that the computers recognize to ensure the story does not enter the computer of the competing paper. It is boldfaced, flush left, with codes in all upper or all lower.

TOR OUT
YYY

HFX OUT
hqq

19. **NewsAlert** – Gives editors a headline description of a news break and alerts them to a bulletin or urgent that will follow immediately.

BC-ALERT
code:1
CP NewsAlert
     TORONTO – Back-to-work legislation for transit workers is defeated.

Catchlines and pickup lines

1.   **Catchlines** are links to previous stories or portions of stories. They are in boldface and flush left. Included are the placeline, identifying slug, CP editor's log number and the last word or two of the previous copy to help locate position in the story, which may already be in type.

AM-Mayor, 1st add
CALGARY — 1st add 420 . . . bums."

PM-Yugoslavia-Rdp, 2nd Ld 6th add
UNDATED — 6th add 2nd Ld—545 . . . lost.

BC-Dog-Show, Insert
TORONTO — 136 INSERT after para 3 (names other competitors) . . . poodle.

Note: When the pickup word is a common one, use more than one word to help locate the line: **. . . soon," he said.**

2.   **Pickup lines** identify the location in previously transmitted copy where new information fits. Pickup lines are boldface with paragraph indent.

IN A PREPARED . . . para 4 — 625
HE RECALLED . . . para 8 DL — 832
"ARSON WAS . . . para 15 2nd Ld — 250, including insert 237

Handling business news

What designation?

Business news often affects people's lives directly. It frequently finds its way on to general news pages. Examples include stories about interest rates, companies closing down or expansion projects. These are best filed as general news items and flagged: **EDS: Business Interest**.

File stories with a business designation only when they have little direct interest to general readers — like longer trading hours on the stock exchanges, a new twist in options trading or a routine company report.

Avoid duplication

Some companies and organizations make the same announcement in two or more cities. Occasionally a company president will visit several places within a few days, delivering the same message to different audiences. CP should avoid duplicating coverage of basically the same event. But we should watch for regional angles that might be presented in one place and not another. If in doubt, check with the Business Editor or Main Desk, or do a Newstex search.

Illustrations

With the growing emphasis on illustration, reporters should think about possibilities for a good graphic or photograph at the beginning of their business-news assignment. Request a photographer, or send figures and details to the graphics artists as early as possible so the illustration can be produced in time to go with the story.

Annual meetings of companies can be a good source of people photographs, whether of a reclusive chairman or an angry shareholder. Well-designed charts and graphs can summarize and simplify complex financial information.

A reporter going to a company's annual meeting should provide graphics artists with some basic information for a QuickFacts box.

Foreign currencies

The daily item slugged **BC-Tab-Foreign-Exchange** can be used to convert many currencies into Canadian dollars.

In stories from most parts of the world, it is best to convert amounts into Canadian dollars. Allied agencies usually provide U.S. dollar figures. Convert them and use phrases like **the equivalent of $50 Cdn** to avoid giving the impression that people elsewhere use the Canadian currency. The **Cdn** is usually necessary only on first reference.

There are exceptions:

1. U.S. dollar figures may be retained in copy with U.S. placelines. Again, specify this on first reference.

NEW YORK (CP) — Orion Pictures said Friday its biggest shareholder has agreed to pump $50 million US into the company.

Orion also said its bondholders have agreed to swap their $267 million in subordinated debt for a 70 per cent equity stake in the company.

---

2. Some commodities like gold and oil are traded on world markets in U.S. dollars. In routine financial items it is acceptable to retain U.S. dollar prices. In more detailed stories, it may be desirable to include a Canadian dollar equivalent in one or two examples.

Precise figures

Precise figures are preferred in routine financial items. But in business stories it is acceptable to round out figures.

BURNABY, B.C. (CP) — Consolidated Paper Clips, which made a breakthrough in recyclable products two years ago, reported a profit of nearly $1.25 million in 1991.

Net earnings

The Business Department prepares a daily roundup of financial results (three months, six months, nine months and annual) reported by Canadian companies whose securities can be bought by the public. Most of these are listed on Canadian stock exchanges.

Bureaus are encouraged to message to the Business Department information that might be included in the roundup, slugged **BC-Earnings**. This item is an example of where precise figures must be used.

Consolidated Paper Clips Ltd., year ended Dec. 31: 1991, $1,247,125, $1.24 a share; 1990, $975,000, $1.05 a share. Revenue: 1991, $10,350,250; 1990, $9,542,000.

Occasionally, a brief clarification may be needed, such as when comparison of per-share profit is distorted by a substantial change in the number of issued shares:

> Consolidated Paper Clips Ltd., year ended Dec. 31: 1991, $1,247,125, $1.24 a share on one million shares; 1990, $975,000, $1.05 a share on 900,000 shares. Revenue: 1991, $10,350,250; 1990, $9,542,000.

Details of per-share earnings and revenue may be omitted when they are not provided by the company.

Dividends

Dividends declared by companies are carried in a daily financial item, slugged **BC-Dividends**, prepared in Toronto. Bureau contributions are welcomed, and should be messaged to the Business Department. Format:

> Canadian China and Cutlery Ltd., common $.20, extra $.05, June 15, record May 15; pfd. $.25 May 15, record April 15.

Dividends are quarterly unless otherwise noted. If an extra dividend is declared, always say so.

Foreign filing

The more diverse the CP world news report, the better.

The basic file is naturally heavy on political and diplomatic developments. But newspapers want to know much more than that about the rest of the world.

The World Desk should watch closely for departmental news of interest to Canadians: Business, Entertainment, Lifestyles, Religion, Travel, Agriculture — even Sports when that desk is not staffed.

News about people is most important of all. The daily Budget of world news should routinely include stories that take an offbeat approach to life in a foreign country. Elements of description and personality should be given priority in the editing of political and other copy.

No newspaper can publish more than a fraction of the average world news file provided by CP. But papers will make room for well-written stories with human interest. When there's a choice between working a bit longer on a story to make it more appealing, or producing even more copy that's dutiful but dull, editors should polish up the best stories. Others can be made into briefs, or ditched, to provide the time needed for better editing.

CP's staff correspondents and stringers abroad should be encouraged to weave atmosphere into their daily reports, blurring the too-sharp distinction between features and spot news.

AP and Reuters routinely include vivid description in their files during the days when the world's attention is focused sharply on some major development abroad, such as the rise of western democracy in Eastern Europe. Their reporters talk to ordinary citizens as a matter of course. They provide background and personality on the political leaders.

But once the spotlight has shifted, the files can become a tedious chorus of government pronouncements, parliamentary debates and other institutional news. The people disappear.

Faced with an example of *institutional* reporting, editors should consider reviving some of the human-interest touches of the past. When a certain foreign minister speaks about a threat to civil rights, it's surely relevant (as the *Newstex* electronic library shows) that he spent three years in prison under a former regime and emerged gaunt and confused.

A sharp eye on the television monitor can also reap atmosphere and detail. An editor who notices some interesting emphasis by a speaker on TV, or sees some telling reaction from the audience, can improve a dull story by working such color into the agency report about the speech. And the phones can be worked to get quotes and color from the scene.

Points to watch

1.   When Canadians are involved in major events abroad, their role needs to be kept in perspective. In a plane crash, for example, to suggest that Canadian victims are somehow more important than dozens of people from other nationalities is insensitive.

Not: Three Canadian missionaries died Thursday when an earthquake levelled dozens of villages in mountainous Peru. The Red Cross said the death toll is likely to be in the hundreds.

But: An earthquake struck high in the mountains of Peru on Thursday, levelling dozens of villages. The Red Cross predicted there would be hundreds of victims found. Three Canadian missionaries were among the first listed as dead.

2.   Travels abroad by CP staff should be signalled in advance to newspaper editors. An advisory should be sent promptly after a decision is made to staff a major international conference, so the papers can take CP's plans into account. When a feature-writing trip is involved, an advisory can be sent as soon as projected dates are known for the copy to be available.

➤ See **Advisories**, page 358.

3.   World Desk editors should remind themselves of the changing complexion of Canada's population. Most newcomers now come from Hong Kong, the Philippines, South Korea and other countries outside the traditional European sources. Their interest in their birthplaces is natural and should influence the selection of news for CP's world report.

➤ See **Locating the news**, page 146.

4.   In reports of polls and statistics from abroad, information is rarely available on the margin of error, the size of the poll and other essentials. The stories should specify that fact. The wording of stories from abroad should be no more categorical than from Canada.

➤ See **Polls**, page 72; **Statistics**, page 89.

5.   Stories from abroad frequently include currency figures, usually expressed in U.S. dollars. For Canadian readers, the figures should normally be translated into Canadian currency and rounded off. Style is to use *Cdn* and *US* immediately after the currency figure, without periods.

6.   CP follows an essentially metric style, with a few exceptions such as personal weights and heights. When copy, particularly from the United States, provides imperial measures, they should normally be translated into metric. However, don't put metric into the mouths of people who use imperial measures, even in indirect speech. And since measures from elsewhere in the world may already have been translated from metric to imperial, the numbers should usually be rounded off when translated back to metric.

➤ See **Metric**, page 253.

Language

Some language points to watch in editing international news agency copy:

1. CP wants the time element to fall naturally in a sentence, as it would in a spoken phrase.

Not: President Bill Clinton Thursday ordered an inquiry . . .

But: President Bill Clinton ordered Thursday that an inquiry be started . . .

2. World copy should follow CP spelling style, even when that means changing the spelling of common-noun elements in proper names: **Lincoln Centre** (not **Center**), the **U.S. Defence** (not **Defense**) **Department**, the **British Labor** (not **Labour**) **party**.

3. CP has no reluctance to separate a verb from its auxiliary. Our preference is to write it the way it's normally spoken: **she is apparently convinced** (not **apparently is**), **he has often gone** (not **often has**).

4. CP capitalization style tends to prefer lowercase where there's a reasonable option: **the foreign affairs committee of the House of Representatives** (not **the House Foreign Affairs Committee**).

5. In words deriving from direction, CP style is **the East, the West** when referring to geographical areas, but **east** and **west** when meaning mere direction. It's also **Eastern Europe, Western Canada, Central Asia**. But when used adjectivally, it becomes **eastern European governments, western Canadian weather, central Asian refugees**. And it's **easterners, northern lights, western boots**.

➤ See **Capitalization**, page 177.

6. While most copy from Britain and other Commonwealth countries has been edited for North America by the time the CP World Desk sees it, examples of British usage can slip by: **goods** (for **freight**) **train, lift** (for **elevator**), **dust bin** (for **garbage can**), **roundabout** (for **traffic circle**).

Place names

The *National Geographic Atlas of the World* is CP's authority for spelling of non-Canadian place names, with the exceptions listed in this book and its companion volume, *(CP) Caps and Spelling*.

Many countries and cities have changed names. CP accepts such changes when they are likely to be enduring and when they appear to be accepted by the people of the country concerned and by the international community. Usually it's essential to remind readers for some time afterward of the former name.

AP copy usually follows *National Geographic* as well. However, AP's exceptions don't always match CP's. Reuters copy includes some place names whose spelling originated in the colonial era, especially in the Middle East. When in doubt, check.

The greatest confusion in spelling usually occurs when languages with different alphabets are involved: Arabic countries, the Soviet Union, China, and so on. Transliteration is inevitably complicated and requires care to ensure consistency of spelling.

➤ See **Place names**, page 282.

Legal

Keeping the news report free of legal problems presents special challenges for World Desk editors. After hours spent looking at copy on American crime cases in which the accused is all but convicted before charges are laid, it takes an alert eye to recognize the legal risks of a similar story that has Canadian elements.

World editors should be familiar with the legal sections of this book.

Any story dealing with Canadians, abroad or at home, or with people who have financial interests in Canada can be dangerous if it unfairly damages their reputations or interests.

The laws of libel in the United States, in particular, permit statements that would be extremely dangerous in Canada. U.S. police seem free to blacken the reputations of arrested people before they come to trial. People in sports and the entertainment world talk freely about other people's drug habits, honesty and truthfulness.

World Desk editors mustn't let their judgment be dulled by all the slanderous and contemptuous material that crosses their desk. The editor who passes a libellous story is as vulnerable to a lawsuit as CP itself — and so is every newspaper that uses the story.

The rules: Check with a supervisor or legal counsel before releasing doubtful material. Kill any story found to be dangerous. Withhold any story that has given rise to legal questions.

➤ See **Legal**, page 95, 111, and 117.

Sports handling

Slugs

1. Slugs must be informative. A well-chosen slug can whet the appetite of an editor and also simplify the search for a specific story.

2. All slugs begin with a *cycle designator*. Stories earmarked for morning papers are designated **AM** and for afternoon editions, **PM**. Secondary items and most agate, which will stand for both cycles, are slugged **BC**.

3. The second element of the slug — all caps and no longer than five characters — identifies major sports. Secondary sports are grouped under the generic **MISC** slug, with the specific sport identified in subsequent slug words. For game copy involving established leagues, the league abbreviation substitutes for the sport designator. Here are the major sports and leagues and their keyword slugs:

Sports

AUTO	auto racing
BBL	baseball
BKBL	basketball
BOX	boxing
CANOE	canoeing
CRKT	cricket
CURL	curling
CYCLE	cycling
DIVE	diving
EQUE	equestrian
FTBL	football
GOLF	golf
GYM	gymnastics
HARN	harness racing
HKY	hockey
RODEO	rodeo
ROW	rowing
RUGBY	rugby
SAIL	sailing
SKTG	skating (figure and speed skating)
SKI	skiing
SOC	soccer
SWIM	swimming
TEN	tennis
THBRD	thoroughbred racing
TRACK	track and field (athletics)
VLBL	volleyball
MISC	all other sports

Leagues

AHL	American Hockey League
AMN	American League (baseball)
APSL	American Professional Soccer League
CFL	Canadian Football League
CIAU	Canadian Interuniversity Athletic Union
CSL	Canadian Soccer League
IHL	International Hockey League
MSL	Major Soccer League
NAT	National League (baseball)
NBA	National Basketball Association
NBL	National Basketball League
NFL	National Football League
NHL	National Hockey League
WBL	World Basketball League
WLAF	World League of American Football
WVL	World Volleyball League

Multi-sport events

OLY	Olympics
GAMES	Other multi-sport events such as the Pan-Am, Commonwealth or Canada Games

4.   The next elements of the slug identify specific subject matter. For example, a story aimed at morning papers and dealing with a world-record swim by Canadian Nancy Sweetnam might be slugged: **AM-SWIM-Sweetnam-Record**. Or, a feature on Canadian table tennis champion Gideon Joe Ng might carry a **PM-MISC-Table-Tennis-Ng** slug.

In game stories, the second element of the slug identifies the league and the third and fourth elements the two competing teams (the visiting team listed first). For example, an NHL game with the Vancouver Canucks visiting the Winnipeg Jets would be slugged: **AM-NHL-Vcr-Wpg.**

➤ See **Slugs**, page 398.

Agate

General

As the design and focus of sports sections continue to evolve, the demand for agate increases.

Agate, or scoreboard, pages allow newspapers to present the essential aspects of a game or competition concisely. In many instances, they provide the option of not carrying a story on the event. These pages also satisfy the appetite among sports readers for more background statistics and comparison tables.

Reporters and editors should think constantly of ways to supplement stories with agate tables, fact boxes and graphics.

All CP-tabulated material carries a **Tab** identifier in the slugline immediately following the cycle designator. Unedited AP tabular copy does not take the Tab slug.

Tabulation

Standings that aren't justified properly lead to unaligned columns of figures and frustration for readers. Tabular material must include the proper typesetting symbols.

Lines containing tabular material must include two such symbols — the tab line indicator *(TLI)*, often referred to as a tapefeed, and the tab field indicator *(TFI)*, or vertical rule.

As the name implies, the TLI, which begins the line, signals the newspaper computer that the line that follows contains tabulation. The TFI then identifies the actual field of information that's to be tabulated and appears immediately before the first column of figures.

Other typesetting symbols — *thin spaces, en spaces* and *em spaces, en leaders* and *em leaders* — provide the proper spacing between columns.

How these symbols are displayed on the computer screen will vary depending upon the software. For demonstration purposes, the following symbols will be used here:

†	tab line indicator (TLI), or tapefeed
▌	tab field indicator (TFI), or vertical rule
‖	thin space
D	en space
○	em space
•	en leader
••	em leader

The TFI signal sends all information that follows it to the far right side of the agate column. As a result, when a figure increases in width, there must be a corresponding decrease in the spacing that precedes it so that all figures in the column remain aligned.

An *en space* is one-half an *em space,* and a *thin space* is roughly one-half an *en space.* When the figure in a column increases by one digit, the preceding spacing must be reduced by an *en space.*

(*En leaders* and *em leaders* replace *en spaces* and *em spaces* respectively in boldfaced lines of tabulation, such as column headers in standings. Most capitalized letters are slightly wider than an en leader and so are preceded instead by a thin space.)

Note in the following example that Edmonton's win total, a double-digit figure, is preceded by an en space, whereas there is an em space preceding Calgary's single-digit win total of 9.

†		▌ G •‖ W •‖ L •‖ T••‖ F ••‖ A ••‖ P
†Edmonton	▌16 D 10 ○ 5 ○ 1 ○ 80 ○ 56 ○21
†Calgary	▌16○ 9 ○ 5 ○ 2 ○ 77 ○ 50 ○20

When first setting up tables such as standings or scoring leaders that will change as the season progresses, determine the maximum probable width of each column by the end of the season. Then ensure each column will be separated by at least an en space at season's end.

For example, by the end of the NHL season, each team will have double-digit totals for games played, wins, losses, and possibly ties. Goals for and against will each be triple-digit figures and so will some points totals. The samples below show how the tabulation would differ between the opening and final nights of the season.

Initial standings:

NHL
Campbell Conference
Smythe Division

†	G	W	L	T	F	A	P
†Edmonton	1	1	0	0	8	3	2
†Calgary	1	0	0	1	6	6	1
†Winnipeg	1	0	0	1	6	6	1
†Los Angeles	0	0	0	0	0	0	0
†Vancouver	1	0	1	0	3	8	0

Final standings:

†	G	W	L	T	F	A	P
†Edmonton	80	52	22	6	390	236	110
†Calgary	80	48	29	3	377	249	99
†Los Angeles	80	32	37	11	295	301	75
†Winnipeg	80	30	41	9	227	335	69
†Vancouver	80	22	55	3	200	368	47

Accuracy

It is essential that all agate items be *proofed* before being transmitted. Such things as shots on goal in a hockey summary, score by quarters in a football summary or runs scored in a baseball linescore can be checked in seconds. Others, such as standings, are more involved. Keep a calculator handy.

For standings involving such sports as hockey, football and soccer — where goals (or points) scored and allowed by each team are recorded — check each team line and ensure that:

• The total number of wins, losses and ties equals the number of games played.

• The figure in the points column equals the number of points awarded for all wins (usually two each) plus the number of points for all ties (usually one each).

Also, do an overall league check. Ensure that:

• The total number of goals (or points) listed in the *F* column for the entire league equals the total for the *A* column.

• The total number of wins, plus losses, plus ties (which must always be an even number) equals the total number of games played.

For sports such as baseball or basketball, where standings often record percentages of games won rather than award points for victories, ensure that:

- The league totals for games won and lost are identical.

- Percentages are achieved by dividing the number of games won by the number of games played. Round the figure off to three decimal places.

Some standings, especially baseball, also include a GBL *(games behind leader)* column. This is calculated by comparing a team's won and lost totals with those of the first-place club. The differences in each column are added together, then divided by two to arrive at the GBL. For example, if Toronto's won-lost record was 48-33 and Boston's was 39-41, the two differentials would be 9 and 8 for a total of 17. Divided by two, the GBL becomes 8½. The reason for the half game is the fact the two teams have not played the same number of games (Toronto 81, Boston 80).

Results formats

Most results are presented in one of three formats: **bare score**, **field result** or **head-to-head result**. An example of each is given here for fast reference. Individual sports sections will specify which format is appropriate.

Note: The word **Tab** is incorporated into the slugline — immediately after the cycle designator — for all agate, with the exception of AP copy transmitted in unedited form and not meeting CP justification standards.

Canadian results in international competitions are boldfaced. Home towns for Canadians are provided; others are listed by country.

Bare score

The winning team is listed first, with the exception of British soccer results where the home team is listed first, regardless of the outcome.

BC-Tab-HKY-Rslts
Wednesday's list

By The Canadian Press
NHL

Toronto 3 Montreal 3

Adds go as follows:

BC-Tab-HKY-Rslts, add
Add Wednesday's list
Add NHL
Calgary 6 Vancouver 4

Field result

BC-Tab-TRACK-World-Cup-Rslts
BRUSSELS (CP) — Results Wednesday from a World Cup track and field meet:
MEN
100 metres: 1. Linford Christie, Britain, 9.38 seconds (world record; previous record 9.40 set by Leroy Burrell, U.S., 1990 Zurich); 2. Dennis Mitchell, U.S., 9:75; **3. Bruny Surin, Montreal, 9.89.**

Note: Where the field is particularly large, such as in a marathon or an auto race, results are broken into paragraphs, approximately of equal length. For example, a 20-member field would be broken into two paragraphs of 10 competitors each. The first paragraph would end with a period, not the semicolon used within each paragraph to separate competitors.

Head-to-head result

BC-Tab-TEN-Wimbledon-Rslts
LONDON (CP) — Results Wednesday from the Wimbledon tennis championships (seedings in parentheses):
WOMEN
Singles
Third Round
Steffi Graf (1), Germany, def. Zina Garrison (9), U.S., 6-3, 6-3.
Helen Kelesi, Richmond Hill, Ont., def. Jennifer Capriati (4), U.S., 3-6, 6-4, 6-2.

Athletics   ➤   See **Track and field.**

Auto racing

1.   Report Grand Prix racing in kilometres, but stock-car, Indy-car and drag racing in miles.

2.   Results use the field format.

BC-Tab-AUTO-Cdn-GP-Rslts
MONTREAL (CP) — Results Sunday of the Canadian Grand Prix auto race, 69 laps of the 4.43-kilometre Circuit Gilles-Villeneuve, with lapsed time of drivers finishing race, laps completed by non-finishers and winner's average speed:
1. Nelson Piquet, Brazil, Benetton Ford, one hour 38 minutes 51.490 seconds (185.520 km-h); 2. Stefano Modena, Italy, Tyrrell Honda, 1:39:23.322; 3. Riccardo Patrese, Italy, Williams Renault, 1:39:33.707; 4. Andre de Cesaris, Italy, Jordan Ford, 1:40:11.700; 5. Bertrand Gachot, France, Jordan Ford, 1:40:13.841; 6. Nigel Mansell, Britain, Williams Renault, 68; 7. Pierluigi Martini, Italy, Minardi Ferrari, 67 . . .

Baseball

1. Write **American League, National League, American League East**, etc.

2. In sluglines on game stories, use **AMN** (all caps) for the American League and **NAT** for the National League, followed by the abbreviations of the teams involved, visiting team first.

AM-NAT-NY-Mtl
    MONTREAL (CP) — A ninth-inning homer . . .

For non-game stories, use the generic **BBL** as the keyword in the slug.

3. Use these team abbreviations:

American League: **Bal** (Baltimore), **Bos** (Boston), **Cal** (California), **Chi** (Chicago), **Cle** (Cleveland), **Det** (Detroit), **KC** (Kansas City), **Mil** (Milwaukee), **Min** (Minnesota), **NY** (New York), **Oak** (Oakland), **Sea** (Seattle), **Tex** (Texas) and **Tor** (Toronto).

National League: **Atl** (Atlanta), **Chi** (Chicago), **Cin** (Cincinnati), **Col** (Colorado), **Hou** (Houston), **LA** (Los Angeles), **Fla** (Florida), **Mtl** (Montreal), **NY** (New York), **Pha** (Philadelphia), **Pgh** (Pittsburgh), **StL** (St. Louis), **SD** (San Diego) and **SF** (San Francisco).

4. Scores are normally carried as part of standings. In instances where stand-alone scores are warranted, use the bare scores format.

5. The first linescore of the day follows this style:

BC-Tab-BBL-Linescores
Thursday's list
                    By The Canadian Press
                    AMERICAN LEAGUE
Toronto   004 221 020—11 15   2
Cleveland   110 000 213— 8 11   1
    Guzman (W,9-2), Timlin (8), Ward (S,12) (9) and Borders;
Nagy (L,3-3) and Skinner, S. Alomar (6). **HRs:** Tor — White (5),
Carter 2 (13); Cle — Belle (15).

Note 1: A *thin space* is inserted after every three innings to break up the figures and make them more readable.

Note 2: There is no spacing around the dash in the team lines, but there is when listing the home runs.

Note 3: Team abbreviations may be necessary for extra-inning games to avoid team lines spilling over.

Subsequent linescores do not carry specific add numbers, such as **1st add**, **2nd add**, and do not carry catchwords.

BC-Tab-BBL-Linescores, add
Add Thursday's list
Add AL etc.

6. In boxscores, the visiting team is on the left. Each player is shown in the last position he played. Figures in parentheses are the player's total in that category for the season.

Note: CP relays AP boxscores in unedited form. Consequently, they do not take **Tab** in the slugline.

BC-AMN-Box-Tor-Bal
  BLUE JAYS 8, ORIOLES 4
TORONTO　　　　　　　　　　　　**BALTIMORE**

TORONTO	ab	r	h	bi	BALTIMORE	ab	r	h	bi
White cf	4	2	1	1	Anderson lf	5	1	2	1
RAlomar 2b	5	1	2	2	Davis dh	4	0	1	1
Molitor dh	4	1	2	0	CRipken ss	5	0	3	0
Carter rf	4	0	2	3	McLemore rf	3	0	0	0
Olerud 1b	2	0	2	1	Buford rf	1	0	0	0
Green ph	0	0	0	0	Gomez 3b	4	0	1	0
Sprague 3b	4	1	0	0	Hoiles c	3	0	0	0
Knorr c	5	1	1	0	Segui 1b	1	0	0	0
Huff lf	3	0	0	0	Reynolds 2b	4	0	1	0
Delgado ph	1	1	0	0	Hulett 2b	3	0	0	0
Gonzalez ss	5	1	3	1	Carey pr	0	1	0	0
					Voight cf	3	1	2	0
					Hammonds ph	1	1	1	2
Totals	37	8	13	8	Totals	37	4	11	4

Toronto	101 000 060—8
Baltimore	002 000 002—4

　　E—Huff (1), Sprague (6). DP—Toronto 2, Baltimore 1. LOB—Toronto 10, Baltimore 9. 2B—Knorr (5), Olerud (7), Molitor (7), CRipken (4). 3B—Anderson (2). HR—Segui (9). SB—White (11), RAlomar 4 (18). CS—Gonzalez (2).

	IP		H	R	ER	BB	SO
Toronto							
Guzman W,9-2	7		9	2	2	2	3
Timlin	1		0	0	0	0	1
Ward	1		2	2	2	1	0
Baltimore							
McDonald	6	2-3	8	2	2	4	4
Eichorn		1-3	0	0	0	0	0
Poole L,0-1		1-3	2	4	4	2	0
Mills		2-3	2	2	2	2	0
Smith	1		0·	0	0	0	1

　　Umpires — Home, Ford; First, Clark; Second, Barnett; Third, Kosc. T—3:21. A—25,569.

Note: For weekend games, the day of the week is included in the slugging to assist editors in differentiating between the Saturday and Sunday games.

BC-AMN-Box-Tor-Bal-SAT

7.   Standings for major league baseball are transmitted twice during the night — once following eastern games for early morning editions and again at the conclusion of play — and are slugged accordingly (**Early** and **Final**).

Standings follow this style:

BC-Tab-BBL-Stdgs-Final
Sunday's standings
By The Canadian Press
(All times EDT)
AMERICAN LEAGUE
East Division

	W	**L**	**Pct.**	**GBL**
Toronto	92	63	.594	—
Boston	90	65	.581	2
Detroit	81	73	.526	10½
etc.				

Sunday Results
Toronto 7 Cleveland 6 (11 innings)
Boston 4 Detroit 1

Saturday Results
Toronto 4 Cleveland 0
Detroit 5-4 Boston 3-6

Note: In doubleheaders, combine the two scores for each club, listing the opening game score first.

Monday Games
No games scheduled.
Tuesday Games
Toronto at Baltimore, 7:35 p.m.
Boston at Milwaukee, 8:35 p.m. . . .

8. **Top 10**

At the conclusion of play each day, the Top 10 feature, listing the hitting and pitching leaders in each league, is carried. This item lists the top 10 hitters graded by average, in tabular form, plus the top five players in 10 separate categories, listed in paragraph form.

```
BC-Tab-BBL-Top-10
Top 10
                        By The Canadian Press
                         AMERICAN LEAGUE
                         G     AB    R    H    Pct
CRipken, Bal            68    270   46   95   .352
Baines, Bal             61    214   37   72   .336
Molitor, Tor            64    267   51   88   .330
Puckett, Min            68    275   46   90   .327
      . . .
```

Runs — Palmeiro, Tex, 51; DHenderson, Oak, 48; . . .
RBIs — Fielder, Det, 56; Thomas, Chi, 55; . . .
Hits — CRipken, Bal, 95; Puckett, Min, 90; . . .
Doubles — RAlomar, Tor, 23; Palmeiro, Tex, 21; . . .
Triples — Molitor, Tor, 6; Polonia, Cal, 5; . . .
Home runs — Fielder, Det, 22; Carter, Tor, 17; . . .
Stolen bases — Polonia, Cal, 27; RHenderson, Oak, 27; . . .
Pitching (6 decisions) — Erickson, Min, 12-2, .857, 1.39; Langston, Cal, 10-2, .833, 3.34; . . .
Strikeouts — Clemens, Bos, 106; Ryan, Tex, 97; . . .
Saves — Aguilera, Min, 20; Eckersley, Oak, 20; . . .

9. Probable Pitchers

This feature, moved for AMs editions, lists the pitchers expected to start and the times of major league games and is carried one day in advance.

AM-Tab-BBL-Pitchers
Monday's probable pitchers
                         By The Canadian Press
   Probable pitchers, with won-lost records, for major league baseball games today (all times EDT):
                         AMERICAN LEAGUE
   Baltimore (McDonald 12-12) at New York (Perez 8-7), 2 p.m.
   Detroit (Wells 6-2 and Gullickson 3-3) at Milwaukee (Wegman 6-3 and Navarro 7-8), 5:35 p.m.
   Oakland (Welch 9-3) at Toronto (Stewart 13-7 or Timlin 2-2), 7:35 p.m.

10. Roundups are written for PMs papers on both the American and National leagues. When play in one league consists of only one or two games, a combined major league roundup may be considered. If such a roundup is contemplated, inform members by advisory as soon as possible.

Basketball

1.   Write **National Basketball Association** (**NBA** also acceptable on sports pages), the **Pacific Division of the Western Conference**, the **Central Division of the Eastern Conference**, etc. On subsequent references: **the NBA West**, etc.

2.   Use these NBA team abbreviations in slug lines and the like: **Atl** (Atlanta), **Bos** (Boston), **Cha** (Charlotte), **Chi** (Chicago), **Cle** (Cleveland), **Dal** (Dallas), **Den** (Denver), **Det** (Detroit), **GS** (Golden State), **Hou** (Houston), **Ind** (Indiana), **LAC** (Los Angeles Clippers), **LAL** (Los Angeles Lakers), **Mia** (Miami), **Mil** (Milwaukee), **Min** (Minnesota), **NJ** (New Jersey), **NY** (New York), **Orl** (Orlando), **Pha** (Philadelphia), **Pho** (Phoenix), **Por** (Portland), **Sac** (Sacramento), **SA** (San Antonio), **Sea** (Seattle), **Tor** (Toronto), **Utah** (Utah), **Vcr** (Vancouver), **Wash** (Washington).

3.   For results, follow the bare score format.

4.   Standings follow this style:

BC-Tab-BKBL-Stdgs
Friday's standings

By The Canadian Press
NBA
(All Times EDT)
Eastern Conference
Atlantic Division

	W	L	Pct.	GBL	
Philadelphia	51	9	.850	—	
Boston	44	17	.721	7½,	etc.

Central Division

| Milwaukee | 41 | 21 | .661 | — | |
| Atlanta | 32 | 31 | .508 | 9½, | etc. |

Western Conference
Midwest Division

| San Antonio | 39 | 25 | .609 | — | |
| Denver | 34 | 30 | .531 | 5, | etc. |

Pacific Division

| Los Angeles | 45 | 16 | .738 | — | |
| Phoenix | 37 | 26 | .587 | 9, | etc. |

Friday Results
New York 107 Seattle 98
Atlanta 110 Portland 93, etc.

Tonight's Games
Portland at New York, 7:30 p.m.
Cleveland at Milwaukee, 8:30 p.m.

Sunday Games
New York at Boston, 7:30 p.m.
Cleveland at Milwaukee, 8:30 p.m.

Note: Some leagues use a format that includes a games column and award two points for a win and one for a tie. For such leagues, follow the format for hockey standings.

Bobsled, luge

Use a field results format.

> **Two-man:** 1. Chris Lori, Windsor, Ont., and Bill Smith, Toronto, four minutes 26.15 seconds; 2. Greg Haydenluck, Toronto, and Jack Wilson, Winnipeg, 4:27.32; etc.

Boxing

1. These are the Olympic weight categories: *light flyweight* (to 48 kg), *flyweight* (48-51 kg), *bantamweight* (51-54 kg), *featherweight* (54-57 kg), *lightweight* (57-60 kg), *light welterweight* (60-63.5 kg), *welterweight* (63.5-67 kg), *light middleweight* (67-71 kg), *middleweight* (71-75 kg), *light heavyweight* (75-81 kg), *heavyweight* (81-91 kg), *super heavyweight* (more than 91 kg).

2. These are the major pro weight categories: *flyweight* (to 112 lb.), *bantamweight* (113-118 lb.), *featherweight* (119-126 lb.), *lightweight* (127-135 lb.), *welterweight* (136-147 lb.), *middleweight* (148-160 lb.), *light heavyweight* (161-175 lb.), *cruiserweight* (176-195 lb.), *heavyweight* (196 lb. or more).

3. Use a revised head-to-head results format, stating whether the victory was by **decision, knockout (KO)** or **referee stopped bout.**

Note: In pro bouts, the **technical knockout (TKO)** is used instead of **referee stopped bout.**

> **Light flyweight (48 kg):** Ivalio Hristov, Bulgaria, def. Michael Carbajal, U.S., 4-1; **Scott Olson, Edmonton,** etc.
> **Welterweight (67 kg):** Robert Wangita, Kenya, def. Laurent Boudouani, France, bout stopped, 0:44 second; etc.
> **Heavyweight (91 kg):** Ray Mercer, U.S., def. Baik Hyun-man, South Korea, KO, 2:16 first; etc.

4. The tale of the tape follows this style:

MONTREAL (CP) — The tale of the tape for the World Boxing Council heavyweight championship Saturday between champion Mike Tyson and challenger Razor Ruddock:

	Tyson	Ruddock
Age	24	27
Weight	216	238
Height	5-11½	6-3
Reach	71	82
Chest normal	43	47
Chest expanded	45	49
Biceps	16	16½
Forearm	14	15
Waist	34	34
Thigh	27	26½
Calf	18	18
Neck	19¾	17½
Wrist	8	8
Fist	13	13½
Ankle	11	10

Canoeing

Use a field result format. Categories are listed as *C-1* (canoe singles), *K-2* (kayak pairs), etc.

BC-Tab-CANOE-Rslts
   NOTTINGHAM, England (CP) — Results Tuesday at the world canoeing championships:
WOMEN
   K-1 500 metres (Heat 1): 1. Sharon Smith, Britain, two minutes 7.35 seconds; 2. **Karen Jones, St. Catharines, Ont., 2:08.55**; 3. etc.

Cricket

Coverage of cricket is generally restricted to Test matches (between national teams) and one-day international matches. Test cricket consists of five six-hour playing days.

Cricket is played by two 11-member teams.

An explanation of some common cricket terminology:

Innings — An innings (singular) is completed when: (1) 10 of a team's batsmen have been dismissed; (2) the batting captain "declares" (voluntarily ends the innings); or (3) a specified number of overs have been bowled.

Overs — consisting of six or eight balls, delivered from alternate wickets.

Wickets — three stumps topped by crosspieces (called *bails*) situated at either end of the pitch (field) and from which the ball is bowled.

Curling

1. Rinks are named in this order: *lead, second, third* (or *vice-skip*), *skip*.

2. Do not write *curling bonspiel*.

3. Abbreviations when necessary in linescores are: **Alta, B.C., Man,** **N.B., Nfld, N. Ont, N.S., Ont, P.E.I., Que, Sask** and **Terr** (Territories)

4. Linescores follow this style:

BC-Tab-CURL-Women-Rslts
   MOOSE JAW, Sask. (CP) — Linescores Tuesday at the Canadian women's curling championship:

	Round 10
P.E.I.	001 010 201 1 — 6
Manitoba	200 101 010 0 — 5

Adds go as follows:

BC-Tab-CURL-Women-Rslts, add
MOOSE JAW, Sask.— add linescores

	Round 11
Nova Scotia	103 021 010 x — 8
Newfoundland	020 200 101 x — 6

   Bye: Territories.

---

5. Standings follow this style:

BC-Tab-CURL-Women-Stdgs
   MOOSE JAW, Sask. (CP) — Standings after the 11th round at the Canadian women's curling championship Wednesday:

	W	**L**	
Alberta	7	0	
B.C.	7	1	
Ontario	7	1	
Nova Scotia	6	2	
N. Ontario	5	3	etc.

Cycling

Use a field result format.

BC-Tab-CYCLE-Tour-Que
   QUEBEC (CP) — Results Sunday from the Tour de Quebec men's
cycling series:
   220-kilometre third stage: 1. Czeslaw Lukaszewicz, Toronto, three
hours 32 minutes 10 seconds; 2. Chris Koberstein, Hudson, Que., same
time; 3. Alex Stieda, Vancouver, five seconds behind; 4. John Harris,
New Zealand, 0:17 behind; . . .
   Overall standing: 1. Koberstein, 5:51:05; 2. Stieda, 5:51:10; 3. Colin
Davidson, Winnipeg, 5:51:41; . . .

Diving

Use a field result format.

BC-Tab-DIVE-Cda-Cup-Rslts
   WINNIPEG (CP) — Results Sunday from the Canada Cup diving
meet:
                                    WOMEN
   Three-metre: 1. Annie Pelletier, Montreal, 477.33 points; 2. Jennifer
Mitchell, Winnipeg, 469.55; . . .

Equestrian

1.   Identify events as *show jumping*, *dressage* or *three-day event*.
2.   Use basic field result format.

Fencing

1.   Identify events as *épée*, *foil* or *sabre*.
2.   Use head-to-head result format.

Football

1. Avoid **major** as a synonym for touchdown. A major was an old scoring play worth five points. Use **touchdown** or, in subsequent references, TD.

2. For results, use a bare score format.

3. Style for game summary:

BC-Tab-CFL-Sums-Tor-Ham
HAMILTON (CP) — CFL Thursday night:
SUMMARY
First Quarter
Tor — TD Clemons 15 run (Chomyc convert) 0:45
Ham — TD Winfield 27 pass from McPherson (Osbaldiston convert) 2:10
Second Quarter
Tor — Single Ilesic 55 7:18
Tor — Safety McPherson tackled 13:15
Third Quarter
Ham — FG Osbaldiston 47 4:15
Ham — TD Zatylny 95 kickoff return (two-point convert failed) 12:12
Tor — TD Harding blocked punt in end zone (Chomyc convert failed) 13:42
Tor — Safety Osbaldiston conceded 15:00
Fourth Quarter
No scoring.

Toronto	7	3	8	0—18
Hamilton	7	0	9	0—16

Attendance — 16,485.

---

4.   Style for game statistics:

BC-Tab-CFL-Stax-Edm-Wpg
   WINNIPEG (CP) — Statistics from the Edmonton-Winnipeg CFL game Friday night:

	Edm	Wpg
First downs	14	22
Yards rushing	156	88
Yards passing	255	280
Total offence	411	368
Team losses	25	15
Net offence	386	353
Passes made-tried	20-37	21-37
Returns-yards	5-95	2-22
Intercepts-yards by	0-0	2-22
Fumbles-lost	0-0	0-0
Sacks by	2	1
Punts-average	6-41	5-44
Penalties-yards	7-70	4-25
Time of possession	26:45	33:15

   Net offence is yards passing, plus yards rushing, minus team losses such as yards lost on broken plays.

Individual
   Rushing: Edm — Foggie 11-84, Marshall 13-54, Smith 1-11, Soles 1-8, Walling 1-minus 1; Wpg — Richardson 11-55, Dunigan 7-26, Hudson 4-7.
   Receiving: Edm — Smith 8-131, Brown 4-46, Cyncar 2-24, Soles 2-17, Wright 1-11, Walling 1-10, Smith 1-8, Marshall 1-6; Wpg — House 6-17, Tuttle 3-70, Hudson 4-66, Hull 2-26, Streeter 2-17, Richardson 1-14.
   Passing: Edm — Ham 20-37, 253 yds, 1 TD, 3 int; Wpg — Dunigan 18-31-286-3-0, McManus 2-2-66-1-0, Garza 1-4-15-0-1.

5.   Style for rosters provided before the opening of the season, or as game lineups for the Grey Cup:

BC-Tab-CFL-Grey-Cup-Lineups
   VANCOUVER (CP) — Lineups for the CFL Grey Cup game Sunday between the Edmonton Eskimos and the Winnipeg Blue Bombers (x-denotes import):

EDMONTON
2.	x-Henry Williams, wr
4.	Ray Macoritti, p-k
6.	x-Warren Jones, qb
9.	Damon Allen, qb
14.	x-Rickey Foggie, qb . . .

WINNIPEG
3.	Trevor Kennerd, k
4.	x-Danny McManus, qb
6.	Bob Cameron, p
9.	x-Sammy Garza, qb
10.	x-Rod Hill, db . . .

Golf

1. Write **par 4, par-4 hole, five-iron** or **No. 5 iron, three-wood** or **No. 3 wood, 1 over par for the round, shot a 1-over-par 73, parred, birdie, birdied, bogey, double-bogey, triple-bogey 7, bogey-free** (not **bogey-less**), **bogeyed**.

2. There are two basic types of play: *match* and *medal* (or *stroke*).

In *match* play, the individual or team wins a hole by taking fewer strokes than the opponent. The entry winning the most holes wins the match. Stroke totals are not kept.

In *medal* play, the individual or team keeps a running total of strokes taken at each hole. The one taking the fewest strokes overall is the winner.

3. Match-play tournaments follow this style in head-to-head results:

> Bill Richardson, Creston, B.C., def. Ian MacDonnell, Antigonish, N.S., 3 and 2.

(Richardson had an insurmountable lead of three after 16 holes. As a result the final two holes were not played.)

> Bill Richardson, Creston, B.C., def. Ian MacDonnell, Antigonish, N.S., 1-up.

(Richardson led by one after 18 holes or after extra play. If two players are tied after 18 holes, play continues until a hole is won.)

4. Medal-play tournaments follow this style for results (lowest scores are listed first; home towns are listed, indented on a second line, for major national tournaments):

For first round:

Cheryl Richardson	33-35—68
Creston, B.C.	
Heather MacDonnell	36-34—70
Antigonish, N.S.	

For second round:

Cheryl Richardson	68-69—137
Creston, B.C.	
Heather MacDonnell	70-68—138
Antigonish, N.S.	

For third round:

Heather MacDonnell	70-68-69—207
Antigonish, N.S.	
Cheryl Richardson	68-69-71—208
Creston, B.C.	

For fourth round:

Heather MacDonnell	70-68-69-70—277
Antigonish, N.S.	
Cheryl Richardson	68-69-71-71—279
Creston, B.C.	

5. In professional tournaments, prize money is included and golfers' first names are reduced to initials to accommodate a single column results format. Some unusually long surnames may also require abbreviation.

G. Norman, $250,000   70-73-72-70—285
A. Forsb'd, $175,000   74-72-70-72—288

6. Team standings for men's and women's interprovincial competitions follow this style:

ST. JOHN'S, Nfld. (CP) — Final interprovincial team standings after play Thursday at the Canadian amateur women's golf championship (top three individual scores each day are counted):

NEW BRUNSWICK

Marilyn Smith Campbellton	70-72—142
Jennifer McDougall Sackville	68-74—142
Sandy Garson Shediac	75-75—150
Heidi Green Moncton	76-81—157
Total: 434	

SASKATCHEWAN

Bev Richards Saskatoon	73-74—147
Sally Oneschuk Prince Albert	75-72—147
Pamela Gordon Regina	79-77—156
Rosemary Hart Moose Jaw	80-77—157
Total: 450	

Gymnastics

1. Identify events as *side horse, floor exercises, vault, rings, parallel bars, high bar, uneven bars, balance beam, team, all-round,* and ensure it's clear whether it's *team, individual combined* or *individual competition.*

2. Use a field result format.

WOMEN

All-round: 1. Lori Strong, Whitby, Ont., 38.250 points; 2. Stella Umeh, Toronto, 37.650; 3. Janine Rankin, Mississauga, Ont., 36.950; . . .

Hockey

1.   A three- or four-letter abbreviation is used to identify teams in slug lines and in the *penalties* section of the game summary. For team bench penalties, spell out the team name.

For the NHL, use: **Ana** (Anaheim), **Bos** (Boston), **Buf** (Buffalo), **Cal** (Calgary), **Chi** (Chicago), **Dal** (Dallas), **Det** (Detroit), **Edm** (Edmonton), **Fla** (Florida), **Hart** (Hartford), **LA** (Los Angeles), **Mtl** (Montreal), **NJ** (New Jersey), **NYI** (New York Islanders), **NYR** (New York Rangers), **Ott** (Ottawa), **Pha** (Philadelphia), **Pgh** (Pittsburgh), **Que** (Quebec), **SJ** (San Jose), **StL** (St. Louis), **TB** (Tampa Bay), **Tor** (Toronto), **Vcr** (Vancouver), **Wash** (Washington), **Wpg** (Winnipeg).

2.   For results, use the bare score format.

3.   Style for game summaries:

BC-Tab-NHL-Sums-NJ-Ott
code:4
   OTTAWA (CP) – NHL Saturday night:
First Period
   1. Ottawa, Daigle 11 (Cunneyworth, Yashin) 10:20 (pp)
   2. New Jersey, Carpenter 5 (Driver) 11:18 (sh)
   Penalty – Cole NJ (holding) 10:10.
Second Period
   3. Ottawa, Daigle 12 (Gaudreau) 14:53
   4. New Jersey, Cole 4 (MacLean, Broten) 19:38
   Penalties – Guerin NJ, Dahlquist Ott (double roughing), Huffman Ott (third man in, game misconduct) 13:35.
Third Period
   5. New Jersey, Richer 17 (Carpenter) 3:27
   6. New Jersey, Guerin 9 (Dean, Chambers) 16:50
   Penalties – Peluso NJ, Levins Ott (fighting) 2:55, Dahlquist Ott (interference) 14:48, New Jersey bench (too many men; served by Peluso) 18:42.
   Missed penalty shot – Daigle Ott, 6:15 third.
   Shots on goal by
New Jersey 11 16 9–36
Ottawa   8 8 6–22
   Goal (shots-saves) – New Jersey: Brodeur (W,11-8-5); Ottawa: Beaupre (L,4-18-2).
   Power plays (goals-chances) – New Jersey: 0-1; Ottawa: 0-2.
   Referee – Dan Marouelli. **Linesmen** – Pierre Racicot, Pierre Champoux.
   Attendance – 9,582.

Note 1: The number after a scorer's name is his season goal total. The *(pp)*, *(sh)* and *(en)* notations designate *power-play, short-handed* and *empty-net* goals.

Note 2: The time of each goal is computed from the start of the period.

Note 3: The winning goaltender is the one in net when the winning goal is scored. The NHL defines the winning goal as the goal which is one more than the opposition's final total. For example, if the final score is 8-4, the fifth goal scored by the victorious team is the winner.

4. At the end of each night's play, results are grouped by league in descending order of significance. Junior leagues are listed geographically, east to west.

BC-Tab-HKY-Grp-Rslts
Monday's list
                    By The Canadian Press
                              NHL
Quebec 5 NY Rangers 4
Detroit 4 Hartford 2 . . .
                              AHL
Cape Breton 6 St. John's 3
Cornwall 4 Syracuse 3 . . .
                      QUEBEC MAJOR
Hull 4 Chicoutimi 3
Trois-Rivieres 6 Sorel 5 . . .

---

5. Style for standings:

BC-Tab-HKY-Stdgs
Monday's standings
                    By The Canadian Press
                              NHL
                   WESTERN CONFERENCE
                     Central Division

	G	W	L	T	F	A	P	
Minnesota	12	9	2	1	54	37	19	
Chicago	12	6	2	4	52	43	16	. . .

Pacific Division

	G	W	L	T	F	A	P	
Winnipeg	12	9	2	1	54	37	19	
San Jose	12	6	2	4	52	43	16	. . .

EASTERN CONFERENCE
Northeast Division

	G	W	L	T	F	A	P	
Quebec	12	9	2	1	54	37	19	
Montreal	12	6	2	4	52	43	16	. . .

Atlantic Division

	G	W	L	T	F	A	P	
New Jersey	12	9	2	1	54	37	19	
Washington	12	6	2	4	52	43	16	. . .

Monday Results
Quebec 6 Montreal 5 (OT)
San Jose 4 Winnipeg 4

Adds are slugged as follows:

BC-Tab-HKY-Stdgs, add
Add Monday's standings
                              AHL
etc.

Horse racing

1.   Terms to watch include *colt* (an uncastrated male aged four or less), *horse* (an uncastrated male aged five or more), *stallion* (an uncastrated male, especially one used for breeding), *gelding* (a castrated male of any age), *filly* (a female aged four or less), *mare* (a female aged five or more), *quarter-horse* (a horse bred to run a quarter-mile), *standardbred* (bred chiefly for harness racing; a pacer or trotter), *thoroughbred* (of pure or pedigree stock; chiefly for flat racing and steeplechase).

2.   This results style is used for thoroughbred, standardbred or quarter-horse racing:

BC-Tab-HARN-Greenwood-Rslts
   TORONTO (CP) — Greenwood Raceway results Wednesday night:
   First — $2,900, mile, pace
Fiddlers Belle (Sloan)   20.60 8.90   5.30
Roberto GB (Strauss)   9.40   7.30
Pet Rock (Condren)   4.30
   Time 2:05
   Carry The Cash, dq-Wil Lor Harry, Echo Vic, Peter Puck Herbert, Wil Lor Kal also started.
   Scratched: Broadway Star.
   dq-disqualified, finished 3rd, placed 5th, lapped on break.
   Second — $6,600, mile, trot
Mauras Pride (Davies) 7.40   5.50   3.70
Minto Stirrett (Gassien)   3.10   2.50
Durita Hanover (Arthur)   6.40
   Time 2:06 2-5
   Kawartha Neon, Borne Eliminator, Darby Demon, Performance Plus, Miway Herbert also started.
                    Daily Double (2-9) paid $141.10
                       Exactor (9-4) paid $25.80
   Attendance: 7,138; **handle**: $1,067,492.

---

3.   Race charts are used primarily for the U.S. Triple Crown (Kentucky Derby, Preakness Stakes and Belmont Stakes) and the two major thoroughbred races in Canada (Queen's Plate and Rothmans International). The chart, provided by the *Daily Racing Form,* is copyright and must be acknowledged as such at the bottom.

BC-Tab-THBRD-Preakness-Chart
  BALTIMORE, Md. (CP) — Chart of the 107th running of the Preakness Saturday at Pimlico:
  Eighth Race: 1 3-16 miles for three-year-olds. Purse $200,000 added. Conditions: Stake: all 126 pounds. Value to winner $209,900. Second $40,000. Third $20,000. Fourth $10,000.

Horse	1/4	1/2	3/4	Str.	Fin.
Aloma's Ruler	1-1	1-1	1-1	1-1hf	1-hf
Linkage	4-1	3-hf	3-hd	2-6	2-6¾
Cut Away	3-hf	4-1hf	4-hf	6-5	3-2
Bold Style	2-hf	2-hf	2-1	3-hf	4-2
Laser Light	7	7	5-1hf	5-hd	5-no
s-Reinvested	5-hf	5-hf	7	4-hd	6-4
Water Bank	6-4	6-2	6-hf	7	7

  s-Supplementary nomination.
  Winner: Ok b or br c by Iron Ruler-Aloma by Native Charger.
  Times: :23 4-5, :48, 1:12, 1:36 2-5, 1:55 2-5.
  Off: 5:41 EDT. Start good, won driving. Track fast.
  Scratch: Cupecoy's Joy.
  Mutuels Prices:
7-Aloma's Ruler   15.80   4.60   3.60
6-Linkage   2.60   2.60
2-Cut Away   6.00
Exacta (7-6) paid $30.40

Aloma's Ruler broke in stride and was quickly angled to the rail, taken in hand and relaxed nicely while setting the pace. He turned back Bold Style entering the far turn and accelerated to increase his advantage under light rousing approaching the stretch. Aloma's Ruler then continued resolutely in response to alternate right and left handed whipping to determinedly hold off Linkage.

Linkage, reserved snugly outside, was always within striking distance. He responded willingly when set down entering the stretch and closed steadily in a game effort.

Cut Away raced along the rail, eased out between horses at the top of the stretch, split foes near the eighth pole and finished willingly.

Bold Style broke sluggishly and slightly in the air, was rushed to prompt the early pace outside Aloma's Ruler, was sent up to challenge entering the far turn and fell back.

Laser Light circled wide to reach contention midway round the far turn and weakened in the drive while bumping repeatedly with Reinvested.

Reinvested, in hand behind horses to the far turn, swung outside entering the stretch and bumped with Laser Light the final sixteenth. Water Bank was not a factor.
  Copyright: Daily Racing Form Inc.

Judo

1.   Weight categories are *extra lightweight* (up to 60 kg), *half lightweight* (up to 65 kg), *lightweight* (up to 71 kg), *half middleweight* (up to 78 kg), *middleweight* (up to 86 kg), *half heavyweight* (up to 95 kg), *heavyweight* (over 95 kg), *open category* (no weight limit).

2.   Use field result format.

Lacrosse

Use the **Hockey** summary style.

Motorcycle racing

Follow the **Auto racing** style.

Rowing

1. A *regatta* is a knockout competition ending with a race or races between two or more finalists. A *repechage* is a second chance to qualify, used only in the preliminaries. The boats used in sculling and rowing are *shells*, not sculls.

In sculling (*singles, doubles* or *four-member crews*), each competitor rows with two oars called *sculls*. In rowing (*pairs, fours, eights*), each competitor uses one oar.

Fours and eights are *crews*, never teams. The competitors are *scullers* or *oarsmen* or *oarswomen*, never rowers. The terms *rowing* and *oars(wo)men* may be used in a general sense referring to regattas and the scullers who take part.

2. Identify events as *single sculls, double sculls, coxless pairs, coxed pairs, coxless fours, coxed fours, coxless eights, coxed eights.*

3. Use a field result format.

Rugby

1. Carry scores on major international matches only.

2. Use a bare scores result format. List the home team first in international matches.

Shooting

1. Identify events as *free pistol, fullbore, rapid-fire pistol, skeet, smallbore rifle* and *trap.*

2. Use a field result format.

Skating, figure

1.   Most figure-skating competitions comprise *men's singles, women's singles, pairs* (man-woman) and *ice dance* (man-woman). *Singles* consists of two elements — a compulsory short program and a free-skating long program. The short program is worth one-third and the free-skating segment two-thirds. In the short program, skaters must attempt eight predetermined jumps or movements in not more than two minutes 40 seconds. In free skating, competitors put together their own combination of jumps, spins and steps and skate to music of their choice. Program length varies between three and four minutes, depending on whether it's a men's or women's competition and on the age group. Judges assign two marks, one for technical merit and one for artistic impression.

Pairs skating consists of a short program in which seven elements (jumps, spins, etc.), announced in advance, must be attempted, and a free-skating portion which contains moves similar to singles skating but executed simultaneously by both competitors. Free skating accounts for 75 per cent of the final mark and varies in length from three to four minutes, depending on the age group.

Ice dancing, in simple terms, is ballroom dancing on ice. It is easily distinguished from *pairs* skating in that there are no jumps, spins or lifts above the waist. The couple seldom separate. The program has three elements — compulsory dances (variations of such dances as the waltz, tango and foxtrot) skated to designated rhythms and patterns; the original set pattern (three repetitive sequences of steps), and the free dance in which competitors select their own moves, steps and music.

2.   Some of the more common jumps (named after their inventors and, therefore, capitalized):

Axel: Skater, facing forward, takes off on the outside edge of either foot, rotates up to four times and lands on the outside edge of the other foot, facing backward.

Lutz: Skater, facing backward, takes off on the outside edge of either foot and, after up to three reverse rotations, lands on the outside edge of the other foot, facing backward.

Salchow: Skater, facing backward, takes off from the inside edge of either foot and, after up to three rotations, lands on the outside edge of the other foot, facing backward.

3.   Use a field result format.

Skating, speed

1.   Speed skating consists of *outdoor* (long track) and *indoor* (short track) events. Race distances include 500, 1,000, 1,500, 3,000 (women only), 5,000 and 10,000 metres (men only).

2.   Use a field result format.

Skiing

1.   Skiing is divided into four categories: *alpine, nordic, biathlon* and *freestyle*. Alpine includes downhill, slalom, giant slalom, super giant slalom and a combined event. Nordic includes cross-country, ski jumping and a combined event. Biathlon combines cross-country skiing with rifle shooting. Freestyle includes ballet, moguls and aerials.

2.   Use a field result format.

BC-Tab-SKI-WCup-Rslts
   KITZBUEHEL, Austria (CP) — Results and standings following a World Cup men's downhill ski race Saturday:
   1. Pirmin Zurbriggen, Switzerland, two minutes 6.68 seconds; **2. Rob Boyd, Calgary, 2:07.01; 3. Brian Stemmle, Aurora, Ont., 2:07.12**; . . .
   Downhill standings: 1. **Boyd, 95 points**; 2. Zurbriggen, 80; 3. Leonard Stock, Austria, 77; . . .
   Overall standings: 1. Stock, 110; 2. Conrad Cathomen, Switzerland, 105; **3. Boyd**, Zurbriggen, **95 each**; . . .

Note: When a competitor appears a second time in standings, his first name and country are dropped.

Snooker

Use a head-to-head result format.

BC-Tab-MISC-Snooker-Rslts
   DUBLIN (CP) — Results Friday from the Dublin Classic snooker tournament:
   Cliff Thorburn, Toronto, def. Bill Werbeniuk, Winnipeg, 3-2 (114-6, 95-26, 6-67, 9-99, 90-25).

Soccer

1.   British standings and results lists require some team abbreviations to ensure material does not spill over on to a second line. The necessary abbreviations are:

English League: Bristol City (**Bristol C**), Bristol Rovers (**Bristol R**), Crystal Palace (**Crystal P**), Manchester City (**Man City**), Manchester United (**Man United**), Nottingham Forest (**Notts F**), Queen's Park Rangers (**Queen's PR**), Sheffield United (**Sheffield U**), Sheffield Wednesday (**Sheffield W**), West Bromwich Albion (**West Brom**), Wolverhampton (**Wolves**).

Scottish League: Dundee United (**Dundee U**), East Sterling (**E Sterling**), Glasgow Celtic (**Celtic**), Glasgow Rangers (**Rangers**), Hearts of Midlothian (**Hearts**), Queen of the South (**Queen of S**).

2. For scores, the home team is listed first in British and European play. Results style is as follows:

BC-Tab-SOC-British-Rslts
    LONDON (CP) — British soccer results Saturday:
                    ENGLISH LEAGUE
                        Division 1
    Aston Villa 4 Luton 1
    Man United 1 Everton 2 . . .
                        Division 2
    Derby 1 Chelsea 0
    Leicester 0 Leeds 1 . . .
                    SCOTTISH LEAGUE
                        League Cup
                    Quarter-finals, first leg
    Celtic 4 Partick 0
    St. Mirren 1 Hearts 1 . . .
                        Division 1
    Alloa 1 Airdrie 1
    Dunfermline 1 Clyde 1 . . .

---

3. For standings, use this style (note order for *T* and *L* reversed from standard North American tables):

BC-Tab-SOC-British-Stdgs
    LONDON (CP) — British soccer standings following play Saturday:
                    ENGLISH LEAGUE
                    Premier League

	W	T	L	F	A	P	
Liverpool	21	6	3	73	24	69	
Watford	18	4	9	60	37	58	
Man United	14	9	6	39	25	51	. . .
Division 1							
Wolves	18	7	6	56	33	61	. . .
SCOTTISH LEAGUE							
Premier Division							
Aberdeen	20	4	4	59	21	44	. . .

Squash

Use head-to-head format.

Swimming

1. Identify events as *men's 100-metre freestyle, women's 4x100-metre medley relay*, etc.

2. Use a field result format.

Tennis

1.   Use head-to-head results format. Grouped results should be graded in order of seedings. See example page 420.

2.   Tiebreakers are used to avoid marathon sets. The first player to win six games wins the set, unless the opponent has won five games. In that case, the player with six games may take the set by winning the next game. If that player loses it, (a) play can continue until either player wins two straight games, or (b) a tiebreaker may be played in which the winner is the first player to score seven points with at least a two-point lead. If the score reaches 6-6 in the tiebreaker, play continues until one player leads by two points.

Track and field   (Athletics)

1.   Olympic and other international events are measured in metric, although some imperial distances are still raced in the United States. Distances and heights in such field events as the high jump, long jump, pole vault, shot put, discus, hammer and javelin should be reported in metres. But the 100-yard dash, for example, is not converted to the 91.44-metre dash.

2.   Use the metric distance for marathons — 42.195 kilometres (not 26 miles 385 yards).

3.   Use a field result format. See example page 420.

Volleyball

Use head-to-head result format.

BC-Tab-VLBL-Rslts
Friday's list
                    By The Canadian Press
                        WORLD LEAGUE
        Canada def. Brazil 3-2 (15-12, 16-14, 8-15, 12-15, 15-10).

Weightlifting

1.   Olympic and most other amateur competitions are divided into 10 weight categories: *52 kg, 56 kg, 60 kg, 67.5 kg, 75 kg, 82.5 kg, 90 kg, 100 kg, 110 kg* and *over 110 kg.*

2.   Use a field result format.

Wrestling

1. Identify by category: *light flyweight* (to 48 kg), *flyweight* (to 52 kg), *bantamweight* (to 57 kg), *featherweight* (to 62 kg), *lightweight* (to 68 kg), *welterweight* (to 74 kg), *middleweight* (to 82 kg), *light heavyweight* (to 90 kg), *heavyweight* (to 100 kg) and *super heavyweight* (to 130 kg).

2. Identify events as *Greco-Roman* or *freestyle*.

3. Use head-to-head result format.

Yachting

1. Following are Olympic-sanctioned yacht classes: *Soling* (three-person keel boat), *Star* (two-person keel boat), *Tornado* (two-person catamaran), *Laser* (one-person dinghy), *Finn* (one-person dinghy), *International Europe* (one-person dinghy), *470* (two-person dinghy) and *Mistral One-Design* (windsurfer).

2. The America's Cup, possibly the most prestigious yachting series in the world, is a *formula* class event. For a yacht to qualify for this challenge series, its size must not exceed a given limit. That limit, which approximates the length of the boat, is arrived at using a complicated mathematical formula that factors in such things as length, draft and sail area. In 1992 a 24-metre limit was set.

3. Where names of yacht classes include an imperial measure (e.g. *Whatsis 30:* a 30-footer), a sentence of explanation may be necessary if there's a risk of confusion.

4. Some races are still measured in nautical miles. Convert these to kilometres but retain an initial nautical-mile equivalent in parentheses. A nautical mile is equivalent to 1.852 kilometres.

Writing for cable, etc.

General

Close to three million Canadians get their news and information directly from The Canadian Press and associated companies. Cable TV viewers, businesses, government departments and Canadian embassies around the world use CP services to stay informed.

CP principles apply to all news services. But some style allowances are made to meet individual requirements of the news services provided.

Cable TV news

Up-to-the-minute news, weather and sports are available in households and offices across the country on the cable news service, displayed in text form on television screens.

Cable news goes directly to the public, and editors meet the challenge of informing viewers of breaking news before others can get on the air or in print.

With the exception of story size, filing the cable service is similar to handling other news services — get it to the customer quickly and accurately.

The cable editor has access to all stories available from CP and Broadcast News, as well as incoming raw copy from other sources. Stories are selected, edited to cable format and inserted into a 15- to 20-minute cycle.

The cable service is geared to the visual display equipment at the cable TV companies. Each screen has a maximum of seven lines and each line is up to 29 characters wide.

Tight writing is the key. Headlines are two lines in length. Stories are limited to seven lines per screen, but a good story runs more than one screen.

Avoid generalities — screen space is at a premium. All sentences need substance. Don't write that the federal government brought down its budget today. Tell the viewer what was in the budget.

Some changes in style are used. Brevity means **first** becomes **1st**. Screen readability in the capital-letter-only display results in **UN** becoming **U.N.** Desk memos explain format and style for this service.

Bulletins interrupt the cycle when a major story breaks. **THIS JUST IN . . .** is used to introduce immediacy to the news break story.

Canadian Press Information Network

To stay competitive and informed, businesses need to know what the stock market is doing, what government representatives are planning, what business decisions are being made . . .

The Canadian Press Information Network gives business and government agencies an edge, delivering news and financial information to their offices as it breaks.

Detailed reports of federal and provincial budgets, minutes after they are released, are examples of the CPIN service.

Editors cull the CP news database for routine business and market reports and major events affecting Canadian business, whether of a legislative, economic or general news nature.

Subscribers to the service keep the CPIN desk up to date on their particular interests and the editors make certain any news falling into these areas of interest is directed to the client.

Writing for the CPIN service generally follows CP style but tends to stay with the present tense whenever possible.

In addition to news stories, there are financial data, hourly headline packages and a feature run at the end of the day to round out this service.

Bibliography

These works have been consulted in the preparation and shaping of the *CP Stylebook:*

Allen, R.E. (ed.). *The Concise Oxford Dictionary of Current English.* Oxford University Press. Oxford, 1990.

Barzun, Jacques. *Simple & Direct: A Rhetoric for Writers.* Harper & Row. New York, 1975.

Bernstein, Theodore M. *The Careful Writer: A Modern Guide to English Usage.* Atheneum. New York, 1973.

Canadian Trade Index. The Canadian Manufacturers' Association. Toronto, 1990.

Collins-Robert French-English English-French Dictionary. William Collins Sons & Co. (Glasgow) and Dictionnaires Le Robert (Paris), 1987.

Colombo, John Robert. *Colombo's Canadian References.* Oxford University Press. Toronto, 1976.

Copperud, Roy H. *American Usage and Style: The Consensus.* Van Nostrand Reinhold. New York, 1980.

Crane, David. *A Dictionary of Canadian Economics.* Hurtig Publishers. Edmonton, 1980.

Eerdmans' Handbook to the World's Religions. William B. Eerdmans Publishing. Grand Rapids, Mich., 1982.

Evans, Bergen and Cornelia. *A Dictionary of Contemporary English Usage.* Random House. New York, 1957.

Evans, Harold. *Editing and Design; Newsman's English.* Heinemann. London, 1973.

Fowler, H.W. *Modern English Usage.* Revised by Sir Ernest Gowers. Oxford University Press. Oxford, 1978.

French, Christopher W. *The Associated Press Stylebook and Libel Manual.* The Associated Press. New York, 1987.

Guide du journaliste. La Presse Canadienne. Montreal, 1992.

Gunning, Robert. *The Technique of Clear Writing.* McGraw-Hill. New York, 1968.

Hohenberg, John. *The Professional Journalist.* Holt, Rinehart and Winston. New York, 1973.

Holley, Frederick S. (ed.). *Los Angeles Times Stylebook.* Los Angeles Times. Los Angeles, 1979.

Jacobi, Ernst. *Writing at Work: Dos, Don'ts and How Tos.* Hayden Book Co. Rochelle Park, N.J., 1976.

Jordan, Lewis (ed.). *The New York Times Manual of Style and Usage.* New York Times Books. New York, 1979.

Kidd, Paris M. and Huber, Wolfgang. *Living With the AIDS Virus*. HK Biomedical Inc. Berkeley, Calif., 1990.

Manser, Martin H. *Good Word Guide*. Bloomsbury Publishing. London, 1988.

Manual of Style. U.S. Government Printing Office. Gramercy Publishing. New York, 1986.

Marsh James H. (ed.). *The Canadian Encyclopedia*. Hurtig Publishers. Edmonton, 1985.

McFarlane, J.A. and Clements, Warren. *The Globe and Mail Style Book*. Info Globe. Toronto, 1990.

Metric Press Guide. Metric Commission Canada. Ottawa, 1981.

Nickles, Harry G. *Dictionary of Do's and Don'ts*. McGraw-Hill. New York, 1975.

Onions, C.T. (ed.). *The Shorter Oxford English Dictionary*. Oxford University Press. Oxford, 1933.

Partridge, Eric. *You Have a Point There*. Hamish Hamilton. London, 1953.

Perrin, Porter G. *Writer's Guide and Index to English*. Scott, Foresman. New York, 1942.

Robertson, Stuart M. *Robertson's Newsroom Legal Crisis Management*. Hallion Press. Dunedin, Ont., 1991.

Rose, Turner. *Stylebook for Writers and Editors*. U.S. News and World Report. Washington, 1984.

Ross-Larson, Bruce. *Edit Yourself*. W.W. Norton. New York, 1982.

Sabin, William. *A Reference Manual*. McGraw-Hill Ryerson. Toronto, 1978.

Schibsbye, Knud. *A Modern English Grammar*. Oxford University Press. London, 1967.

Shaw, Harry. *Dictionary of Problem Words and Expressions*. McGraw-Hill. New York, 1975.

Skilling, Marjorie E. and Gay, Robert M. *Words Into Type*. Meredith Publishing. New York, 1964.

Strunk, William Jr. and White, E.B. *The Elements of Style*. Macmillan Publishing Co. New York, 1979.

Timmons, Christine and Gibney, Frank (eds.). *Britannica Book of English Usage*. Doubleday. Garden City, N.Y., 1980.

Warner, Alan. *A Short Guide to English Style*. Oxford University Press. Oxford, 1965.

Webb, Robert A. *The Washington Post Handbook on Style*. McGraw-Hill. New York, 1978.

Worth, Sylvia (ed.). *Rules of the Game*. St. Martin's Press. New York, 1990.

Acknowledgments

What more appropriate for a co-operative news agency than a co-operative stylebook. CP staff across the country shared the updating and revising of individual chapters from the previous edition. Others contributed new chapters. For many, it was work fitted around their regular workload. And people from every bureau tossed in ideas for improvements. All recognized the importance of making the CP Stylebook as authoritative and helpful as possible.

The greatest debt for any new edition of the CP Stylebook is undoubtedly to the past. The earliest workers and managers for The Canadian Press established the traditions of quality, integrity and consistency for the news agency.

Beginning more than 50 years ago, style rulings were first gathered into book form. Senior managers of the past like Gillis Purcell, Charles Bruce and John Dauphinee put their various personal — and sometimes eccentric — stamps on CP style. More recently, Bob Taylor contributed an enviable knowledge and a distinctly human touch to regular updatings of the stylebook.

For this edition, Ian Donaldson, Jim Poling and Dan Slovitt carried particularly heavy burdens with thoughtfulness and good humor. Mike Fuhrmann's unmatched proofreading skills spared us embarrassment and worse.

The following CP people will readily recognize their substantial contributions in the final product: Heather Boyd, Jim Dalziel, Linda Drouin, Scott Edmonds, Al Gibson, Ross Hopkins, Kirk LaPointe, Mike Lawson, Paul Loong, Brian McKenna, Malcolm McNeil, Diane Menzies, Annita Newell, Steve Nicholls, Jack Picketts, Patti Tasko, Lorraine Turchansky, Shawn Waddell and Scott White.

Such people as Bill Anderson, Mark Bastien, Dean Beeby, Morris Brown, Neil Davidson, Keith Leslie, Elaine McCluskey, Nelle Oosterom, Stephen Thorne, Sheryl Ubelacker, Jamie Underhill, Paul Woods and Heather Zeppieri also answered the call for help in a variety of important ways.

Stuart M. Robertson of O'Donnell, Robertson and Sanfillippo provided crucial advice for all the legal revisions.

For CP, Kent Jones kept the look of the book in mind throughout and saw it through production. Laural Carr and colleagues at Impagination worked with wit and patience on all aspects of its design.

The editor salutes them all and takes full responsibility for any shortcomings or errors in the finished work.

Index

abbreviations 169-176. *See also* acronyms;
    metric symbols
  Agence France-Presse 181
  Associated Press, The 181
  awards, after name 175
  Bible, books of the 175
  bracketed 169
  in broadcast copy 164
  Canadian Press, The 181
  common 169
  compound 170
  currency 170
  dates and times 171
  degrees, university 175
  foreign 170
  honors, after name 175
  lowercase 170
  measurements 172
  members of Parliament 169
  military 260-263
  mixed 170
  names, first 175
  names of leagues 81
  names of organizations 172
  names of teams 425, 434, 440
  names, scientific 285
  names, single letter 175
  periods, with or without 170, 175
  place names 173-174
  political affiliations 175, 211
  Presse Canadienne, La 181
  saint, sainte 208
  serial terms 175
  ships and planes 175
  single-letter 170
  sports 81, 415-416
  streets 174
  style 170
  time zones 290
  titles 174, 177, 200
  U.S. states 173
aboriginal 22. *See also* native peoples
abortion 24
Access to Information Act 303-305
accounting terms 43
accuracy
  agate 418-419
  CP policy 13
  editing 160
  fast-breaking stories 129, 130
  legal privilege 114
  polls 73, 74
acronyms 169-171
  business 44
active verbs. *See* active *under* verbs
active voice 136-137
AD 171
addresses 208, 217, 219
advances 378-381

advisories 378, 381
  embargoes, broken 379
  leads 378
  priority codes 399
  slugs 379-380
  speeches 378-379
advertising. *See* publicity
advertising, political 48
advisories 354-366
  advances, embargoes 378, 379
  breaking news 129-130, 354-356
  bureau duty 352
  Calendar 360-361
  correctives 393
  designators 355
  foreign plans 412
  Fronts 361-363
  long-range 358
  Look-Ahead List 352, 360-361
  Main Desk 351
  News Budget 363-366
  newspage copy 375
  obituaries 70
  photo networks 342
  planned events 356-357
  publishable, non-publishable 357
  spot breaks 355-356
  terrorism stories 34
  Top Copy (slug) 354
  updating 364
AFL–CIO 62
agate 416-419
  accuracy 418-419
  tabulation 417-418
age 19
  as identifier 215
  CP policy 19
  figures, use of 218
  in obituaries 69
Agence France-Presse
  abbreviation 181
  capitalization 181
AIDS 287-288
  accuracy 24
  confidentiality, legal 107
  obituaries 69
aircraft 249
  altitude 254
  identification, figures in 219
Algonquian 267
Algonquin 267
altitude 254
AM (cycle designator) 400
America 283
American Federation of Labor–Congress of Industrial
    Organizations (AFL–CIO) 62
analyses 37-39
  byline 382
  style 39

Anglo-Quebecer 207
anglophone 207
animals 178, 254
anniversaries 55
anonymous sources 26-29
anthem, Canadian 213
apology
 legal 116-117
 with corrective 393
apostrophe 228-229
 for omissions 228
 plurals 228-229
 possessives 81, 226, 227, 228
appeals, civil 108-109
appeals, criminal 97, 98, 104
arbitrator 64
arithmetic. *See* numbers
armed forces. *See* military
arraignment 101-102
artist, graphic 346, 347, 348, 408
arts 51-54
Asian names 216
Asked (slug) 406
Aspirin 286, 296
Associated Press, The
 abbreviation 181
 byline style 383
 capitalization 181
 foreign news 3-4, 56, 411
 photos, international 330
 place names, spelling of 413
 terrorism stories 34
At-a-Glance 367-368
athletics. *See* track and field 442
Attn (slug) 406
attribution 13, 141
 accuracy 17, 131
 Analyses 39
 breaking news 130
 captions 340
 dash, use of 236
 editing 159
 overattribution 159
 quotations 16-18
 say, told 140-141
 unnamed sources 25-29
 vagueness 132
 writing checklist 155
attrition 65
auto racing 420
awards
 capitalization 179
 entertainment 52, 53, 205
Axel (skating) 439
Backgrounders 40-41
 vs. Analysis 37, 40
 style 41
bafflegab 16, 139, 156. *See also* jargon; journalese
bail hearing 101-102
bands, Indian 267
bare score format 419
baseball 421-424
 abbreviations, team 421
 agate 419

boxscores 422
 roundup 424
 slugs 421-423
basketball 419, 425-426
BC (dates) 171
BC (both cycles) 400
beaver (Canadian emblem) 213
bias 15, 20-21, 22-24, 37-38, 56, 114. *See also* sensitive
 subjects
biography 75
black (race) 21
blasphemy 18
BN Audio 4
bobsled, luge 426
bomb, mortar 251
bonds 44
books
 capitalization 178, 179-180
 French titles 205-206
 reviewing 54
 The in title 198
Borderline language 18, 21
boxing 426-427
brackets 229-230
 abbreviations 169
 capitalization 230
 in captions 340
 constituency names 211
 identification 229
 measurements 230
 nicknames 216, 229
 numbering 229
 political affiliations 229
 with other punctuation 230
 translations 205, 230
brand names 181, 201, 296-298
break (code) 396, 398
breaking news 129-134. *See also* foreign news
 accuracy and speed 129
 advisories 355-356
 At-a-Glance 368
 broadcast copy 165
 cable TV news 444
 equipment 134
 first steps 133
 guidelines 129-132
 Main Desk 129, 133
 newspage copy 375
 PhotoNet 335
 procedures 133
Britain, British Isles 283
broadcast
 privacy 121
 writing 162-165
broadcasters, news from 377
Broadcast News Ltd. 4
 BN Style Guide 165
 BN Cable 444
budget lines 364
Bulletin 402
 breaking news 129-130
 completes 387
 Kill 391

priority code 399
withhold notes 390
bullets (format) 369
bureaus
advisories 356, 361
dividends, reporting of 410
editorial symposiums 373
News Budget 363
business news, handling 408-410. *See also* business
news, reporting
CP Information Network 445
designation 408
dividends 410
duplication, avoiding 408
figures, precise 409
foreign currencies 408-409
illustrations 408
net earnings 409
business news, reporting 42-45. *See also* business news,
handling
company meetings, reports 45
context 42
legal considerations 111, 117
newspage copy 375
organizations, capitalization 191
pitfalls 43-44
sources, unnamed 25
terminology 44-45
terminology, French 209
buyout 65
bylines 382-386
in budget lines 364
captions 339
guidelines 382-383
Highlights 369
multiple 382, 383, 386
pickups 278-279, 377
placelined stories 279
Quicks 370
removal of 382
style 383-386
cable TV news 398, 444
Calendar 352, 360-361
calibre 251
campaigns, political 47, 48
Canada, flag etc. 213
Canada Labor Code 63
Canada Labor Relations Board 64
Canadian Auto Workers 63
Canadian Federation of Labor 62
Canadian Labor Congress 62
Canadian Press Information Network (CPIN) 445
Canadian Press, The 3-4, 181
Canadian Union of Public Employees 62
candidates, political 47
canoeing 427
capitalization 177-201
abbreviations 170, 181
acronyms 171
alliances 178
animals, birds 178
awards 179

buildings, other structures 179
following colon 231
compositions 179-180, 188-189
courts 180
CP, PC, AP, AFP, Reuters 181, 383-386
decorations 179
derivatives 181
food, drink 181-182
foreign copy 413
French 206
genus and species 285
geography 183-184
government 184
guidelines, rules 177-178
headlines 196
historical terms 185
holidays 185
laws, documents 186
legislative bodies 186
letters as words 228
medical terms 286
metric 255
military 187-188
music 188-189
names, foreign personal 182
names, proper 9
nationalities, peoples, races, tribes 21, 22, 189
newspapers, magazines 190
nicknames 190
numbers 190
organizations 191
placelines 278
plants, fruit, vegetables 192
politics 192-193
quotations 193, 201
religion 194-196
schools, universities 196
slogans 196
space 197
sports 81, 197
structures 179
the 198
times, seasons 198
titles 199-200
trade names 189, 191, 296-298
capitals, foreign 270-276
captions 339-341
error 341
freelance photos 342
photo specials 345
position 340
style 339
writing 340
cartoons 345
cartridge (case) 251
cash flow 44
Catchline 389, 407
Celsius. *See* metric
Central America 283
Centrale de l'enseignement du Quebec 62
Centrale des syndicats democratiques 62
ceremonies 213, 264
chair, avoid 7
championships 81, 86

change of venue (legal) 102
checkoff 63
Chinese names 216
civil cases 108-109
    appeals 108-109
    damage suits 109
    examination for discovery 109
    vocabulary 108
claims, civil 108
Clarifications 351, 394-395, 410
cliché 144
    foreign news 57
    sources, describing 29
    sports 80
    writing checklist 156
climate 299-302
clip (magazine) 252
closed shop 63
coat of arms, Canadian 214
code:# (slug) 396, 398
coding 396-407
cola (cost-of-living allowance) 61
colon 230-231
    amplification 230
    citations 231
    lists, tables 230
    question-and-answer 231
    quotations 230
    in sports times 87
    subtitles 231
color (race) 20, 21
color adjustment (photos) 335
colt 436
columns 46, 278
comma 232-235
    between adjectives 232
    in apposition 233
    between clauses 232
    and dash 235, 236
    in dates 234
    in direct address 233
    with measurements 87, 235
    numbers, spelled out 220
    with numbers 221, 233, 234, 259
    marking omissions 234
    around paraphrase 233
    with place names 234
    before quotations 233
    inside quotation marks 235
    and semicolon 244
    in series 232
    with time 235
    before version field 401
comment, fair 117
commissions of inquiry 115
commissions, royal 115, 187
commodities 409
common faults 135-145
    active vs. passive 136-137
    arithmetic 142
    attribution 141
    clichés 144

everyday words 140
formula lead 139
front-end loading 138
headline language 142
hidden angles 136
jargon 139-140
lazy words 140
mind-reading 145
overloads 138-139
paragraphs 136
place names as adjectives 234
prepositions 145
say and variants 140-141
sentences 136
split infinitives 145
that–which 143
time element 143
trippers 137
unanswered questions 135
verbs ending in *-ize* 142
who, whom 144
word order 145
company meetings 45, 408
company names. *See* names of organizations
company reports 45
comparison (statistical) 89, 90
compilations 383
Completes 387-388
composite person 28
compositions
    capitalization 179-180, 188-189
    entertainment 51-54
compound words 202-203
    hyphenation 238-240
    plurals 223-224
    possessives 227
concessions, labor 60, 61
conciliation 64
Concise Oxford Dictionary, the 182, 248, 297
Confederation of Canadian Unions 62
Confederation of National Trade Unions 62
confession, criminal 100, 102, 103, 110
confidential material 161
conflicts of interest 25
Conseil des syndicats nationaux 62
consistency in style 6, 8
consolidated statement 44
contempt of court 110-111
    administration of justice, criticism of 104
    criminal proceedings, influence on 98
    police statements, reporting 99
contract disputes 59, 60-61
contractions 164, 228
contracts with sources 27
controversy
    in advances 379
    cartoons 345
    fairness 15, 26
conversion (currency) 408-409, 412
conversion (measures) 256-257
    Celsius and Fahrenheit 259

gallons and litres 259
nautical miles to kilometres 251, 443
recipes 259
round figures 254
in sports 87
copyright 119-120
court 108
photos 342-343
corporate names. See names of organizations
Corrections 389-391
advances 378
breaking news 130
CP policy 13
pictures 341-342
style 389-390
Correctives 392-395
apology and retraction, legal 116
clarifications 394
Main Desk 351
sources of error 392
style 394
supervisory attention 14-15
countries, regions 271-277
courts
capitalization 180
civil 108, 109
criminal 97-98
labor 63-64
martial 264
privilege 115
cover, right to 114-117
CP Backgrounder. See Backgrounders
CP News Analysis. See analyses
CP news report, the 349-445
CP policies 11-34
ethical behavior 15
fact, not opinion 14
hostage-takings 33-34
impartiality 15
principles 13-15
quotations 16-18
reliability and speed 13
sensitive subjects 19-24
sources 25-26
staff responsibility 13-14
taste and tough calls 30-32
terrorism 33-34
CP style notes 5-9
consistency 6
member preferences 5
names 9
popular usage 6
sensitivity 6-7
credit. See also bylines; permission; copyright
freelance, legal 120
photography, freelance 120, 340, 342
pickups 377
crew (rowing) 438
cricket 427
crime 95-107
appeals 97-98, 104
arraignment 101-102
bail hearing 101-102
before charges 98-99

change of venue 102
criminal cases, guidelines 96-98
foreign cases 111, 117
identity of suspects 99
inquests 100
young persons 105-106
pré-enquête 101
preliminary inquiry 102-103
racial minorities 20
retrials 105
sensitive cases 107
trials 103-104
young persons 105-106
criminal record 99, 110
Crown 180, 200
curling 428
currency. See money
cycling 429
damage estimates 132
damage suits 109
dash 235-236
minus sign 255
Datafile 397
dates 289-290
abbreviations 171
comma 234
contracts, labor 61
Correctives 393
editing 160
figures 218
hyphen 240
polls 74
day. See dates
Day Budget 364
death 68-70
death, cause of
AIDS 69, 287
inquests 100
medical 286
suicide 69
death tolls 132
debentures 44
debt financing 45
decimals 218, 255. See also fractions
defamation 112
defence. See military
deferred priority 398
denial 14, 26, 393
designators 400-401
completes 387
cycle 400-401
departmental 400
editorial symposiums 374
Desk Book 352
Developing (slug) 364
Developing Sked 353, 360
dialects, in quotes 16
direction (points of) 183, 413
disabilities 6, 19
disclosure
privacy 121
sources 27
diseases 19, 286

distance
    auto racing 420
    marathon 442
    measurement in sports 86-87
    track and field 442
    yachting 443
dividends 410
diving 429
divorce 107
documentation, sources 26, 130
double translation 208
Dr. (title) 174, 292, 293
drag racing 420
drama. *See* reviews, entertainment
drink names 181-182
drugs (medical) 201, 285-286
editing 157-161
    accuracy 160
    agate 418-419
    brightening 159-160
    byline, removal of 382
    changing copy 157
    editorializing 161
    fairness 161
    foreign copy 413
    how to 157-158
    overediting 157
    pictures 334-335
    principles 157
    sensitive material 161
    shortening stories 157
    style 160
    tightening 158-159
editor. *See also* editing
    advising 354-366
    breaking news 133, 134
    libel suits 112
    pictures 85, 336, 342
    responsibility 13
editor's note. *See* notes (to editor)
editorializing 38, 161
editorial symposiums 373-374
-*elect* 211
elections 47-50
    Analyses 39
    cleanup 50
    context, color, detail 48
    election day 49, 185
    hype 50
    issues 47
    legal considerations 48, 116
    planning 50
    polls restricted 48
    preparation for 47-48, 49
    results 49
electronic picture desk 330, 335, 338
ellipsis 17, 236-237, 374
em leader, em space 417
embargo 378-381
emblem, national 213
en leader, en space 417
entertainment 51-54, 146
equestrian 429
equipment, bureau 134
equity financing 45

equivalents, metric 230, 253
error. *See* Corrections; Correctives; margin of error
Espy (slug) 406
estates 108
estimates
    in disasters 129, 132
    poll-based statistics 89
    sports 87
ethics
    in journalism 15, 107
    in libel 113
    with sources 27-28
ethnic groups 20-21
examination for discovery 109
exclamation mark 237-238
exclusive material 120, 141, 377
extraordinary items (business) 44
fact (not opinion) 14
fair comment 117
fairness
    CP policy 14, 15
    editing 161
    legal term 114
    unnamed sources 26
fanciful names 183, 193, 213
Far East 283
fashion 66-67
Federal Court of Canada 108, 109
federations, labor 62
feminine variants 23
fencing 429
field result format 420
figures. *See* numbers
filly 436
financing (business) 45
First Lady 213
1st Lead 131, 393, 403-405
first person
    byline 382, 383
    travel writing 92
flags
    Canada 213
    military colors 264
    Quebec 207
Flash (slug) 401-402
Flashbacks 55
Fleur-de-lis 207
flex time 60
food 66-67, 181-182, 259
football 430-431
    agate 418
    game statistics 431
    game summary 430
    imperial measure 254
    lineup, rosters 431
foreign currencies, tables of 270-276. *See also* money
foreign names 182
foreign news 56-58, 411-414
    advisories 412
    chasing 58
    currency 412
    guiding principles 57
    language 413
    legal considerations 111, 117, 414

measurements 412
national origin 412
photos 338
place names 270-276, 413-414
polls, statistics 412
sensitivity 412
foreign nouns, plurals of 224
fractions
    figures, use of 218
    hyphenated 239
    metric, small 255
    spelled out 87, 220-221, 255
Franco-Albertan 207
freebies 15
freelance
    bylines 384-385
    copyright 120, 342-343
    foreign 56
    photos 120, 330, 336, 339, 342-344
    travel 91-92
French 204-209
    awards 179
    capitalization 206-207
    companies, organizations 204, 206, 209, 226
    family names 208
    language law 204
    municipalities 207
    newspapers 190, 206
    place names 81, 174, 206, 207, 280
    possessives 226
    Presse Canadienne, La 4, 56, 181
    saint, sainte 208
    streets 208
    titles of art works 189, 205-206
    translation 18, 208-209
    union names 63
front-end loading 138
Fronts advisories 361-363
funerals 31, 70, 264
    military 264
    obituaries 69, 70
    privacy 31
game-over stories 80, 82, 416
games, capitalization 81, 197
gauge (shotgun) 251
gay 23, 287-288
gelding 436
gender 6, 23
General Desk 351, 352, 373
generic drugs 285-286
genus and species 285
German
    names 282
    titles of compositions 189
golf 431-433
    imperial measure 254
    match play 432
    medal play (stroke) 432
    team standings 433
    tournaments, professional 433
good faith 117
government 210-214
    Canadian 213-214
    capitalization 184, 186

ceremonies 213
constituencies 211
election background 49
First Lady 213
first minister 212
information briefings 26
jargon 214
laws, documents 186
leaks 25
legislatures, national and provincial 210-211
monarchy 212
nationhood 213
political affiliations 211
privilege 115
succession 213
governor general
    head of state 212
    salute, vice-regal 213
    title 295
Grand Prix racing 420
graphics 346-348. *See also* pictures
    advisories 356
    breaking news 129, 130
    business stories 44, 408
    charts, graphs 344, 408
    entertainment stories 51
    error 341
    faxing sketches 348
    information sources 347-348
    lifestyles stories 67
    News Budget 363, 364
    Newsmakers 79
    newsmap 130
    Profiles 79
    Quicks 370
    sidebars 348
    sports stories 85, 416
GraphicsNet 330, 346
guest columnist 46
guns 251-252, 265
gymnastics 433
handicap, people with 19
head of government 212
head of state 212
headers. *See* designators
headings 241
headline language 142, 369
headlines
    cable TV news 444
    capitalization 196
    quotation marks 244
head-to-head format 420
hearing, preliminary 102-103
height 254
Highlights 367, 369
historical events 55, 185
hockey 434-435
    agate 417-418
    standings 435
    summaries 434
    team names 434
Hold (coding) 398

holidays
   capitalization 185
   under contract 61
homosexual 23-24
Honorable 295
horse racing 436-437
   imperial measure 254
   results style 436
   terms 436
hostage-takings 33-34
humor, tasteless 21
hunting 251
hype 50, 159
hyphen 238-240
   aircraft, weapons 249
   broadcast copy 164
   compound words 202-203
   figures 219
   French place names 81, 174, 207, 280
   keyword slug line 401
   metric symbols 255
   numbers spelled out 219, 221
   in obscenity 18
   when to hyphenate 202-203, 238-240
ice dancing 439
identification
   brackets 229
   broadcast copy 163
   common names 215
   long quotations 243
   obituaries 69
   public notices 115, 122
illustrations. *See* cartoons; graphics; pictures
immigration 20, 108
impartiality 15
imperial
   abbreviations 172
   conversions 256-257, 259
   foreign filing 412
   metric equivalents 253
   recipes 259
   sports 86, 87
indecency 107
independent unions. *See* unions
indexation (wages) 61
Indian Act 267
Indians. *See* native peoples
infinitives, split 145
indictable offence 97, 124
indigenous 21-22
Indy car racing 254, 420
information, access to 303-305
   cost 303
   exemptions 303-304
   inclusions 304
   recourse 305
   search strategies 304-305
initials 170, 215-216
inquests 100, 115
inquiry, preliminary 102-103
Insert (slug) 406
international news. *See* foreign news
Internet 29
Inuit, Inuk. *See* native peoples
Inuktitut 269

-*ion* 140, 159
Ireland 283, 284
Israel, capital of 284
Italian capitalization 189
its and *it's* 227
-*ize* 142, 214
jargon 139-140. *See also* bafflegab; journalese
   editing 159
   government 214
   Highlights 369
   medical 82
   newspage copy 375
   writing checklist 155
job protection 61
journalese 139. *See also* bafflegab; jargon
judges, criticizing 104, 111
judo 437
jury
   absent 103, 111
   civil cases 108, 109
   criminal cases 97
   deliberation 100, 111
   hung 105
   impartiality 102
   influence 97
   inquests 100
   interviewing jurors 100, 111
   prejudiced 99
   sequestered 103
juvenile crime 95, 105-106
   adult court 106
   in camera hearings 104
   publication ban 105-106
   Quebec law 100
Keyword slug line 400-401. *See also* Slugs
Kill 391
   foreign stories 414
   legal considerations 95, 112
   pictures 341-342
kilometre. *See* metric
Korean names 216
labor 59-65
   affiliations 62-63
   conciliation 64
   conditions of work 60-61
   courts 63-64
   departments of 64
   laws 63-64
   lockouts 64
   organizations 62-63
   strikes 64
   union membership 63
   vocabulary 65
   the new workforce 59-60
   the new workplace 60
lacrosse 438
ladies (in sports) 84
Lady, the title 295
Laser transmitter 337
Latin America 283
Latin titles 189
layoffs 61, 65
leads, slugs 403-405
leads, writing
   age 19

breaking news 131-132
broadcast 162
clear 151
corrections 389
formula 139
"grab-bag" 41
hidden angles 136
improving 157-158
overloaded 138
placelined story 279
specific 151
time element 289
writing checklist 155
league abbreviations 81
leaks 25, 28
legal considerations 112-118, 119-120, 121, 122-123,
    342-344. *See also* editor; information, access to;
    legal reporting; *separate entry for* libel; Main
    Desk; supervisor
  business 111, 117
  copyright 119-120
  correctives 393
  editing 161
  foreign filing 414
  libel 112-118
  pictures 342-344
  police 122-123
  privacy 121
  privilege 114-116
  rules for reporting 95
  sports 82, 116-117
  unnamed sources 27, 28
  wiretaps 121
  writing checklist 155
legal reporting 93-125
  capitalization 180, 186, 198
  civil cases 108-109
  contempt of court 110-111
  crime 95-107
  foreign cases 111, 117
  French terminology 204, 209
  not, use of 160
  privileged information 114-116
  Quebec law 100, 108, 109, 113, 114, 116
  rules 95
  sensitive cases 107
length. *See* sentences; wordage
lesbian 23
letter as word 228
Letters to the Editor 120
libel 112-118
  business, politics, sports 116-117
  captions 340
  defences 114, 117-118
  elections 48
  fair comment 117
  foreign filing 117, 414
  good faith 117
  kill, withhold 112
  Main Desk 351
  of the dead 113
  police statements, reporting 98, 99
  privilege 114-116
  provincial statutes 116

  Quebec law 113
  responsibility 113
lieutenant-governor 213, 295
lifestyles (news, features, profiles) 66-67
  graphics 67
  language 67
  promotion 67
  stereotypes 67
  trends 67
light-year 254
Lloyd's *Register of Shipping* 250, 251
local unions. *See* unions
Locals out (slug) 365, 407
locating the news 146-147. *See also* capitals, foreign;
    geography *under* capitalization; newsmap; place
    names; streets
  breaking stories 130
  writing checklist 155
locator maps 130, 346-348
lockout 64
long-range advisories 358
Look-Ahead List 352, 360-361
Lord, the title 295
Lutz (skating) 439
magazine (firearm) 252
magazines, capitalization 190, 198
  French 206
Main Desk 351-353
  breaking news 129, 133
  budget notes 364
  Correctives 393
  denials 393
  Developing Sked 353
  editorial symposiums 373
  Look-Ahead List 360
  pictures, doubtful 342
  proofing for bureaus 352
  responsibilities 351-352
malice, absence of 113, 114, 116, 117
man 23
management 59-65
Maple Leaf 213
maps. *See* pictures
marathon 420
mare 436
margin of error 72-74
marital status 22, 293
marking papers 351, 352-353
mass (weight) 256-258
measurement 253-259
  abbreviations 172
  altitude 254
  calibre (arms) 251
  commas 235
  distance 254
  gauge (shotgun) 251
  height 254
  land 253
  marine 251, 254
  metals, precious 253
  metric 253-259
  personal 87
  pressure, atmospheric 300
  sports 86-87, 254-255

weight 254
wind speed 299
mediator 64
medical terms 286
  capitalization 181
  drugs 201, 285-286
  sports 82
medicine 66-67
member newspapers 376-377
  bureaus 352
  CP style 5
  editorial symposiums 373
  elections 48
  local photos 330
  taste, tough calls 31
members of Parliament 186, 210
members of provincial legislatures 186-187, 210
mental disabilities 20
Métis. *See* native peoples
metric 253-259. *See also* conversions; metric symbols
  altitude 254
  distance 254
  equivalents 253
  exceptions 253-254
  foreign filing 412
  height 254
  in idiom 254
  marathon 442
  in quotations 253, 254, 412
  in recipes 259
  speed 254
  in sports 86-87, 254-255
  track and field 442
  units, names of 255, 258
  weather 299-300
  weight 254
metric symbols 258
  capitalization 255
  period, do not use 170, 241
  plural (no *s*) 255
  on second reference 255
  table of 258
  in tabular matter 255
Middle East 283
military 260-266
  aircraft, ships, guns 249
  Americanisms 265
  bases 260
  capitalization 187-188
  ceremonies 264
  courts 264
  decorations 264
  female personnel 262
  ranks 261-263
  rank vs. appointment 265
  regiments 261, 265
  retired officers 263
  terms, use of figures in 218
  titles 262-263
  units 261
minister (government) 177,184-185, 210
minority groups. *See* race
misquotes 16

misrepresentation 26
monarchy 212, 213
money
  abbreviations 170
  converting 408-409, 412
  currencies, foreign 270-276
  estimates with benefits 61
  figures, use of 219
  pictures of 343-344
  style, international 259
  U.S. dollars 409
months, abbreviations 171
MORE (slug) 130, 406
motorcycle 254, 438
MP, MHA, MLA, MNA, MPP 169
Mr., Mrs., Miss, Ms. 5, 293
music 188-189, 205-206
names 9, 189, 215-216. *See also* drugs (medical);
    magazines; names, French; names, non-English;
    names of organizations; names in sports;
    newspapers; nicknames; place names; titles;
    trade names
  aircraft, weapons 249
  animals, birds 178
  astronomical, celestial, meteorological 197
  in At-a-Glance 368
  in broadcast copy 163
  capitalization 9, 189
  common 215
  constituencies 211
  derivatives 181
  first 19, 216
  on first reference 292
  government departments 172, 184
  in obituaries 69, 215
  of people 215-216
  peoples, races, tribes 21, 189
  plants 192
  plurals 177, 216
  political parties 211
  preferred by individual 22, 216
  prefixes 239
  promotional 215, 296
  pronunciation 216
  proper 216, 413
  religious 194-196
  saints 208
  schools, universities 196
  scientific 285
  sponsors 86, 298
  sports events, trophies 197
  streets 217
  victims of crime 32
names, French 204-209
  capitalization 206-207
  family 208
  municipalities 81, 206, 207
  newspapers 206, 190
  possessives 226
  Quebec companies 206, 226
  saints 174, 208
  streets 208
  unions 63

names, non-English 216. *See also* names, French
  Asian 216
  German 282
  peoples, races, tribes 189
  personal 182
  proper 174
  Russian 216
  Spanish, Portuguese 216
names of organizations 172, 191
  abbreviations 169, 172
  capitalization 9, 189, 191, 296
  French 204-205, 206, 226
  geographical element in 184
  month spelled out in 171
  pitfalls (business) 43
  possessives 226
names in sports
  capitalization 197
  events 197
  golfers 433
  leagues 81
  sponsors 86, 298
  teams 80
  teams, hockey 434
  trophies 197
national origin
  capitalization 189
  foreign news 412
  identification 20
National Union of Provincial Government Employees 63
nations, peoples 271-277
nation vs. *country* 213
native 22
native peoples 21-22, 267-269
  CP policy 21-22
  Indians 268-269
  Inuit 269
  languages 267
  Métis 269
  writing about 268
nautical miles 251, 253, 254
negative transmitter 337
net earnings 45, 409-410
net profit, income, earnings 45
NewsAlert 129, 407
News Analysis, CP. *See* analyses
News Budget 363-366
  descriptive lines 364-365
  graphics, photos 356
  Main Desk 351
Newsmakers 75-79
newsmap 130
newspage copy 81, 375
newspapers 190. *See also* member newspapers
  French 206, 207
  style for names 190, 229, 374
news report, the CP 349-445
NewsStream 398
next-cycle stories 154
nicknames 190
  capitalization 190
  military 188
  parentheses 216

  political 193
  sports 81
Night Budget (lines) 364
NO PICKUP (slug) 403
no-comment stories 377
North America 283
not (legal use) 160
notes (to editor)
  byline 385
  publishable, non-publishable 357
  questionable material 21, 31
  slug 406
  withhold 390
notes on style 5-9
notes, tapes, preserving 26, 130
nouns, plurals 222-225
numbering 175
numbers 190-191, 217-221. *See also* decimals; fractions;
    measurement; metric; money; percentages; roman
    numerals; statistics
  agate 416-419
  apostrophe 228
  arithmetic 142
  broadcast copy 164
  business news 43, 409
  capitalization 190
  commas 233, 234
  common faults 142
  editing 160
  estimates 87
  figures, use of 217-218
  graphics, source for 348
  hyphen 239
  international style 259
  large 221, 254, 255
  in names 217
  odds 87
  polls 72-73
  range 221
  rounding 254, 409, 412
  sequence 175, 219
  series 175, 229
  singular or plural 246
  spelled out 219
  sports 86-87
  wages 61
oarsmen, oarswomen 438
obituaries 68-70
  age 19, 69
  death, cause of 69
  funerals 69, 70
  identification 69
  language 70
  length 68, 69
  names 69, 215
  next-cycle stories 68
  prepared obits 70
  race 21
  spot stories 68
obscenity 16, 18, 156
odds 87, 218
offences, criminal 97, 116. *See also* crime
official, government 26

official vs. *spokesman* 28
off the record 28
Ojibwa 267
open shop 63
opinion
   avoid 14
   in columns 46
   in editorial symposiums 373
   legal issues 117-118
organizations 172, 191
-or vs. *-our* 7-8
Oscar awards 52
OUT (slug) 339, 407
overline 339
overloads 138-139, 160
overwriting 138-139
pairs (skating) 439
paragraphs
   At-a-Glance 368
   common faults 136
   Highlights 369
   quotation marks 242
paraphrase
   punctuation 233
   quotations, direct 27
   quotations, French 208
   union names, French 63
parentheses (brackets) 229-230
parole 99
parties, political 211
   affiliations, designations 211, 229, 236
   capitalization 192-193
   elections 47
   names of 211
   polls 73
part-time reviewers 53
passive voice 136, 159, 162
passports 134
past tense. *See* verb tense, past; verb tense, past and
     present
patent law 108
patient 20
pay equity 61
pension protection 61
peoples, names of 271-277
percentage points 73, 142
percentages. *See also* statistics
   business 43
   common faults 142
   editing 160
   elections 50
   loss or gain 217
   wages 61
period 240-241
   in abbreviations 170
   At-a-Glance, ending 368
   and dash 236
   in decimal fractions of a second 87
   in decimals 259
   and exclamation mark 238
   in field result format 420
   Highlights, ending 369
   initials without 215
   with time 290

permission
   to use cartoons 345
   for Letters to the Editor 120
   for news or exclusives 120, 121
   for pickups 278
   to quote 26-28, 119
   to record 121
-person 6-7, 293
photographer. *See also* pictures
   business news 408
   copyright 120, 342
   credit 340
   sports stories 85
   weekend coverage 336
PhotoNet 335-336
   breaking news 335
   history and description 330
   money, pictures of 343
   specials 344-345
   useful photos 336
photos. *See* pictures
picket 65
Pickup lines 407
pickups from members 377
Picture Desk
   breaking news 335
   fax 348
   Kills, Corrections 341
   specials 344
   weekend coverage 336
Picture Service Plan 343
pictures 329-345. *See also* cartoons; graphics
   advisories 356
   business news 408
   Canadian Press BBS 336-337
   captions 339-340
   composition 334
   content 331-332
   copyright 342-343
   entertainment news 51
   freelance 120, 330, 336, 339, 342-344
   funerals 70
   good illustrations 330-334
   legal considerations 342-344
   maps 130, 329, 346-348
   of money 343, 344
   photo manipulation 334-335
   PhotoNet 335-336
   quality 332-333
   specials 344-345
   sports 85-86
   taste 30-31
   transmitting photos 336-338
   travel 92
pistol 251
placelines 278-281
   American 280-281
   bylines 382
   Calendar 360-361
   Canadian 173, 279-280
   captions 339
   columns 279
   Corrections 389
   Correctives 394

foreign, non-U.S. 279, 281
Fronts advisories 363
Highlights 369
locating the news 146, 147
Look-Ahead List 361
News Budget 364
pickups 278
Quicks 370
spot stories 278
style 278
unconventional 279
withhold notes 390
place names 173-174, 183-184, 270-277, 282-284
abbreviations 173-174
as adjectives 234
Canadian 282, 284
capitalization 183-184
commas 234
descriptives, provincial 276
descriptives, U.S. state 277
foreign filing 413-414
foreign table of 270-276
French 81, 174, 206, 207-208, 280, 282
German 282
regions 283
spelling 282, 284, 413
use of *the* 198, 281
planned events 356-357
plant closings 61
plants 192
plural 222-225, 245-247
apostrophe 228-229
capitalization 177, 184
compounds 223-224
editing 160
expressions 225
foreign nouns 224
irregular nouns 248
military ranks 261
misrepresenting sources 131
numbers and letters 191, 249
possessives 226
sex, to avoid specifying 23
sports 80, 81
titles 200
words as words 225
PM (cycle designator) 400
point-form 41
police 122-123
co-operation by press 122
newsroom searches 122-123
public statements 99, 111
terrorism, hostage-takings 33, 34
policies, CP. *See* CP policies
politics. *See also* elections; foreign news; parties,
political; polls
capitalization 192-193
libel 116
polls 72-74
during elections 48
election background 49
foreign filing 412
pitfalls 74

reporting 72-73
statistical reports 89
Pope, the 199, 294
portable color transmitter 337
possessives 226-227
CP, AP 181
sports 81
Precede 405
Pré-enquête 101
preliminary hearing, inquiry 102-103
premier vs. *prime minister* 212
prepositions 145
present tense. *See* verb tense, present
president-elect 211
Presse Canadienne, La 4, 56, 181
pressure, atmospheric 300
prime minister
-*designate* 211
Right Hon. 295
salute, general 213
vs. *premier* 212
Princess of Wales 212
principles. *See* CP policies
priority codes 398
prison terms 97
privacy 30, 31, 121. *See also* public interest
privilege 114-115, 116
newsroom searches 123
protection 114-115, 116
provincial statutes 116
Quebec law 116
Profiles, Newsmakers 75-79
color and description 76-78
defined 75-76
graphics 79
slugs 78
promotion 67
public, contact with 14, 25-27
public good 28
public interest, the
fair comment 118
hearings *in camera* 104
identity of victim 32
previous convictions 99
privilege 113, 114
Quebec law 113
unnamed sources 27
publicity 67, 86
public meetings 115
public notices 115, 122
public opinion. *See* polls
Public Service Alliance of Canada 63
Public Service Staff Relations Board 64
punctuation 228-244. *See* apostrophe; brackets; colon;
comma; dash; ellipsis; hyphen; period; question
mark; quotation marks; semicolon
quarter-horse 436
Quebec law
civil suits 108, 109
inquests 100
libel 113, 116
privilege 114, 116
Queen, the 212, 213
question-and-answer 231, 244, 370

464

question mark 241-242
Quicks 367, 370-372. *See also* sidebars
    business 44, 408
    lifestyles 67
    News Budget 364, 365
    polls 73
    sports 85, 416
    style 372
quotation marks 242-244
    colon 230
    comma 233
    direct quotations 242
    editorial symposiums 244
    headlines without 244
    mid-sentence quotations 242
    paragraphs 242, 243
    question-and-answer 244
    slang 17
    texts 244
    titles without 179
    words and phrases 242-243
quotations 16-18, 193-194, 242-243. *See also* quotation
    marks
    attribution 17
    bafflegab 16
    broadcast copy 164
    capitalization 193-194
    colon 230
    commas 233
    copyright material 119-120
    CP policy 16-18
    dash 236
    derogatory terms in 21
    dialects 16
    double translation 208
    editing and writing 150, 155, 161
    editorial symposiums 374
    ellipsis 236-237
    foreign measurements 412
    grammar 16
    metric 253, 254
    news or exclusives 120
    obscenity 18
    QuickQuotes 371-372
    religious titles 295
    reviews and critiques 119
    slang 17
    spelling 16
    tampering 16
    translation 18, 205, 206, 208
    unnamed sources 26, 27
    vulgarities 16race, racism 6, 20-21, 96, 122. *See also* sensitive subjects
Rand formula 63
ranks, military 261-263
readability
    capitalization 9, 215, 289, 296
    paragraphs 136
    on cable TV news 444
    sentences 136, 148
Recast (slug) 403
recipes 182, 259
recording conversations 121
records (sports) 87

regatta 438
regional news 352
release (advances) 379-380, 381
Release Withhold (slug) 391
religion. *See also* sensitive subjects
    capitalization 194-196
    crime 96
    explanation needed 20
    titles 294-295
repechage 438
reserves, Indian 267
residences, official 174, 211
responsibility of staff 13-15, 95. *See also* bureaus;
    editor; legal; Main Desk; supervisor
results formats (sports)
    bare score 419
    field format 420
    head-to-head 420
retouching (photos) 335
retraction 116
retrials 105
Reuters
    byline style 383
    capitalization 181
    foreign news 3-4, 56, 411
    placelines 386
    place names, spelling of 413
    terrorism stories 34
Rev. (title) 174, 292, 294, 295
reviews, entertainment 53-54
    byline 383, 385
    French titles 205, 206
    quotation, copyright 119
Richter scale 288
rifle 251
rifle hunting, avoid 251
roman numerals 220
    period, omit 241
    proper names 190, 215
    sequence 190
roundup (slug) 278
rowing 438
Royal Family, the 212
rugby 438
Russian names 216
saint, Canadian patron 214
Saint, Sainte 208
Salchow (skating) 439
salutations 231
salutes 213
say and *said* 140-141, 159
schools, universities 196
scoreboard. *See* agate
Scot, Scottish 283
scullers 438
searches, police 122-123
seasons 198
security, national 100, 104, 303
    hearings *in camera* 104
    information, access to 303
    inquest closed 100
See (slug) 405
See also: (budget lines) 365
semicolon 244

senate 186-187, 210-211
senior citizen 19
sensitive subjects 19-24, 107, 161. *See also* age; AIDS;
    death, cause of; disabilities; funerals; legal
    reporting; native peoples; obituaries; race; sexism;
    taste
sentences
    broadcast copy 162-165
    common faults 136
    dependent clauses 153
    incomplete 164
    length 148, 153, 368, 369
    overloaded 160
    writing checklist 155
separates. *See* Quicks
sequence (numbers) 179, 190, 219
serial terms 175
series 229, 232
sex
    animals and birds 178
    either-sex names 215
    vs. gender 6
sexism 22-24
    language 6-7, 21
    ships 250
    sports 84
sexual offences 96, 107
sexual orientation 23
share (corporate) 45
shell (artillery) 251
shell (rowing) 438
ships 219, 250-251
shooting (sport) 438
shotgun 251
sidebars. *See also* Quicks
    business stories 44
    concise writing 154
    game coverage 80
    News Budget 363, 364
singles (skating) 439
singular 245-247
    agreement 160
    vs. plural 131, 245-247
    possessives in sport 81
    team names 80
Situational. *See* Backgrounders
skating, figure 439
skating, speed 439
skedlines 364
skiing 440
slander 112
slang 17, 243
slugs 396-407, 415-416
    adds, advances 379-380
    Asked 406
    At-a-Glance 368
    Attn 406
    Borderline 21
    Bulletin 402
    business 408, 409, 410
    captions 339, 342
    catchlines 407
    Clarification 394-395
    Correction 389-391

    CP Backgrounder 41
    CP Flashback 55
    CP News Analysis , 39
    Day Lead 403
    designators 400-401
    Espy 406
    1st Lead 403-405
    Flash 401-402
    Highlights 369
    Insert 406
    keyword slug line 400-401
    Kill 391
    MORE 130, 406
    News Budget 363, 364
    Newsmakers 78
    Night Lead 403
    NO PICKUP 403
    Note 406
    OUT 339, 407
    pickup lines 407
    Precede 405
    priority codes 398
    Profiles 78
    Quicks 371-372
    Release Withhold 391
    See 405
    sports 415-416, 421, 422
    Sub 391
    Undated 279, 370
    Urgent 402
    version field 401
    With 406
    Withhold 390
snooker 440
soccer 440-441
sources 25-29
    analyses 38
    breaking news 130
    broadcast copy 164
    computer sources 29
    confidential material 161
    CP policy 13, 14
    entertainment news 51
    ethics 27-28
    fictitious or composite 28
    Flashbacks 55
    Head Office 28
    of photos 343
    others' sources 28
    release times 379
    searches, police 123
    singular vs. plural 131
    unnamed 25-29
    women as 29
South America 283
Southeast Asia 283
space 197
Spanish names 216
specials, photo 344
speeches 378-379
speed (measurement)
    metric 254
    sports 86
    wind 299

speed (and reliability) 13, 129
spelling 248
  compounds 202
  CP style 248
  foreign copy 413
  national preferences 7-8
  -or, -our 7-8
  place names 282, 284, 413
  in quotations 16
  Russian names 216
  sports terms 88
  transliteration 216, 414
  troublesome words 248
split infinitives 145
spokesman vs. official 28
sponsorship 86, 298
sports 415-443. *See also* sports handling and reporting
  athletics. *See* track and field 422
  auto racing 420
  baseball 421-424
  basketball 425
  bobsled, luge 426
  boxing 426-427
  canoeing 427
  cricket 427
  curling 428
  cycling 429
  diving 429
  equestrian 429
  fencing 429
  football 430-431
  golf 432-433
  gymnastics 433
  hockey 434-435
  horse racing 436-437
  judo 437
  lacrosse 438
  motorcycle racing 438
  rowing 438
  rugby 438
  shooting 438
  skating, figure 439
  skating, speed 439
  skiing 440
  snooker 440
  soccer 440-441
  squash 441
  swimming 441
  tennis 442
  track and field 442
  volleyball 442
  weightlifting 442
  wrestling 443
  yachting 443
sports handling and reporting 80-88, 197, 415-443. *See also above for handling of individual sports*
  agate 416-419
  amateur, recreational 83
  as business 83
  capitalization 197
  dates 289
  libel 116-117
  measurement 86-87
  more than a game 82-84

newspage copy 375
Notes 237
  points to watch 80-82
  records 87
  results formats 419-420
  slugs 415-416
  spellings to watch 88
  sponsorship 86
  times 87
  women 84
squash 441
stallion 436
standardbred 436
statistics 89-90. *See also* percentages
  agate, sports 416
  American 90
  foreign filing 412
  graphics, sports 85
  pitfalls 89-90
  polls 73
  trends 89
status Indians 267-269
stocks (corporate) 45
stock-car racing 420
street addresses 146, 208, 217, 219
strike (labor) 64
Sub (slug) 391
subtitles 231
succession to throne 213
suicide 69
suit for damages 109
summary conviction offences 97
supervisor
  analyses 39
  breaking news 133, 134
  Developing Sked 352, 353
  elections 48, 50
  legal reporting 99, 102, 103, 106
  member co-operation 376
  police searches 122-123
  responsibility 13
  terrorism, hostage-takings 33-34
Supreme Court of Canada 98, 109
swimming 441
symposiums, editorial 373-374
Syndicat des fonctionnaires provinciaux du Quebec 63
tab field indicator (TFI) 417
tab line indicator (TLI) 417
tabulation 417-419
  days of the week 171
  measurements 172
  metric symbols 255
  months of the year 171
  political parties 211
  sports handling 417-419
Tale of the Tape (boxing) 427
tampering with quotes 16
taped conversations 121
tapes, notes 26, 122, 123, 130, 161
taste 30-32
  CP policy 13
  obituaries 69
  writing checklist 156
taxation (Federal Court) 108

technical terms 285-288
 AIDS 287-288
 burns 287
 drugs 285-286
 explaining 90, 139, 161, 285
 medical 181, 286, 287
 Richter scale 288
 scientific 285
telephone books 131
 Foreign Affairs 58
 travel agency 58
 unofficial sources 131
television 51-54, 444
Telex 58
temperature
 and dash 236
 figures, use of 219
 weather 299
tennis 442
tenses. *See* verbs
term contract employees 60
terminology. *See* words
terrorism 33-34
text, quoted 17, 236-237
that and *which* 143-144
the 198, 281
theirs and *there's* 227
thin space 236, 417
Third World 57. *See also* foreign news
thoroughbred 436
time 289-291
 abbreviations 171
 Britain 291
 broadcast copy 163
 capitalization 198
 colon 231
 commas 235
 common faults 143
 day, date 289-290
 daylight 291
 editing 160
 embargoes 379
 figures, use of 219, 290
 foreign copy 413
 Greenwich mean 291
 leads 289-290
 news cycles 289
 releases 379-380
 statistical studies 89
 when to specify 290
 zones 290
titles 199-200, 292-295
 abbreviations 174
 books, French 205-206
 bylines 382-383
 capitalization 199-200
 compositions 188-189, 198, 243
 couples 293
 courtesy 293
 doctor 292, 293
 false 292
 first reference 292
 French 206
 government ministers 210

Honorable, Lady, Lord 295
 joint 239
 members of Parliament 210
 members of provincial legislatures 210
 military 262-263
 movies, French 205-206
 Mr., Mrs., Miss, Ms. 5, 293
 -person 6-7, 293
 professional 293
 religious 294-295
 subtitles 231
 surnames 22
 teams 80
 TV programs, French 206
 -woman 6-7, 293
to be 159
tonnage 250
Top Copy notes 354
tough calls 30-32
track and field 442
trade names 296-298
 alternatives 297-298
 Canadian Trade Index 201, 297
 capitalization 201, 296
 Federal Court 108
 food and drink 181
 pitfalls 43
trademarks. *See* trade names
translation 204-206, 208-209
 brackets, use of 205, 230
 double 208
 quotations 18
 titles of works 189, 205, 206
transliteration 216, 414
transmitters, photo 337-338
travel stories 91-92, 385
treaties, Indian 267
trials, criminal 103-104. *See also* legal
 appeals 98, 104
 retrials 105
tribunals, federal administrative 108
trippers 137
trophies 81
typesetting symbols 417
umlaut 282
Undated (slug) 279
union shop 63
unions 62-63. *See also* labor
United Food and Commercial Workers 63
United Kingdom 283
United Nations 172
United Steelworkers of America 63
universities 196
unnamed sources 25-29
Urgent (slug) 387, 399, 402
usage, popular 6, 189, 191
venue, change of 102
verbs. *See also* active voice; first person; passive voice;
  verb tense
 active 155, 159
 agreement 80, 160, 245-247
 apostrophe 228

broadcast writing 162
  compounds 203
  ending in -ize 142, 214
  indicate, suggest 72
  separating from auxiliary 413
  to be 159
verb tense, past
  alternative forms 248
  avoid in obituaries 70
verb tense, past and present
  breaking stories 133
  reporting on polls 73
verb tense, present
  At-a-Glance 368
  breaking stories 133
  captions 339
  Highlights 369
version field 401
vertical rule 417
vocabulary
  business 44-45
  French 209
  labor 61, 63, 65
  legal 124-125
  technical 285-288
  weather 300-302
  words 306-325
voir dire 103, 111
volleyball 442
voting day, legal 48. *See also* elections
vulgarities 16, 18
wages 61
warrant
  for arrest 98
  search 122-123
weapons 251-252, 265
weather 299-302
  metric 299-300
  terminology 300-302
weight (measure) 254, 256-258. *See also* tonnage
weight categories
  boxing 426
  judo 437
  wrestling 443
weightlifting 442
which and *that* 143
who, whom 144
whose and *who's* 227
wildcat strike 65
Will be Lead (slug) 364
wills 108
Wirephoto 330
wiretaps 121
With (slug) 406
withhold
  legal doubts 95, 112
  pictures 342
  style 390-391
witnesses to crime 99, 106
-woman 6-7, 293
women
  feminine variants 23
  sexism 22-24

as sources 29
in sport 84
wordage 154
  broadcast lead lines 162
  Bulletin 402
  editorial symposiums 373
  game-over stories 80
  News Budget 363, 364
  Quicks 371
  travel stories 92
word order 137, 143, 145, 160
words 306-325. *See also* bafflegab; jargon; journalese;
    vocabulary
  business 44-45
  business, French 209
  correct or preferred 306-325
  feminine variants 23
  foreign plural 224
  government 210-214
  guns 251-252
  labor–management 60, 61, 63, 64-65
  legal 108, 112, 124-125
  legal, French 209
  obituaries 70
  overcharged 139
  ships 250-251
  sports 88
  weather 300-302
workers. *See* labor
workplace 60
world news. *See* foreign news
wrestling 443
writer
  breaking news 133, 134
  captions 339
  freelance 120, 385
writing 148-156
  be clear 151
  be concise 154
  be direct 152-153
  be human 148-150
  be specific 150-151
  broadcast 162-165
  cable 444
  captions 340
  checklist 155-156
  common faults 135-145
  locating the news 146-147
  next-trick stories 154
yachting 255, 443
years 218, 219
Yiddish 248
young offender 104, 105-106
Young Offenders Act 104, 105
your and *you're* 227
youth 19

United States

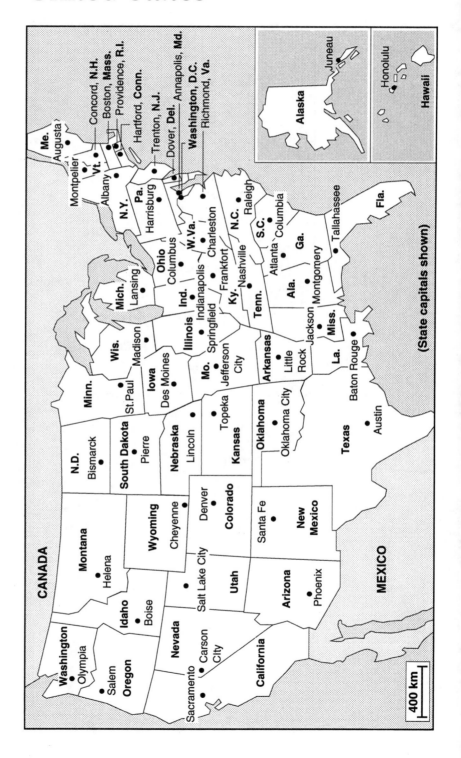

(State capitals shown)

Western Canada

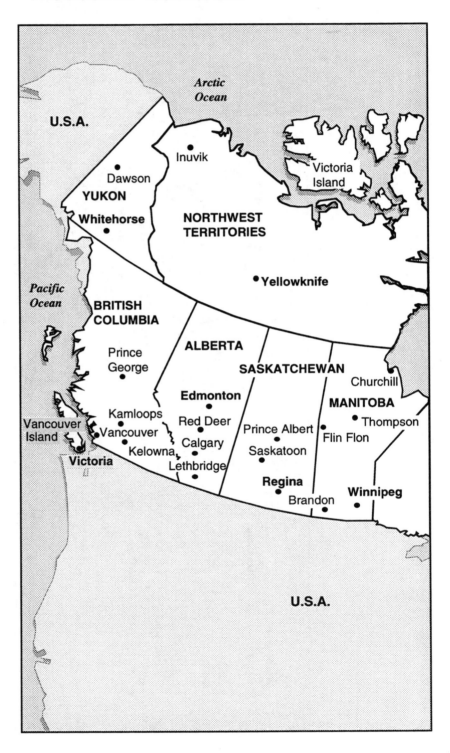

U.S.A.

Arctic
Ocean

Inuvik

Dawson

Victoria
Island

YUKON

Whitehorse

NORTHWEST
TERRITORIES

Pacific
Ocean

Yellowknife

BRITISH
COLUMBIA

Prince
George

ALBERTA

SASKATCHEWAN

Churchill

Edmonton

MANITOBA

Kamloops

Red Deer

Prince Albert

Thompson

Vancouver
Island

Vancouver

Calgary

Flin Flon

Kelowna

Saskatoon

Victoria

Lethbridge

Regina

Brandon

Winnipeg

U.S.A.

Eastern Canada

Baffin Island

Cape Dorset

Hudson Strait

Atlantic Ocean

Nain

LABRADOR

Hudson Bay

Goose Bay

NFLD.

QUEBEC

St. John's

James Bay

Sept-Îles

ONTARIO

Chicoutimi

P.E.I.

Sydney

Noranda

N.B.

Charlottetown

Thunder Bay

Fredericton

Quebec

Halifax

Sault Ste. Marie

Hull

Montreal

Saint John

NOVA SCOTIA

Lake Superior

Sudbury

Lake Huron

Kingston

Ottawa

Lake Michigan

Lake Ontario

London

Hamilton

Toronto

Windsor

Lake Erie

U.S.A.

500 km

Printed in Canada
Design and cover art by Laural Carr, Impagination, Toronto
Printed by Imperial Press Ltd., Mississauga, Ont.

Use these order forms for
more copies of the *CP Stylebook*

You can also get: *(CP) Caps and Spelling* listing hundreds of tricky names and spellings.
Guide du journaliste for French-language writing.
BN Style Guide for broadcast writing.

Mail to: Book Orders   Phone: (416) 364-0321
The Canadian Press   Fax: (416) 594-2163
36 King St. E., Toronto, Ont. M5C 2L9   http://www.canpress.ca

Cheques are payable to The Canadian Press. Prices are subject to change without notice.
Bulk-order rates available.

➤➤➤

Name _____   Address _____

City _____   Prov. _____   Postal Code _____

_____ copies of the *CP Stylebook* $29.95 each _____   TOTAL $ _____
_____ copies of *(CP) Caps and Spelling* $17.00 each _____
_____ copies of *Guide du journaliste* $20.00 each _____   plus 7% GST _____
_____ copies of the *BN Style Guide* $15.00 each _____   TOTAL ENCLOSED $ _____

➤➤➤

Name _____   Address _____

City _____   Prov. _____   Postal Code _____

_____ copies of the *CP Stylebook* $29.95 each _____   TOTAL $ _____
_____ copies of *(CP) Caps and Spelling* $17.00 each _____
_____ copies of *Guide du journaliste* $20.00 each _____   plus 7% GST _____
_____ copies of the *BN Style Guide* $15.00 each _____   TOTAL ENCLOSED $ _____

➤➤➤

Name _____   Address _____

City _____   Prov. _____   Postal Code _____

_____ copies of the *CP Stylebook* $29.95 each _____   TOTAL $ _____
_____ copies of *(CP) Caps and Spelling* $17.00 each _____
_____ copies of *Guide du journaliste* $20.00 each _____   plus 7% GST _____
_____ copies of the *BN Style Guide* $15.00 each _____   TOTAL ENCLOSED $ _____